RELIGIONS IN PRACTICE

Sixth Edition

RELIGIONS IN PRACTICE
AN APPROACH TO THE ANTHROPOLOGY
OF RELIGION

John R. Bowen
Washington University in St. Louis

Boston   Columbus   Indianapolis   New York   San Francisco   Upper Saddle River   Amsterdam
Cape Town   Dubai   London   Madrid   Milan   Munich   Paris   Montréal   Toronto
Delhi   Mexico City   São Paulo   Sydney   Hong Kong   Seoul   Singapore   Taipei   Tokyo

Editor in Chief: Ashley Dodge
Publisher: Nancy Roberts
Editorial Assistant: Molly White
Director of Marketing: Brandy Dawson
Executive Marketing Manager: Kelly May
Marketing Coordinator: Jessica Warren
Managing Editor: Denise Forlow
Program Manager: Mayda Bosco
Senior Operations Supervisor: Mary Fischer
Operations Specialist: Mary Ann Gloriande
Art Director: Jayne Conte
Cover photo: © Robert Harding World Imagery / Alamy
Cover design: Bruce Kenselaar
Director of Digital Media: Brian Hyland
Digital Media Editor: Rachel Comerford
Digital Media Project Manager: Tina Gagliostro
Full-Service Project Management and Composition: iEnergizer/Aptara®, Inc.
Printer/Binder: Courier Corp.
Cover Printer: Courier Corp.
Text Font: Palatino LT Std 10/12

Credits: pp. 13, 21, 71-72, 143, 145-147, 158, 164: Scripture taken from the NEW AMERICAN STANDARD BIBLE®, Copyright © 1960,1962,1963,1968,1971,1972,1973,1975,1977,1995 by The Lockman Foundation. Used by permission.

Photo Credits: pp. 36-37, 56: John Bowen; pp. 41, 126, 192: John Renard; p. 46: Jane Atkinson; pp. 61, 121: Image copyright © The Metropolitan Museum of Art. Image source: Art Resource, NY; pp. 99-100, 103-104: Diane Mines.

Credits and acknowledgments borrowed from other sources and reproduced, with permission, in this textbook appear on the appropriate page within text.

Library of Congress Cataloging-in-Publication Data
Bowen, John R.
  Religions in practice: an approach to the anthropology of religion/John R. Bowen. — Sixth edition
    pages cm
  Includes bibliographical references and index.
  ISBN-13: 978-0-205-91766-2
  ISBN-10: 0-205-91766-6
1. Religion.   2. Anthropology of religion.   I. Title.
  BL48.B625 2013
  306.6—dc23   2013004233

10 9 8 7 6 5 4 3 2 1

ISBN-10:   0-205-91766-6
ISBN-13: 978-0-205-91766-2

For Family and Friends

CONTENTS

PREFACE

Whether we are interested in individuals praying, in how a small group heals through trance, or how Catholics have organized the mass over the centuries, I think that we learn the most when we look at how people engage with the practices of their religions: how they speak, cry, govern, or pontificate. I emphasize the appropriateness of an anthropological approach for large-scale religions, which for too long were studied mainly by historians and religious studies scholars but avoided by anthropologists: thus the treatment of Catholic and Protestant faiths within Christianity, as well as the running analysis of Islam, my own research specialty.

NEW TO THE SIXTH EDITION

Although I have revised and updated many sections of the book, here are some of the major changes.

- A new treatment of Islam in Chapter 13.
- A new chapter on Orthodox Judaism (Chapter 10), with attention to how rules and rituals shape the gendered development of the self; here I draw on the emphasis on the formation of the self discussed (new to this edition) in Chapter 2.
- New sections on Christianity in small-scale societies (Chapter 11).
- Rewritten chapters on healing and sorcery (Chapters 5–6) incorporate new material.
- I have added boxes summarizing the main features of seven religious traditions, and new sections for discussion and media resources at the end of each chapter.
- MySearchLab, an online resource for student research that includes access to articles from the EBSCO/ContentSelect database, can be packaged with this edition. Please see your Pearson sales representative for more information.

This text is available in a variety of formats—digital and print. To learn more about our programs, pricing options, and customization, visit www.pearsonhighered.com.

STUDENT AND TEACHER RESOURCES

MySearchLab with eText
A passcode-protected website that provides engaging experiences that personalize learning, MySearchLab contains an eText that is just like the printed text. Students can highlight and add notes to the eText online or download it to an iPad. MySearchLab also provides a wide range of writing, grammar, and research tools plus access to a variety of academic journals, census data, Associated Press news feeds, and discipline-specific readings to help hone writing and research skills.

Instructor's Resource Manual and Test Bank (0-205-92940-0)
For each chapter in the text, this valuable resource provides a chapter outline, lecture topics, research topics, and questions for classroom discussion. In addition, test questions

in multiple choice and essay formats are available for each chapter; the answers are page-referenced to the text.

MyTest (0-205-92942-7)
This computerized software allows instructors to create their own personalized exams, to edit any or all of the existing test questions, and to add new questions. Other special features of this program include the random generation of test questions, the creation of alternative versions of the same test, scrambling question sequences, and test previews before printing."

ACKNOWLEDGMENTS

I would like to thank the following reviewers for their work on this book: Mark Webb, Texas Tech University; Derrick Lemons, the University of Georgia; James Findlay, California State University Northridge; Eric Rovie, Georgia Perimeter College – Newton Campus; Sean O'Neill, the University of Oklahoma; Frances Purifoy, the University of Louisville; and Annapurna Padney, San Jose State University.

Studying Religion through Practice

In late 2010 some residents of Murfreesboro, Tennessee, became alarmed when their long-standing Muslim neighbors decided to build a new mosque. They tried to have the city council block the project, and when that failed they filed a lawsuit. Already feeling uncomfortable with Muslims in the town, they claimed that the new mosque would bring in shariah law. They were convinced that this was already happening elsewhere in America. "It's creeping in," said one leader of the anti-mosque faction (CNN, "Unwelcome: The Mosque Next Door," March 27, 2011). Local contractors boycotted the mosque project, and someone torched the building equipment. The lawyer representing them in court claimed that Muslims mistreat women and that therefore Islam was not a real religion. To this point, the story seems to illustrate the inability of some Americans to accept Muslims in their midst.

But the story is not finished. At the same time that the anti-mosque folks were suing and demonstrating, other (non-Muslim) townspeople staged counter-protests, urging the town to support the Muslims' constitutional rights to religious freedom. The judge overseeing the lawsuit ruled that Muslims had the same right to worship as did those of other faiths, and that the mosque could go ahead.

In the Murfreesboro story appear some of the challenges faced in countries where citizens practice many different religions. We may feel uncomfortable with new people and their beliefs, even fearful, and fear can lead us to accept arguments that justify our discomfort (Muslims beat their women, shariah is coming to America). Blindly accepting such arguments can contribute to violent actions, as when in July 2011, Anders Behring Breivik opened fire on youth members of the Norwegian Labor Party, killing 69 teenagers, and bombed government buildings in Oslo, killing 8 others. Breivik had written a long set of statements espousing hatred for all that he saw as destroying a properly Norwegian way of life. In his statements, he repeated claims found in the writings of far-right, anti-Islam activists from the United States and Europe. But in Murfreesboro, laws and constitutional principles proved to provide the best bulwark against hate speech. The judge applied the law and people were granted their constitutional rights.

But even if Muslims win their rights in court, they continue to encounter suspicions that they, unlike everyone else, base all their actions on their sacred texts and, so, cannot be accepted as citizens. Commentators often suggest that their religion leads Muslims to have many children, or to react violently to events, and so we find Muslims rioting (as in Paris in late 2005), carrying out jihad, and continuing to have large families. Some suggest that Europe will be 50 percent Muslim by 2050, and that Muslims will rise in unison to take over European capitals.

Now, there is a lot to object to in these claims. For one thing, the best demographic information shows that Muslim women born in Europe are having about the same number of children as non-Muslim Europeans—just what research in immigration and fertility would predict. But I was, and am, more interested in the assumptions many current writers make about the causal force of religious texts in the everyday lives of Muslims. If we assume that Muslims shape everything in their lives around sacred texts, then we could legitimately read those texts to understand Muslims' actions. But Muslims draw on their scriptures in much the same ways as Christians, Jews, and Buddhists draw on theirs. Some pay close attention to their holy books; others don't read them at all. Some worship frequently; others never do. And, as with Christians, Jews, and others, Muslims interpret their scriptures in varying and changing ways. Moreover, even most highly religious people have a lot of secular aims in their lives: eating well, holding down a job, bringing up children, and so on. These were the issues behind the 2005 Paris riots, which involved many non-Muslims and people of European backgrounds, who all were enraged by problems of unemployment, discrimination, and police harassment; religion was not among their concerns (Bowen 2012).

I begin on this note because of the sense of immediacy I have about the importance of correctly understanding the role religion does and does not play in modern public life, and the contributions the anthropology of religion can make to this understanding. The issue arises most pressingly with regard to contemporary armed conflicts, from those in the Balkans in the 1990s, through the continuing struggles in parts of the former Soviet Union, Kashmir, Indonesia, and Palestine, to the post–9/11 security debates about Islam in the United States and Europe. Are people fighting because of their religion? Does their religion shape how they think and act? Or is it just a way of mobilizing support? How far can religions be stretched to adapt to new ways of life?

These basic questions are less often posed than are the answers to them simply assumed. In less dramatic ways, many people living in Europe and North America continue to search for new forms of religiosity within or alongside established religious organizations. The fast-rising Christian churches in Melanesia, Africa, and Latin America are posing new challenges to indigenous religions. Muslims are engaging in internal deliberations about how to rethink issues of gender, the public sphere, and their religion's place in European and North American societies. Practitioners of smaller-scale religions throughout the world find themselves struggling for recognition or survival.

WHAT IS "RELIGION"?

Discussions of religion are often based on knowledge of only a few familiar religions. Many U.S. politicians and school officials who support a moment of silence for prayer in schools, for example, assume that all religions include the practice of silent individual prayer to a god; some people find the Islamic practice of five daily prostrations before God disruptive. German officials have declared that Scientology is not a religion. Indonesian officials exclude animist beliefs and practices from the category of religion.

What then is "religion"? I view religious traditions as ever-changing complexes of beliefs (including those authoritative beliefs called "doctrine"), practices (including formalized rituals), and social institutions. But how do we decide which beliefs, practices, and institutions are to be called "religious"?

In most Western traditions, we find two very common definitions. One emphasizes an individual's beliefs; the other, his or her emotions. The former defines religion as a set of shared beliefs in spirits or gods. The latter identifies religion in terms of a sentiment of awe and wonder toward the unknown. I do not think we need a hard-and-fast definition of religion. This book examines a wide variety of ways in which people in different societies and times have thought about the world beyond the immediate sense-world. Some posit a set of deities; others do not. Some have a distinct sphere of life called "religion"; others do not distinguish religion from the rest of life.

Sufficient for our purposes is that the phenomena we will study—prayer to God, uses of magic, death rituals—all involve the idea that there is something more to the world than meets the eye. This definition is much broader than standard Western usage. What if we said that religion was anything that involves a stated belief in spirits or gods? In those cultures strongly shaped by modern Christianity, people do indeed tend to think of religion in these terms. But the idea of a separate religious sphere is recent even in the West. In other societies, people define the world in different ways, treating as a natural part of everyday life actions and ideas that we would want to include in a cross-cultural category of religion.

Consider the practices of the Azande people of the southern Sudan that ethnographers have labeled "witchcraft" (discussed further in Chapter 6). According to the Azande, some people carry in their bodies a substance called *mangu*. This substance is inherited, and it sends out emanations when the person feels jealousy, anger, or other negative emotions toward another person. The substance causes things to happen, and it fits into everyday ways of explaining misfortune: "I tripped at a place where I never trip; it must be witchcraft that caused me to trip."

When the person causing a particular misfortune is discovered (by using oracles), he or she is asked to blow water from his or her mouth and say: "If I was doing harm, I certainly did not mean to, let it be gone." And that is the end of the matter. The Azande do not concentrate on blame or intentions, but on the particular problem at hand and how to solve it. Indeed, they believe the substance sometimes acts on its own without the person's knowledge.

What do we make of these practices? From a Western point of view, they refer to a reality beyond the immediately verifiable, and thus we may legitimately include them in a comparative study of religions. The Azande, on the other hand, see mangu and oracles as everyday, ordinary aspects of reality. Some of the Azande who have converted to Christianity continue their use of oracles and accusations of mangu precisely because they do not see those activities as part of a separate religion, but more in the way that an American Baptist or Catholic might regard the use of an astrological chart.

The diversity of ideas about what constitutes a particular religion places any student of religion in a difficult position. If I write about a particular religion as the symbols, statements, and practices of a particular group of people, I will almost in-evitably differ with some of them as to what their religion is. The perspective of an outside observer, who wishes to include a wide array of opinions and activities, may be much broader than that of a practitioner, who may insist on his or her own view of what properly lies within the boundaries of the religion in question.

I have frequently met with objections to the way I define "Islam" when describing certain Sumatran village practices to Indonesian Islamic scholars. For example, many villagers gather at ritual meals to ask ancestral spirits for help in healing the sick or in ensuring a good rice crop. These practices may have their origins in pre-Islamic times, but villagers view them as consistent with their understandings of Islam and they ex-plain them in terms of prophets and angels. Much as Catholics ask saints to intercede for them because they are presumably closer to God, these Muslims ask pious ancestors to do so. For this reason, I include them in my own writings about Sumatran Islam. But for Islamic scholars, these practices conflict with proper understandings of Islam. "Those practices are what we try to teach them to throw aside," they say. For some of them, my own writing could become part of the very problem they are trying to solve, that is, an overly broad idea of Islam.

How do we respond to these challenges? My own response has been to realize that definitions of religion are not just academic matters but part of the very social real-ity we are studying. I thus refrain from giving too precise a definition for religion (or for Catholicism or Islam), and instead look at issues and debates among practitioners about where the boundaries of religion indeed lie, recording what they say and what is at stake for them. Baptists and Catholics do not agree about how to interpret Biblical texts, but we nonetheless speak about "Christianity" because both groups do refer to the Bible and do share a history.

Indeed, the boundaries of "religion" are no clearer when we look closer to home. Some people living in the United States would consider modern forms of witchcraft to be a religion; indeed, the Rhode Island state legislature passed a law making it so in 1989. People continue to debate about the limits the state should place on religious freedom, no more so than in cases of Christian Scientists denying medical treatment to their children. (Until August 1996, treatment given by Christian Science practitioners was considered "medical" for purposes of Medicare and Medicaid reimbursements, on grounds that to deny them that category would be to violate their religious freedom.)

I propose to define religion in two stages. First, we can use an extremely broad definition, such as "ideas and practices that postulate reality beyond that which is im-mediately available to the senses." This is a broad definition—too broad, as it includes string theory in physics (although some physicists do consider such untested theories to be akin to religious belief!). Second, for each society we study, we ask how *these* peo-ple construct their world. They may have a shared set of beliefs in spirits and deities and thus fit squarely into Western definitions of religion. Or, they may speak about impersonal forces, such as the East Asian idea of a life force or *chi* that permeates the natural and social world. Or, they may not focus on describing beliefs at all, but rather concentrate on carrying out rituals correctly, with a general understanding that the ritu-als are important.

What we call *religion* may look quite different from one society to another—in the relative importance of a shared belief system, in the degree to which religious practice involves strong emotions, and in the social functions and contexts associated with religious practices.

AN ANTHROPOLOGICAL APPROACH TO RELIGION

What is the peculiarly anthropological approach to the study of religion? These days, most of us reach across disciplinary boundaries to engage with colleagues in other disciplines. As I work on my own current questions, which in 2013 include debates in Europe and Southeast Asia about religion, law, and politics, I consult the work of specialists from sociology, history, politics, law, and so forth. And yet I find that multidisciplinary research highlights rather than hides the distinctive contributions made by each discipline. Three closely connected features guide an anthropologist's study of any topic.

First, anthropology is based on a *long-term relationship with people* through fieldwork. We live for a fairly long time, more than one year and sometimes many years, in a particular place. During that time, we develop friendships with some people and gain, we hope, the trust and respect of many more. I have spent about six years in Indonesia, and much of that time was spent with the Gayo people in the highlands of Aceh on the island of Sumatra. My experience is not unusual. I developed a very close and continuing friendship with a Gayo family that has continued through the years, and which is now global in scope. The eldest daughter of the Gayo family now lives in the United States. She began her career with Procter & Gamble in Jakarta, moved to Cincinnati to continue her career, and then, with her Egyptian husband, moved to Sunnyvale, California. After the 2004 Indian Ocean tsunami that devastated much of Aceh, she created a foundation to build orphanages in Indonesia, and then extended her work to Pakistan, Bangladesh, and Haiti. My children call her "Cousin Evi"; one of them used to babysit her children in California.

Close relationships are not only the joy of fieldwork but also help us to interpret social life. We trust certain people to report what they think truthfully, and we know enough such people to be able to check our interpretations with people who might be expected to disagree in their views on things. For example, I know people who have very different perspectives on religious rituals, and I can depend on them to disagree with whatever I see. One can compare this source of reliability to that which psychologists obtain by repeating experiments.

Second, anthropologists start studying a topic by learning *local perspectives.* Rather than studying the economy by creating a model of what people might do and then seeing whether they do it, or studying religion by reading scripture and then seeing whether ordinary people believe it, we begin with the ideas and practices we learn about in the field: how they grow rice or recite scripture. Then we follow the connections to larger institutions like government agencies, religious schools, or national banks—but we always start from local views of those institutions.

When I study Islamic law in Indonesia, for example, I begin with how particular individuals—Gayo villagers or Acehnese state judges—define Islamic law vis-à-vis customary rules or state, non-Islamic law. I look at how people make references to particular legal concepts and texts when resolving conflicts, or pursuing conflict in courts. I learn about colonial law, contemporary civil law, and Islamic codes, but only after studying everyday social life, in order to anchor these codes and institutions in local practices. This feature distinguishes anthropology from disciplines that usually begin with historical, religious, or legal texts, or with national political institutions.

Finally, anthropologists study *connections across social domains.* Rarely do we look only at the economy, or at literature, or at religion. We might wish to focus on one of these domains (indeed, it is required when writing a doctoral dissertation), but when we do, we usually discover that our chosen domain is connected to other domains. Suppose I want to learn about rice cultivation and discover that the planting and harvesting is tied to the performance of elaborate religious rituals and that work on the irrigation system depends on local political structures. I have to investigate religion and politics in order to understand how rice is cultivated.

Conversely, my study of Islam in Gayo society involved learning about how rice is grown, how the major rice-growing regions were allocated among villages, how healing takes place, the origins of political parties, and the short history of a poetic genre written in Arabic script—all because they were part of local practices that people explained by referring to Islam. Indeed, I focused on Islam only as a third research project; I was brought to it because the topics I came to study—social structure and oral literature—were interwoven with Islamic ideas about society and history. Even when we work in new kinds of sites, we retain these features in our work. When by 2000, the civil war raging in Aceh had made fieldwork no longer possible, I began working on Islam, law, and politics in France. I began to sit in religious schools along with Muslim students, interview French political actors, and analyze newspaper stories and law review articles. I no longer worked in a village or even in a single neighborhood. Now I am doing similar work on Islam in England.

How is what I am doing different from the work of a political scientist? Well, it comes close to the approach of some of my French colleagues in political science—the French version of that discipline having developed more attention to everyday life than has its more behaviorist American cousin—but it retains a critical difference. I focus on how a wide range of Muslims and non-Muslims talk about matters of importance to them—schools, mosques, political coalitions, and so on—in private and public contexts. The "local" setting in which I work is multiple: a set of institutions and events across France and England in which people deliberate and debate. Starting from these deliberations and debates leads me to look at law, politics, jurisprudence, ethics, the history of immigration, and the perspectives of French and English social scientists on their own society—in other words, the connections across domains. A French political science friend once said to me, her eyebrows slightly raised, "You're studying us, too, aren't you?" That it was so more intrigued than troubled her; it was a way of marking our disciplinary differences and transoceanic differences in perspective, alongside our shared interests in French Islam.

How Is Anthropology Distinctive?

Consider how scholars in different disciplines approach a question about why people believe the (religious) things they do. As I said before, most anthropologists approach the question through fieldwork. Susan Harding (2000), for example, set out to understand how it is that people become "convicted" (that is, convinced) followers of the Reverend Jerry Falwell's Fundamental Baptist community. Her ethnographic approach was to spend a lot of time in the community, listening to what people said and how they said it. She worked to counteract her basic skepticism toward Falwell by "bracketing," as the phenomenologist Husserl put it, her preconceptions and trying to accept his statements as true. This approach allowed her to perceive the complexity and the force of the arguments made by the Baptists. It also gave her a strong, personal sense of what it meant to have a soul and to know that Satan is real. She did not convert, but she gained a felt sense of conviction.

Harding's work fits the overall account of the anthropological approach that I offered earlier. She got to know people well enough to be able to discuss a wide range of topics with them and to grasp how they saw the world. She tried to start with their concerns, rather than bringing her own categories and ideas to the field. And she did not limit her study to one specific domain, but investigated ritual, schooling, gender issues, and politics.

Most anthropologists of religion teaching in North America or Europe carry out at least their initial fieldwork outside those areas, reflecting the general anthropological emphasis on grasping the widest possible range of human experiences, practices, and ideas. This centrifugal tendency also means that they must study and explain to their readers the social and cultural context within which they find religion: kinship and marriage systems, local and national political structures, and broad cosmologies and ideologies. One could limit one's reading to the subfield of the anthropology of religion and nevertheless gain a good understanding of all of social anthropology.

Even though many sociologists carry out fieldwork, the fundamental orientation of their discipline is different from that of anthropology, with a greater interest in developing general propositions about social life, but (one might say ironically) less of a concern with broad-based comparative studies. Most sociologists of religion teaching in the United States study the organization of religions, changes in religious attitudes and beliefs, or new religious movements, usually focusing on people and institutions found in the United States. This focus means that they can assume general knowledge of institutions and ideas on the part of their readers, and that they often pitch their writings to generally held concerns, such as the decline in attendance at mainstream churches or the rise in New Age religions.

Penny Edgell Becker's (1999) study of congregations illustrates one sociological approach. She asked how congregations in the United States manage internal conflict. Her concern thus was primarily organizational. She selected a sample of churches in Chicago, choosing her sample so that it would contain variation in size, organizational structure, and liberal–conservative orientation. Her concerns were primarily to develop a general model consisting of types of church organizations and concomitant types of conflict resolution. These goals were motivated by a broader theoretical literature in sociology concerning institutions and their cultures in the United States. Along the way, she discovered interesting histories of each church and ways of preaching and worshipping, but each of these miniethnographies was inevitably partial, useful only to the extent that it contributed to her particular question.

Psychologists more rarely study religion, but a few anthropologists have taken up the methods of experimental psychology to pursue research into why people believe certain religious propositions. Pascal Boyer (2000, 2001), for example, observed that people around the world have a strikingly small number of basic ideas about supernatural beings: that they behave much as ordinary beings or objects do except for a slight variation in their properties. Thus, one has supernatural agents who are very much like people except that they can go through walls, remain invisible, hear everything, or live forever.

We do not find gods who exist only every other day, or who exist in six dimensions, or who think about everything in the world at once, including the contents of all our refrigerators. Why is this? Boyer and others hypothesized that people have an easier cognitive time working with a limited set of god-concepts. They then tested this idea through experiments with children and adults and found that it held across a number of different cultures. This work resembles that of other psychologists in that it is carried out through controlled experiments and tests some universal propositions about human minds, but it joins long-standing anthropological concerns with the question of what it is that humans share in their religious beliefs. (See the discussion of Tylor in Chapter 2.)

PRACTICES, CONTEXTS, AND DIVERSITY

In the chapters that follow, I examine religious life from different perspectives: the relations of doctrines to rituals; the role of religions in explaining misfortune, overcoming grief, and extending human powers; the ways that rituals of pilgrimage, preaching, and sacrificing shape religious belief and experience; the ways that images and taboos can be used to organize religious life or change it; and the role of religions in public life.

The emphasis on practice includes the study of doctrines, focusing on how doctrines are embodied in texts or other forms and how they are understood; this relation of doctrine to practice is examined in greater detail in Chapter 3. Religious practices often invoke texts: A person may read, chant, recite, or sing a text. These textual practices are critical in linking local practices to broader religious traditions.

Certain practices are especially characteristic of one or more religious traditions, and in some chapters I analyze at length those traditions. For example, images are particularly central to Catholicism, and the analysis of Catholicism in Chapter 8 focuses on imagery and worship as the basis for a more general discussion of imagery.

The particular contribution of ethnographic and social historical studies to knowledge of religion lies in the attention to interconnections among domains of social life—among religion, economy, marriage, politics, and so forth—and to the ways that cultural ideas and social institutions shape activities in many of these domains. The importance of such cross-domain connections was underscored by the social theorists Émile Durkheim and Karl Marx, who continue to have a strong influence on many anthropologists (see Chapter 2). A particular religious practice such as worship may structure communities in particular ways, or lend a religious interpretation to existing social divisions, as when a Hindu priest distributes consecrated foods according to caste standing, or when men and women worship separately in a Muslim mosque, or when church pews are reserved for those who have contributed to the church.

The interpretation of texts and doctrines is strongly shaped by local factors, as Clifford Geertz (1968) showed in contrasting Islam in Morocco to Islam in Java, a contrast I revisit in Chapter 4. Comparing two or more cases of a practice can help to highlight these shaping processes, and in each of the following chapters I engage in such comparisons. In Chapter 4, for example, I contrast treatments of death in Japan, New Guinea, and Sumatra; in Chapter 6, patterns of sorcery in Africa and Asia; in Chapter 14, Muslim migrations to different counties in Europe; and in Chapter 15, the relationship of religion and state in Germany, France, Britain, and the United States.

Finally, I consider the diversity of religious understandings and practices even in small-scale societies. This internal diversity includes questions of how knowledge and ideas are distributed in the society—between men and women, or adults and children, or across other social groupings—as well as the debates among people about how best to understand the norms and forms of religious culture. Anthropology has often been insufficiently attentive to internal diversity. This insufficiency has been due in part to the idea that a "culture" is an integrated whole, an idea inherited from German nineteenth-century cultural studies, and in part due to ways of carrying out research by concentrating on a small number of "key informants"—or even, in some extreme cases, one such informant.

We know that the same practice may be interpreted in myriad and diverse ways. Beginning from particular religious practices and then examining diverse interpretations allow us to capture these diversities, and in some cases explain them in terms of accompanying social differences and changes. Certain religious traditions allow a particularly broad diversity of practices to flourish—the case of Japan is explored in Chapter 3. Debates within Islam are explored at several points in this book. I draw on my own fieldwork with the Muslim Gayo of Sumatra and on Islam in Europe in some of these chapters. I also examine debates within Christianity: concerning the role of the Virgin Mary in Chapter 8 and the nature of divine election in Chapter 11.

The final chapter returns us to the broad debates concerning the place of religion in public life with which I began this chapter. It is with an eye to these debates that I write this book. A great deal of misunderstanding and, to my mind, wrong-headed public policy in many countries, but certainly in the United States, has been based on ideas about religion that ignore diversities, debates, and possibilities. For example, particular features of certain strata of Middle Eastern societies (the role of women, views on Islamic law, etc.) are frequently confused with Islam in general. Religious beliefs are all open to debate and transformation; attending to those debates reminds us of a sense of the open-ended nature of religious ideas.

Conclusions

Anthropology approaches any social phenomenon in the terms outlined here: through long-term knowledge of people, wherein they learn local perspectives, and by looking for interconnections across domains. This perspective entails studying religious ideas and texts as they are written, read, and referred to in social life. It prevents us from assuming that we can discover something about a religion only by reading its scriptures, because we learn nothing from doing that about how people understand their scriptures. We give a broad definition of religion here, and then ask for each society we study: How do *they* cut up the world? Do they have concept of "religion"? How does it differ from other areas of social life?

Discussion Questions

You may have rituals you carry out in everyday life to ensure good luck; are these practices religious to you? Why or why not?

Take a current newspaper article that refers to a religion, or that identifies someone as a Catholic, a Muslim, or a Jew. What questions would an anthropologist want to pose to the author of the article?

Media Resources

The related controversies about "shariah law in America" have been covered at Jurist: http://jurist.org/paperchase/2011/09/federal-appeals-court-considers-oklahoma-sharia-law-ban.php

The Twin Transformations of "Religion"

We write about religions today against a long background of history, including two major transformations in how people practice and understand what we now call "religion." One such transformation occurred about 2,500 years ago along a broad band of civilizations stretching from Greece to China. The other occurred over the past two centuries, as colonial powers sought to regulate religions, and scholars based in those powers sought to classify them.

AXIAL AGE TRANSFORMATIONS

It was the philosopher Karl Jaspers, writing in 1949, who first drew attention to an extraordinary thing: that in a relatively short span of human history, between about 800 and 200 B.C.E., people living across Eurasia radically changed how they thought about divinity and how they acted toward it. He termed this period the "pivotal" or "axial" age, and saw it as the beginning of our own cultural world. In broad terms, this new age included the early great philosophers of Greece, Iran, India, and China, who began to ask general questions about who we are and what the purpose of our lives might be.

In more specific, "religions in practice" terms, the transformation involved placing less emphasis on sacrifices and offerings, and more on attending to divine commandments. Whereas before people undertook rituals, usually sacrifices, in order to propitiate the gods (or God), now people began to question why powerful gods would need burnt offerings. Would not obedience to their word be more in keeping with their strength and our weakness? Prophets and sages began to ask questions about social justice and ethics. Why is there oppression? What does God (or gods, or the Heavens) intend, plan, and create?

We will look at the ideas more deeply later, but let's start from where Jaspers did, by noting who was living and teaching during that time. On the early side is the Biblical prophet called the second Isaiah, who (around 740–700 B.C.E.) urged the Jews to obey the Law rather than offer up burnt sacrifice. Three major Asian figures arrived about a

11

century and a half later: Gautama Buddha in South Asia (563–483 B.C.E.), and Lao Tse (sixth century B.C.E.) and Confucius (551–479 B.C.E.) in China. On the more recent end is Socrates (469–399 B.C.E.), who radically challenged established truths in Athens. What did these figures have in common? Two elements: the argument that power lay in a transcendent realm (heaven and God) and that truth lay in an ethical code. On an intellectual plane, some people in Greece, Israel, India, and China at this time were engaged in theoretical thinking or what we might call "second-order thinking." How can we prove a theorem in geometry? How do we proceed to know something about the good life? These are questions about how we do and how we should reason through tough issues, and they laid the bases for philosophy.

Why were similar questions posed, and a similar emphasis on the transcendent posited, at roughly the same time across this large expanse of societies? Well, in this area people were trading, traveling, and moving—sometimes against their will—much more than before. Specialized agriculture and small craft production gave rise to lively trade, largely managed by small urban structures and small states that remained outside of large empires. Market society was growing and bringing with it new questions about ethics and meaning. Coinage, laws of commerce, and translation across languages and across belief systems were part and parcel of the movements across boundaries that trade encouraged. (Gore Vidal's novel *Creation* concerns fictive encounters among these great thinkers.) The empires in Persia, North India, and China assimilated some peoples and pushed others outwards.

As people began to move around more and seek points in common with others, they emphasized the more universalistic elements of their religious traditions. Movement and exchange lead people to seek "common denominators." A command to sacrifice a goat on such and such a hill is fine when you live near that hill, but not when you are exiled (as were the Jews to Babylon in the sixth century B.C.E.) or when you travel long distances to trade—for example, along the various segments of what came to be called the Silk Road, expanded through Persia in the seventh and sixth centuries B.C.E., and in Asia Minor under Alexander the Great and his successors in the fourth century B.C.E.

The new philosophies and theologies converged on ideas of a transcendent source of morals and order, but they differed as to how they saw the world. For example, Chinese philosophy does not posit a radical break between this world and another, whereas the Jewish theology found in the second Isaiah does do that. But the Chinese idea of the Heavenly mandate does locate power, well, in the heavens. In the Confucian Analects (II.3), we read:

> The Master said: "Guide them by edicts, keep them in line with punishments, and the common people will keep out of trouble but will have no sense of shame. Guide them by virtue, keep them in line with rites and they will, besides having a sense of shame, reform themselves."

When the ruler cultivates virtues, there is social harmony and order in the realm. Religion, *li*, is part of what the ruler dictates for the social good, for when the people worship spirits and keep rites and ceremonies, they will cultivate order in themselves and around them.

Israelites

Let us consider the Jewish case more closely. Unlike in China, at issue here was a personal relationship between a God and his people. Jewish ritual had been organized around sacrifice, first mentioned when God takes Abel's offering and refuses Cain's in Genesis, an event that introduces homicide and guilt to the world. David and his son Solomon united the tribes of Israel into a kingdom during the tenth century B.C.E. and built a Temple in Jerusalem, where sacrifice regularly took place. At least by the seventh century B.C.E., when Josiah forbade sacrifices "in the high places," meaning the scattered local altars, sacrifice had become exclusively centered on the Temple.

But Israelites were also considering other ways of reshaping political and religious society, and at this time we also read emerging criticisms of the notion that God is best worshiped through sacrifice. The prophet known as first Isaiah, writing sometime before the exile, quotes God as wearily castigating his sacrificing flock (1:11):

> *What to me is the multitude of your sacrifices?*
> *says the Lord;*
> *I have had enough of burnt offerings of rams*
> *and the fat of fed beasts;*
> *I do not delight in the blood of bulls,*
> *or of lambs, or of he-goats.*

God then orders his people to stop approaching with hands "full of blood," but instead to focus on their own purity (1:16):

> *Wash yourselves; make yourselves clean;*
> *remove the evil of your doings*
> *from before my eyes;*
> *cease to do evil.*

Sacrifice was made impossible when the Babylonians destroyed the Temple and sent the Jews in exile to Babylon ("by the waters of Babylon …") in the sixth century. Some dreamed of a restored Temple, where sacrifice would once again be carried out—Ezekiel (45–46) speaks in great detail of how the Temple will be rebuilt and burnt offerings made. But after the end of exile, when Cyrus of Persia permitted the Jews to return to Jerusalem, religious practice became primarily about maintaining the laws of ritual purity. Ezra, the chief creator of a post-exile life, was himself a priest and a scribe, not a hereditary king. Furthermore, many Jews continued to live outside of Judea, in the diaspora areas of Syria, Egypt, and Babylonia. If they did not have the Temple close at hand, they did have the Law of Moses as contained in the first five books of the Bible, the Pentateuch. It was in the period after return from exile that this Law was compiled in roughly the form we know it today. The Law, with its emphases on obedience to transcendent commands, reflects the new social reality of a scattered people.

Over the final centuries before the Common Era, Judea passed from Persian to Greek Rule, and the Jewish community itself became more and more internally differentiated. Even as the upper classes moved into the political and cultural world of the Greeks, others emphasized the importance of hewing to the Law. These groups included various pious groups of *hasidim*, the Maccabees (leaders of a successful revolt against the Greek rulers in 167 B.C.E.), and the later Pharisees, students of the Bible and strict followers of the laws of ritual purity.

Debate ensued over the question "what is a Jew?" Is a Jew anyone who claims to be a Jew, or only those people who maintain ritual purity? The Pharisees held to the latter position, and their answer prevailed: A Jew was someone who observed the Law as it had been handed down from Moses to the authorities of the day.

Religion had shifted from the group's sacrifice of animals, to each individual's avoidance of certain tabooed animals. From destroying life in atonement for sin, religious life was refocused on living according to the Law. This change was further intensified when Roman rulers destroyed the second Jerusalem Temple in 70 C.E. and then expelled the Jews from the city in 135 C.E. Gone was the possibility of worship through sacrifice. Religious scholars, rabbis, became the leaders of the community, and sought to rebuild religious life around the idea that by obeying the Law in their homes, Jews could experience the divine without a Temple. A general, shared religious life could be created through the medium of the Law, and observing the proscriptions contained in it would also keep the Jews separate and distinct. Taboos and boundaries became central elements in everyday life.

We will turn to the South Asian case in Chapter 7 when we examine the parallel transformation of Hinduism, from a religion based on sacrifice to one based on the avoidance of violence. But at present let us look at the second transformation, occurring much later.

ENLIGHTENMENT TRANSFORMATIONS

For most of Western Christian history, religion was regarded as an individual's personal piety or faith, not as a set of systems of belief and practice. Current ways of regarding religions and of studying them date from transformations traceable to the European Enlightenment and to the expansion of European power through trade, travel, and colonial rule.

The word *religion* comes from the Latin word *religio,* whose early meaning appears to have been "a power outside the individual, or a feeling relative to such a power." *Religiosus* meant a powerful place and conveyed a sense of mystery. The term also came to refer to the particular pattern of worship, the *religiones,* due a certain god (Smith 1978, 19–31).

The early leaders of the Christian Church adopted these usages from the Romans. Roman authorities forced the early Christians to participate in the traditional Roman cultic ceremonies. If they refused, they were often put to death. So, the key issue about religion was how to worship: the Roman way or exclusively the Christian way—the choice was literally a matter of life and death. This focus on one's own religious rituals as opposed to those of other people gave rise to the new idea that there was more than one way to practice religion: our way of worship (*nostra religio*) as opposed to the *religiones* of outsiders. In this context, the phrase "the Christian religion" was often used to mean the Eucharist, the central ritual performed by people considering themselves Christians.

The concept of religion might then have developed its current meaning, as a term used to refer to the system of beliefs and practices of each of a number of societies. But it did not develop in this way, and the word *religion* itself virtually passed out of existence for a thousand years. (An exception is St. Augustine, whose *De Vera Religione* we might translate as "On Proper Piety"; it concerned the bond between an individual and God and not a system of beliefs and practices.) People did not write books about religion, but about faith, on the one hand, and the institutions of the church, on the other.

Despite the general impression, true in many ways, that the European Middle Ages were an age of religion, it appears that no one ever wrote a book using "religion" in the title or as a concept during this period. Not until the fifteenth century, during the Renaissance, was the term taken up again, and then with the sense of a universal capacity for piety and worship common to all human beings. There was to be only one kind of *religio*, but it would exist in different degrees in different people.

The Reformation continued this line of thought; both Martin Luther and John Calvin stressed the importance of individual piety and faith over and against any external religious system, by which they meant the Catholic Church. Luther inveighed against any "false religion," or putting faith in religion rather than in God. Indeed, Luther inaugurated a tradition in the German language of avoiding the term "religion" altogether in favor of *Gottesdienst*, "service to God" (Smith 1978, 35).

Religions as Objects of Study

The idea of religion as a system of beliefs, as opposed to personal piety, did not take hold until the seventeenth century. The change was partly the result of efforts during the Enlightenment to classify and understand the world. It was also because of a growing diversity of religious claims within Europe and the increased awareness, because of trade and travel, of religious traditions beyond Europe. By the eighteenth century, treatises on religions of the world began to appear, introducing the fact of religious pluralism. The plural form "religions" is possible only when we think of religion as a cultural system rather than a personal one. There are no plural forms for "piety," "reverence," or "obedience."

As Europeans began to study other religions, they tended to use the religions most familiar to them, namely Judaism and Christianity, as a general model. They assumed all religions would have three central elements: a central *text*, *exclusivity*, and *separation*. The central text was assumed to be a collection of doctrines or beliefs that all adherents shared, ideally, written in a sacred book that had been inspired by a god or gods. Exclusivity meant that a person was a member of one and only one religion, at least at any one time. Separation indicated that religion constituted an area of social life distinct from politics or economics.

The idea of religion as a separate domain developed in modern Western Europe, partly in response to the destructive religious wars of the seventeenth century. John Locke, writing in the late seventeenth century, advocated the separation of state and religion as a way of ensuring toleration and religious freedom. His argument became the basis for the principle of separation of church and state in the United States; nowhere else was it so fully realized. But long before Locke, the struggles for power between kings and Popes made it difficult to think of the world as constructed around a single religious truth. As Charles Taylor (2007) argues, the modern age is "secular" in precisely this sense that religious believers live in the awareness that there are alternatives, that the world cannot be defined in religious terms, because it contains followers of other religions (in the modern sense) as well as those who follow no religion.

While this model of religion as a separate domain may have worked well to meet the changing perceptions and desires of Europeans, it fit poorly with the religious situation in India, China, or Japan. In each of these large geographical zones, no single book did or does provide a shared creed for practitioners of religion; instead, people refer to one or more of a variety of teachings on diverse aspects of life, and they choose distinct teachers or organizations. Today we know these collections of texts and teachers under the general rubrics of *Hinduism, Buddhism, Taoism,* or *Shinto*, but these labels are modern inventions.

Nor does the idea of exclusivity fit these societies. In Japan today, for example, people routinely bring offerings to shrines dedicated to local gods (practices associated with the label *Shinto*) and, in the same temple complex, venerate Buddha figures (see Chapter 3). The same people may marry in a Christian church. The idea of a separate religious sphere is also alien to many other religious traditions. Many Muslims argue that all of life should be conducted in accord with God's commands. Hinduism involves ideas of purity and pollution that permeate all of social life.

But despite these problems with the European model of religion, modern European attempts to understand these other religions worked from the European model. By the nineteenth century, books appeared about other religions and they introduced the names that we use today. *Buddhism* was first used in 1801 and *Hinduism* in 1829. (Before then writers referred, more accurately, to "the wisdom of the Japanese" or to "Hindu teachings.") The term *Islam* also began to be used in Europe; previously, Europeans referred to *Muhammadenism,* treating Islam not as a religion, but as allegiance to a false prophet (Smith 1978, 51–79).

The nineteenth-century European notions of what counted as a religion have powerfully shaped how other religions and other countries have viewed religion. For, with few exceptions, the creation of terms for *religion* and for particular religions has been the result of Western, Christian influence, transmitted through colonial domination.

Take what we often refer to as Hinduism. In India today, religious practice and the precise formulations of doctrine vary from place to place. Indeed, it is a central tenet of religious teaching in India that one should follow the inspiration derived from one's teacher in pursuit of enlightenment. Thus, there is no, nor is there supposed to be, one single formulation of Hindu Religion.

The word *Hindu* itself was not used by ancient Indians to refer to their religion. It is a word meaning "river," and in particular is used as the proper name for the Indus River. Foreigners—Greeks, then Muslim conquerors—came to designate the people living near that river as "Indian" or "Hindu." Under Muslim rule, the term came to be used to refer to all non-Muslims in the country, including Buddhists and Jains. Only recently has *Hindu* been used as a residual term to designate those people, and their beliefs, who are residents of India but who are not Jains, Sikhs, Christians, Muslims, or animists. But in the 1980s and 1990s, some politicians made the creation of a "Hindu India" their party platform, and they succeeded in rallying large numbers of supporters to their cause. Whatever was once the case, today "Hindu" is experienced by many Indians as a unitary social as well as religious category (see Chapter 7).

The Chinese, too, had no word corresponding to the Western idea of religion. They eventually borrowed a word from the Japanese, *Tsung-Chiao,* which the Japanese themselves had created to accommodate the Western concept. Nor did Chinese have words meaning Confucianism, Buddhism, or Taoism in the sense of religions that one joined or left. Instead, people were aware of collections of teachings that could be followed in trying to find a path toward truth. These teachings included the sayings of Confucius, Buddha, and Lao Tse (a possibly mythic figure who urged followers to find the true path, or Tao).

In a rather neat exchange of terms, foreigners seeking to refer to indigenous traditions in Japan used a term, *Shinto,* that came from Chinese. Japanese themselves use a translation of the Chinese borrowing—*kami no michi,* or "the way of the spirits or gods"—to refer to these practices (Reader 1991, 23). What is and is not included in the definition of religion is a matter of much public interest in Japan today. At the end of the nineteenth century, the Japanese government declared that the indigenous, or Shinto, worship at shrines was not a religion. But what came to be called State Shinto, to which the cult of the emperor was central, became an ideological pillar of twentieth-century Japanese efforts to modernize society, and for that reason the cult was abolished under the post–World War II occupation.

The boundaries of religion were again debated when the new emperor, Akihito, succeeded his father, Hirohito, in January 1989. According to Shinto creed, the emperor is the descendant of the Sun Goddess, and he performs certain rituals at the goddess's shrine when he takes office. Are these rituals to be taken as religious? If so, they imply his claim to be the chief priest of Shinto and the intermediary to the Sun Goddess. But this status was abolished under the occupation, in the Constitution. Are they just political rituals? There was a fierce debate in Japan over this question, and the matter (which we consider in Chapter 3) remains unsettled.

The names for religions were often provided by outsiders—one can add to the preceding examples that the term *Judaism* is Greek, not Hebrew. The name *Islam,* used from the beginning by the religion's adherents, is the major exception. However, the term means "submission to God," not the set of beliefs and practices themselves. Indeed, the religious scholar Wilfred Cantwell Smith (1978, 114) has argued that if one believes in God as a Jew or Christian, and realizes that from an Islamic perspective Muslims, Christians, and Jews worship the same God, then one cannot truthfully say in Arabic, "I am not a Muslim." One submits to God, after all, in whatever language. Fred Donner (2010) argues that early Muslims spoke of al-muslimûn, "the believers" to refer to all those who believed in God, a way of looking at faith and submission that corresponded to Muhammad's rule over a Medina that included Jews and others.

SOCIAL THEORY AND THE ANTHROPOLOGY OF RELIGION

As Europeans were beginning to think of "religions" as distinct sets of beliefs and practices, European social scientists and theorists began to ask new questions about these phenomena. The question "why religion" came to be posed within the context of different theories about society, culture, and psychology. Theorists such as E. B. Tylor focused on the distinctive ideas that characterize religions, and asked why people hold certain religious ideas and not others. We continue, today, to ask this question, for example, within cognitive anthropology and evolutionary psychology. Other theorists, such as Émile Durkheim, focused on the social realities (and, he thought, origins) of religious practices and groups. Much of the sociology and social anthropology of religions grow out of the questions asked by Durkheim: Why do people join, and remain part of, organized religions? Other social theorists came to look at religion as part of broader theoretical preoccupations. Karl Marx and Max Weber asked how modern capitalism came to dominate the world. Each had his own approach, and his own ideas of religion fit into the picture: for Marx, as part of the structures that subtended a particular form of economic organization; for Weber, as a source of outlook on life that animated much of what people did in their economic and social lives.

RELIGION AND MIND

One dimension of religion is the intellectual: What do people think exists, and why do they think those things? These questions are still with us and justify turning to some of the major figures who posed them.

In the mid-nineteenth century, the early years of anthropology as a formal discipline, scholars in most disciplines tried to explain the diversity and complexity of today's religions by postulating a process of religious evolution. They were strongly influenced by German idealist philosophers, who saw human history as the development of a set of human essences. These philosophers understood religion as a unity of thought and feeling, intellect and emotion that had developed historically from initial germs. The philosopher Hegel postulated a universal idea of religion that preceded its particular historical manifestations. As it developed over time from an initial germ, it became increasingly complex. This idea of development or evolution did not concern the history of a particular religion or a particular people, but the evolution across time and space of an idea, independent of particular cultures.

This theory of general human cultural evolution provided the intellectual framework for the early anthropology of religion, as well as for social anthropology more generally. The comparative study of religion in the late nineteenth century was based on two assumptions: that religion progressed from the simple to the complex and that one could reconstruct the origins of religion by studying "primitive peoples" in the world today. Many students of the origins of religion did not subscribe to the universal truths offered by their churches, and their accounts were more or less subtle ways of discrediting the absolute truth of Christianity. If Catholic or Anglican beliefs evolved from something very simple, then they looked much less absolute than if they had been delivered through divine revelation.

E. B. Tylor and the Origins of Religious Ideas

The most famous study along these lines was *Primitive Culture* (1970 [1871]) by Edward B. Tylor (1832–1917). Tylor was the first person to be appointed to a university position in anthropology in England, in 1884 at Oxford. He argued that primitive people acted as proto-scientists when they created religion, constructing concepts to explain what they perceived through their senses. Tylor (1970, vol. 2) asked: "What is true of all religions?" He looked around him and saw that all religions employed a belief in spiritual beings. The higher ones had souls, gods, angels, and so on, while the more primitive ones had spirits and ghosts. The primitive form of this belief he called animism. He saw this belief as basic to religious development.

"Why do people come to hold such a belief?" he then asked, and answered that it might well be because they perceive things that lead them to suppose these spiritual entities. They perceive different states of consciousness (wakefulness, sleep, and death), dreams (and the appearance in them of places and persons), and shadows. Then they think up things to explain these appearances. "Soul" explains the different states of consciousness, because as the soul sleeps, or leaves the body, we lose consciousness or pass into death. "Ghost" or "spirit" explains the phenomenon of dreams, because as we sleep, our ghost or spirit leaves the body and travels to other places, and we vaguely remember these wandering perceptions when we wake. Finally, shadows are one form taken by souls and ghosts.

Tylor was able to amass a large body of evidence to support his claims. Religion was due to "the plain evidence of men's senses" for Tylor, and as it develops, it continues to build on perceptions and logic. People reasoned that because animals, too, have life, they must have souls as well. If they are killed, their souls can follow those of their masters to the world of the beyond, and there do work for them. Burial practices from such diverse civilizations as Egypt and China attest to this belief. Furthermore, because plants also live and die, they must have souls as well. All living things, concludes Tylor's primitive thinker, thus have souls; such is the origin of "animism," the belief that all living things are "animated" by souls.

But how is it, asks Tylor, that such ideas have survived until today? One way is through psychological development. As children, we have the very same experiences, and make the very same inferences, as did primitive people: We have dreams and we attribute life to things and play with them as if they were alive. When we grow up, we are thus prepared to accept as true, because in some sense natural, the claims of the religions we are taught. We do so because—and here is the second way the early ideas survived—the ideas of advanced religions are merely further elaborations of the primitive ideas. Tylor offers the example of the Eucharist, the Christian ritual wherein bread and wine become, or symbolize, Christ's body and blood. This ritual might appear to be far from primitive religion. But, he argues, it is but the further development of the idea of sacrifice, which itself was based on the notion that the soul of the sacrificed animal or person would travel to the world beyond.

Tylor's account of religion captures elements that one does, indeed, find throughout the world. The ideas of soul, spirit, dreams that he described as basic or primitive do indeed animate many religious systems. Tylor's weakness, from our contemporary perspective, is that he emphasized an essential commonality to all religious beliefs and thus played down what most anthropologists emphasize today, namely, the diversity of ways in which humans have constructed their religious beliefs and practices. But by analyzing the logic of a set of beliefs, Tylor did inspire his successors to analyze the different ways people have constructed their understandings of the cosmos, their "world views."

An eminent successor to Tylor in this enterprise was James Frazer (1854–1951) whose massive compendium of religion and myth, *The Golden Bough* (1981 [1890]), first issued in 2 volumes and later expanded to 12, brought together in a readable style much of the knowledge of the day about comparative religion. Frazer followed Tylor in sharply distinguishing among science, magic, and religion as distinct modes of thought. Religion, in their view, involves acts intended to appease deities; magic, like science, assumes impersonal relationships between certain actions and their outcomes. Magic rests on two basic, albeit mistaken, ideas. The first idea is that of similarity, that is, like causes like (a green stone will cure jaundice). The second idea, contagion, implies that contact between two objects allows someone to control one through manipulating the other: A person's hair-clippings can be burned, for example, thereby harming the person. Magic is thus pseudoscience; religion proper involves a qualitatively different kind of activity.

Tylor and Frazer's intellectualist legacy was to focus anthropological energies on understanding how particular people view the world, taking their world view seriously as an intellectual or philosophical enterprise. Most anthropologists continued to pose these questions thereafter. Notably, in the United States, Franz Boas and his students developed cultural anthropology around a twofold approach to studying small-scale societies. On the one hand, they sought to discern the patterns of each culture as they were reflected in art, myth, kinship, and everyday ways of speaking. On the other hand, they traced the historical processes through which people transmit cultural ideas across societies and also change them. This dual focus on both ideas and empirical processes reflects Boas's own German training in both empirical sciences and idealist philosophy.

Claude Lévi-Strauss and the Structure of Mythic Thinking

Boas's complex approach to myths probably was best continued by the French anthropologist Claude Lévi-Strauss. Lévi-Strauss drew from Tylor's analysis of the intellectual operations detectable in myth-making, but he also, following Boas, sought to trace transformations of myths as they have passed from one society to another. Myths, in his analysis, are composed according to intricate codes, each of which concerns a distinct level of local life and awareness: a code of flora and fauna, one of geography, one of social institutions, and so on. These codes are structured as oppositions among categories: cold versus hot, high versus low, mother's versus father's relatives, and so forth. Moreover, neighboring peoples often tell contrasting versions of these myths, and these contrasts across societies indicate that myths reflect differences in local social life, and that they may function to underscore the boundaries between peoples.

In one of his best known analyses, Lévi-Strauss dissects a myth told among several peoples of the Northwest Coast of North America, the "Story of Asdiwal" (1976). The myth is structured around four distinct codes of geography, economy, society, and cosmology. Events often concern all four codes at once: for example, a marriage involves geographical movement, fishing, a particular kind of marriage institution, and movements between earth and sky. Lévi-Strauss argues that the myth depicts in especially salient ways the contradictions that are the basis of Tsimshian society. Marriages among families of chiefs, for example, were supposed to create or reaffirm relations of hierarchy among them, but precisely who was superior to whom was debated fiercely at each marriage. The myths depict such chiefly marriages as ending in death and battle, thus representing in heightened form problems inherent in the social structure. The myths also try out alternative realities, such as trying to inherit from one's father and one's mother, "in order to show that they are untenable" (1976, 173).

Differences between two versions of the myth show how myths, as they are transferred from one place to another, are recast in light of local conditions. One version was collected along the coast, from people who make a great seasonal migration from one region to another to catch candlefish in the spring from one river and salmon in the summer from another. In their version of the myth, characters travel great distances and they engage in very different economic pursuits, as do the humans telling the myth. Lévi-Strauss points out that this version of the myth is characterized by strong oppositions between categories along geographical and economic codes. But oppositions are also strong along the social and cosmological codes (for example, featuring people who are distantly related to each other), as if to follow the oppositions generated by the codes of economic life and geographic movement. This priority of some codes, the economic and geographic, over others is mentioned by Lévi-Strauss in referring to himself as a Marxist.

In the versions of the myth that were collected along a river where the residents made fewer movements in the course of the year—they hunted candlefish but not salmon, for example—the oppositions were weaker, again along all four codes. This comparative analysis thus supports Lévi-Strauss's conclusions that codes of a myth are internally integrated and that they all differ in a systematic way across societies. Others, especially James A. Boon (1990), have used this insight in their own ethnographic analyses of how people structure religious and social life through their use of oppositions and contrasts. In these studies, myths are seen as extended commentaries on the practice of everyday social life.

Max Weber and Suffering

Mind is broader than the intellectualist accounts might suggest. Max Weber (1864–1920) sought to provide an account of the broad orientations individuals might develop toward the world as a consequence of their reflection on their religious doctrines, not as a simple consequence of that doctrine. In particular, he wished to explain how different religious orientations toward the world would produce different economic ethics, leading to different kinds of economic organization. In particular, he sought to explain how Protestant ideas spurred on modern capitalism in Europe—most particularly the early Protestant ideas of "unknowable election," that some people were elected to heaven and others condemned to hell, but that no one could know his or her category nor change what God had preordained. Weber argued that this doctrine, taught by the theologian John Calvin, was so unsettling that people worked hard to succeed in this world, grasping at the idea that the material signs of their success also were signs of God's favor. The "Protestant ethic" was thus the psychological consequence of a specific doctrine, and it, not the doctrine itself, was a key element in the rise of modern capitalism.

Weber thought that the idea of predestination also served to affirm the absolute, transcendent power of God over his creations. The idea explains the presence of evil in the world by stating that God's motives are beyond human understanding. The idea is basic to one of the most powerful and enigmatic of the Bible stories, the story of Job. The story concerns how Job retains his faith in God through a series of terrible tests—he loses his family, health, and wealth. God wagers with Satan, allowing Satan to inflict these sufferings, with Job's faith as the prize. Job has done nothing to deserve his suffering, but suffer he does. Others voice to Job their belief in a rule-bound God: "Does God pervert justice?" asks one. But of course God does do precisely that, or, rather, he stands above human norms of justice. It is human self-righteousness that leads people to challenge God: "Will you condemn me that you may be justified?" answers God out of a whirlwind (40 Job v.8). The point of the story is to show the reader or listener someone who loses everything and yet keeps his faith—and finally understands the total power of God and his demand for total submission to him.

The Book of Job offers to those who read it a sense that their own suffering is not to be argued with but accepted. This acceptance may provide a psychologically powerful, perhaps comforting way to survive suffering. One finds similar narratives in other religions. For many Muslims, the story of the martyrdom of Husain at the Battle of Karbala plays this role. The story concerns how Husain, the grandson of the prophet Muhammad, died through treachery in battle. The story is important to those Muslims who believe that Muhammad's descendants are his rightful successors. Every year, these Muslims, called the *Shi'i*, or "Shiites," celebrate Husain's martyrdom as an enacted narrative of their own suffering, and their position today as a minority within the Muslim world. The processions in which Husain rides his horse through large crowds of celebrants, while some beat themselves bloody with sticks or chains, dramatize and religiously contextualize suffering (Waugh 1977).

Elsewhere, Christians stage similar reenactments of Christ's suffering on his way to crucifixion. In some societies people volunteer to play the role of the crucified Christ, enduring great suffering as they are hung from crosses. These "passion plays," public dramatization of suffering and death, remind the faithful of the human drama captured in the phrase, "he died for your sins."

Each of these stories and reenactments represents suffering as part of a broader framework, one that not only transcends but also adds meaning to human societies. We can see these stories as some responses among many to the general human problem of how to endure suffering. They can enable us to place our own problems "in perspective."

Religion Explained by Emotions

Other social theorists have based their approaches to religion more completely in psychology than did Weber. Although the notion that religion springs from emotions is ancient, an important modern argument along these lines came from David Hume, the philosopher of the Scottish Enlightenment. In his *Natural History of Religion* (1757), Hume argued that religion first came from "the incessant hopes and fears which actuate the human mind." Religion thus offers one way of overcoming anxiety.

This idea was given ethnographic substance by Bronislaw Malinowski (1884–1942), one of the first anthropologists to carry out long-term fieldwork. Malinowski worked in the Trobriand Islands, today part of Papua New Guinea, between 1915 and 1918. He distinguished between the practical, rational knowledge and skills that Trobrianders employ to carry out their everyday tasks and the religion and magic they call on to supplement their knowledge and powers. Ideas about the afterlife help people live despite their knowledge that death awaits them, wrote Malinowski, and funeral rituals add further authority to the idea that something awaits them after death. These rituals and ideas "save man from a surrender to death and destruction" (1954 [1926], 51). Ideas about the powers of spells and prayer to change the world also serve a psychological function; they reduce the anxiety that comes from uncertainty, allowing people to carry on their practical life. Religion and magic are thus not pseudosciences; rather, they arise in response to deep-seated, innate human fears and concerns.

Malinowski was influenced by the psychologist William James (1842–1910). In his *Varieties of Religious Experience* (1972 [1901–1902]), James defined religion in terms of a set of individual human attitudes, as "the feelings, acts, and experiences of individual men in their solitude, so far as they apprehend themselves to stand in relation to whatever they may consider the divine." James advocated *pragmatism* in philosophy and science; in his version of this approach, the experiences one accumulates, whether in the laboratory or in everyday life, are the basis for deciding about truth and falsehood. Since belief in God works toward the general good, it is "true." Religious beliefs are validated when they are shown to have beneficial consequences, such as reducing anxiety and fear.

References today to innate or unconscious psychological impulses usually draw on the writings of Sigmund Freud (1856–1939), the founder of modern psychoanalysis. Freud argued that the psyche was more than the conscious. Powerful drives for self-preservation and pleasure often shape our actions and conscious ideas in ways of which we are only half-aware. These drives in the individual run headlong into societal norms, creating repression and neuroses. Freud's (1930) own views on religion were largely negative. Born of infantile feelings of helplessness and society-caused suffering, religion only keeps us from rationally critiquing and rebuilding our social lives, he wrote. But Freud's ideas about the power of religious symbols have been used by some anthropologists to explain why certain objects—hair, the color white, blood, and so on—have the frequent and powerful positions they do in religious rituals.

Other theorists and historians of religion have taken up the issue of how and why certain symbols have widespread power. Among them are theorists who stress the irreducible nature of religious experience. Carl Jung (1875–1961), a student of Freud, saw religion as an experience of awe at the power of the divine, a submission to a superior power that is later codified into doctrines and rituals. Jung followed William James and the theologian Rudolf Otto in finding the truth of religion in these religious experiences. But Jung then postulated a "collective unconscious" of humankind that contains all religious symbols. These symbols stem from "archetypes" that are innate in every human being and that make possible the translation of religious experiences across persons and cultures. These archetypes—the hero, the earth mother, gods, and so on—form the basis of the universal religious experience.

Also viewing religion in terms of archetypes is Mircea Eliade (1907–1986). Eliade exemplifies the "phenomenological" study of religion, that is, bracketing what we think we know of the external world to focus our study on experience itself as an irreducible phenomenon. For Eliade (1954 [1949]), religious objects, acts, and roles are symbols that have multiple meanings but that eventually come together in a cosmological unity. This unity is mainly about the primordial creation of the universe. Eliade examines myths and rituals from many societies, interpreting each as fundamentally about the creation of life, order, and the world. The view of religion in terms of universal archetypes has become even more popular through the writings of Joseph Campbell (1949) on myth. As with Tylor's intellectualist approach, however, this approach points to broad patterns but is unable to provide an analytical foundation for understanding specificities: how people have come to create and understand particular religious forms in particular times and places.

RELIGIONS IN SOCIAL LIFE

Although neither Tylor nor Lévi-Strauss conceived of religious ideas and practices as divorced from society, they underscored the intellectual dimension of religious ideas. Boas, too, and especially his students, emphasized the ways in which religious and other ideas cohere in patterns. As we will see, this emphasis on the cultural patterning of religion has retained a central role in anthropology.

But certain social theorists argued that religious ideas, sentiments, and orientations had developed out of specific social conditions. Each of the three major social theorists of modern Europe—Durkheim, Marx, and Weber—crafted some distinctive ways of understanding religion's relationship to broader social processes. All three theorists were primarily concerned with explaining features of modern life—the rise of modern capitalism, challenges to social solidarity, and the peculiar nature of rational and legal authority. In the process of developing their theories, they also tried to explain the role of religion in premodern societies.

Émile Durkheim on the Social Origins of Religion

Some scholars continued Tylor's quest for the origins of religion, but sought those origins in social life. The sociologist Émile Durkheim (1858–1917), for example, saw the birth of religion in the ideas and emotions generated out of collective social action. "Religious representations are collective representations that express collective realities," he wrote (1995, 9). Durkheim was not entirely the originator of this general idea. Aristotle, after all, had declared that "men create the gods after their own image." The French historian Fustel de Coulanges (1830–1889) and the Scottish scholar of Semitic societies W. Robertson-Smith (1846–1904) had linked social organization to religious ideas in ancient societies. Robertson-Smith had argued that the earliest societies had been totemic; that is, they had been organized into clans, each of which had a special relationship to a species of animal—"my clan is a wolf." Sacrificing this animal was a way to communicate and commune with the deities, and at the same time it was a means to strengthen the emotional bonds among clan members.

Durkheim drew from these earlier writers to argue that knowledge in general, and religious knowledge in particular, has a social foundation. His argument was philosophical, against Kant's idea that humans had innate categories of the understanding, by which he meant categories such as causality and temporal succession that people apply to everything in the world around them. But it was also social and moral, and grew out of the concerns of the day (Lukes 1973). Durkheim wrote at a time of great social and moral turmoil in France, when older certainties about God and Church had been excised from public and legal life by the Revolution but no alternative moral certainties had yet replaced them. The country appeared to be polarized between urban agnostics and rural Catholics. Battles were especially sharp over the future of the school system: Should it be secular or Catholic, and if secular, what would be its moral content? No wonder that in his first articles, Durkheim was deeply sensitive to the problem of social cohesion in contemporary society: "A society whose members are not bound to one another by some solid and durable link," he wrote in 1886, "would resemble a loose pile of dust which could at any time be dispersed by the slightest wind to the four corners of the world" (quoted in Alexander 1982, 82). But what are these bonds? And how do they unite people in societies that have not undergone the sort of schisms experienced by France?

As one would expect given the evolutionary way of thinking in vogue at the time, Durkheim sought his answer in a study of *The Elementary Forms of the Religious Life*, the title of his 1912 book. The book posits an early type of social consciousness in those societies where everyone is for all important purposes alike: Everyone has the same statuses, duties, and roles. In such societies, people's feelings are also alike, and thus strongly reinforce each other whenever people gather together. Moral sentiments, religious beliefs, and other cultural ideas are all very strong, and law, religion, and social norms are strong as well.

Durkheim postulated that religious beliefs and sentiments must correspond to something real and that they could not be purely illusory or mistaken, as Tylor and Frazer had concluded. These beliefs clearly were false if taken at face value. The problem then was to go underneath the symbol to the reality that it represents and that gives it its true meaning. Doing so required redefining the very idea of "religion."

Rather than defining it as the belief in spirits, as did Tylor and Frazer, Durkheim viewed it as involving a fundamental division of the world into sacred versus profane things. Religion is thus a collective reality that concerns how the members of a particular society divide up the world, rather than an individual reality consisting of what a person believes. But *how* the world is divided into sacred and profane varies greatly from one society to the next; what determines this division?

Here Durkheim accepts Robertson-Smith's thesis that totemism was the earliest basis for social organization and the wellspring of religion. He turns to the religions of Australian aborigines to prove his thesis. In these societies, specific groups perform rituals at sacred sites that are associated either with ancestral spirits or with mythical beings that lived during the ancient "dream time" that came before the time we know. Each group also has objects made of wood or stone engraved with symbols of these ancestors or mythical beings, and these *churinga* objects themselves have sacred powers.

Each such social group also has a special ritual relationship toward certain species, such as kangaroo, or certain natural phenomena, such as rain or wind. Members of the group may have special rules regulating their activities with respect to these species, the group's *totem*, and the group can carry out rituals that increase the species' numbers. These rituals sometimes involve eating an item of the species, and Durkheim thought that this practice confirmed the theory that sacrifice and communal eating were the earliest, basic forms of religious ritual.

Durkheim argued that the general idea of spiritual force that underlay totemism existed prior to ideas about spirits or souls, and he cited related ideas from other societies, such as the notion of impersonal force or *mana* in Melanesia. (He also could have cited the Chinese idea of life force, or *chi*.) This same force, at later stages of development, gives rise to ideas of souls, ancestral spirits, and God, stated Durkheim.

Durkheim set out his argument on two different levels. First, he explained the variety of religious ideas by arguing that particular features of societies give rise to particular features of their cultures and religions. Religion thus represents society. So, there are "societies in Australia and North America where space is conceived in the form of an immense circle, because the camp has a circular form." The early division of society into two halves or *moieties* gave rise to ideas of the cosmos as dualistic. In societies such as the Australians just discussed, where people were organized into clans, people often postulated an animal, or sacred place, or force, as the totem of that clan. These totems were the projections onto a spiritual place of a sense of belonging together in the clan. As the society grew and spread over a wider area, giving rise to a sense of a broad social group with shared interests that spilled over the boundaries of the clan, totemic representations synthesized into the idea of one or more gods, "the god being only a figurative expression of the society," Durkheim summarily stated (1995, 227).

This level of argument presumes that there already is a general religious idea that can be shaped by society. So arguing at a second level, Durkheim tried to explain the emergence of general religious ideas and sentiments in the first place. People sense a moral force that is exterior to them, he argued. This idea is given social content in those moments when people come together in social assemblies, such as dances, meetings, or festivals. These assemblies create a social effervescence out of which religious ideas are confirmed and given stronger emotional meaning. A qualitative change takes place and people began to feel themselves transported to an altered state.

Religion serves the function of strengthening social solidarity by communicating specific ideas and sentiments and by regulating and strengthening social relationships. A totem, for instance, reminds you what kind of person you are (a member of a certain clan) and thereby regulates relations among individuals. It also gives you a feeling of strength—speaking of one Australian society, Durkheim wrote: "The Arunta who has properly rubbed himself with his churinga feels stronger; he is stronger" (1995, 229).

This functionalist perspective on religion gave Durkheim a way of discussing the place of religion in modern society. Religion is no longer a satisfactory *cognitive* solution to the "problem of meaning," in which science is now the master. But religion continues to be *symbolically* important: Cult and faith are essential to any society's social solidarity, including our own, and that explains its continued hold on us. (This logic is what we mean by "functionalism": The positive social consequences of the beliefs or practices explain why they continue to exist.)

Durkheim emphasized the cognitive, emotional, and social aspects of religious ideas and practices. His *Elementary Forms* focuses on the social origins of religion by way of a theory of collective emotions; but there and in other writings, Durkheim also emphasizes the logical nature of religious classifications. In *Primitive Classification* (1963 [1903]), Durkheim and his nephew Marcel Mauss (1872–1950) compared the symbolic classifications found in Australian, native North American, and Chinese societies. The Zuni Pueblo people of the U.S. Southwest, for example, assign to each of the cardinal directions (plus center, and the zenith and nadir of the sun's apparent motion) a color, a season, and a kind of weather, together with a general force such as creation or destruction, a specific group, and an animal. Durkheim and Mauss claimed that members of these societies have created totalizing religious systems; these systems unite the social, natural, and cosmological realms. Their comparison of logical similarities across these societies inspired later anthropologists to make more detailed studies of symbolic classification.

Durkheim's legacy in the field of religious studies was twofold. First, he connected the religious to the social, leading later anthropologists to look for social origins or functions of specific religious practices and ideas. This strain of his legacy was a foundation of British social anthropology, from A. R. Radcliffe-Brown through Edmund Leach and Mary Douglas. For Mary Douglas, for example, the key to understanding food taboos, whether in the Hebrew Bible or in the societies of central Africa she studied in her fieldwork, is to look for the social functions such taboos may have served. She argued that by separating the sacred from the profane, and then by restricting membership in the community to those who observed the rules, food taboos make group membership sacred.

Durkheim also emphasized the ways that participating in collective religious practices confirm faith, and this insight remains compelling. Consider how many European Catholics find visions of Mary to be central events cementing their faith, or perhaps their hope within their faith. In less spectacular ways, the good feelings of participating in something with friends and neighbors may also make the religion particularly "true." Particularly important is the way in which public ritual generates religious commitment. A religious service in which many people worship together can be a wonderfully compelling context, generating a sense of being together and being in the presence of something else. Such feelings, perhaps most startlingly displayed when Christian worshipers speak in tongues, lay behind Durkheim's claim that coming together as a social group gave rise to the earliest ideas of the supernatural. Most people, however, most of the time, experience their activities of carrying out worship, consulting oracles, or avoiding tabooed foods as routine actions. It may indeed be the case that the routine nature of most of the religions' demands, the integration of religion into everyday life, provides a social and psychological comfort. (Perhaps you can think of moments when a religious gathering provokes heightened feelings of belonging together.)

Second, Durkheim connected the religious to the intellectual, in this respect continuing Tylor's emphasis on the intellect, but inverting it, explaining features of the intellect in terms of their origins in religion, seen as a *social* activity. "The essential notions of scientific logic are of religious origin," he wrote in *Elementary Forms* (1995, 431).

This last statement has broadly echoed in cultural anthropology throughout the world, and most notably by Claude Lévi-Strauss, who saw classificatory systems as the product of intense, imaginative intellectual activity. Rather than seeing totems and totemic social organization as a primitive form of identification that then gave rise to higher forms of society and religion, Lévi-Strauss considered them, in his *Totemism* (1963a [1962]), as one among many ways of classifying the world in order to understand it. Particular plants or animals are chosen to be totems not because they have utility or excite awe in themselves, but because they provide a usable symbolic template through which to make distinctions in the natural, social, and cosmological worlds.

Karl Marx on Religion in Capitalist Europe

Durkheim's approach to religion assumed that society, and therefore religion, was an integrated whole. But what if society is not like that, and instead consists of several groups whose interests and ideas are in conflict? How then ought we to understand the social origins and functions of religion?

This question lies behind the work of both Karl Marx and Max Weber. Karl Marx (1818–1883) emphasized the historical process by which different social groups come to dominate social life. The key to this process was the interplay between the material forces of production and the social relations of production: how things were produced and how their production and distribution was organized. Each historical period in European history has thrown up its own distinctive dominant ideology: politics in classical Rome, the Catholic Church in the medieval period, and capitalism as ideology in the modern period. Marx and his collaborator, Friedrich Engels, saw religion not only as serving ideological functions in all periods, as providing social cement in the face of class divisions, but also as expressing class interests (Marx and Engels 1965 [1846]).

Studies of religion inspired by Marx have looked for the material interests served by movements gathered together under the banner of religion. Engels (1956 [1850]) argued that the religious wars of the fifteenth and sixteenth centuries in Germany, although couched in the language of religious dissent, were motivated by the disparate interests of the nobility, burghers, and peasants. Among these movements were those millenarian Christian movements that prophesied the imminent moment (the "millennium," or thousand years) when the corrupt leaders of the church would face the Day of Judgment. German millenarian prophets combined apocalyptic teachings with calls for the end of the feudal system, supporting Engels's thesis that material interests and religious ideas were intertwined. Engels thus showed the power of religion to subvert as well as to confirm the existing social order. His study launched a distinguished tradition of investigations (for example, Worsley 1968) into the material and religious sources of those radical religious movements whose leaders preach an imminent radical transformation of society, if not the end of the world—"millenarian" in today's general sense of the term.

Max Weber on Religion in Modern Civilizations

Max Weber also analyzed the relationships between particular interest groups and religious ideas. Weber (1978 [1956]) took the social action of the individual as his unit, distinct from Durkheim's emphasis on social structure and function and Marx's emphasis on changing modes of production. Weber wrote that one can only come to understand social action by, first, discovering the meaning of the action for the individual and, second, by explaining it in terms of the social conditions and actions that preceded it. Social science thus involves both interpretation and causal–historical explanation.

Religion provides one major source of ideas and orientations for the actor, and Weber devoted much analysis to the comparative study of religions. His interest was not religious doctrine per se, but the spirit or *ethos* that was produced in individuals by their adherence to one faith versus another, as well as the social conditions that allowed new types of religious orientation to emerge. Weber saw the development of Western society as the progressive *rationalization* of society, a concept that implies both the increasing differentiation of social life into functionally defined domains or spheres—family, economy, religion, and so on—and the systematic reorganization of each domain around a single set of values or rules. Economy gradually became reorganized around the maximization of profit; family, around the general solidarity of kin; religion, around the worship of God. In Weber's view of Western world history, religion gradually shed its "magical" character and developed a set of universalistic doctrines about a divine order and a set of ethical principles that apply to everyone, everywhere.

Weber's theory of religious history is both sociological and universal. Weber carried out separate studies of India, China, Islam, ancient Judaism, and modern Europe. He saw each of these societies as characterized by a distinctive set of religious beliefs, a particular economic ethic, and a specific set of interest groups; his research concerned the interplay of these three elements. In his study of India, for example, Weber argued that the caste system and the doctrine of *karma*—the idea that one's actions in this or a previous life determined the course of one's life—inhibited the development of a rational economic ethic because it led religious energies away from this world and directed them toward the "other world." Only with the development of Calvinist Protestantism in Europe did there arise a religion-driven energy to rationally remold the world; this energy pushed forward modern capitalism.

Weber traced similar developmental processes within each socioreligious system. In the larger-scale societies he studied, prophets arose to challenge an older way of thinking, often in the name of a universal creed and god. But with the demise of the prophet, followers had to "routinize" the movement, creating a religious community or congregation. The eventual development of a rational, differentiated religious system required the parallel development of a bureaucratic state, whether in India, China, or Europe.

Weber's analysis rested on the "ideal types" he created—the other-worldly mystic and the this-worldly prophet. These types give us an initial, clear sense of the contrasts in dominant ideas among large-scale religions. But they are less useful in analyzing the many ways in which people reinterpret and transform those ideas. Weber's ideal types have been questioned by later students of each society. For example, Weber based his claims that the Indian doctrine of karma would retard economic development on the assumption that the doctrine contained in religious texts was also what ordinary people believed. But popular Indian ideas about fate and action in the world are not the same as the textual doctrines (Babb 1983), and they have not prevented people from engaging in modern industrial development (Singer 1964).

Symbols between Society and the Individual

Among anthropologists seeking to integrate sociological and psychological dimensions of religious practices was Victor Turner (1920–1983), whose work has focused on symbols and meanings. Turner is attentive to unconscious meanings and near-universal symbols, but he emphasizes the ways that ritual and social uses of symbolic objects shape their meanings for particular people.

Turner (1967) analyzes the meaning of symbols from three distinct perspectives. He begins by asking how members of the society explain a ritual or unpack the meaning of a statue. He then asks how objects are used in ritual processes and in interpreting their use. Finally, he examines the place of the object in a system of symbols. The meanings he derives from these three perspectives themselves are arrayed between two poles: one around which cluster meanings that relate to general human emotions and desires, especially those of a natural or physiological sort, and a second pole of social norms and values.

Turner's most famous symbolic analysis illustrates this process. His ethnographic work was done among the Ndembu of Zambia, a society organized around matriliny, that is, the continuity between mothers and children. When a girl reaches puberty, the Ndembu hold an initiation ceremony, during which they wrap the girl in a blanket and place her at the foot of a tree, the *mudyi*, known for its white latex. This ritual is thus known as a "white" ritual.

Turner understood the "native symbolic meaning" of the symbols largely from many discussions with one "key informant," a man named Muchona. Based on these discussions, he concluded that the tree stands for human milk, for the ties between the girl and her mother, and for the principle of ties through women, more generally. These meanings seem consistent with other Ndembu statements and practices, although discussions with a broader range of Ndembu men and women might have introduced a greater diversity of meanings into the analysis.

These symbolic meanings include both physiological and social poles: aspects of the human body and of social institutions. Turner then considers the way the tree is used in ritual practices, and here he finds several distinct meanings: In one event, the tree is the center for all-female activities from which the men are excluded (meaning of women versus men); in other contexts, it is associated with the girl undergoing initiation.

Finally, Turner examines the broader system of symbols, and finds this tree to be one among several trees that are used in ritual activities, each associated with white, red, or black. Each color calls forth associations with natural substances: black with putrefaction and feces, red with blood, white with milk and semen. Although these associations are "natural" in the sense that blood is indeed red, the values placed on these associations are cultural and relatively arbitrary. Is blood good? Powerful? Polluting? The Ndembu highlight certain values and play down others. Red is linked to power and wealth, black to pollution and disease, and white to purity and life. They can then interpret the value of various ritual and medicinal objects in terms of this color scheme. Medicines made from the "white" mudyi tree, for example, aid a woman having difficulties breastfeeding.

For the Ndembu, then, the three primary colors provide a template for much of social life, just as do the four cardinal directions for the Zuni. Turner's account of religious ritual situates the ritual in its matrilineal social context, analyzes the Ndembu explanations of rituals and symbols, and considers the emotional power of Ndembu ritual associations. Other anthropologists, for example Gananath Obeyesekere (1981), emphasize the ways that personal, sometimes unconscious, meanings of key symbols in a culture shape the lives of individuals. For these and other writers, symbols are studied for their roles in the lives of individuals in particular societies.

Clifford Geertz (1926–2006) occupies an important place in late twentieth-century anthropology for his efforts to bring together Weber's emphasis on cultural orientations, often born of religious ideas, with a semiotic emphasis on the symbolic mediation of ideas and social forces. In his *Religion of Java* (1960), as well as in other works on Indonesia and Morocco, he analyzed the diversity of religious beliefs in large Muslim-majority societies.

Geertz draws from Weber's emphasis on the answers that large-scale religious doctrines provide for life's key questions, such as: Why is there evil in the world? Who gets to heaven and why? But whereas Weber worked largely from the writings of religious figures and other literate men—those who formed what Robert Redfield (1956) was to call the urban "great traditions"—Geertz relies on the testimonies of ordinary village and townspeople, those people participating in what Redfield called the rural "little tradition." Geertz looks at the diversity of ideas in a single society. In this respect, Geertz laid the groundwork for subsequent anthropological studies of everyday practices of Islam, Buddhism, Hinduism, and other large-scale religions.

Geertz's method in his early writing on Java was to define three "streams" of Islam, each situated in a different institutional context: a set of village understandings that focused on spirits and community rituals; a more scripturally oriented Islam of the religious school and the market; and a focus on status and etiquette among noble Javanese. Although criticized for not emphasizing that people in all three streams were Muslims and that many read works of Islamic doctrine and spirituality, his analysis was able to capture both the variety of ways Javanese men and women talked about religion and society, and the ways that large-scale institutions of politics, economics, and religion shaped their understandings and actions.

Geertz's approach has been especially influential in the anthropology of religion. Today many anthropologists place even more emphasis than he did on the ways that villagers and religious experts ("culture brokers") interpret and reshape the texts and ideas of religious traditions in their societies. For example, Stanley Tambiah (1970) studied the uses that monks and other villagers make of Buddhist texts in northeastern Thailand. Dale F. Eickelman (1985) traced the career of a rural Moroccan judge. In these and other studies, anthropologists have situated large-scale changes in specific towns and villages and with respect to specific people. I also began my work in Indonesia strongly influenced by Geertz's capacities to draw on social theory (largely Weber) as he interpreted events and debates, creating a sense of which ideas and which emotions were central to everyday preoccupations.

RELIGION, SOCIETY, AND POWER

By the 1990s, the symbolic approach associated with Geertz, Turner, Mary Douglas, and their students began to be challenged by those examining religion through the lenses of power and subjectivity. The touchstone for this new approach was the writings of the philosopher Michel Foucault (1926–1984) on forms of power. Foucault examined the interactions between forms of knowledge and forms of power, emphasizing the former in much of his work on science and on sexuality, and the latter in his writings about madness, the state, and the prison. But the two were always linked: categories of knowledge are part of an overall system of control. Whereas control is often located in "the state," Foucault (1977, 2011) emphasized its location both in centralized means of control, and through the actions of individuals, insofar as they develop "technologies of the self" designed to form the self in accord with a certain set of ideas about ethics and power.

The starting point for many current anthropological studies of religion and power is Talal Asad's (1982) attack on the idea that there could be transhistorical definitions of religion. The attack proceeded on two levels. First, Asad argued that the dominant modern Western categorical structure, in which politics and religion are taken to be two distinct domains, cannot constitute an analytical starting point for anthropology, because it is a particular way of thinking that follows from certain modern political processes. (This is the argument that I rehearsed above.) Second, Asad criticized one particular, well-known definition of religion provided by Clifford Geertz, which postulated a causal relationship between religious symbols, on the one hand, and the religious ideas and emotions shaped by those symbols, on the other. Geertz said that certain powerful religious symbols create "moods and motivation" in the followers of a religion. This argument was highly Weberian (as noted earlier) but focused the attention of the anthropologist on the key symbols in that religious environment: the Eucharist, for example, or the Islamic pilgrimage.

Asad reached back to the teachings of the Christian Church Fathers to identify a very different perspective. Augustine of Hippo, in particular, emphasized the necessity of discipline, administered through law, family, and schools, to induce the proper capacity to understand and absorb Christian teachings. Symbols did not induce faith; discipline did. Augustine's emphasis on teaching and discipline was part of his battle against the Donatists to make Church ritual objectively efficacious, that is, effective in providing the means to salvation regardless of the state of mind or moral purity of the priest. Moral purity was not a precondition to religious labor bur rather its outcome.

Here we join Foucault's admonition to attend to the work of ethical self-fashioning that underlies any system of government, including religious government but also extending to all systems, ancient and modern. Augustine here can be read as a particularly apposite historical case of taking religious instruction and learning to be a species of ethical labor (see Chapter 10). Asad refers to the Augustinian perspective for a different reason, however: It provides both an influential idea of religion that dislodges Geertz's definition from its putative universality, and it lies at the root of the Western world's progression of attitudes toward Christianity. This progression eventually leads to a privileging of private *credo*, belief, and to the modern notion of religion we discussed above. Its inspection reminds us that making belief (or the more extensive idea of "moods and motivations") the starting point for an anthropological definition of religion risks privileging this rather unique modern Western notion over other possible religious ideas. Asad concludes by urging us to situate symbols and meanings in the social practices that produce, sustain, and transform them, as we do in this book.

Conclusions

The anthropology of religion has drawn from a wide range of social theories but seeks to test them against evidence from fieldwork, where we have the capacity to see disagreements and doubt over key ideas, and to follow change in how people practice what we then call "religion." But we do so in the knowledge that our own analytical categories—religion, ritual, symbol, and myth—derive from a very particular history, a history I have called the twin transformations. In succeeding chapters, we will see some of the rough edges that our predicament produces: one person's religion may be another's science, magic, or simply unremarkable facets of everyday life.

Discussion Questions

Many of the central rituals of major religions have their histories. The Islamic pilgrimage probably emerged as a combination of two older rituals, one involving the harvest. A similar set of combinations and changes lie behind the Jewish Passover. But in their texts both religions treat these rituals as unchanged since their birth, and born out of divine intervention. Do we devalue a religious practice by showing it to have been transformed over time? How can practitioners square the historical study of the practice with a belief in its divine origin? Does this arise for your own religion, or for those of your friends and relatives?

Media Resources

On the Axial Age you can consult any one of a number of sites on important dates in world religions, such as the site at http://www.sacred-texts.com/time/origtime.htm. A very readable book by Karen Armstrong tells the story in a great amount of detail—good for students expressing a particular interest in the matter: Karen Armstrong, *The Great Transformation* (Anchor, 2007). She has a particular perspective, which comes through clearly in a short clip (http://www.youtube.com/watch?v=uKi7bB4Xgxl).

A good handbook for the theories of religion discussed here is Brian Morris, *Anthropological Studies of Religion* (Cambridge, 1987).

Domains and Boundaries of Religion

In the last chapter, we saw that only with the advent of the European Enlightenment, world travel, and colonialism was there the emergence of a notion of religions as distinct belief systems in Western Europe and North America, as well as the emergence of social sciences of religion. But what are the boundaries of "religion"? When does it become politics, or magic, or medicine? And who decides these and other questions? How much do these boundaries shift as we move from one country to another?

We will return to these questions throughout the rest of this book, but here I want to explore them directly. Let's begin with a country that has a lot of practices and ideas that surely we would consider to be religious, but where most people say they do not have a religion—Japan!

COMBINING RELIGIOUS PRACTICES IN JAPAN

In practice, Japanese freely blend elements from indigenous practices, state-inspired Shinto, and the traditions of Buddhism, Confucianism, and Taoism, with a bit of Christianity thrown in from time to time. Few would argue for maintaining boundaries between these religions. Indeed, most people speak of a division of labor among the religions; a common saying sums it up as "born Shinto, die Buddhist," referring to the daily appeals to Shinto spirits during one's lifetime and the Buddhist priest's responsibility for carrying out funeral rites (Reader 1991). Marriages are increasingly conducted in Christian style, and many Japanese consult practitioners of the New Religions for solutions to recurring illnesses. These sects themselves combine ideas and practices from many sources, including Hinduism, Japanese nativist writings about racial superiority, and indigenous healing practices. To take an extreme example: It seemed not at all unusual or striking to Japanese that the Aum Shinrikyo sect responsible for the 1995 nerve gas attack in Tokyo combined Buddhist and Hindu texts.

Practice and Belief

Across many surveys, from 65 percent to 85 percent of Japanese people say that they have no religious beliefs (compared to fewer than 10 percent in the United States). Only 20–30 percent say they believe in the existence of *kami* (spirits) or in souls of the dead. But 76 percent of these respondents have in their homes either a Shinto altar devoted to kami, or a Buddhist one devoted to the souls of the dead; 45 percent have both. Eighty-nine percent say they visit the graves of their ancestors to pray for them (Reader 1991, 5–12).

These results are very puzzling to Western readers if we assume that people think of their beliefs as governing their practices. One problem is with the word *religion*, which in Japanese is *shukyo*, a word originally devised to answer pesky missionaries who asked Japanese to state what their religion was. Japanese meant it to refer to a separate set of beliefs, removed from everyday life, and not to some everyday activity like stopping for a moment at a shrine to make an offering. Thus, asking someone in Japan if she has a religion or religious beliefs is akin to asking someone in the United States or Germany if she is a member of a religious movement, a question that would elicit denials even from many devout churchgoers.

Students of Japanese culture have also emphasized that ideas about beliefs and morality are more focused on specific events and situations than is true for European cultures. Anecdotes from World War II relate how Japanese prisoners of war, having once been bent on killing Allied troops, suddenly became model prisoners of war. In their eyes, the situation had changed and so had their responsibilities.

Finally, a pragmatic try-it-and-see attitude underlies the approach taken by many Japanese toward religious ritual. This approach emphasizes the importance of sincerity for the ritual to work, but not a general "belief," and certainly not an exclusive commitment to that religion and no other. It is thus relatively easy, within the Japanese religious world view, to try a new healing religion without abandoning offerings to household spirits and Buddhist deities. This willingness to participate in more than one religion lies behind the common practice of declaring oneself to census takers as both Buddhist and Shinto, marrying in a Protestant church, and attending sessions of a healing sect to seek a cure for an illness. And it is evident in figures about religious membership: No doubt thinking in practical terms, the Japanese government has classified about 75 percent of the population as Buddhist, 95 percent as Shinto, and over 10 percent as members of New Religious movements (Reader 1991, 6). Japanese do affiliate with religious organizations, and usually with more than one.

Perhaps, then, answers to surveys underplay the extent to which Japanese assume that there are spirits at work in the world. It would appear that the practices of keeping an altar at home and reciting prayers for one's ancestors at graveside imply such a set of beliefs. And yet haven't we all engaged in practices for which we are unsure of whether we agree with the associated doctrines? As we saw in Chapter 2, modern Western religious culture emphasizes the importance of believing in the doctrines behind practices, in the paramount importance of creeds of faith, and this emphasis may make it quite difficult for some people in the United States, for example, to deny belief in God to a survey taker, whatever their doubts might be. Japanese religious culture does not make this same emphasis; consequently, denying the belief while going along with the practice may be easier for the Japanese person than for the American.

This religious–cultural emphasis on practices over doctrines makes it easier for Japanese to combine elements from different religious traditions. We will explore the roles played by two major traditions—Shintoism and Buddhism—and how people's actions may imply their belief in a proposition about the spiritual world without them directly expressing that belief.

Shinto and Spirits

Basic to the Japanese Shinto tradition are spirits, or *kami* (Earhart 1982), which are located in specific places in the empirical world: in a boulder, or a house, or a shrine. One Japanese estimate is that there are "eight million spirits"—meaning they are innumerable. When foreigners asked Japanese to name their religion, in order to distinguish it from Buddhism, they called it "the way of the *kami*," although it came to be called Shinto in the West (Reader 1991).

The term *kami* refers both to the sense of power felt in things of the world and to particular spirits. A waterfall is a powerful kami; calling it a kami communicates the sense an observer has of its immense power. Space may also contain kami and may be demarcated by rocks, or by a shrine with boundaries and a gateway. One sees these *torii*, Shinto gateways, with two pillars and one or two crossbeams, throughout Japan and in many U.S. cities. A Japanese rock garden works similarly, demarcating a sparsely filled space rather than, as in European-style ornamental gardens, featuring a dense collection of plants. Although kami can be anywhere, they are not everywhere; these boundaries serve to separate the sacred from the profane.

Perhaps the most important spirits are those in the house. They occupy particular places and protect the members of the household when in those places: The kitchen god lives in the kitchen, the latrine god in the latrine, and so forth. There is also a guardian deity of the household as a whole; this spirit is made up of many ancestors who have merged to guard the household as a corporate unit that exists over time. The village has a guardian deity, often a fox god or an ancestor of a founding member. The village, like the household, is a corporate group, with control over irrigation, cooperative use of some land, and religious festivals. Villagers will ask the village god for help in their rice harvest or for success in schooling. Village elites once controlled the shrine festivals for the village gods, but today, with many villagers engaged in urban pursuits, their importance has diminished.

Also important to everyday life is the spirit of a rice field. This spirit lives a dual existence, as the figure of Inari, the rice deity, and also as the spirit guarding each particular field. Spirits of the fields and of rice live in the mountains and come down in the spring when the soil is tilled. They guard over the rice, and return to the mountains in the fall after the harvest. They are sometimes represented as fox spirits, probably because foxes, also associated with rice, sexuality, and fertility, were thought to come down from the mountains in spring.

People create new spirits as needed. When the Tennis Players' Association was created in Japan before World War II, someone suggested the creation of a new god, to be named "Heavenly God of Speedy Ball." And in a less individuated way, all equipment, from computer chips to cameras to automobile production machinery, are thought to have a spiritual side. The machines are blessed by a Shinto priest before they are used, and in 1990 engineers met at Tokyo's Chomeiji temple to thank their used-up

Temple complex near Narita, Japan, with Shinto and Buddhist shrines, and shops selling amulets, books, and other items. *(Courtesy of John Bowen)*

equipment for the service it had given them. Photographs of the cameras and video recorders were burned as a Buddhist priest chanted verses. Even in the electronics industry, Shinto and Buddhism are mixed (Sanger 1990).

Kami can also be the spirits of deceased persons. Sometime famous people will become deified as kami and have shrines built to them, but for a mixture of reasons. One ninth-century court official, for example, had died at the hands of his rivals for power. As a spirit he wreaked havoc with their lives until they built a shrine to him.

Spirits and Social Change

Japanese relationships to spirits developed in a civilization centered on enduring social units: the household, the village, and the Imperial House. Household spirits stood for the continuity of the household over generations. Households in a village were protected by community spirits. And everyone was under the protection of the unbroken imperial line, itself said to come from the Sun Goddess and dating at least back to the seventh century C.E. Although these continuities have been disrupted by massive migrations to cities, older orientations toward spirits of the collectivity—including the emperor and his temples—continue in Japan.

Many kami are venerated in shrines, and some shrines, such as the great shrine at Ise to the Sun Goddess, are the focus of national veneration. The Ise shrine is rebuilt every 20 years as part of a cycle of national renewal of life and fertility; the last rebuilding, in 1993, was widely publicized by banners erected throughout Japan.

Parents routinely take their newborn babies to the local shrine to be placed under the care of the spirit guarding the local community. An offering is placed on the altar, and the shrine priest says prayers requesting these blessings. In the older, agrarian world in which Japanese religions developed, they also carried out rites at this shrine to ensure the fertility of the crops. The shrine also served as the place for community meetings and recreational activities; it was thus the center of social life. Often the community shrine was said to be a branch shrine of a famous national shrine, such as that at Ise. Performing rituals at the shrine thus linked the individual to the community and the nation-state.

Since World War II, Japanese have flooded from country to city and from farming to other occupations. In 1950, 62 percent of all Japanese families lived in rural areas, of which 50 percent were full-time farmers. By 2011, only 24 percent of families lived in rural areas, and only 5 percent of these families were still engaged in full-time farming. This rapid shift in population led to the realization that a civilization and a set of religious practices that had developed around stable rural households now had to be modified for urban living. The Shinto shrines, however, have been part of this transformation. People who commute to the city from suburbs or rural areas still visit the shrines to seek blessings for their babies and to seek further spirit protection for young children, though now they may dress in Western-style clothes and record the occasions with expensive video cameras.

Worship at a shrine, Narita temple complex, Japan. *(Courtesy of John Bowen)*

People living in the cities may return to their ancestral villages for harvest festivals and for the New Year's festival, when they acquire new amulets from the shrines to protect their homes during the coming year. For two years, Ian Reader (1991, 61–64) watched proceedings at the Katano shrine midway between the cities of Osaka and Kyoto in what has become a commuter village. He records that on festival days, hundreds of people took trains from both cities to the shrine to seek blessings and purchase amulets. A shrine priest could call on office girls to work as temporary "shrine maidens" on these occasions; at one festival, Reader found himself being blessed by one of his own students who had been engaged to work as such a shrine maiden during the holidays. Businesses sent rice, or sake, to be placed on the altar for blessings (and afterward quickly consumed by visitors). The same priest was called upon to bless a new university building nearby. He had a temporary altar to the shrine spirit constructed inside the new building for the occasion.

Increased ease of transport has meant that Japanese increasingly visit the more famous shrines in larger cities. Several million people visit these shrines each year, while some rural shrines, those not on commuter lines and unable to afford priests, have closed. The social ties affirmed by attending a shrine are less and less local and increasingly national in scope.

Buddhism and Souls

Most of the people frequenting these shrines with their newborns, or at festivals, also participate in rituals drawn from Buddhism (Saunders 1964). The Buddhist religion came into existence in the sixth century B.C.E. in what is today northern India, when the historical Buddha, Siddhartha of the clan Gautama, found enlightenment after long meditation. The followers of Buddha also seek enlightenment; his teachings provide examples and practices to follow rather than creeds to which followers must adhere.

> Buddhism is based on teachings by Siddhartha, of the Gautama clan, called the Buddha, in about the sixth century B.C.E. in today's eastern India. Buddhism's "three jewels" are the Buddha, Dharma or rules for right conduct, and the Sangha or community. Following the Buddha's example is designed to lead to eventual escape (moksa) from the wheel of suffering. The two major streams of Buddhism specified different roles for the Sangha. Theravada Buddhism spread southward through Sri Lanka and into Southeast Asia, and stressed the role of monks in mediating between laypersons and Gautama Buddha, hence the importance of donations to the monasteries. Mahayana Buddhism spread northward, through Tibet to China and Japan, and stressed the availability to everyone of pathways toward the status of bodhisattva or Buddha in becoming, hence a practical emphasis on every individual's actions, including donations and chanting vis-à-vis a particular member of the pantheon of Buddhas.

In South Asia, Buddhism diverged into two major streams. One, called "Theravada" (the elders), emphasizes the role of the monastic community in mediating between laypersons and Buddha. This stream spread from Sri Lanka to mainland Southeast Asia. The other stream was called "Mahayana," or "Greater Vehicle," for its universalistic approach to salvation. In this stream, individuals are encouraged to engage in practices that lead to their salvation and to enter directly into contact with Buddhas and other deities.

The Mahayana stream of Buddhism spread northward from India through Tibet and China. Japanese scholars learned about Buddhism in China, and for that reason, Japanese Buddhism adopts the Mahayana orientation. Mahayana Buddhism emphasizes the illusory character of the world and orients the individual toward a transcendent reality in which he or she might achieve salvation. One sees this emphasis in paintings, where individual Buddhas are depicted floating above the world we live in, transcendent of its specific concreteness. These diverse Buddhas—Fudo, Amida, Maitreya—provide multiple sources of divine aid and also multiple paths for individuals to seek salvation.

Each of the several major schools of Buddhism in Japan—Zen, Shingon, Nichiren, and others—combines a set of spiritual disciplines that lead to salvation (Reader 1991). They all evince a special concern for death and treatment of ancestors. Zen Buddhism, the best known in the West of these schools, emphasizes meditation. Indeed, the word *Zen* itself means "meditation." Zen teachers point to the example set by the historical Buddha, Gautama, who achieved enlightenment in this world by sitting and meditating. Zen practitioners may use *koan*, problems that appear unsolvable, as a way of breaking down the barriers that everyday linear thinking places in the path to enlightenment. They practice together in communities of meditators, engaging in strenuous physical labor—scrubbing floors, chopping wood—as additional aids to enlightenment. Laypeople may participate in retreats at Zen temples, and businesses routinely send their employees on special retreats that incorporate some of the austerities of temple life.

Japanese Buddhism's emphasis on individual meditation and enlightenment provides a counterpoint in religious practice to the overall Japanese cultural emphasis on the value and continuity of the group. But Buddhism also adapted itself to those values by assuming responsibility for the care of family ancestors. Even if they have no other contact with Buddhism, and would not state that they believe in Buddha, most Japanese "die Buddhist"; that is, their children or other relatives seek out the service of a Buddhist priest to perform a funeral service. The main activity at most temples is in fact not meditation but performing memorial services for the dead. Most Japanese households are affiliated with a particular temple for this purpose.

Before Buddhism, Japanese people considered that each person's soul traveled to a world of the dead, where it continued to watch and intervene in the lives of its relatives. People carried out rituals designed to ease the transition to the other world and to keep the spirits happy. When Buddhism came to Japan, people saw the priests as possessing spiritual powers due to their activities of meditation. They began to call on those priests to perform the funeral ceremonies. Priests added new practices to the rituals, practices designed to guide the spirit toward enlightenment after death. The priest and his associates cremate the body to rid the soul of its impurities and chant Buddhist texts and prayers to lead the soul toward the state of enlightenment. The word for dead soul, *hotoke,* also means a Buddha.

These ancestors continue to affect the lives of their kin, and both Buddhist priests and practitioners of New Religions are concerned with keeping the ancestors happy and resolving problems that occur when they are not. (See Chapter 5 for an example.)

Buddhism coexists with Shinto in Japan. The temple complex at Nara, which I have visited, contains both Buddhist temples and Shinto shrines, and visitors stop at both. Temples may include images of kami alongside those of a Buddha, although the former are said to no longer contain spirits but only to represent them. The two kinds of entities are represented in clearly contrasting ways. In paintings, for example, kami are depicted in a realistic manner as specific, human-looking personages, sometimes identifiable as historical figures, always standing near or on the place with which they are associated. Buddhas and bodhisattvas, by contrast, are abstract in their appearance and not confined to specific spaces. Often they are painted as floating above the ground or on clouds.

Two other religious traditions have also influenced Japanese ideas and practices. Taoism (from *tao*, the "way" in Chinese) developed in China as an approach to understanding the way of the universe. Taoism includes methods of divining good or bad days by consulting calendars. Japanese adopted some of these practices—there was even a bureau of divination in early Japan—but no Japanese would identify himself or herself as a Taoist.

Confucianism, based on the teachings of the Chinese philosopher Confucius (551–479 B.C.E.), has played an important role in shaping Japanese social and moral values (Smith 1983, 37–67). Confucius taught that social order and welfare depended on maintaining the proper hierarchical relationships between persons, particularly those of father to son and ruler to subject. In Japan, these ideas strengthened the notion of the family as a corporate entity, with succession passing from father to the eldest son, and that of the nation as a family-like entity headed by the hereditary emperor.

THE STATE AND RELIGION

Japan's rulers have added to their legitimacy by drawing on Shinto and Buddhism. The state has variously promoted one or the other of these two complexes of religious ideas and practices. In its encounter with outside cultures and in particular with Christianity, the Japanese state has created indigenous alternatives—systems of ideas and practices that looked like religion as defined in the West.

State promotion of religions began between the sixth and ninth centuries with the adoption of Chinese ideas that the emperor is both divine and the active ruler of society. Just as village guardians often were thought to be the ancestors of the village elite, the emperor declared himself (or herself) the descendant of the Sun Goddess. (These borrowings were a major source of Confucian influence in Japan.)

Scholars began to teach Buddhism in Japan during the Nara period (710–784 C.E.), named after the capital city of Nara. Emperor Shomu (reigned 724–749) quickly made Buddhism the state religion. Buddhism appealed to the emperor and his advisers because it came from China, along with the writing system and ideas of the divinity of the emperor, and also because it could be made the basis of a state-centered system of religious temples, with scriptures and priests. The preexisting religious practices were decentralized, with local spirits and shrines. Buddhism offered the possibility of constructing a religious hierarchy under imperial control.

In 728, the emperor built the Todai temple in Nara (just south of present-day Kyoto) as the first national temple. The statue of Buddha inside the temple, called "Lochana," still stands as the largest Buddhist statue in the world. Lochana, or Dainichi, is the Sun Buddha. When he was building the statue, the emperor had to seek approval from his ancestress, the Sun Goddess Amaterasu, at her temple in Ise. Reportedly, the goddess told the emperor that the Sun Buddha was the same as the Sun Goddess and approved building the statue.

Todai temple, Japan, with statue of the Buddha Nyiori. *(Courtesy of John Renard)*

The emperor then ordered two temples built in each province, one as a monastery and one as a nunnery. Monks and nuns were recruited to these temples to recite Buddhist scriptures and accumulate merit, and then to pass on the merit to the nation as a whole. This form of mediated merit was not part of the Mahayana tradition imported by the state; it was created by the emperor for his own project of state building. By venerating the Sun Buddha, the emperor managed to link Buddha to his own Sun Goddess ancestor. By constructing a national temple system, he linked acts of individual merit-making to the welfare of the nation as a whole, and forged a religious connection between the people and the state. But the temples and their priests, particularly at Todai temple, grew more and more powerful, and the decision to move the Imperial capital to Kyoto in 784 was in part to establish a separate power base away from the temple.

In succeeding centuries, the influence of state-sponsored Buddhism waned along with the power of the emperor. But in 1600, the warlord (*shogun*) Tokugawa Ieyasu consolidated power throughout Japan, ending the many centuries of political disorder, and reduced the emperor to a figurehead. Ieyasu once again promoted Buddhism as the state religion, building a new hierarchy of temples. All Japanese were required to register at a temple, proclaim their religion, and use the services of Buddhist priests for funeral services. These state actions were not motivated by religious piety, but intended to tighten state control and exclude Christianity as a disruptive, foreign ideology. Thus, Buddhism was promoted as the best alternative to Christianity, as "not-Christianity."

In 1868, a coalition of warlords and a rising economic elite took power in the name of the Emperor Meiji and sought to reduce the influence of Buddhism because of its association with the old regime. The Meiji Restoration combined economic restructuring with the creation of a cult of the emperor. A hierarchy of Shinto priests was created, and the result has come to be called State Shinto. Shrines were created to appeal to popular opinion. Foremost among these new shrines were Yasukuni, founded in 1869, where those soldiers who have died for the honor of the state are enshrined and deified, and the Meiji shrine, built in 1920 to honor the deceased emperor. Both produced talismans for people to take home with them, and people were also required to have talismans from Ise in their homes (Hardacre 1989, 79–99).

These efforts were meant to create a religious plane on which individual households would be merged into the state. The Confucian value of filial piety was emphasized, as well as the common descent of all Japanese, as in the following section from a teacher's manual used in the 1930s:

> The connection between the Imperial House and its subjects is thus: one forms the main house and the others form the branch house, so that from ancient times we have worshiped the founder of the Imperial House and the heavenly gods. Our relationship to this house is sincerely founded on repaying our debt of gratitude to our ancestors. (quoted in Smith 1983, 32)

After World War II, the American forces that occupied Japan insisted that the new Constitution remove the aura of divinity from the emperor. The Constitution states that the emperor is not divine, but only "the symbol of the state and of the unity of the people." The Nobel Prize-winning writer Kenzaburo Oe has written of his and others' astonishment when on August 15, 1945, they heard the emperor speak over the radio: "The Emperor speaking to us in a human voice was beyond imagining in any reverie. The Emperor was a god, the authority of the nation, the organizing principle of reality" (Oe 1995, 103).

The Occupation forces also proclaimed Shinto to be a religion and that because people ought to be able to choose their religion freely, it could not be taught in the schools or be supported by state funds. And yet despite this new official ideology, the Sun Goddess Amaterasu continues to be worshiped at the great shrine at Ise. Each time the shrine is rebuilt, the ancient mirror that is thought to embody the Sun Goddess's spirit is moved into the new shrine. Six and a half million Japanese visit the shrine each year. Japanese visit Ise the way that Jews visit Israel and Muslims visit Mecca, as a journey to a sacred place.

The precise status of Ise and the nature of the emperor's relationship to the Sun Goddess (if any) became major political issues when Emperor Hirohito died in January 1989. At Hirohito's funeral the following month, the Shinto rites were performed behind curtains, evidently so that visiting dignitaries would not have to acknowledge them. Yet many in Japan criticized these proceedings as tantamount to worship of the emperor and thus a violation of the 1946 Constitution.

Then, in November 1990, Hirohito's son and successor, Akihito, was enthroned. Part of the enthronement procedure is the "great food-offering ritual," in which the new emperor offers special foods to the deities of the heaven and earth and performs a ritual of union of sorts (left ambiguous in official accounts) with the Sun Goddess. The last time this ritual had been performed was in 1928, when the emperor was still considered a god. At Ise he is still thought of as the chief priest of Shinto. There was a great deal of protest from those who considered the ritual to be religious, and thus to violate the Constitution's mandate that state and religion be separated (Weisman 1990).

Similar controversy continues to surround the Yasukuni shrine to the war dead. Prime ministers regularly visit the shrine, located next to the Imperial Palace in central Tokyo, to venerate the war dead, sometimes in their official capacity. In August 1985, Prime Minister Nakasone with his cabinet made an official visit to the shrine to pay tribute to the war dead. But here Japan's difficulty in facing its wartime history surfaced, because major ("Class A") war criminals executed by judgment of the 1946–1948 Tokyo Trial are among the two and a half million people listed as gods in the shrine's record book. Furthermore, the Rape of Nanking is among the events celebrated, a fact that led China to protest this attendance. Protests by many Japanese led Nakasone to forgo additional state visits to the shrine, but from 2001 to 2006, Prime Minister Junichiro Koizumi made annual visits, although as a private citizen and not as head of government. In 2010, far-right European politicians, including the leader of France's National Front, Jean-Marie Le Pen, paid the shrine a visit.

Veterans' groups continue to enshrine and deify the spirits of Japanese soldiers. In 1988, the Japanese Supreme Court backed up one such group over the objections of the widow of a soldier about to be deified. She was Protestant and protested that the deification violated her religious beliefs, but the Court claimed that her religion had no bearing on the group's freedom to carry out the ritual. The idea of religious exclusivity—that one religion excludes others—is not part of the Japanese legal tradition (Haberman 1988).

Death practices, indeed, have all along been important elements in the state–religion nexus. The eighth-century ascendancy of Buddhism was accompanied by a change from burial to cremation for emperors and empresses, following Buddhist practice. During the 1600–1868 Tokugawa period, Shinto nationalists were gradually able to reduce Buddhism's official status—after 1654, although burial rites for the imperial family continued to follow Buddhist practices, the bodies were interred rather than cremated. Only at the funeral of Emperor Meiji's father, Komei, in 1867, were all Buddhist elements eliminated from the funeral, and thus one could say that the funeral ushered in the new Shinto-dominated Meiji era. The government prohibited cremation entirely in 1873, as part of its effort to drive out Buddhism, but it was forced to rescind the order as people pointed out that Japan already lacked sufficient space to bury intact bodies (*Far Eastern Economic Review,* March 16, 1989, 66–70).

The place of religion in public life, even the definition of what religion is, continues to be the subject of debate in Japan. What *is* clear in Japan is that lines between religions are fuzzy or, rather, that religions are not defined by the individual's exclusive commitment to one set of doctrines as opposed to others. Japan challenges our idea of what religion means for the individual, for the nation, and for the state.

IMPOSED DEFINITIONS OF RELIGION

Many modern states in Asia, Africa, and Latin America have drawn their ideas of religion from Western, Christian, and, to some extent, Islamic models, and often imposed these ideas on local people who think about their beliefs and practices in quite different ways.

Let us turn to Indonesia to consider these problems of state-imposed definitions of religion. Indonesia, the world's fourth largest country, has about 240 million people living on thousands of islands and speaking more than 300 distinct languages. About 85 percent of the people call themselves Muslim, and the remaining 15 percent includes important Christian and Buddhist minorities as well as practitioners of indigenous religions.

The Indonesian government has "belief in one God" as one of the planks of its ideology. The state defines religion as having a sacred book, a monotheistic foundation, exclusive boundaries (such that one person cannot belong to two religions at the same time), and as transcending ethnic boundaries (rather than being essentially an aspect of a hereditary culture).

This model came by way of several large-scale religions. In the early centuries of the present era, rulers adopted the symbols and ideas of Hinduism and Buddhism, sometimes both together. The Indonesian word for religion, *agama*, comes from Sanskrit, and means "text." The agama of a person was the set of texts from which he or she derived teaching and religious direction: the books of Hinduism, Buddhism, Islam, or others. The idea of a central text does not require that the religion have exclusive boundaries; that idea came later, in the fourteenth through sixteenth centuries, when many rulers began converting to Islam. Islam does insist on absolute exclusivity and on the idea of one and only one true foundational text, the Qur'ân. Christianity, brought to Indonesia at about the same time, shares these ideas.

By the time of Indonesian independence, then, the major religions supported this model of religion. The state decreed that everyone should belong to one of five religions: Catholicism, Protestantism, Islam, Hinduism, or Buddhism; Confucianism was recognized, then removed, and re-added in 1998. One might be surprised to hear that Hinduism, with its many vividly represented deities, stood for monotheism; the Indonesian resolution of this problem—supported by some Hindus—was to declare that the various Hindu gods were all manifestations of a single absolute deity.

Today, any Indonesians who practice local religions that do not conform to the official model are pressured to join one of the state-recognized religions, although this pressure has begun to ease since the fall of President Suharto in 1998. Those who do not convert may be accused of being atheists and therefore communists, a dangerous label in this strongly anticommunist state. So defining one's religion is a matter of great concern, and for some a matter of sheer survival (Kipp and Rodgers 1987).

What do people who practice other religions do? Some nominally convert but retain some older practices, such as ways of healing that involve calling on spirits to possess a healer and speak through him or her. Other people work to have their indigenous practices counted as a world religion, usually as Hindu. In one such case, a group of people on the island of Sulawesi did manage to become recognized as Hindus, despite the fact that there were few resemblances, other than a few words of Sanskrit, between their religion and anything practiced in India. A problem arose when one member of this group was elected to the local parliament. Members of parliament need to be sworn in on "their book." So what was this fellow's scripture? Well, because the book had to be Hindu, as the group's practices were called that, the parliament wrote to a Hindu association in Jakarta asking for their book. The association sent along a book in Sanskrit (I could not determine what book it was), and the new member was duly sworn in using it. Appearances were saved, and the religion's credentials established: They had a Book.

Wana Practices and Indonesian Definitions

Some people reshape their indigenous ideas in response to state pressures to convert. The 5,000 Wana people of Sulawesi, described by the anthropologist Jane Monnig Atkinson (1987, 1989), practice forms of divination and shamanism, and their ideas about spirits and possession surface in many domains of everyday life. They do not have a distinct domain called "religion."

Central to Wana efforts at dealing with the spiritual domain are the performances called *mabolong*. These rituals of possession and healing are performed by shamans, ritual experts who are possessed by spirits. Shamans are called on to perform mabolong when someone is ill and requires supernatural assistance. Often many people attend these performances. The shaman is invited to feast from a tray of food, and he in turn invites his "spirit familiars" to join him in enjoying the food. He then asks these spirits to discover what is ailing a patient, to rid the patient of foreign objects, and to go with him on a spirit voyage to recover souls or dream spirits that the patient has lost.

Shamans have greater inner powers, and they draw on these powers to keep people healthy and to increase their own social standing. They are heroes in their community. Indeed, they often create new social communities as people seek to live near them. It is in these rituals performed by shamans that ordinary humans engage the spirit world. The Wana have no written texts that prescribe doctrines or beliefs, and their narratives concerning the spirit world are many and varied. What brings their diverse ideas and stories together is collective attendance at shamanic rituals.

But Wana also face intense pressure from Muslim officials and from Christian missionaries to convert to a state-recognized religion, an agama. Wana come into contact with Muslim peoples living on the coast and serving as local state officials, and, more recently, with Christian converts living in other upland regions.

As they have come to understand what is meant by agama, some Wana have constructed their own ideas of what their religion must be. These constructions are not about healing and possession, but about what distinguishes Wana from Muslims and Christians: diet, burial practices, and ties to government among them. Most saliently, Wana are people who, unlike Muslims, do eat pork, and, also unlike Muslims, kill chickens by wringing their necks rather than slaughtering them by knife.

Wana have also constructed a set of beliefs along the lines of Muslim and Christian beliefs, but distinct from them. They claim, for example, that they have a single God and that this God is the same as the Muslim and Christian creator. They recently invented a heaven that corresponds to the images of heaven taught to them by Muslims

Wana shaman during possession at a healing session, Indonesia. *(Courtesy of Jane Atkinson)*

and Christians but reverses those groups' teachings about the destiny of the Wana. In the Wana notions, Wana lead poor lives on earth and therefore they will have the best places in heaven. Muslims, by contrast, they believe, will live in pig excrement because they avoid it here. Christians will have only scraps of clouds to eat (an idea probably derived from pictures of Jesus in the clouds in Bible schools).

Most Wana have so far resisted conversion, but even in resisting they have transformed their religion in accord with the dominant, ultimately Western, model of proper religion.

Conclusions

If Japan shows us how the categories that inform social life do not necessarily conform to the modern Western notion of religion, with its requirement of exclusive membership, Islam shows us how difficult it is to agree on the boundaries of religion even for an example of that modern idea. These difficulties occur all around us. We all know that "freedom of religion" is guaranteed for citizens of the United States, France, Britain, and many other countries. But what is it that is guaranteed? France declared that schoolgirls may not wear headscarves to school even if they considered wearing them to be part of their religion, because the state protects something more limited: religion as practiced in places of religion, such as mosques and churches. But in Britain, wearing religious dress is protected in schools and indeed for civil servants, because the state protects the individual's actions in any place. These two countries work from different conceptions of the domain of religion, of what the freedom of religion refers to.

Discussion Questions

In modern Western societies, we have created distinct domains of education, religion, politics, and so on. We believe that institutions in each of these domains ought to have some degree of autonomy in carrying out their missions: schools to teach, religious institutions to transmit their teachings, and politics to represent citizens in public deliberation. We disapprove of interference by one domain in another's affairs. But things are not always clear. Consider the role of education in the United States. What is the proper role of religion in education? Should parents have the right to censure teachings that conflict with their religious beliefs? Should they be able to homeschool their children in a way that exposes them to religion but not to, say, modern biology? If we say that education is to prepare children to be citizens, are there limits on what freedom of religion should permit parents to do? Or, are parents to be the best judge of how to prepare their children for the world?

Media Resources

Among full-length films, *Shinto: Nature, Gods and Man in Japan* beautifully introduces the beliefs and aesthetics of the Shinto tradition and its relationship to Japanese Buddhism. *Japan: Past and Present: Buddha in the Land of the Kami* traces the ways in which Buddhism was assimilated into preexisting beliefs. I often use short clips interspersed in a lecture, and then allow time for discussion. A clip at: http://www.youtube.com/watch?v=D3ikvSZOOw0 introduces Shinto in under four minutes; a decent two-minute clip is at: http://www.youtube.com/watch?v=iOynXOWvkU8.

On Buddhism, other than the first film mentioned above, there are short clips on important temples; I would recommend the following silent tour of Todaiji temple in Nara, mentioned in this chapter, at: http://www.youtube.com/watch?v=x1tpVaekWi8 (you need not show the entire clip). If you want resources on Buddhism more generally, a BBC 50-minute documentary on the life of Gautama Buddha is available at: http://www.youtube.com/watch?v=bfuWXqX1sbE.

Rituals of Transition

Now we turn from studying the ideas about religion to the analysis of key elements of religions. We start with those fixed sequences of actions that we often call "rituals." People carrying out a religious ritual try to conform to certain rules to get the ritual right. In some cases, they are seeking to accomplish a specific end, such as healing, pleasing a deity, or restoring fertility. In other cases, they perform rituals out of a sense of obligation. We will consider these and many other types of rituals in this book, from pilgrimage to prayer to "rituals of rebellion." In this chapter, we consider rituals that mark transitions of various kinds and explore the way such rituals shape, or are motivated by, emotions.

In most, perhaps all, societies, people mark transitions or life stages by carrying out certain transition rituals or rites of passage. These rituals often have a religious dimension, and they tend to cluster around several points in the life cycle, particularly birth, puberty, marriage, and death. Rituals that mark the passage into adulthood may involve changes in name, membership in a new society of initiates, bestowal of new social rights and duties, or, in the category of religiously competent persons, conferral of supernatural powers. Death is also ritually represented as a transition in most societies; death rituals are usually intended to ease the passage of the spirit to another social state and possibly to another world. Many other kinds of rituals are also concerned with transitions. The beginning of an agricultural cycle or the succession to an office may be ritually enacted in ways that resemble life-cycle transition rituals.

We find three aspects across many distinct transition rituals. First, they often emphasize the *creation of life*: new persons, life after death, or the soil's fertility. Initiation rituals that move people from an immature to a mature state are of course directly concerned with reproduction and biological fertility. But funeral rituals may also tie death to the regeneration of life, refocusing attention and emotions on life and fertility rather than on death and loss.

Second, the content and sequence of rituals *shape specific emotions* in the participants. Feelings of grief are given well-specified forms of expression, sometimes a prescribed period of mourning followed by a break from mourning, sometimes the reverse:

stoicism followed by an emotional release. The promise of new life gives hope after loss, and rituals that structure time support the notion that humans can control natural processes of growth, maturation, and death.

Finally, transition rituals *represent the social order* in a particular way, often an idealized or partial way, and often as if the rituals themselves produce or shape the social order. Relations and differences between men and women, or superiors and inferiors, may be projected onto a cosmic plane, or produced in the ritual itself, especially in initiation rituals that create adolescent or adult men and women. Initiations often reveal secrets, the mere possession of which is the basis for initiates' claims to supremacy over noninitiates. Secrecy creates status and boundaries across a range of social institutions. From members of initiation societies in Africa and New Guinea, to Mormons and Masons, those "in the know" can claim superiority, power, or at least special status. Death rituals often have a different social design—to restore social order after a loss.

RITES OF PASSAGE

The sociologist Arnold van Gennep pointed out in 1908 (1960) that across many societies, transition rituals display a similar sequential structure. Rites marking birth, puberty, marriage, and death, he remarked, as well as many other rituals of initiation or succession, often are structured temporally as three distinct stages.

The first stage separates the person from the ordinary social environment. It may involve rites to purify the body, seclusion, cutting hair, or simulating death. The separation may amount to the social recognition of a natural event, such as the onset of menstruation or death. Separating one group of people from others may create a peer group, such as a group of boys or girls to be initiated. It may define a geographical space, as when Muslims exchange their ordinary identities and clothing for the garb of pilgrims when entering the sacred precincts of Islam in Arabia.

Next comes a stage of marginality, the transitional or *liminal* ("threshold") stage during which the person is outside of normal social life. The liminal person may have to observe certain taboos, be isolated, be subjected to beatings and insults, or be elevated to temporary high status. This stage may be as short as a brief baptismal ceremony in a Christian church or as long as certain New Guinea initiation cycles lasting 10 years or more. It is a period of social work, where the liminal person is transformed in bodily or spiritual status.

Finally comes the reincorporation of the individual into society (or into an afterlife society), now possessing a new status. A girl may have become a woman, or a boy a man; a candidate is now a king; the loose soul of a dead man takes up its place in heaven.

The middle or liminal period has a key importance in this sequence of events. Consider what happens when a signal event occurs: a girl's menstruation begins; a man dies. The event changes the natural condition of the individual in a way that underscores the limits of society's control over nature. Such events are often thought of as polluting. Ritual removes the person from everyday life and provides time for people to define the event and its consequences: to transform the person in body, mind, and status, and then to define the new state—as a fertile woman, or a soul proceeding to the world of the dead.

Of course, some events that are sequenced as transition rituals are not unplanned acts of nature at all: the initiation of a group of 10-year-olds, or a baptism, or a pilgrimage. Yet the liminal stage of these rituals, too, provides the setting for a dramatization of the individual's recasting into a new form, a convincing statement that the old has died and the new is born.

THE PILGRIMAGE TO MECCA

Let us look in some detail at one well-known ritual, the pilgrimage to Mecca. Each year during the pilgrimage month of the Islamic lunar calendar, more than a million Muslims from throughout the world gather in the holy places in and around Mecca. These men and women have traveled to Mecca to carry out their religious obligation to make the pilgrimage. All the pilgrims must carry out a series of very specific actions, moving and worshiping together, before completing their task and returning home. The principal goal of the pilgrimage is to obey God's commands, as they were made clear to humans through his messenger, Muhammad.

> Islam or "submission" to God grew out of the recitations by Muhammad (570–632) to his followers of God's message, first at Mecca and then in Medina, then collected as the Qur'ân. These revelations and Muhammad's own sayings and deeds are the basis for Islamic ways of life, including the "five pillars" of confessing the faith, daily worship, fasting for the month of Ramadan, giving alms and, if possible, making the pilgrimage to Mecca. The division into Sunni and Shiite Muslims reflects a split over authority some 40 years after Muhammad's death. By the mid-eighth century Muslims ruled the lands from Spain into central Asia, and by the sixteenth century, much of southern and southeastern Asia was ruled in the name of Islam. Today, most Muslims live in Indonesia, Pakistan, Bangladesh, and India; others are spread through Africa, Asia, and, increasingly, Western Europe and North America.

Muslims consider the Qur'ân to be God's major gift to humans, and in this respect the Qur'ân's role is similar to that of the Torah for Jews and that of Christ for Christians. But Muslims also consider as divinely inspired the actions of the Prophet Muhammad—not because he was divine himself, but because he spoke and acted as God's messenger. The collection of reports about his statements and actions is called the "hadîth." These reports supplement the Qur'ân as the second basic source for guidance and law in the Muslim community. Much of Islamic ritual as well as everyday life is based on what Muhammad did as contained in these reports, and it is in this way that Muslims developed the pilgrimage, or hajj.

Why Make the Hajj?

The pilgrimage is meaningful for Muslims in the first place as a repetition and commemoration of the Prophet's actions, "following in his footsteps," as many pilgrims who had completed the hajj said to me. But it was also dictated by God in his revelations to Muhammad. Several years after Muhammad and his followers had fled from Mecca to Medina to escape persecution came the first revelation concerning the pilgrimage, quoted in the last chapter of the Qur'ân:

Say: 'God has spoken the truth; therefore follow
the creed of Abraham, a man of pure faith and no idolater.'
The first House established for the people

was that at Mecca, a place holy, and a guidance to all beings.
Therein are clear signs—the station of Abraham,
and whosoever enters it is in security.
It is the duty of all men towards God to come
to the House a pilgrim, if he is able to make his way there.
As for the unbeliever, God is All-sufficient nor needs any being.
(Qur'ân 3:90–92)

The house mentioned in this passage is the large cubic structure called the "Ka'ba," which is draped in gold-bordered black silk cloth. The Ka'ba is the centerpoint of the religious world for Muslims. It is toward the Ka'ba that Muslims worship five times daily, and it is around the Ka'ba that they walk when they make the pilgrimage. In Islamic tradition, the Ka'ba dates back to the prophet Abraham, who journeyed to Mecca with his son, Ishmael, and Hagar, Ishmael's mother. (In the Islamic version of the sacrificial trial of Abraham, it was Ishmael, not Isaac, whom he was ordered to sacrifice.) Abraham built the Ka'ba on God's command. The angel Gabriel then brought down a black stone to place in its corner. The stone, it is said, was white, but turned black on contact with the sinful world.

By the seventh century C.E., Mecca had become a trading center in the Arabian peninsula, and it was here that Muhammad was born, grew up, and received his first revelations. His triumphant return to Mecca from Medina marked the victory of Islam over the polytheistic Meccan elites, and his first pilgrimage, in 632, the year of his death, became the model for all pilgrimages since (Peters 1994).

Making the pilgrimage is one of the five ritual obligations, or *rukns* (pillars), of Islam. The pilgrimage has always attracted Muslims from all over the world, but the development of steamship travel in the nineteenth century and air travel in the twentieth century have led to a boom in pilgrimage activity. By the mid-twentieth century, about 30,000 people made the journey each year; today, over about 2 million pilgrims, from the 60 or more countries with sizable Muslim communities, arrive in Mecca each year. Pilgrims come from near and far: The largest delegations are from Nigeria, Pakistan, Turkey, and Yemen, and then Iran, Indonesia, and Iraq. Some pilgrims stay on to study and teach; most return home bringing new ideas and trade goods. Islam was founded by a trader amid vast networks of desert caravans; the contemporary pilgrimage enlarges those networks of trade and communication to the scale of the entire world.

Precisely because these holy cities occupy such a central place in the Muslim popular imagination, they have sometimes been the targets of political movements. During the 1979 pilgrimage, an armed group seized control of Mecca's Grand Mosque and broadcast denunciations of the Saudi government over a citywide loudspeaker system. Iranian anti-American demonstrations at Medina in 1982 led to arrests and revived debates about whether religion and politics could legitimately be separated in Islam. Since then, the Saudi government has prohibited delegations from making the pilgrimage when they feared political disturbances (or health risks, as in the 1996 ban on Nigerians during an epidemic in Nigeria).

Pilgrimage Stages

Although the details of the hajj are taken one by one from accounts of that first pilgrimage, the steps can be sorted into the three stages of rites of transition. Indeed, Victor

Turner (1974, 182) argues that in larger-scale societies, pilgrimages perform some of the same social functions that are filled by initiation rituals in smaller-scale societies, in providing the place for a religious experience outside the bounds of everyday social life. The pilgrim separates himself or herself from ordinary social life, enters a liminal stage in which distinctive everyday identities are exchanged for the shared identity of the pilgrim, and then returns to the social world. Each transition point is marked by clear religious duties.

Rites of Separation

Although a Muslim may visit the holy places in Mecca and Medina at any time during the year, the pilgrimage itself may be performed only on the eighth, ninth, and tenth days of the last month of the Islamic lunar calendar—the pilgrimage month, Dhu'l-Hijja. (Because the lunar year is 11 days shorter than the solar year, the pilgrimage season cycles back through the solar year.) Unlike pilgrimages made by Christians, Jews, or Hindus to their holy cities, the hajj is a series of ritual actions performed together, simultaneously, by all the Muslim pilgrims for that year (Ruthven 1984, 23–48).

Weeks or even months before these key days, pilgrims have been gathering and departing from villages, towns, and cities all over the world. In Indonesia, as in many other countries with large Muslim populations, each group receives an official send-off from a local government official. As recently as two generations ago, departing pilgrims from the Gayo highlands received a different kind of send-off. They were fed at a ritual during which prayers for the dead were recited on their behalf, because most people who made the journey were older, and many would not survive the two- or three-month sea voyage. The ritual was held before they left because otherwise they would not receive one.

Travel, whether by land, sea, or air, is for much of the way a secular affair. Only when approaching the port or airfield of Jiddah must pilgrims take steps to enter the state of consecration, or *ihram*. Each pilgrim announces his or her intention to undertake the pilgrimage; renounces shaving, cutting the hair, and sexual intercourse; and changes clothes. The new pilgrim's clothing consists of identical, simple, white seamless garments. Men leave their heads uncovered, and women must not have cloth touching their faces. Some pilgrims even ride roofless buses once they approach Mecca. Each of these measures maintains an unbroken physical link between the pilgrim's head and God, and signals his or her surrender to God.

Moving in the Liminal State

Wearing identical clothing, renouncing normal relationships to their bodies, and concentrating their lives on worshiping God define the pilgrim's position during the days of pilgrimage. In the liminal state, between their previous lives of various occupations, nationalities, wealth, and status, and their future lives as returned pilgrims, these men and women live and move as equals, sharing some rudimentary Arabic, simple accommodations (for most pilgrims, anyway), and the same daily objectives.

The clothes mark the fact that all pilgrims are religiously equal. As Muhammad's grandson Husayn stated, "The pilgrim offers himself to God as a beggar." Pilgrims mingle with one another even while onboard ship or plane as pilgrims, leaving ordinary social status aside.

Once in Arabia, they gather in groups by country and are led through the pilgrimage steps by a group leader, usually someone from their country. For many pilgrims, this is their first international experience, rubbing shoulders with others whose language they cannot understand. Arabic prayers and a few short greetings are usually the only form of verbal communication across these groups. Even the American black Muslim leader Malcolm X (1973, 339) was shocked by this universalism, as he wrote in a public letter to his mosque in Harlem. "For the past week, I have been utterly speechless and spellbound by the graciousness I see displayed all around me by people *of all colors."*

Pilgrims arrive steadily at Mecca. As they do, they make seven left-hand circles (tawaf) around the Ka'ba. Indeed, the root meaning of hajj is "to describe a circle." Huge masses of pilgrims move slowly around the silk-draped structure. Each tries to touch or kiss the black stone set into its eastern corner. The Iranian scholar Ali Shariati (1977, 31) described the experience of the tawaf as that of "a small stream merging with a big river. . . . Suddenly, you find yourself floating and carried on by this flood. You have become part of this universal system. Circumambulating . . . Allah, you will soon forget yourself."

The Ka'ba already served as a holy site before Islam, but its guardian was the deity Hubal, whose statue was kept inside the structure. Many other deities were worshiped as well, and the circumambulation was part of worship. Muhammad retained this practice and the veneration of the black stone when he undertook the first pilgrimage, and his followers, though surprised that he did so given the stone's association with paganism, followed suit. The rigorous logic of following the Prophet's actions won out, here as elsewhere.

After the tawaf, the pilgrim does the *sa'y,* "running," which does indeed consist of simply running (or, for the older, walking) back and forth, seven times, along a street in Mecca. The running commemorates the time when Hagar was abandoned under a tree at Mecca by Abraham. When her food and water ran out, she began to run wildly between two high points, pleading with God for help. When Ishmael raised his hand, there was a well, which became known as the well of Zamzam. The well marked the spot where Mecca was then built. Pilgrims collect water from the Zamzam well and bring it home with them; often diluted with rainwater, it will be used to heal or bless others. The running covers about two miles, and some pilgrims must be pushed in wheelchairs.

The circumambulation, also called the *'umra,* is sometimes performed separately out of season as the "little hajj." Travel agencies throughout the Muslim world offer 'umra packages—a Muslim may travel to Saudia Arabia at any time of year, circumambulate the Ka'ba, visit the holy sites, and return home.

The Hajj Proper

Pilgrims then begin the events that constitute the pilgrimage proper, the events that are performed only on the prescribed days. They must travel to the plain of 'Arafat by sunrise on the ninth day of the month. It is at 'Arafat, a barren plain about two miles from Mecca, where Adam and Eve were reunited after their expulsion from heaven. Here, too, Muhammad delivered his final sermon in 632, in which he set out most of the details of the hajj. A vast tent city is erected on this plain on the days before to the ninth, and there the pilgrims are assigned quarters.

At 'Arafat the pilgrims spend the ninth day in prayer and meditation, gathering around the Mount of Mercy at the edge of the plain. After performing the midafternoon worship, the millions gathered together stand, awaiting sunset, shouting cries of "God is great." This standing (*wuquf*) is the central event of the hajj proper. The special status enjoyed by this rather unspectacular (relative to the tawaf that precedes it and the sacrifices to follow) event comes from its role in replicating Muhammad's final sermon, and from the shared sense pilgrims derive from it of showing humility before God.

Pilgrims then disperse and return toward Mecca, stopping to spend the night in the city of Muzdalifa, where they are to rid themselves of all resentments toward others. There, too, they collect pebbles, which they use the next day to throw at three pillars near Mina, on the return road to Mecca. This *rajm*, or stoning, of the statues is understood to be a stoning of devils. No mention is made of it in the Qur'ân; as with the veneration of the black stone in the Ka'ba, it is performed solely because Muhammad did it on his pilgrimage. As interpreted by most participants, it commemorates Abraham's resoluteness to obey God, for it was on this spot that he prepared to carry out God's command to him to sacrifice his son. The devil appeared to Abraham, and tried to instill doubt in his heart about the sacrifice. Abraham stoned the devil until he fled. After the crowding and rushing of the previous two days, the stoning also undoubtedly releases tensions. Some commentators have harnessed the energies visible during the stoning to religious mission; Ali Shariati urged pilgrims to think of the pebbles as bullets used to kill one's enemies.

Pilgrims then carry out a sacrifice in memory of Abraham's submission to God's will. Usually they buy a goat on the spot and arrange to have its throat cut. The meat is distributed to the poor, much of it immediately frozen on the spot by Saudi authorities. The day after this event is called the *yaum an-nahr*, or day of sacrifice, and it is celebrated throughout the Muslim world by similar sacrifices. The pilgrimage is thus both a duty for all Muslims and the occasion for a worldwide ritual observance.

Reintegration to Normal Life

The pilgrimage proper is complete at this point, and the pilgrims gradually make the return to normal social status. They begin by cutting some of their hair. Women snip off just a bit, but men often have their heads shaved. Now all prohibitions are lifted except for that on sexual intercourse. Pilgrims return to Mecca, perform another circumambulation of the Ka'ba, collect Zamzam well water for the return trip, and now can again engage in sexual intercourse. They are urged to spend several days in "eating, drinking, and sensual pleasure." This urging emphasizes that the pilgrims are now leaving the state of consecration and returning to normal society—the rite of passage has ended.

Those pilgrims who return home immediately find themselves enjoying a new status, that of hajji (male) or hajjiyah (female), someone who has made the pilgrimage and returned to society. Many now wear white for everyday activities or when they attend the mosque to signal this new status. Their status may lead to other achievements: They are probably looked on with greater favor by their local bank; they may be chosen for office. They certainly have much to tell about from their journey. But they also enjoy a sense of religious accomplishment, having fulfilled the most difficult of God's commands.

How Is It Meaningful?

Ordinary Muslims undertake the pilgrimage for a variety of reasons—they are obeying a divine command; they are fulfilling a duty expected of them socially; they may be advancing their own social status. But is this all we can say? In what ways is the pilgrimage with its many component actions meaningful?

The pilgrimage presents a challenge to our usual ideas of the meaning of a religious act. It is not performed with a separate goal in mind, such as atonement or cleansing. The religious historical event that is commemorated in each segment of the ritual is sometimes but not always clear. The only overall, uniting idea of the pilgrimage is that it is made up of actions that were performed by Muhammad on his first (and only) pilgrimage.

Scholars do suggest parallels with earlier rites, either those performed on the same spot as a contemporary ritual and taken over by Muhammad, or parallel rituals within the Semitic ritual tradition that were adopted by Muhammad as properly monotheistic. For example, the wuquf, or "standing," was part of earlier Hebrew practice. Muhammad made the entire plain of 'Arafat a place of standing before God. The *'umra* was originally a sacrifice of firstborn livestock and was held in the early spring, much as with Passover, in the month of Rajab (at that time the lunar calendar was made concordant with the solar, so that Rajab always occurred in the spring). The sacrifice was carried out at the Ka'ba. As late as the twelfth century C.E., local Muslims were still carrying out this older sacrificial 'umra in the month of Rajab.

In fact, although the 'umra is thought of as a little hajj, 'umra and hajj were once distinct events. The essence of the 'umra is the tawaf, the circumambulation of the Ka'ba, while the essence of the hajj is the standing before God at 'Arafat. In origins, the one is sacrificial; the other is an act of submission to God. Muhammad then tied them together in one long series of events.

This kind of explanation may provide a historical account for why certain events became part of the overall pilgrimage. They do not account for the meaning of the rite for those people who take part in it. Muslim commentators have offered several broad lines of interpretation.

One interpretation links the performance of the hajj to the overall meaning of Islam as *surrender*. According to the important twelfth-century theologian Al-Ghazali, devotion to God demands self-abnegation, surrender to his will. Therefore, God has imposed on the Muslim actions that in themselves have no emotional or intellectual appeal, such as the running back and forth between two points, or sa'y.

A second interpretation identifies symbolic or iconic meanings for each individual place or object that the pilgrim encounters. The Ka'ba is the House of the Lord. You will meet God in a seamless shroud, so you meet him today wearing such garments. The tawaf resembles the movement of angels that encircle the Throne of God, which itself is situated directly above the Ka'ba in heaven. Ali Shariati (1977) sees the "running" as standing for purposeful activity on the earth.

A third line of interpretation seems to me to be closest to the ways in which pilgrims themselves interpret their experience. This approach locates meaning not in the events but in their historicity, as commemorations of past events. The running commemorates the moment when Hagar was looking for water for Ishmael and Gabriel created the Zamzam well. The stoning marks the moment when Abraham stoned the devil. The sacrifice commemorates Abraham's willingness to sacrifice his son. At the very least, every event commemorates Muhammad's pilgrimage—and this insight returns us to a key element of Islam, that practices and texts constantly refer back to the life of the Prophet for their authenticity.

And what is the specific goal of the pilgrimage? Despite the fact that worship is always done facing the Ka'ba in Mecca, and that "Mecca" has become a shorthand for a central place or goal, in fact, the central event in the pilgrimage, the standing at 'Arafat, takes place outside Mecca itself, as does the sacrifice, both in places that are virtually uninhabited during the remainder of the year. Within the hajj framework, for instance,

Man returned from the pilgrimage proudly displays his new clothing, Isak, Sumatra. *(Courtesy of John Bowen)*

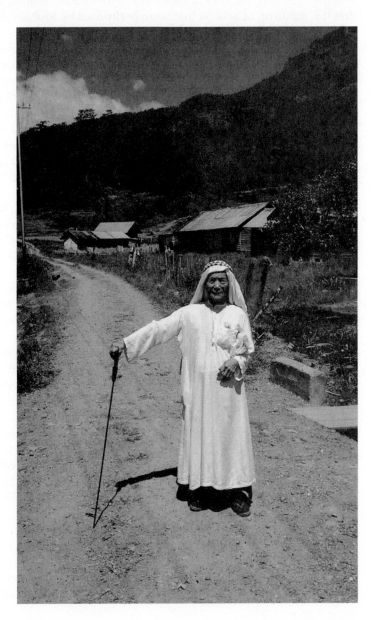

the pilgrim is never still, but is hurried around the Ka'ba, down the road to 'Arafat, back to Mina and then to Mecca, around the Ka'ba again, and then home. What the pilgrimage is really about is commemoration of Muhammad's actions, not the visit to the holy places (which, one should again note, can take place at any time of the year).

Pilgrims expand this sense of historicity from particular commemorations to a more diffuse sense of being in the place where their religion was born, being "at the source." "Everywhere," writes the Pakistani religious leader al-Maudûdî of the typical pilgrim, "he sees the relics of those who lived God, and sacrificed their lives for His sake. Every grain of sand witnesses the glory and grandeur of Islam, and every piece of stone declares: 'This is the land where Islam took birth, and whence God's word rose high'" (quoted in Cragg 1980, 60). As the leader of U.S. Muslims, Warith Deen Muhammad said in conversations in St. Louis in 1996, "On the pilgrimage you come near to God; you are visiting Him."

DEATH RITUALS AND SOCIETY

If performing the pilgrimage links the Muslim to his or her history, death rituals across societies can be seen as highlighting ideas about the individual's relationship to the collectivity. If an individual leaves society, is he or she to remain part of it? In the answer to that question, people often highlight their picture, real or ideal, of society and of an individual.

In much of China and Taiwan, villagers conceive of the spiritual world as composed of three beings: ghosts, gods, and ancestors. Each is dealt with differently, for example, offered different kinds of food or money. These three beings are also associated with three kinds of humans. Gods are dressed in the garments of officials, and they can punish people and be bribed. They keep records; they are clearly bureaucrats. They are worshipped in temples (Wolf 1974). Ghosts, by contrast, are worshiped outside, with large offerings of food or clothing, and they resemble bandits or beggars—strangers, in other words. Ancestors are, well, ancestors. You owe them a debt for your own life and prosperity, and you feed them as you would feed a human visitor to your home. This close correspondence between society and supernatural beings suggests that in different Chinese settings, people would interpret these beings somewhat differently, and they do: The god who is a police official today may have been an influential country gentleman in the past.

From Spirit to Household God in Japan

For an extended example of this general idea, let's return to rural Japan. If the living individual is thought of as a member of a household and of a community, at death he or she becomes a spirit (kami) as well as a Buddha (hotoke). Funerals are performed by Buddhist priests, but death ritual also involves pre-Buddhist ideas of pollution and ritual. A long transition stage allows the spirit to progress from an individual's spirit to one element in the household deity. Death ritual thereby reinforces the notion of spirit collectivity (Plath 1964; Smith 1974).

Death begins a three-stage process of transforming the deceased into a part of the spirit collectivity. At death the body may be cremated or buried; urban Japanese inevitably cremate. In either case, bodily death pollutes the spirit (shirei) as well as the close relatives of the deceased. Death ritual helps to separate the spirit from the pollution. The grave receiving the body is located far away from the residential part of a village and is called the "abandoned grave." In some parts of Japan, a second, "ritual grave," consisting of a headstone is built nearer the house. This grave may be tended without encountering the pollution of the dead body. Urban Japanese must rely on funeral parlors. (Today the combined expenses of burial, home altar with tablets, and the services of a Buddhist priest can amount to a middle-class family's one-year pretax income!)

The memory of the deceased individual is preserved for the first 49 days after death. The survivors set up a mortuary tablet on the household altar, together with a photo of the deceased, incense, bells, and other objects. Buddhist memorial services are held for the individual every 7 days until the 49 days are completed. The soul also wanders near the house during this period, before leaving on the 49th day.

Sometimes the soul takes some action on its own on the 49th day to settle scores with the living. In an eighteenth-century puppet play called *The Woman Killer and the Hell of Oil*, Yohei murders Okichi, but no one knows that Yohei is the murderer. Yohei arrives on the 49th day of the ritual, just after a rat has run along the rafters of the room, dislodging a scrap of paper with evidence of the murderer's guilt; and the husband of the dead woman exclaims that this was a sign from the dead person: "This I owe to Buddha's mercy," he says.

At the end of this initial period, the family performs a series of rituals to transform the spirit of the dead into an ancestral spirit (*sorei*). The photo is put away and the temporary tablet disposed of, replaced by a permanent tablet, usually an upright wooden plaque four to six inches high, lacquered in black or gold, and inscribed with a special posthumous name of the deceased and the date of his or her death. (Buddhist temples provide these after-death names.) This tablet is placed with the other tablets on the altar.

The altar and tablets stand for the house's history (Smith 1974, 1978, 152–165). The household (*ié*) is thought of as a corporate group, the headship of which passes from father to son over the generations. The tablets are the first objects to be saved (standard newspaper accounts of fires say that "flames swept through the building so rapidly that the residents only had time to carry out the altar and tablets"). The tablets are even more important than the Buddha image. As one man put it, the ancestors need help like anyone else, whereas the Buddha can take care of himself.

But the tablet itself is impermanent. After either 33 or 50 years (depending on the region of Japan), the tablet is destroyed and the spirit becomes a god. The spirit is sometimes transferred to the household god in a noteworthy ritual in which the tablet is cast into a river and then a pebble is picked up from the river bed and placed on the household god's altar. This collection of pebbles represents the spirits merged into the guardian god of the household as a collectivity.

Thereafter, services are held for the collective dead, without identifying them singly, both with daily offerings of flowers and on seasonal occasions, in particular New Year's on January 1 through 3, Obon or the Festival of the Dead or of Lanterns on August 13 through 15, and the equinoxes in late March and September.

The Obon festival, when the ancestors come down from where they live to their villages, has been celebrated at least since the year 606 c.e. One dedicates temples and recites Buddhist verses and makes offerings to ancestors. One category of ancestor is especially grateful for these offerings: Ancestors who committed misdeeds in past lives may end up on the plane of existence called *gaki-do,* or Plane of the Hungry Ghosts. They suffer from hunger and thirst, and they alone out of all one's ancestors may benefit from offerings one makes to a holy or virtuous person.

But Obon generally is the time to make offerings to the ancestors. The ritual grave near the house is cleared and a path is swept leading back to the house. The household altar is cleaned and a dance (today in decline) is held in the village. People return to their ancestral villages to participate in the festival and end the ritual by taking lanterns and small boats to the graveyard or to a mountain or river to see the spirits off on their return to their abode. Japanese overseas also celebrate Obon. In St. Louis, where I live, it is the time for a Japanese festival at the Botanical Gardens, with the lighting of lanterns around the lake in the Japanese garden.

The long transition stage in Japanese death rituals supports the idea of a gradual melding of the individual into the collectivity and thus also supports the general cultural importance of the collectivity.

REGENERATING LIFE FROM DEATH

Death rituals also frequently feature images of journeys to new worlds, enactments of rebirth, or the disinterment and reburial of bones (Bloch and Parry 1982). Images of journeys are sometimes the material focus of religious innovations. As Sumatran Toba Batak people left their ancestral homeland for big cities, they began to use their new wealth to build elaborate family tombs back home. These tombs were carved in the shapes of boats and other images of soul journeys, and the tombs kept alive a sense of attachment to the homeland and a promise of rejoining the family for the journey to the afterworld. In Ghana, a man named Connie Kway began to carve elaborate, painted coffins in the shapes of boats or birds during the 1970s. These coffins sold for the equivalent of a year's average wage and were snatched up by the rich. They were an innovation; Ghanians had not used fancy coffins before, but because they dramatized the comforting and spirit-raising belief that the dead were going to a resting place where loved ones would see them again, they quickly became popular and spawned imitators. (In 1996, a museum tour of the coffins swept the United States, where they were competed for as treasured folk art objects.)

Death is often linked to life and fertility in the transition stages. This linking may take different forms. Bloch and Parry (1982, 7) argue that death rituals tend to revitalize "that resource which is *culturally conceived* to be most essential to the reproduction of the social order." The resource may be the land, human fertility, or some combination of the two. Thus, in four African hunter-gatherer societies compared by James Woodburn (1982), social reproduction was thought to depend most importantly on control over nature, and the ritual response to death was to reawaken the productivity of nature.

For the Merina of Madagascar, studied by Maurice Bloch (1982), reproducing the society requires that members of a descent group have their bones buried together in ancestral tombs. Because these related individuals do not live in the same place, they are initially buried where they die. Their bones are later dug up and moved to the ancestral tomb. The initial burial is attended by sadness and mourning, but the subsequent "regrouping" of the body with the ancestors is full of joy and dancing. While dancing, women repeatedly throw the brittle bones to the ground, smashing them to bits. These actions merge the physical remains of the individual with the ancestral groups as a whole. The ritual also employs the symbolism of birth, entering into and emerging from the tomb as if it were a womb.

Asmat Headhunting and Birth through Death

Consider in more detail the case of the Asmat, a society of about 50,000 people living in the swampy plains of West Papua in Indonesia. The Asmat are best known in the West for the tall *bis* poles, made out of sago palm, examples of which are to be found in many Western museums (Kuruwaip 1974).

The Asmat (Sudarman 1984) call themselves the "tree people." Their environment is wood; stone or metal for tools must be acquired from elsewhere. Canoes, poles, housing are all from wood. Their staple, sago, is also wood. Every four or five days, the men of a clan will spend an entire day looking for a large (45-foot-high) sago palm tree in the forest, cutting it down; removing the pith; and then pounding, washing, drying, and roasting the pith into large cakes of sago to be pounded into sago flour. Sago is regarded as a human being. The sago palm resembles a woman: Life comes from within it, and the white, milky sago resembles breast milk. When an Asmat man carves a sago palm into a pole, he considers his work similar to what he does to help produce a baby. Asmat hold that the father does not cause conception, but molds the child through frequent intercourse into the shape he or she eventually has at birth (Gerbrands 1967).

Much of the Asmat men's time used to be spent in warfare between clans, fueled partly by their practices and beliefs surrounding death. Asmat believe that deaths are due to malevolent actions by others, that people in other clans kill your own relatives either in an observable way (in a raid, for example) or through sorcery. The spirits of the dead demand retribution or revenge for their deaths (Zegwaard 1959). The Asmat once took revenge for a death by taking a head in a raid on another clan, thus continuing the cycle of death and retribution. The relative taking the head would have carved for him a long, 15- to 20-foot *bis* pole. The clan would then drum and dance to entice the spirit into the pole. The relative would dedicate the pole to the deceased, and cry out (for example): "Oh mother, I have killed a man from [place name]." Then the spirit of the dead person, which would have remained in the village until avenged, would begin its journey out of the village and toward an island somewhere off the western coast, later to be reborn as a new human (Kuruwaip 1974).

Today, headhunting is prohibited, and Asmat seem to have abandoned the practice. But they continue to carve images of deceased relatives onto the long poles, to drum the spirit into the pole, and to erect the pole and publicly dedicate it, calling out for the spirit to leave the village.

Through their myths, the Asmat believe the acts of producing sago from palms, carving wood poles, and cutting heads to be situating their lives in the universe. Taking a head reenacts a sacrifice made at the beginning of time. In a widely told story, a being who was both god and man killed his brother and cut off his head, immediately causing the universe to come into existence, and all of culture with it. (In some versions of this story, the god–man cut off the head of a crocodile in order to create non-Asmat people.) Taking a head thus caused life to emerge (Zegwaard 1959).

In practice, the skulls of the dead help to bring about a new birth. In past times, the skull used would have come from a headhunting expedition, and thus the same skull would accomplish two important functions. First it would allow the spirit to leave

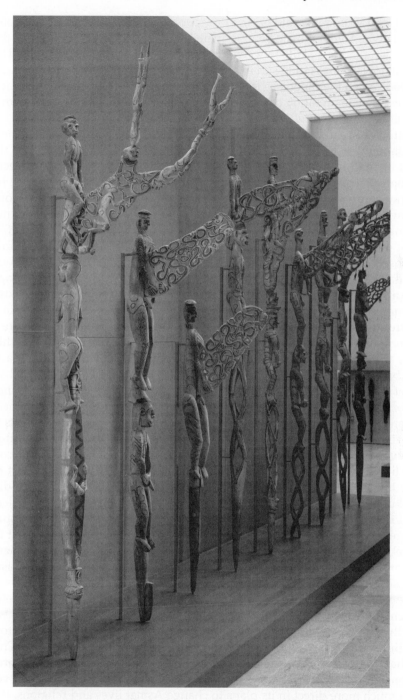

Bis Pole. Mid-twentieth century. New Guinea, Irian Jaya, Faretsj River, Omadesep village, Asmat people. Wood, paint, fiber, H. 216 in (548.6 cm). The Michael C. Rockefeller Memorial Collection, Bequest of Nelson A. Rockefeller, 1979 (1979.206.1611). *Image copyright © The Metropolitan Museum of Art/Art Resource, NY*

the world, and second it would bring a new person into it. Today, the skull would come from a relative. A young male being initiated into manhood sits for days in the men's house, contemplating a skull between his legs, pressed against his genitals. Then he is carried out toward the setting sun in a canoe, following the journey made by the spirits of the dead. When the canoe has traveled far enough from the shore, he lies at the bottom of the canoe in imitation of someone who has just died. Then he is thrown into the water, still holding the skull, to resurface as a newly born initiated man.

Cutting the sago is also likened to taking a human head and releasing energy. The palm is thought to have the same spirit as a human. Men attack the palm, throwing spears at it, and butcher the starch. Asmat also draw on these ideas to project human actions onto the animal world. They see an analogy to headhunting in the behavior of the praying mantis. The insect is seen as human in its movements (think of how its stance gave rise to its English name), and the female bites off the head of the male during mating.

Not only is the mantis's cannibalism like taking a head, but it also reminds the Asmat observer of the mock, or part-mock aggression enacted by women toward men in everyday life. For when the Asmat men return along the river with the sago palm, women carry out an attack on the canoes from the village shore. The attack is ostensibly to keep malevolent spirits from entering the village along with the palm, but in practice women throw their spears hard and accurately and, not uncommonly, men are injured.

Drumming the spirit of the dead into the *bis* pole also replicates a mythic event. The very first man on earth was called Fumeripits. He drowned in the sea but was brought back to life by War, the name of the white-tailed eagle, who pressed smoldering bits of wood against his body. Then Fumeripits built a large men's house and carved images of men and women. He began to drum, and they came to life, dancing. The carvers and drummers of today cannot create life, but they can attract spirits through their carving and drumming, thereby reenacting Fumeripits' deed on the spiritual level.

In everyday life, too, Asmat experience the link between heads and the continuity of life. All adults sleep on skulls, usually skulls of close relatives, and report feeling a continued tie to the deceased through this skull-sleeping. Some men will (or did) sleep on the skull of a powerful enemy, claiming that they absorb some of the deceased's power at night. Carving the pole and cutting heads thus not only frees the spirit from the village (and the village from the spirit) but also signifies to the living that the dead will be reborn and life will continue. The ritual also gives the bereaved a concrete way to care for the spirits of their relatives. And since they practice it together as a social group, a single individual's death strengthens the power of their origin myths.

The ritual as it once was carried out allowed the individual to complete a logical and emotional circle: A death, avenged by taking a head, was completed when the skull of the victim was used to release the spirit from the village and then to cause a rebirth. But now the circuit has been shorted at the point of headhunting. The Dutch (when they controlled the territory) had already prohibited headhunting throughout the region, but they had little direct sway over the Asmat. The Indonesian government has been much more direct in its plans to change Asmat lives and religions: It encourages missionaries to promote the adoption of proper religion, with a book, a creed, but no violence. The missionaries offer salvation through communion (which might be interpreted by Asmat as a different kind of cannibalism) and rebirth through baptism (a different path to rebirth through immersion in water).

Secondary Burial

The "regrouping" of bones practiced by the Merina, and described above, provides one example of a widespread practice of secondary burial, or the removal and reburial of a corpse. This practice is intended to provide material signs of the transition from life to an afterlife in the form of the state of the bones of the dead after decomposition is supposed to have set in. Secondary burial is relatively rare, but it is found in culturally unrelated areas throughout the world—Greece, Africa, Siberia, Indonesia, the Americas, and in early Jewish practice. Medieval Christian burial in Europe often included the display of bones in an ossuary.

Peter Metcalf (1982) provides a detailed description of the practice from the Berawan society in Borneo. In this society, a body is stored in a large jar right after death. After several days, the bones are cleaned of flesh and stored in the longhouse or on a platform outside. Months or years later (Metcalf records a range of eight months to five years), the bones of some of the dead, but not others, are removed and placed in a permanent death monument. For the Berawan, the display of bones stands for the passage of the spirit of the dead outside the community. It confirms that the spirit has reached the land of the dead.

Robert Hertz (1960) wrote a comparative essay on the practice in 1907. Hertz used material from Borneo and Indonesia but also made reference to similar practices elsewhere. Based on his reading of available ethnography, Hertz argued that people take the natural fact of bodily decomposition as the basis for thinking about the process of death, the transition from the loss of soul to the passage to another place. Just as the body decomposes, so the spirit gradually leaves the body, transformed to a new state in which the spirit is definitively separated from the body.

The process of decomposition, then, defines three moments in the death process, each of which serves as a sign of the unobservable process through which the spirit leaves the body and the community. At the moment of death, the spirit has left the body. During decomposition, the spirit is uncertain as to its final home, and during this period it may haunt the living and roam the community. But when the bones are seen to be clean, the spirit has left for its new home.

Hertz noted that people have a horror of the corpse throughout the world, but that it is not a physical repugnance. The same people fear the corpse but wash it, sit with it, even drink the wash water. The fear is for two reasons. First, the death tears a hole in the community, and the social fabric must be mended and order restored. The more important the person, the more ritual work needs to be done, so only some bones are subjected to secondary burial. Second, the soul remains near the corpse and until it has left the community, it will continue to haunt the living. The rites of secondary burial enact the finality of the passage out of the community.

This analysis explains why Berawan people evinced horror at the practice of embalming when Metcalf described it to them. Embalming for purposes of viewing the body in a "lifelike" state is seen by Berawan as delaying the process of decay and thereby retarding the successful separation of the soul from the community.

Similar concerns are found in the official policy on burial of the Greek Orthodox Church. Bodies must not, commands the church, be buried in airtight caskets lest the natural, and God-ordained, process of decomposition be halted. In rural Greece today, relatives exhume the bones of the deceased five years after the body is buried, and remove the bones to the village ossuary (Danforth 1982). If the bones are clean and white, relatives are assured that the soul has passed to heaven. If decomposition has not been completed, villagers wait for another two years and then repeat the process. Meanwhile they say prayers for the forgiveness of the person's sins; it is these sins that have retarded the soul's passage and the body's decomposition.

In these and other cases, people feel ambivalent about the passage of the soul from the community. People may wish loved ones to remain near them, but they also wish for closure in the process of dying and mourning. Death rituals not only demonstrate to the living that the dead have left the community, taking danger with them, but also that they remain close by and that they can be called on to help the living. The soul of a Berawan person remains ready to aid the living in times of illness or other need. Asmat send the spirits of the dead away from the community to an island off the coast, but people continue to sleep with the skulls of deceased loved ones and sense that the person continues to remain with them. For people in many societies, death involves desires for both finality and remembrance; death rituals give those desires a material form.

GRIEF AND RITUAL FORM

Transition rituals marking events such as initiations or deaths are emotional times. Often the emotions are produced by the rituals themselves. The sociologist Émile Durkheim (1858–1917), stressing the social base for much of religious life, argued that ritual action, especially when in a group, channels and determines emotions. Durkheim maintained that although there might be natural emotional responses to death, they are highly subject to social shaping. Is this view correct? How culturally different are those emotions? What role does ritual play in the interior lives, the feelings, and the grieving of the survivors? Do rituals create emotions or do emotions determine what kind of rituals people create?

Consider the contrast between the ways in which two Muslim peoples mourn the loss of a close relative. In Java, where people typically value the control of their emotions, Clifford Geertz (1960, 73) reports a man he knew well, distancing himself from the loss of his wife, describing how he kept his emotions inside him. A girl who wept softly after her father died was told she could not participate in the funeral events unless she stopped crying. And yet, in Morocco, another Muslim society, the expected behavior is just the opposite. People in mourning tear their clothes and hair and wail loudly and publicly (Westermarck 1968 II, 34–42).

These marked differences in public behavior are between two peoples with the same religion. Ritual forms, linked to dominant cultural values, prescribe sharply contrasting patterns of mourning behavior.

But we cannot assume from such publicly observed contrasts that the emotions and the grieving process experienced by the individual are correspondingly different (Rosaldo 1984). Many Moroccans may feel indifference; many Javanese, great sorrow. Yet men and women in each society are expected to act in certain standardized ways regardless of their feelings. Many people in the United States report feeling quite different from what their public mourning behavior would suggest. Some feel guilty at the gulf between their mixed emotions and the expressions of grief that they are expected to display. Others adhere to religions that urge their followers in a different direction, to maintain a hopeful attitude consistent with a strong belief in the afterlife. Mormon services reflect this attitude, and Christian Scientists argue that bereaved people can and should lift themselves out of sorrow through the sheer force of the will. Yet many adherents to these faiths do grieve, and may find their social networks not offering the support they need (Palgi and Abramovitch 1984).

Is Grief Universal?

Perhaps the most devastating loss to an American adult is the death of a child, and here cross-cultural variation is striking. Psychologists (Bowlby 1980) argue that parents in all societies develop attachment to their children and experience grief at the loss of children. The attachment and the grief seem to have a basis in the evolution of social relationships. Both features are found in nonhuman primates as well as in humans. And yet in many societies the deaths of newborns are not accompanied by the same expressions of loss and grief as are the deaths of older children or adults. In many societies, children are not named until some number of days have passed after birth, and a death before that time is treated very differently than later deaths. Do these practices indicate that parents feel the loss less? How strongly does such a cultural practice shape emotions?

Two studies in anthropology have addressed this question but reach distinct conclusions. Nancy Scheper-Hughes (1992) argues that some poor Brazilian parents do feel loss less than do most middle-class parents. She emphasizes the cultural malleability of emotions—cultural practices shape emotional response. Unni Wikan (1990), emphasizing the distance between public expressions and inner emotions, finds that Balinese people feel strong grief emotions, but that they follow culturally prescribed practices of working on their grief through laughter and sociability. These and other studies underscore the emotional importance of rituals and other practices during the transition stage after a death—and also the difficulties in generalizing about "private" emotions.

Nancy Scheper-Hughes lived, worked, and studied in a very poor region in northeastern Brazil in the 1960s and then again in the 1980s. Many in the area had little to eat, and infant death was common. Mothers, fathers, and siblings developed an attitude of "letting go" toward those infants who seemed near death, often drawing on an elaborate catalogue of symptoms that pointed to an inevitable death.

Scheper-Hughes tried to make sense of the families' emotionally flat responses by challenging the Western view about attachment and mourning. In that view, attachment is a basic instinct that structures relationships between all human mothers and their children. The death of a child triggers natural responses of mourning, which must be worked through if the survivors are to be able to carry on in a healthy way. But Scheper-Hughes (1992, 400–445) argues that many mothers in fact have an ambivalent attitude toward their newborns. When the mother–infant experience is positive, and when nurturing all of one's children is possible, parents invest emotionally in their children and feel great loss at a death. But in poor Brazil and some other places, a "lifeboat" ethic leads parents to choose, reluctantly, to nurture only those who have a chance at surviving. Cultural practices reinforce this survival strategy: Parents delay naming their infants and hold them much less often than do middle-class mothers.

Death ritual also plays an important part in this survival strategy. In some parts of Brazil, lower-class men and women treat the death of a very young child as a blessing. The child will be taken to heaven, is already a little angel, they say. The wake held for the little child, who is dressed in a white or blue shirt with curled hair and floral wreaths, includes joyous music and samba dancing. Although much more sober in tone in the community where Scheper-Hughes worked, the "angels" were a "transitional object" for these women, she points out (1992, 421), both because the infant is in transition from life to death, and because the dressed-up corpse and coffin allows the woman to let go of her child by giving her an idealized heaven-child to hold onto. Women told Scheper-Hughes: "I feel free" or "I feel unburdened" after the funeral. Grief seemed absent. For some students of Brazilian society, the flat emotional response is a mask, a wall against the unbearable. But Scheper-Hughes takes the responses of these women at face value, arguing that culture and ritual succeed in preventing grief responses. The idea that deaths need to be worked through by a process of open mourning, she says, is applicable only in some societies.

Still, it may be difficult to decide between several possible interpretations of Scheper-Hughes's data—are denials of grief a mask, or are denials accurate reports of feelings? Another study of the same area (Nations and Rebhun 1988) reports very different findings. In many parts of the world, women lose their babies in infancy and yet mourn them deeply and loudly; high rates of infant mortality do not seem to be associated with low rates of grieving. Finally, we should note that arguments for a universal attachment structure are based on cross-cultural research: The major early empirical work (Ainsworth 1967) was not from the West but from Uganda!

Emotions and Their Expressions

Scheper-Hughes's argument was intended to counter universal theories of death, emotions, and ritual. By contrast, anthropologist Unni Wikan draws on her fieldwork in Bali to oppose culturally relativist theories about the malleability of emotions. In Bali, as in neighboring Java, people are expected to preserve a "face" of equanimity at loss or disaster. Anthropologists had long understood the grace and composure of Balinese as a cultural style that focused on beauty and on distancing oneself from emotions. Balinese selves, wrote the anthropologist Clifford Geertz (1966), are quite different from Western ones; they live in a "dramatistic" world composed of masks, roles, and a stage.

Wikan (1990) argues instead that Balinese think and feel their way through the world in ways that are much closer to European ways than earlier anthropologists believed. She describes several months in the life of one woman who lost her fiance in an accident. Her friends laughed and joked with her, insisting that she laugh too. During the following months, she appeared bright-faced and happy, even to her friend Wikan. After several months Wikan did see her cry, and then the woman began to tell of how devastated she had felt through the whole experience. About the same time, her friends began to change their ways of being with her, sympathizing out loud with the distress she must have felt. Her emotions, and their understanding of them, were not all that different after all.

But why did she laugh her way through the first few months, and why did her friends insist that she do so? The key lies in a distinctive set of ideas about the relationship between one's "face"—appearances and behavior—and one's "heart"—emotions and thoughts. For the Balinese with whom Wikan spoke, emotions of sadness and sorrow weaken one's life force. A weak life force opens up the body to all sorts of invasions, but most particularly to attacks from sorcerers. These attacks are always near at hand; half of all deaths are attributed to sorcery. Moreover, these sad feelings can spread from one person to another, endangering the community, so one has a social as well as a personal responsibility to keep sorrow at a distance. How does one do that? Whereas we might think of emotions as having a life of their own—grief inevitably following loss—the Balinese think that behavior, including how one forms one's face and the choice to laugh or cry, shapes the heart and channels emotions. Laughing, then, keeps sadness from welling up, and thereby keeps the person strong against murderous sorcery.

Wikan concludes that Balinese appearances of calm and joy are not due to a theater-like detachment from the world, but rather to their strong fears of sorcery and their ideas about how best to combat it. During the transition period after death, these dangers are at their highest and thus when the practices of laughing together are most required.

Wikan, then, affirms the distinctiveness of Balinese ideas and practices but sees them as responses to a universal emotion of loss and grief. Scheper-Hughes claims that the emotions of the Brazilians she studied are quite different from those experienced by middle-class families, but she does so by way of a general theory about the responses of mothers (and others) to infants and to risk. Both underscore the critical role of culturally sanctioned practices designed to shape the emotions people feel when a loved one dies. Balinese laughing and Brazilian "angel caskets" bridge the transition period between death and the reintegration of the survivors into the ordinary routines of life.

Conclusions

The three-stage model of transition rituals provides a powerful way to compare rituals across societies and across ritual types. We can analyze rituals of initiation, death rituals, and pilgrimages through the same lens. And the evidence suggests that this lens provides a very useful tool for examining rituals and then comparing them. But the debate over emotions also provides a cautionary note. Just because everyone dies and all societies organize the passage from life to death in some way, we do not know that all societies shape emotions in the same way, or that all individuals in one society experience the same emotions at deaths. There remains an important role for in-depth ethnographic study, and for expecting to find considerable variation in experience among individuals in any one society. (You would probably discover such variation in comparing your own experiences at deaths of friends and family.)

Discussion Questions

Most of us have experienced rituals of transition, whether regarding coming of age, marriage, or death. Many of us also have been involved in an initiation of some sort. Map out the steps of these rituals. Why were they designed this way? What emotions do you remember during the ritual?

Funerals tend to be formally structured, with time marked out for worship, viewing, burial or cremation, and so forth. Class discussion could focus on any of these moments: for example, in your experience, was the body viewed ("open-casket") or not? Why or why not? Would you have redesigned the ritual in any way?

Media Resources

To illustrate rites of passage quite different from those discussed here, *Kinaalda: Navajo Rite of Passage* is about the four-day event performed to guide a young girl's ascent to womanhood. The theme of passage to adulthood is of course a staple in American films. A number of films now are available about the Islamic pilgrimage; my favorite is the IMAX 2009 film *Journey to Mecca*. But on YouTube you can get a 46-minute Discovery Channel film called "Revealed—The Hajj," at: http://www.youtube.com/watch?v=9x_WU0-uMns. Many short clips also are available, such as the one-minute report that summarizes the stages at: http://www.youtube.com/watch?v=VJmjkOw8F0I, good value for time.

For Japan, a short clip shows chanting in front of a new household altar just created for a relative (and also can be used for Chapter 5), at: http://www.youtube.com/watch?v=CdhtRcKxbvY. For the Asmat, I use a clip at: http://www.youtube.com/watch?v=ZxDDUK8lDss&feature=related, which is Part 3 of a longer film. I show the segment starting at 4.30, and then continue to Part 4 until 2:30.

Healing through Religion

Across the world, people try to heal themselves or others through religion. In the United States, healing through prayer is widely accepted; polls regularly report that a clear majority of Americans believe that their prayers can help someone else heal, what is known as "intercessory prayer," and higher percentages believe that if a sick person prays it can help recovery. Of course, religion can bring other forms of healing as well, from bedside visits to stories about the causes of illness to focused healing ritual. We explore some of them here.

NARRATIVES AND HEALING

It makes sense that stories and activities that a patient believes have a beneficial effect may have that effect, through the calming effects of the storytelling, or the belief that the story or practice has a direct relationship to healing, or merely because of the presence of a medical helper. Anthropological studies support that idea; we will consider a number of them here.

Giving Birth in Panama and Malaysia

Consider two examples of birthing magic, one from Panama and the other from Malaysia. In both, midwives and shamans help the mother in moving the baby down the birth canal and out into the world. But they do so by drawing on very different sets of images and values. Cuna society, in Panama, holds high the culture of heroes and battles (Lévi-Strauss 1963b). There, a shaman, who can be possessed by spirits, sings to help childbirth. He sings a story of how Muu, the spirit that forms the fetus, has exceeded her usual domain and captured the woman's soul, thereby preventing her from moving the baby down the birth canal. The shaman must carve small figurines, the spirits of which he then leads up the birth canal to overcome wild beasts and defeat Muu and her allies. In his song, the shaman describes in painstaking detail the events leading up to his own arrival at the woman's house—the woman experiencing pain, the midwife coming to call him, his own arrival—and then the journey of the friendly spirits. The journey is in the same concrete detail as the mundane events and, in Claude Lévi-Strauss's analysis, the woman is thus likely made to feel the entry of the spirits as real. She now can identify her pain with specific, well-described animals and spirits lodged in her vagina. The detail makes the journey psychologically real to the woman in pain, giving her a language for her pain and difficulties, organizing her perceptions and feelings.

Now contrast the chants recited by a healer in a Malay village studied by Carol Laderman (1983). As with the Cuna, the ritual specialist intervenes only when the midwife can no longer cope with the difficult birth. Malinowski's idea that most people work on a commonsense basis until they reach the limits of their capacities and knowledge, and only then reach for magic to extend their grasp, thus once again seems to work well. The specialist, called a "bomoh," recites a story about God's creation of the world and of the first couple, and then about the creation of the individual human. These stories follow generally available Muslim lines. They provide for the woman a story that takes place out of ordinary time, placing the woman's suffering also out of ordinary time and giving it a sense of order, naturalness, and harmony. Just as Cuna culture highlights battle, Malay culture stresses the importance of harmony and control.

Even if the woman does not hear every detail of the story, she knows the story's general outline beforehand, says Laderman, and is soothed by its familiar references to the creation story, listing of prophets and mythological figures, and litany of the sequence of days leading to birth.

The story responds to a general cultural emphasis on harmony with the universe. But what happens in the individual? Drawing on work in U.S. hospitals as well as Malaysia, Laderman argues that the psychological response to hearing the story creates a biological response, producing endorphins that reduce pain and anxiety. Endorphins are chemicals found in several areas of the brain, which appear to be responsible for "placebo effect" pain reduction. Not only do these effects benefit the mother, but because anxiety can prevent proper cervical dilation, the reduction of anxiety may directly lead to more productive contractions, and a quicker, easier birth.

Of course, the ways in which imagery, narratives, beliefs, and emotions affect bodily states, from levels of pain tolerance to changes in the immune system, are a topic under considerable current research. On the one hand, fear can lead to death, as Walter Cannon (1942) observed; more recent research suggests that the "fight or flight" adrenaline response induced by fear, though useful in the short term, is debilitating over longer periods, weakening the heart and the immune system. On the other hand, dissociation (the mechanism involved in trance and hypnosis) and positive imagery reduce pain levels. Just how "magic"—and the many other curing techniques now used in the United States and therefore not so labeled—works on the nervous and immune systems is far from being understood, but it is now widely accepted that such mechanisms do exist.

The "placebo effect" is surely part of the explanation for a number of approaches to curing. Sometimes it is even recognized by practitioners, as in the following case. Americans dramatically increased their interest in voodoo in the 2000s. In New Orleans, the grave of a nineteenth-century "voodoo queen," Marie Laveau, has become one of the most visited graves in the United States (Kinzer 2003). Laveau was a free woman of mixed Native American, African, and European descent, and she has come to stand for a mixed heritage of religion, power, and geographical roots similar to that of Brazilian Candomble. As in the Brazilian case, many adherents profess themselves Catholics, and one practitioner stated that Catholic priests come to him for help. Why this recent rise in popularity? Some ascribe it to post–9/11 searches for meaning and others to the constantly shifting search for healing and power. One voodoo priest working in New Orleans for over 20 years said that he performed ceremonies to help people but did not know how they worked. "Have you heard of the placebo effect?" he asked (Kinzer 2003).

The Creative Power of Navajo Song

The view that speech directly confers power flowers fully within Navajo religion. Navajo place speech at the center of religion as the source of creative power.

In Navajo tradition, the individual human being has the power to change the world through language (Witherspoon 1977). A person can do so because the world itself was created through language, when First Man sang the song known as Blessingway. Among the first creatures, the Holy People, were Long Life Boy (thought) and Happiness Girl (speech), to whom First Man said: "You two will be found among everything." Indeed, their names are found in nearly every Navajo prayer and song as signs of the powers to create. They are also the parents of the Changing (or Earth) Woman, the being who is associated with the earth's fertility.

The sung prayers known as Blessingway tell the story of creation. They also reenact creation each time they are told (Wyman 1970). They may be performed as a separate ritual—for example, to bless a house—or be incorporated into other rituals in which, by invoking the events of creation, they endow the ritual with the same creative power. Navajo sand painting also draws its powers from the story of creation. After the Holy People built the first house, they decorated the floor with bits of shale, rock, and mineral dyes. They drew all the forms of life that they eventually were to create, depicting them in the forms of holy people. They then recited a long prayer to these holy people, and in that act created a causal pathway between sand paintings and the sacred powers of creation. Blessingway and many other prayer cycles identify and associate everyday people and conditions with the Holy People and the events of creation. Blessingway contains many lines that link powers given to the Holy People to powers desired by the speaker, such as:

May the power that enables you to inhale also enable me to inhale.

Let the dark flint which arises to protect you always arise to protect me.

Often these sections of the prayer provide long catalogues of body parts and powers, underscoring the identification of the Holy Person's body with that of the prayer reciter. These identifications are intended to transfer the properties of the Holy People to that of the person who is the object of the ceremony. For example, Navajo singers will help ensure a good birth for an expectant mother by performing a Blessingway ceremony that identifies the Holy People of the Earth, themselves associated with fertility and life, with the mother and child (Gill 1981). The singer will collect earth from a cornfield and water from a flowing stream, both nurturing life, and apply them to the woman. The prayers recited include the Earth's Prayer, which underscores these identifications through passages such as the following:

> *Earth's feet have become my feet by means of these I shall live on.*
>
> *Earth's legs have become my legs by means of these I shall live on.*
>
> *Earth's body has become my body by means of this I shall live on.*
>
> *Earth's mind has become my mind by means of this I shall live on.*
>
> *Earth's voice has become my voice by means of this I shall live on.*
>
> . . .
>
> *It is the very inner form of Earth that continues to move with me, that has risen with me, that is standing with me, that indeed remains stationary with me.*
>
> *Now it is the inner form of long life, now of happiness that continues to move with me, that has risen with me, that is standing with me, that indeed remains stationary with me, surprising, surprising.*
>
> (Wyman 1970, 136)

The pair of terms *long life* and *happiness* are the principles personified in the *Holy People Long Life Boy and Happiness Girl* (Wyman 1970, 19–46). They are linked to all the components of the earth. The effect of these pairings is to transfer to the mother and expected child these two essential qualities, long life and happiness.

Prayers such as these are used for healing when Holy People are thought to have been responsible for the illness. If a person has trespassed on a holy site, the Holy People may place a spell on that person; the Holyway ceremony is designed to induce them to remove the spell. The singer addresses a particular holy person by name and makes an offering of tobacco smoke to him. In the Holyway stories associated with the ceremonies, the holy person is sent tobacco, which he smokes, and then agrees to help cure the patient. The holy person addresses the patient as "grandson," placing himself in a relationship, in which he can be compelled to aid the ill person, his "grandson." The prayer draws on the knowledge contained in these stories by demanding, not requesting, that the holy person cure the patient:

> *This very day you must remake my feet for me,*
>
> *This very day you must remake my legs for me.*

The prayer ends by asserting that the cure has occurred:

> *With my body cooled off, I am walking about,*
>
> *with my body light in weight, I am walking about,*
>
> . . .
>
> *As one who is long life and happiness I am walking about*
>
> *Pleasant again it has become,*
>
> *Pleasant again it has become!*
>
> (Gill 1981, 128–129)

In this, its concluding section, the prayer performs the act of bringing the patient to health. The verb is in the progressive mode—"I am walking about"—indicating that the patient will continue to enjoy health. Most importantly, the prayer identifies the patient with Long Life Boy and Happiness Girl: He or she has become "one who is long life and happiness."

Healing practices often turn on the idea that a spirit has possessed the patient and is causing the illness. The cure then involves putting the patient (or sometimes a curer) into a trance state, investigating the reasons for the spirit's actions, and driving out the spirit (or *exorcising* the patient). We turn to an example from Japan.

MODERN MAGIC IN JAPANESE NEW RELIGIONS

In Japan, new forms of healing and worship bring trance mechanisms together with the Japanese cultural heritage to heal patients suffering from what we would call psychosomatic illnesses. These New Religions developed in response to new life situations, particularly in response to the new illnesses and anxieties felt by many newly urban Japanese. Those millions of Japanese who have moved into cities since the 1950s have found themselves cut off from their accustomed places for ritual practice and sources of religious strength. They also found themselves living in a radically new era, with new kinds of pressures on the job and at home.

The New Religions range from the nationally important Soka Gakkai, with its millions of adherents, its own newspaper and university, and its strong ties to a major political party, the Komeito, to smaller sects and cults. Between 10 and 30 percent of Japanese are estimated to follow one of the New Religions. But these New Religions and their healing practices draw on elements from Japan's older religious traditions.

One such religion, studied by Winston Davis (1980), is Mahikari, meaning "True Light." It was founded in 1959 when a man of lower-class origin in Tokyo recovered from illness and debt and received a revelation from God that he was to change his name and bring light and health to the people of Japan. This man, now known as Okada Kotama, began to heal people through the use of amulets (a method he had learned from another group), and the sect grew rapidly in popularity. By the late 1970s, Mahikari had more than 150 dojos (buildings for practicing spiritual disciplines) and somewhere between 50,000 and 100,000 active members. Close to half a million had received its amulet.

Purification and Apocalypse

The major activity engaged in by people who join Mahikari is called "okiyome" (purification). The process of okiyome is designed to rid the body of spirits that have possessed it. These spirits may be those of ancestors, of other people, or of animals, especially foxes and badgers. The process involves divination and then exorcism of the spirit.

People generally come to be healed at Mahikari because of a physical complaint, the roots of which are often psychosomatic: cramps, back pains, headaches, and so forth. In their theory of causes of these illnesses, the healers join physical and psychic explanations. Consider one account of illness:

> "There is much poison around us," said a Mahikari teacher. (Indeed, in the main river in the city where Davis studied Mahikari, fish introduced to the

river die within 3 minutes from industrial toxins!) "We eat poisoned food and the poisons build up inside and cause illnesses. But," he then asked, "why did we eat the poison? Or, given that bacteria can be carried in food and then eaten by us, what led us to eat the infected food?"

The Mahikari world view offers to supplement the scientific world view by bringing the laws of natural cause and effect down to the level of the individual and his or her suffering.

The answer to our suffering is that we are possessed by spirits. Indeed, according to Mahikari, nearly all illnesses are caused by spirits. Each person has an astral spirit, which must burn off its impurities on the astral plane. (Here we see echoes from Buddhism of the planes of existence and the idea of karma.) Burning off impurities is not fun, and many of these astral spirits seek refuge in humans or torment humans for one reason or another.

The power to exorcise spirits derives ultimately from the High God, "Su-God," and also from a Shinto god he created, called Miroku, identified with the bodhisattva figure Maitreya, here called the "Buddha of the Future." Mahikari sees itself as a supplement to other religions. It recognizes that all religions worship lower deities and prophets created by Su-God; some of them have lost their healing powers, however, which Mahikari offers to restore.

The Mahikari ideology also places the individual's suffering on a grand world-historical plane. In its version of history, mankind once was united on the lost continent of Mu, where people existed in five colors. The yellow people were dominant, and within the yellow group, the Japanese. Mu had all the technological advancements of today: telephones, airplanes, and so forth. It was ruined when the races began to intermarry. The present world then developed, but is about to be destroyed.

This story combines an apocalyptic vision of coming disaster with a way out. Because of human wickedness, Su-God has recently put strict gods in power, and signs of this change are to be seen in recent earthquakes, droughts, and so forth. Humankind is to be subjected to even greater torments, and only those possessing the amulets of Mahikari will be saved, to become the "seed people" of the next era.

These kinds of disaster-plus-solution texts appear throughout human history and are often called "millenarian movements" (see Chapter 12). Each of these movements appropriates a set of already widely accepted ideas and traditions—for example, the role of a Buddha or Christ in ensuring salvation—and harnesses them to a small-scale organization, to which are attracted people looking for spiritual guidance, discipline, or health. These movements take the promise of salvation seriously, and set out to get it here and now.

Amulets and Ancestors

Consider in greater detail how healing works for Mahikari adherents. People come to the sect to be healed; they learn why they suffer; and the ideas they learn are an important part of the healing process. They learn that their souls are polluted by spirits and by material pollution and that Mahikari offers them both a temporary, personal solution through healing and a way to prepare for future destruction through continued membership in the sect. People are satisfied that they understand why things have happened to them, that it is not their own fault, and that they can do something about them.

The healers diagnose the patient's ills by detecting the auras around their bodies. Bodies give off electromagnetic waves, they are told, and the shape of these waves can be detected by an "aura meter." Auras come in different shapes and colors. Healers can also detect spirits around the body. But the main activity of the healer is to channel energy into the body that will heal and ferret out spirits bothering the patient.

The healer wears an amulet, a small locket worn on a chain, with a piece of paper inside that has a symbol written on it. This locket is "plugged in" through the central Mahikari organization to God—indeed, the objective properties of the amulet are explained in ways that draw on electric and electronic imagery. If the amulet gets wet, it may disconnect, healers are told, and apology money must be paid to Mahikari for it to be reconnected. Monthly dues must be paid, which are offered to Su-God "to keep the line connected for the next month."

The healer, wearing the amulet, raises his or her hands over the patient's body, concentrating rays from God on the body. The healer begins with the patient's "primary soul" and then looks for parts of the body that seem to need attention, perhaps massaging the body to detect such parts. The healing power of okiyome also works for inanimate objects, such as automobiles or movie projectors. (Of those people belonging to Mahikari who were surveyed, 42 percent had repaired their television sets with okiyome; 29 percent had used it to fix their wristwatches.)

In the case of people, spirits usually are responsible for their ailments. The healer must find out the identity of the spirit and then convince it to leave the patient. The patient must enter a state of trance. The healer chants over him or her, and the patient usually begins to move and cry out in ways indicative of the spirit's identity. The patient's hand movements may be characteristic of a particular animal (serpentine movements indicate a snake and so on). Or the patient may write out words or names on a tablet.

But the healer usually talks to the spirit as well, asking it if it is human, when it died, and, most importantly, why it is possessing the person. The healer scolds the spirit: "Go back to the other world and leave her in peace."

The most common explanation of specific ailments involves relationships with ancestors. Events may have caused an ancestor's spirit to possess you, for one of two reasons. First, you may have neglected the altar of the ancestors in your house. One man's ancestor came back to possess him because the altar was on a filing cabinet and the spirit was disturbed by the noise. In the Mahikari sect, people study proper altar care to avoid these problems. Nothing must be above it (so it must occupy the top story of the house), its flowers must be arranged properly, and it must have proper lacquered tablets and be supplied with food every day. Recall that in rural society the altar was the site of the protective household god, and so the anxiety of ordinary people about neglected altars makes sense.

Second, events that happened to ancestors, or to yourself in an earlier life, may have caused your misfortune and caused you to be possessed by an ancestral spirit. Healers draw on the logic of karma from Buddhism to explain how this works. One woman had been the wife of a warrior (samurai) in a previous incarnation, and when she married he grew jealous and came to bother her. Samurai often appear as the ancestors responsible for possession because they tended to commit all sorts of bad deeds and would be expected to bring misfortune.

But sometimes another kind of spirit is involved: that of a fox or snake, for example. Here, too, there is an explanation of what event caused the spirit to possess the person. One man with cancer of the face was found to be possessed by the spirit of a snake. When he was a boy, he had cut off the head of a snake, and the spirit had chosen appropriate revenge.

Trance Psychology

Central to the patient's experience of being healed is the state of trance into which he or she enters. Trance, like any other altered state of consciousness, begins when one dissociates, or withdraws from ordinary states of consciousness (Davis 1980, 132–144). We have all experienced dissociation during daydreaming, when different, sometimes odd thoughts and images wander into one's consciousness. But in the kind of structured trance settings found in Mahikari or elsewhere, the patient has been trained to expect certain specific symbols, images, or actions to emerge. Mahikari patients study books of spirit images beforehand; some also rehearse the hand movements of different spirits. They then *project* their fears, anger, sadness, or specific problems onto the symbols that have been made available to them. They respond to questions posed to them about ancestors or animals, and can introduce into their answers their own life problems. Finally comes the moment of release, or catharsis, when the person collapses onto the floor and experiences a strong feeling of relief. (Aristotle used "catharsis" to refer to the moment in a drama when pent-up emotions in the audience are released.)

The psychology of the trance-healing session is not specifically Japanese; Felicitas Goodman (1988) documents trance and possession worldwide. Its particular form in Japan draws on older culturally specific practices, however. One is the duet form of the healing: The process always involves an exorciser and a subject, who then exchange roles (rather than, for example, a single healer and many patients). This duet form is found in much older spirit possession–healing cults in Japan and is familiar to patients. It is especially effective in the way it taps the Japanese emotion of "dependence" on another, *amae*. This emotional relation has its prototype in the dependence of a child on his or her mother, and underlies relations to teachers, employers, and, in the past, the emperor. When the emperor was demoted to the role of ordinary human and state symbol after World War II, psychiatrists (Doi 1986) noted that some people became depressed by the loss of a pole for their dependence emotions.

The healing session helps to draw out longings for someone to depend on, in this specific, highly charged sense, and also longings to be depended on. The alternation of roles allows the person who is missing these roles in everyday life to better assume them. For example, one housewife had become so concerned about pollution in food that she could not bring herself to cook for her family. She then became immobilized out of guilt for not doing so, for no longer being depended on. These feelings emerged during trance, and repeated sessions gave her a way to speak these feelings as well as a new setting for dependence–role playing.

Mahikari combines universal psychosocial processes (such as trance) with culturally specific features (such as the focus on ancestors). Simply by participating in a group, regardless of its content, some people gain a stronger sense of the value of their lives. Members also have a legitimate reason to meddle in other people's lives. But, remembering Malinowski, we might pay special attention to the way the process adds confidence and certainty to the making of difficult decisions.

Take the case of Winston Davis's teacher, Yoshida Sensei, and his wife (Davis 1980, 52–63). Yoshida's father had died in the hospital, even though he had asked his son to take him home to die. Several years later, their daughter died in the same hospital. Later, Yoshida's mother died of a stomach ailment, and Yoshida himself developed ulcers. They joined Mahikari and began to be possessed by a number of ancestors and relatives, and through the exorcism procedure learned the causes of their various misfortunes.

Yoshida's father appeared in the form of a badger. He complained of dying in the hospital and said he had caused the daughter's death as revenge, and added his regret that Yoshida had sold off their land. (Yoshida remembered that he had had trouble selling the land and now knew that his father was behind these troubles.) Yoshida requested his father to be a spirit and not trouble them in the earthly world: "Apologize to God and return to the astral world to continue your austerities," he demanded. His father's spirit wept at this. He then agreed that Yoshida could sell some of the land, since it was difficult to farm and surrounded by buildings, as long as he bought some other land as a hedge against inflation. After that the father appeared as a human spirit; he had progressed up the spiritual ladder.

The process addressed the several sources of guilt faced by Yoshida and his wife, explained the series of illnesses, and finally exorcised the guilt by leading Yoshida through a series of emotionally charged sessions. Finally, it legitimated his further action, allowing him to sell off the land with a clear conscience.

Who Joins the New Religions?

Women make up 60 percent of the participants in Mahikari; many of these women are unmarried and in the traumatic period after high school during which society views them as in transition to their next state, marriage. Employers still see most women as temporary employees, biding time until marriage. But some women either wish to pursue careers or have not found suitable husbands, and many psychosomatic illnesses occur then.

Healing can explain why marriage is difficult, perhaps because of possession by a jealous husband from a past life, and can also provide an outlet for repressed emotions and desires. Consider several cases discussed by Winston Davis (1980, 161–200). Tanio lived in fear of men. Her own father was often drunk and violent, and she was raised by her mother. In trance the spirit possessing her declared herself to be that of a woman whose husband she stole in an earlier life. Nakata never married because, trance revealed, she was possessed by spirits of aborted children. Eiko was happily married, but her family resisted her joining Mahikari. Her own ancestors torment her whenever she worships her husband's ancestors. (Here emerged the classic problem of changing ancestral allegiances.)

These women and men found power in an environment of their own general powerlessness. Inside the sect, people experience possession and curing. But outside, as well, they experience miracles. Only 12 of 688 members interviewed said they did not experience such miracles. They found social status within the group. And they found an ideology that explained much of what was happening around them, gave them a way to muddle through it, and promised future salvation.

Whatever we might think about these groups, they are a response to urban ills. Some of them are clearly destructive (and some think even Mahikari to be so). In March

1995, canisters containing the nerve gas sarin exploded in a Tokyo subway, killing 10 and injuring more than 5,000, and the attack was linked to the sect Aum Shinrikyo. Aum Shinrikyo's leader, Shoko Asahara, preaches much the same apocalyptic vision as does Mahikari's Okada Kotama. Aum hands out battery-powered headgear to followers so that they may communicate directly with their leader. (The headgear also attracts recruits from the sciences.) Its teachings combine Buddhism and Hinduism—especially the god of destruction, Shiva. Aum followers had to renounce ties with the outside world and donate all their goods to the cult (Sayle 1996).

The history of state Shinto and its ties to militarism have made the Japanese state very wary of interfering in these sects, even when evidence of criminal actions emerges. In 1989, Asahara was held responsible for killing a lawyer helping to return children kidnapped by the sect. And yet Aum was recognized as a religious body the same year and no steps were taken against its leader. One legacy of state Shinto is thus an extraordinarily lenient attitude toward the new sects.

WHAT DOES SCIENCE SAY ABOUT PRAYER?

The above studies provide powerful evidence of the ways that participating in religious healing would have beneficial effects for ill people. Narratives, trance, beliefs in possession—these and other elements of religion-based healing can have strong psychophysiological effects.

The medical effects of religious practices have come in for a great deal of scientific study in the past decade, usually focused on prayer. The claims and studies bear on two separate questions: What are the health effects when a patient prays, attends church, thanks or blames God, and so forth? And what are the effects, if any, of "intercessory prayer," meaning prayer by someone else for the patient? Although these two practices often are mixed together in articles, they imply two quite distinct mechanisms. If the first set of practices leads to significantly better health, the results can be attributed to a range of psychophysiological mechanisms—for example, the influence of confidence and optimism on the immune system, in essence the same as a "placebo effect." If intercessory prayer leads to greater health, the results are attributed to God.

A number of scientific studies of Christians in the United States support the claim that praying, believing in God, and attending church make people healthier and longer lived than people who do not practice a religion. Studies have been done on large samples, often balanced between white and black Americans. Some studies focus on patients and their postoperative outcomes, others on blood pressure levels, and still others on mortality rates in the general population. Current research reports from mainstream medical journals are listed on the Duke University Center for Spirituality, Theology, and Health (http://www.spiritualityandhealth.duke.edu/). In one National Institutes of Health–funded study (Helm et al. 2000), over 3,000 North Carolina adults were surveyed in 1986 and then monitored over the next six years (1986–1992). The researchers controlled for social support and health behaviors, and found that lack of private religious activity continued to predict a 47 percent greater risk of dying.

Religiosity does not necessarily promote health, however; more important seems to be the relatively positive or negative way U.S. Christians approach a relationship to God. One group of researchers (Pargament et al. 2001) studied what they called "negative religious coping" among black and white patients, a concept that they attributed to patients who wondered whether God had abandoned them, felt punished by God for their lack of devotion, or decided the Devil had made them ill. People who believed these statements experienced 19–28 percent greater mortality during the two-year period following hospital discharge. Positive religious coping, however, has consistently been shown to promote mental and physical health (for example, Koenig et al. 1992). Frequency of church attendance is a powerful predictor of health in many of these studies, for example, of a strong immune system, indicated by low levels of plasma interleukin-6, an immune system messenger that appears in higher levels among people with chronic illness (Koenig et al. 1997).

Although some of these studies attempt to control for the amount of social support the study subjects enjoyed, it also seems that the social side of church attendance contributes to the positive effects of religion on health. The role of organized religion in offering solace during illness may be particularly important in the contemporary United States, given the mobility of its residents and the tendency to rely on institutions for support for elderly relatives. Prayer also "gives patients something to do so that they don't feel as helpless," notes Harold G. Koenig (2002), one of the Duke investigators. Prayer also may lead to greater relaxation that reduces muscle tension (Koenig 2002).

Even within the medical community, debate has arisen about the mechanisms or pathways that link prayer to health. Writing to comment on Koenig's analysis quoted here, a physician and theologian stated that it was the "spirit of God" that provided the healing because of the patient's prayer (Flynn and Fulton 2002). In so doing, they implicitly link prayer by patients to prayer by others on behalf of patients, or "intercessory prayer," prayer to God to intercede on someone else's behalf.

A small number of medical researchers have designed studies to test the idea that if a team of "intercessors" prays for patients, patients will do better than will patients not receiving prayer from the team. These studies have been controlled, in that patients were assigned in random or near-random fashion either to a prayer-receiving group or to a non-prayer-receiving-group, as well as "double-blind," meaning that neither the patients nor the medical personnel knew which patients were in which group.

In one such study, conducted in a coronary care unit in Kansas City, about 1,000 patients were assigned to the two groups (Harris et al. 1999). Fifteen prayer teams of five people each were asked to pray for patients identified by name. Intercessors all agreed to the statement that God "is responsive to prayers for healing made on behalf of the sick," that is, that God intercedes. The intercessors prayed for 28 days for each patient (a time chosen to cover nearly all patients' hospital stays). The researchers then faced the problem of how to measure outcomes. Because the prayers were for a general speedy and complete recovery, they needed a measure of overall goodness of outcome. They devised a scoring system, on which complications added points: the higher the score, the worse the outcome. They then calculated the association between prayer and outcome, using t-tests and accepting $P < .05$ as significant for most tests. Both decisions follow accepted procedures, but were the source of much critique afterwards, as we shall see.

The investigators found an 11 percent reduction in the outcome score for patients who had received prayer, with $P = .04$, thus meeting their conditions for significance. The length of stay was not different between the two groups; the study thus agreed with earlier similar studies. The investigators were able to gain exemption from hospital Internal Review Board (IRB) rules for informed consent on the grounds that simply knowing of the study might create anxiety about not being treated with prayer, and because no clear harm could result from no prayer. They note that because half the patients stated a religious preference, there likely was "background prayer noise" caused by relatives praying for control-group patients, so that the study measured the effects of "supplementary intercessory prayer."

How could such prayer work? The study's authors refrain from suggesting mechanisms: It could be God, or it could be unknown physical forces caused by prayer. They defend themselves against the (correctly) anticipated charges of studying relationships without proposing causal mechanisms by citing the pathbreaking clinical trials conducted by James Lind in 1753 aboard the HMS *Salisbury*, which determined that eating lemons or limes cured sailors of scurvy. He did not know why this was so, they state, but his observations were sound. Cautiously, they conclude: "It was intercessory prayer, not the existence of God, that was tested here."

Well, as one might imagine, a storm of protest appeared in this and other journals. Some questioned details of the study; others stated that $P = .04$ is more acceptable if a causal mechanism is known or proposed than otherwise (a point made widely in the social sciences as well); most argued that science and faith were two different kinds of knowledge and should be kept that way. A few entered into the theological implications of such a study: If God indeed favors people for whom strangers choose to pray, over others, then is he a capricious rather than an all-loving God? (You can continue to follow the thread of these debates on http://archinte.ama-assn.org.)

The cautious entry of medical science into these waters threatens some because it could legitimate studies that show other kinds of practices to have medical effects despite the absence of known causal mechanisms: Homeopathic medicine, which features potions containing minute traces of supposedly effective elements, is the most obvious candidate. Other physicians find the mixing of science and religion ipso facto distasteful. Still others find it enormously welcome that they can speak with patients about the patients' religious beliefs and practices—indeed, most of the medical centers or institutes devoted to religion and healing focus on clinical care and not scientific research.

Mapping the Brain

Another approach from medical science to studying religious experience has been by way of brain mapping rather than experiments. Much of this research has focused on determining how the brain state correlates to states of calm achieved through meditation. People who become adept at meditation report common themes, among them a sense of great calmness, a diminishing of the boundaries between the self and other, and a sense of union with the universe or with God.

Andrew Newberg and his colleagues (Newberg, D'Aquili, and Rause 2001) have used single photon emission computed tomography (SPECT) to measure the blood flow patterns in the brains of Tibetan monks during meditation and Fransiscan nuns while in prayer. The subjects were instructed to give a simple hand signal at the peak of their meditative state. At this signal, a radioactive marker was released into the bloodstream. As the marker passed through the brain, images of the peak moment's effects on the brain were captured.

Most often, the measurements showed marked changes in brain activity during meditation or prayer, and these changes were related to the subjective changes reported by the subjects. In particular, the meditation affected the posterior section of the parietal lobe in the cerebral cortex, an area that receives input from several senses and produces the experience of a three-dimensional self-oriented in space. Normally this area exhibits extremely high degrees of activity. However, at the peak moments it experienced very low activity levels, as indicated by reduced blood flow. These were precisely the moments that the monks and nuns said were characterized by the sense of a diminished self or a union with God.

Conclusions

We have considered only some of the widespread practices of healing that draw from religious ideas and images. Religion-based healing combines effective practices (stories, images, as well as sound and smell) to induce states that certainly can contribute to healing. The felt effectiveness of these healing techniques can also make them particularly sensitive matters in pluralistic societies, or, in monotheistic settings, when they are seen as appealing to spirits other than God. They can also be perceived as infringing on the domain of biomedicine, leading me to pose the following question for debate.

Discussion Questions

In the United States and elsewhere in the world, conflicts arise when parents seek to use religious healing instead of biomedical techniques. In October 2009, for example, a Wisconsin couple were sentenced to jail for failing to treat their 11-year-old daughter for her diabetes because they preferred to pray for her instead. A child was involved in that case, but should we consider an adult who dies after choosing to pray for himself rather than seeking medical care to be committing suicide? And do advocates of prayer-only treatments bear a moral responsibility in such cases? How tolerant should societies be toward religious healing?

Media Resources

Many films explore the scientific evidence concerning religious healing, for example the ABC program *The Power of Belief: Its Impact on Our Minds*. *Jero Tapakan* shows how a healer in Bali (Indonesia) consults with clients; Brujo (shaman) does the same for shamans in Oaxaca (Mexico). You can follow developments in ongoing research on prayer, spirituality, and healing at several centers, such as that at Duke University, http://www.spiritualityandhealth.duke.edu/. A number of artists offer beautiful treatments of Navajo Blessingway chants, such as the translation of the chant with images from the region at: http://www.youtube.com/watch?v=ajC94N0KJSw. The series of seven short documentaries called *Through Navajo Eyes* would be one way to expand that section of this chapter.

I often show short clips of Mahikari practice in different contests. This clip shows two students administering the practice: http://www.youtube.com/watch?v=XPOuQeuxbQg&feature=related. Another shows a practitioner opening up an amulet of the kind used for healing: http://www.youtube.com/watch?v=Pvk_LvyvOX8&feature=related.

Sorcery, Witchcraft, and Modernity

In many societies, people think that unseen powers, usually manipulated by humans, cause illness, death, or just plain randomness in everyday life. Anthropologists have used the words "sorcery" and "witchcraft" to refer to these ideas and practices. But in many cases, people do not consider these unseen powers as always harmful; indeed, often the same person draws on the same powers to heal or harm. Sometimes terms for "sorcery" also refer to a range of healing practices. Consider the many people in Europe and North America who follow "witchcraft" in order to find spiritual energy or ways of healing and recall the figure in Disney's *The Sorcerer's Apprentice*—hardly an evil character.

Here we have a problem with language, for most readers living in Europe and North America will have associated the term "witchcraft" with harm, evil, and Satan, thanks to efforts made in the name of Christianity to demonize heretics and control congregations. Do we retain terms that are so ridden with these powerful negative meanings? How do we translate the many ways of talking about the unseen found across the world into a single language of anthropology? Things are still more difficult, because colonialism introduced European terms for "sorcery" into occupied lands. Thus, in French-speaking areas of western Africa, people use the French word *la sorcellerie*, which corresponds to both English "sorcery" and "witchcraft," to refer to their own ideas about the unseen, ideas that are morally ambiguous.

What do we then do in writing about these things? Most anthropologists writing today use the terms *sorcery* and *witchcraft* (or cognates in other languages), acknowledge the problems that this use poses, and then describe as best they can how things work in the places where they have worked. In fact, this is what we do regarding much of social life: Terms such as *kinship, politics,* and, of course, *religion,* are not so straightforward either!

AFRICAN SORCERY AND WITCHCRAFT

The best way, then, to understand the logics of sorcery and witchcraft is to jump into an account of one society, and then describe how things differ elsewhere and how they change over time.

Maka Djambe

We will begin with the Maka people, who live in the southeastern, French-speaking, forested part of Cameroon. The Maka survived German efforts to extract rubber from the region, and equally coercive French efforts to force people to plant coffee and cocoa. After World War II, rising producer prices led some Maka to plant more of these crops, and some of them became wealthy and powerful.

Throughout this period, Maka have spoken of an unseen power called *djambe,* a force that lives in the belly of some humans in the form of a small animal, like a mouse or a crab. A myth tells of the introduction of the djambe to human society. A hunter found a djambe in the forest. It asked him to give it a little meat and he did so. That day he killed many animals. Every day he did the same, feeding the djambe and enjoying success in hunting. But then his wife followed him into the forest and spoke to the djambe. It entered into her body, promising to make her rich, but then demanded more and more meat. She killed their animals to feed it, and ended up feeding it her children.

As the ethnographer Peter Geschiere (Geschiere 1997) explains, the myth establishes links between greed and killing, particularly of close kinsmen, and it blames women for causing the djambe to become destructive. Maka say that certain people, called *njindjamb,* "bring out their djambe," which means that they leave their bodies and join others of like mind at nighttime rendezvous. There, ordinary social rules are reversed: Men have sex with other men, and women with women, and they finish by eating the hearts of kinsmen. These kin are certain to die if they do not obtain the aid of a healer (*nkong*).

The djambe concept lies at the heart of two problems for the Maka. The first concerns one's kin. The djambe represents the "dark side of kinship." Although if you are to trust anyone it will be your kinsmen, some people, those who "bring out their djambe," eat their kinsmen's hearts. Stories about djambe bring to the surface the possibility that kin may betray one another, a possibility that one sees in everyday life, when kin feel jealousy toward one another and enter into quarrels.

The djambe also brings out the ambivalence of power. One can have access to power only through the use of djambe. No one who exercises authority in the village could do so without having protected himself by drawing on his djambe. Healers, who can counteract the harm done by djambe, also gain their powers through their own powerful djambe. In the past, healers had to sacrifice kinsmen in order to fully obtain their powers. Indeed, if a girl or boy shows signs of having an active djambe—for example, if all one's younger siblings die—then a teacher might try to teach her or him to channel that power into the practice of healing so that she or he becomes an *nkong,* a healer.

The ways of talking about djambe illustrate general human problems: Do we trust or mistrust our close relatives? Can someone who obtains power be presumed to use it only for good, or is its use for evil inevitable? In each society in the world, people articulate and develop these problems in particular ways; often they call on ideas of sorcery or witchcraft to provide language for these anxieties.

Geschiere tells the story of Tsjume to illustrate the "vicious circle of djambe" in Maka society. Tsjume, an elderly man, fell ill and his third wife died. People attributed these misfortunes to djambe and rumors pointed at Nanga, Tsjume's first wife. She, too, became ill, and most people said she was the victim of her own djambe use (although others said she suffered from fear of djambe attack). But then she died, after being taken to her natal village, and now Tsjume was accused of having caused the deaths of his wives. Nanga's and Tsjume's families quarreled violently over the matter of where Nanga would be buried. A few weeks later, Tsjume's second wife died. Tsjume now began to openly accuse a woman who lived in his compound and who enjoyed a spotless reputation. Geschiere heard her reply: "People who know so well what the witches do are the first to leave their bodies in the night."

Tsjume eventually recovered his strength and the matter ended. People assumed that "the witches had settled the whole affair among themselves." The series of accusations showed the social shaping of fear and suspicion in Maka society. People assumed that if a death occurred in the household, that others in the household must be responsible. But how could you decide who is responsible? In the case of Tsjume, people could follow the logic of Maka djambe ideas to decide. They could infer from the fact that Nanga's illness followed closely on that of her cowife that sorcery was responsible: She was either responsible for the misfortunes or next on the list of victims. Most people thought she was causing the illness until she died, at which point the second possible position, that she had been a victim, became the majority view. Tsjume's final accusations, of a woman who otherwise was above suspicion, elicited a reply that tapped into a key Maka idea, namely, that those who best understand the doings of djambe are the ones who bring out their own djambe, that is, who attend nighttime revelries and use their powers for ill.

The slipperiness of accusations rests on the postulate that everyone in the society might well have a djambe. What is at issue is not what is inside you but how you use it: Do you develop it, and bring it out for use against others? Do you draw on it to become a great healer, or a powerful government official? To exercise power or achieve greatness depends on having "a full belly," meaning that you have an active djambe. Or do you just go about your business and trouble others as little as possible?

Sorcery ideas imply that particular individuals are responsible for misfortune, or that others experience rapid success through use of their inner force. In other words, it explains success and misfortune by pointing to characteristics and actions of individuals. And the specific characteristics of djambe—the uncertainties and ambiguities created in its "vicious circle"—fit with Maka local politics. Maka village affairs are set out and, sometimes, resolved in village meetings, at which the greater persuasiveness of some people over others determine the day. People attribute these powers to djambe, but djambe's inherent ambiguity means that such authority is fleeting. One elder, Mpal, could cut off others in debate. It was said that he did this by tightening their throats so that they could not speak. But one day he was challenged on grounds that his overly active djambe had caused the deaths of several boys. On that occasion, another man was able to counter Mpal's powerful djambe by the power of his own indignation.

The moral ambiguity of djambe reminds us of the difficulties of using the English words *sorcery* and *witchcraft*, or the French *la sorcellerie*, a word that encompasses both English terms, because of the sense of evil, or at least maliciousness, that these words convey. The difficulty is further compounded by the fact that Maka use *la sorcellerie* to refer to djambe, and *sorcier* to indicate someone who makes use of his or her djambe, for whatever purposes. A man giving testimony in a court case involving sorcery accusations might give his occupation as *"sorcier,"* a self-description that indicates that he has the knowledge and experience to testify, not that he admits committing malicious acts against others. Geschiere notes the problems and in the end uses *la sorcellerie* to refer to these ideas and practices on grounds that the terms fit reasonably well, and in any case they have entered into Maka use.

Azande Oracles and Mangu

From the Maka case we can take the idea that what matters is not so much what is inside you (does she have djambe?) but how you use it (has she caused sickness?). This same idea underlies practices found in a society in central Africa, the Azande.

Anthropological studies of sorcery and witchcraft always refer back to the pioneering work carried out in the 1930s by E. E. Evans-Pritchard with the Azande. Evans-Pritchard underscored the logic of experience, explanation, and proof that underlies these ideas. In this respect, he followed his teacher Bronislaw Malinowski, who argued that people everywhere are rational in their everyday behavior. However, Evans-Pritchard examined much more thoroughly than had Malinowski how it is that the institutions of everyday life reinforce a specific set of beliefs. In his 1937 book, *Witchcraft, Oracles and Magic among the Azande*, he paid particular attention to the social logic of oracles, or how Azande would interpret the results of divination through the lens of their knowledge of their society.

The Azande case continues to be cited by philosophers with respect to the "problem of rationality," and we will focus here on the logic of Azande practices as Evans-Pritchard studied them. Azande say that some among them have inherited a substance that lives in their small intestine, called *mangu*. Mangu can give forth emanations that cause misfortune, and this can happen, at least sometimes, without the knowledge of the person in whose body it exists, as a direct consequence of feeling envy or hatred. In their theory of causation, Azande ideas thus differ from Maka ones, although in both societies people focus on the use of these powerful substances rather than the mere possession of them.

Although Azande will point to natural or social causes for unfortunate events, they cite mangu to explain why it was this person who was the victim. Using an arresting idiom, they say that mangu provided the "second spear" of explanation, thrown after the first to clinch the matter. A man hanged himself after a quarrel, but people quarrel every day without killing themselves, so the force of mangu is called on to explain why in this case the man committed suicide. People are killed when a granary collapses on them, and it is clear that termites had weakened the structure, but why it had to be these people who died is referred to the causal logic of mangu.

Sometimes Azande simply say "it must be mangu" and leave it at that. When they decide to accuse someone of causing misfortune, they choose the likely targets: People likely to have hated or envied the victim. How is an accusation evaluated? Usually an oracle of some kind is consulted by an expert. Oracles form a hierarchy from the most common (and least expensive to use) to the most tightly controlled (and most costly), but the form of consultation is the same. An expert puts a question to the oracle. The question might be: "Did so-and-so cause my son's illness?" but it might also be on a nonwitchcraft matter, such as: "If I build a house in this clearing will I fall ill?" Among widely available oracles are the stones that when rubbed together either stick or glide in response to questions and the termites that eat parts of a stick pushed into their mound. On the top of the oracle hierarchy is the chicken oracle controlled by princes. When this oracle is consulted, a handler, who works for the prince, administers a strychnine-type poison to the chicken. He then poses a question, directing the chicken to die (or live) if the answer is "yes." The chicken then dies or lives. Sometimes the answer is verified by putting the question the other way around (using a second chicken). Thus, the first time the handler asks the chicken to live if the answer is "yes"; the second time to live if the answer is "no."

How does this oracle, the most important and beyond which there is no appeal, work? Presumably, if the oracles gave random answers to questions, they would come to be perceived as unreliable. There must then be some degree of positive correspondence between outcomes and what those involved already know or suspect. Part of the answer lies in what is asked of the oracles.

Some questions will concern matters about which most people already have some knowledge and about which there is already a great deal of suspicion, such that either answer, yes or no, will fit what people think they already know. For instance, a couple was accused of a specific act of adultery, and the oracle came out against them. They had protested their innocence (and may have indeed been innocent this time) but were known to have been carrying on an affair for some time. Upon being confronted with the oracle's decision, the man blurted out: "It must have been another time!" Still claiming his innocence of this act of adultery, he surmised that the oracle had detected a previous adulterous act on his part. In his eyes (assuming his outburst reflected his thoughts), then, the oracle was mistaken but not disconfirmed. Other questions cannot be easily disconfirmed. A person might ask an oracle: "If I build my house in such and such a place, will I die?" If the answer is yes, he will not build there and there is no test; if the answer is no and he does build there, chances are low he will die soon. Similar is the question, "If I marry so-and-so, will she die within a year?" If they do not marry, the oracle is untested; if they do marry, the chances that she will die soon are again low, and were she to die, an additional explanation could be sought in, you guessed it, witchcraft!

Even if we assume that the handlers do not influence the result by varying the amount of poison administered to the fowl, then, the oracle will appear not random but in accord with common knowledge. And of course some bias may enter in, although Evans-Pritchard claimed he could detect none.

What are the consequences of being found guilty? They can be quite severe; once, Evans-Pritchard was told, a man could be put to death for certain offenses. Today, a person or couple might be put to work for the prince or be fined. But even more commonly, the offender will merely be ordered to make things right. How he or she does so sheds important light on what this business of oracles and mangu is all about. For when one is formally accused of witchcraft—one is presented with the wing of a fowl that died—the correct response is to blow out water and say: "If I possess witchcraft in my belly I am unaware of it; may it cool. It is thus that I blow out water."

Today, younger people are counseled by their elders that, even if they are sure they are not guilty, they should just blow on the wing to show that they bear no ill will. The matter is not about guilt but about setting things right, smoothing over the hurt. Of course sometimes the oracle is right on the money, or only slightly off, as in the case of the adulterous couple, and then a spontaneous confession may result.

In analyzing the Azande system, we are better off considering witchcraft first and foremost as a set of social practices rather than a pseudoscientific system of knowledge claims (as philosophers often do). Individual Azande may or may not be completely convinced of the truth of each statement uttered about witchcraft and oracles, but the overall effect of the way questions are put, the range of responses, and the focus on restitution rather than guilt, is to make the set of practices believable.

This way of looking at it helps to solve the "rationality problem": The set of statements about and practices of Azande witchcraft is a discourse about social problems, one that gives the members of the society a relatively socially harmless way of talking about conflicts and dissatisfactions, bringing them to light, and also resolving those problems. The moment when water is blown by the accused is a moment of catharsis. Tensions between the parties may be released and somewhat relieved. The overall system of power receives an ideological reinforcement, as the prince's oracle has revealed the truth.

SORCERY AND MODERNITY

Ideas about sorcery are neither limited to a particular society nor static. Let us return to Cameroon, where the Maka and their neighbors share a set of ideas about sorcery. One of the major languages of the region, Ewondo, has provided a lingua franca term, *evu*, to designate concepts that correspond to the Maka *djambe*. These societies also share a basic political structure; they are what anthropologists call "segmentary," meaning that they consist of small kinship-based groups, related more or less closely to one another, and much of their political activity is based on these kin ties.

The relevance of local political form for understanding sorcery becomes apparent if we contrast these societies with those lying to the west, in the grasslands portion of Cameroon. These societies were and are organized in a more hierarchical fashion, with chiefs and notables. People living in these societies also believe in an inner force that can be used in a range of ways, but their chiefs have the power and responsibility to ensure that the force remains under control and that it works in the interest of the good. The chiefs can declare when someone is using sorcery in a harmful way, and in the past they could execute them (Goheen 1996). Their power allows them to cut through the "vicious circle" of sorcery force. Of course, they declared their own powers to be beneficial.

In many African societies, sorcery ideas have provided ways to understand contemporary politics and economics. In Cameroon (as elsewhere), the authoritarian character of colonial rule government has continued into the postcolonial period. Intrigues and feuds among national politicians have led to sudden twists and turns, climbs to success and falls from grace. One way to explain these events is through the logic of sorcery. As Geschiere observes, much as Americans continue to search for complete explanations of the assassination of John F. Kennedy, so do Cameroon people try to explain these otherwise opaque fortunes and misfortunes.

Sorcery ideas may also be invoked to explain how some people accumulate riches, and why some of the rich then suffer for it—all the modern houses have gravesites in front of them, noted one man. The phrase coined by Jean-François Bayart (1989) to describe African politics, the "politics of the belly," points to the idea that power comes from "eating" wealth, whether that wealth comes from the outside, in the form of aid or export revenues, or from villagers. It also refers to the means of accumulating those riches, namely, through sorcery, the djambe that lives in the belly. Because sorcery power engenders jealousy and, often, misfortune, sorcery ideas have often caused people to refrain from accumulating visible wealth—even planting coca trees could trigger sorcery consequences.

People also create new sorcery ideas to explain new forms of great wealth, and the existence of wealthy people who appear to live contentedly with their riches. One new idea has been that of the sorcerer who turns people into zombies to work for him. This practice is called *ekong* in the port of Duala, one of the centers of new commercial wealth in Cameroon and also a center for these new ideas. Someone seeking this way to wealth may dream and in his dreams visit a prosperous estate. The owner will offer the estate to him on condition that he offer the life of his mother or another close relative. The victim—the poor mother, for example—will dream that she is led away with her hands tied. It is then time for her to consult a healer to counter the sorcery (de Rosny 1992). These self-described victims are usually people who live in cities and who are experiencing problems with their families. Healers understand these social sources of the ills and the fears, and their work is a type of family therapy, bringing to light family tensions. But, as the circular logic of sorcery implies, these same healers might themselves be responsible for ekong practices. People turn to ever-new possible sources of powerful assistance, whether new healers, chiefs (in the western region), or the state.

As we saw above, chiefs in the western regions can neutralize harm, and this power also allows them to "launder" new wealth that is suspected of having been earned through ekong. Presenting wealth to a chief allows a newly rich person to be accepted by others, as they presume that the chief will work to ensure that the power behind the wealth works only for the good.

Since the 1970s, the Cameroon state has increasingly intervened in sorcery, as have other African states. State prosecution of sorcerers began in the eastern part of the country, where sorcery is reputed to be the most common and where the absence of chiefs has provided the state with the possibility of a new role. These prosecutions were at the behest of local notables—farmers, village officials, and party leaders—who thought they had been the victims of sorcery. In most cases, neither a confession nor the material proof is offered. Judges, assisted by a prosecutor, hear the cases, and most of the time they find the accused guilty. Judges do not make use of healers to see whether the accused does indeed have active sorcery inside him or her, but rely on testimony of accusers and of healers. In other words, the courts cut through the local practices of accusation, counteraccusation, and divination. The healers function not to aid the accused or the sick, but to advise judges on the guilt or innocence of a suspected sorcerer.

Throughout Africa, ideas about sorcery incorporate ideas about social tensions and power, and they have changed along with broader social transformations. Even in precolonial times, accusations of witchcraft were made against women much more often than against men. Some cases of rapid social change exacerbated the attacks on women. In Nigeria, for example, the development of the cocoa economy in the 1940s and 1950s led to the rapid proliferation of women traders, many of whom left the traditional patrilocal compound to pursue their activities elsewhere. These women passed on trading capital to their daughters, bypassing traditional inheritance lines that ran from fathers to sons. Local witchcraft ideas already targeted women; the rapid social and economic change in this period led to an increase in witchcraft accusations and to the 1950–1951 Atinga cult of witch finding that accused thousands of women in Nigeria as witches, forcing them to confess, pay a cleansing fee, and eat a substance that would kill them if they ever practiced witchcraft again. In Andrew Apter's analysis (1993) of the movement, newly powerful male traders financed the cult in part to persecute the women traders with whom they competed.

Accusations of witchcraft continue to be a part of modern urban life in many parts of Africa as a way of talking about evil, particularly the evil brought by strangers (Auslander 1993; Bastian 1993). Tabloids and other newspapers carry witchcraft stories across regions of West and Central Africa. Witches in Zambia and South Africa are accused of causing barrenness and AIDS, sickness, and economic failure. Witch finders, in southern Africa often associated with the Zionist churches, are recruited by young men to cleanse their villages by identifying the elderly women and men who are preventing the younger people from advancing economically. Witches are not killed but cleansed by having potions rubbed into cuts on their bodies. And yet, an exception to this general pattern, young militants in South Africa have used the "necklace"—the burning tire used to kill suspected informants during the struggle against apartheid—as a weapon against accused witches, leading one chief—significantly, a woman—to create a new town as a sanctuary for the accused.

Sorcery and Reciprocity in New Guinea

If we turn to another part of the world, we find very different ideas about sorcery and society. In 1998, when the ethnographer Bruce Knauft last visited them, about 600 Gebusi were living in the forests of southwestern New Guinea. The Gebusi once lived in a world of sorcery, but one that was strikingly different from that inhabited by the Maka. Gebusi were known for their absence of warfare and their overall sociability. And yet, until the mid-1980s they had one of the highest rates of homicide in the world; about one-third of the deaths occurring in the period 1940–1982 were from killing, and the overwhelming majority of these deaths were in retribution for a suspected death or illness from sorcery (Knauft 1985). These killings were all within the group, but, contrary to what one might expect to find, they did not engage in particularly great amounts of internal conflict or backbiting. Clearly, a different cultural logic from that we have studied for Africa was at work here.

Knauft explains how Gebusi social life is shaped by the idea of "direct reciprocity": I give you something and you give me its equivalent in return. Anthropologists find that in many societies two modes of reciprocity underlie many social norms and values, regarding agriculture, material exchange, marriage, relationships with spirits, and general sociability. In direct reciprocity operating in Gebusi society, the movement of goods, a service, or a person in one direction is supposed to be countered by a movement of a similar good, service, or person in the other direction. In marriage, it means that if my village receives a woman (or a man) from another group, we must make sure that a woman (or man) from our group marries one of them. In the case of "generalized reciprocity," giving something to another group will eventually be reciprocated, but perhaps from a different group, in a chain-like fashion. My group might take a spouse from one group, and give a spouse to another group. If direct reciprocity implies closure, generalized reciprocity implies an opening toward the outside.

For the Gebusi, both marriage and sorcery involved direct reciprocity. Marriage was supposed to involve women moving between groups in balanced fashion, and if a marriage in one direction was not followed by one in the other, tensions resulted—and sometimes these tensions led to sorcery accusations. Sorcery itself was structured along the lines of direct reciprocity, for if a woman was the victim of sorcery, then a female sorcerer had to be discovered and killed, and that killing put an end to the matter. Discovery was accomplished through divination and the use of mediums. Mediums also allowed the living to communicate with the spirits of sorcery's victims, who lived in the forest as beautiful birds and animals, the spirit familiars and protectors of the living.

The severe consequences of being suspected of sorcery meant that no one seems to have practiced it, and Gebusi refrained from claiming positions of leadership for fear that their actions would be seen as typical of sorcerers. By the late 1990s, sorcery accusations had nearly disappeared. Most Gebusi had joined one of several local churches and now faced the highly powerful spirit, God. All the people who had acted as mediums to ascertain the identity of sorcerers had died or given up their ties with spirits. If someone did level a sorcery accusation, he or she could be hauled into court and charged with slander. Many people continue to believe in sorcery, but in some places, at least, the practice has ceased.

Why is this so? The contrast with the African cases discussed earlier provides some clues. Maka and other people see a threat in the accumulation of riches and the emergence of inequalities, and sorcery has provided a way of talking about, and sometimes acting against, that threat. The Gebusi with whom Knauft has lived have *welcomed* the introduction of "modernity" in the form of consumer goods, schools, churches, and protection against warfare. They see abandoning sorcery as a way toward that modernity. Many of them did a "direct exchange" between the older spirits and the new god, and see sorcery practices and churchgoing as incompatible. Their new lives bring them into constant contact with people from other ethnic groups at the large station area; these contacts radically alter social life, which now includes a large, depersonalized domain of social interactions at school, office, church, or sports events. The modernity experienced here is attractive, individualizing, but also passivizing—Gebusi now receive lessons, speeches, sermons, all of which instruct them to supplicate and hope for the best (compare the analysis of religion in another small-scale New Guinea society, the Urapmin, in Chapter 11).

This outcome was contingent on the particular experience of the Gebusi and differed across New Guinea societies. Knauft suggests that such locally important elements as the relatively friendly character of the local police and the tolerant attitude of church officials made it seem attractive to Gebusi to ally themselves with these local officials. In the case of the police, this reliance contributed to the decline of sorcery accusations, because accused sorcerers were now sent off for jail terms or released for lack of evidence rather than killed. The legitimacy of these state institutions, itself due to this set of contingent factors, then led to sorcery's decline.

PURITAN WITCHCRAFT

In contrasting African and New Guinea societies, we already see that ideas about causality and social reciprocity give rise to distinct ways of invoking spirits and practices of sorcery in everyday life. We know turn to a very different social context, that of early modern Europe and North America. There, misfortune was thought of in a dualistic framework, where God and his followers confront Satan and those unfortunates who had fallen into his grasp. Witch hunts in various parts of Europe resembled those in Africa today, except that the source of the witchcraft was not the individual but her or his ties with Satan.

In the United States, witchcraft is surely most closely associated with the celebrated 1692 trials held in Salem, Massachusetts. I would argue that witchcraft ideas in New England once functioned much as they do in Azande society, to encourage confession and purge the society of its fears and tensions. But rapid social changes of the late seventeenth century created new fissures in village society that were given strong moral and emotional colorations by Puritan preachers and church members. Much as in contemporary Africa, older tensions were exacerbated, and witch hunts grew in importance.

New England Puritans

The Puritans of seventeenth-century New England held strong religious ideas about the church as a community and about the immanence of evil in the world. A church in this society was not a building or even an association to which one could freely belong. In its narrow and most compelling sense, it was a community of people who felt themselves elected by God, as "saints," who had joined in a covenant that bound each to the other. Church members were responsible for one another, such that the sins of one person would lead to misfortune for others (Miller 1956, 141–152). As John Winthrop put it in his sermon on "Christian charity" delivered to the Pilgrims onboard the Arabella en route to the New World in 1630: "We must be knit together as one man and must delight in each other, make other's condition our own, rejoice together, mourn together, labor and suffer together, always having before our eyes our commission and community in the work" (quoted in Demos 1982, 299).

This sense of common destiny was reinforced by the constant copresence of church members in a village. You encountered your fellow parishioner in his store, where he sold you bread, or near your fields, where you might get along or you might become embroiled in a dispute over boundaries or water. Common destiny and a shared life worked tolerably well as long as everyone prospered tolerably equally. But sharp differences in economic and social standing had begun to emerge, along with ideas of individualism. These new and dangerous ideas were, ironically, exacerbated by the opportunity afforded in the New World: the abundance of land and the fragility of new institutions.

Puritans also held that a strong line divided good from evil in the world. Evil was incarnate in the witch. As the prominent preacher Cotton Mather put it: "There is in witchcraft a most explicit renouncing of all that is holy and just and good." The witch showed "the furthest effort of our original sin" (quoted in Demos 1982, 304). Witches' meetings were imagined as inversions of all that was holy, involving trampling on the cross and defiling the Host. (And, indeed, contemporary Satanic cults do practice some of these rituals of inversion.) In this respect, witchcraft served to sharpen and perhaps to strengthen the moral boundaries between the community and Satan's forces.

In this context, in which all actions were to be scrutinized for their good or evil, ordinary people understandably could experience a great deal of anxiety about whether their actions and feelings came from God or Satan. Puritans believed in predestination, that God has damned or saved us before we were born, but not revealed to us His decision (we turn again to this idea in Chapter 11). Puritans saw the world as full of signs or marks of God's will, such that one might recognize in himself the signs of Election or those of damnation (and indeed becoming a member of the church required that one declare oneself saved). But Satan could be behind such feelings, trying to induce damned individuals to enter the church. Even the most highly placed church member could not easily escape gnawing doubts as to the reliability of his or her own certainty. One story has it that a woman in a Boston congregation, tormented by her uncertainty, threw her child into a well to seek relief of certain damnation. (Hers was, however, an incorrect interpretation of the strictly unknowable nature of Election!)

Evil and Accusations

Puritans held gnawing doubts about their salvation, lived in the presence of Evil, and were acutely aware that they were far from achieving their ideal of a morally as well as socially close-knit community. It is unsurprising that fears of evil within the society were endemic, and that they took the form of accusations of witchcraft. Now, throughout the early modern period in Europe, accusations of witchcraft were an expected part of life. England had somewhere between 300 and 1,000 executions for witchcraft between 1542 and 1736. Accusations fit the general pattern already noted. Most of the accused were women; indeed, in one detailed record for the period 1560–1680 in Essex County, only 8 percent of the persons tried were men. The typical English witch was an older woman, perhaps widowed, from the poorer segment of the community. Often she was a beggar. She was usually accused of bewitching someone in her own village, specifically in her part of the village. Witches were neighbors. The historian Keith Thomas argues that accusers were beginning to chafe at the demands of charity, as the ethics of the time gradually became more individualistic. And yet, moral responsibility for charity was still preached by the church and probably felt as legitimate by the better-off citizens. Harsh words, even curses, by those whose appeals for financial assistance were denied would have spawned some guilt in the hearts of these newly individual-minded villagers, and to assuage this guilt, argues Thomas, they projected it onto the "witch" (Demos 1982, 298–300).

Witchcraft accusations were brought from England to New England—indeed, in particular from Essex County, England, to Essex County, Massachusetts. In seventeenth-century North America, there are recorded 93 witchcraft cases, of which 16 led to hangings, leaving aside the Salem outbreak. If we count the Salem trials as well, the total rises to 234 cases and 36 executions—an "accusation rate" of 7 accusations per 100,000 people in North America, compared to less than 1 accusation per 100,000 in England, and about 5.5 for the most "active" county in England, Essex. Clearly, then, events in Salem pushed the rate of accusations far beyond their usual frequency (Demos 1982, 11–12).

Accusations functioned in similar fashion to what we observed for the Azande. The activity of a witch could explain why an unexpected event happened, even when the physics of the matter were perfectly clear. For example, a man on maneuvers with his militia accidentally discharged his gun, which ricocheted off a tree and struck another man, killing him. The first man was charged with manslaughter, but people continued to ask why the rather odd accident had happened. In the event, a woman was accused of witchcraft. She had owed money to the deceased and had been his landlady: She was thus close to him and yet in a socially ambivalent relationship with him. But to blame a single individual was insufficient to account for the presence of witchcraft in the community, where everyone was in some way responsible for everyone else. And so, on a subsequent Sunday, the preacher widened the field of blame to include the entire community, whose general moral decrepitude, he charged, had permitted Satan to enter among them and do his evil work (Demos 1982, 3–9).

In such a case the matter would rest there, and so it had been in Salem before 1692. Events in that year represent an abnormal, outrageous set of actions. Yet the people involved were ordinary village folk, much like all the other folk peopling the eastern seaboard then and afterward.

The Salem Outbreak of 1692

First, the events: In February 1692, several girls in Salem Village began acting very strangely, alternately prancing about and hiding under chairs, making strange, "foolish" speeches that no one could understand, and taking to their beds, moaning and complaining about pains. The authorities of the village interpreted this behavior as witchcraft. One of the first girls to act strangely was the daughter of the village minister, Samuel Parris. As she lay on her bed, Parris and others began to question her, thinking that she might be a victim of witchcraft. The questions put to her and to several other girls were in the form of: "Was it so-and-so?" Much as with the Zande oracle, certain names were put forward and others were not. The girls were urged to name someone, and they did name several women, including Tituba. Three women were then questioned by two members of the provincial legislature, who lived in nearby Salem Town. Tituba confessed to having committed witchcraft; the other two denied the charges.

The accusations snowballed, and the public hangings began in June of that year. Between June 2 and September 22, 19 men and women were hanged, including a minister, the Reverend George Burroughs. The hangings were finally stopped by the intervention of Boston-area ministers who were troubled by the willy-nilly hangings, though not by the *principle* of hanging witches. On October 12, Governor Phips forbade any more imprisonments for witchcraft, and all prisoners were set free during the following year.

The events raise some troubling questions. First, why were the experiences of the children interpreted as the torment of witches? The nature of the experiences was not all unpleasant, after all. The girls' strange speech suggests the speaking in tongues of the Pentecost spoken of in the Bible and known to the ministers. Indeed, in the very same year a Boston servant girl exhibited similar syndromes: spasms, outbreaks of strange speech, and, upon meeting some of the accused Salem women, violent behavior toward them. But in this case, Cotton Mather drew on her behavior to form a group that met with her, chanted psalms, and had similar experiences, which began to be seen as a kind of religious ecstasy. Only a few years later, the same sort of behavior in Northampton, Massachusetts, was interpreted by the minister of that town, Jonathan Edwards, as a sign of the "pouring out of the spirit of God." This movement led to what came to be called the "Great Awakening," a period during which a wider range of religious experiences and behaviors were accepted (Miller 1956, 153–166).

Second, why were the charges believed? The accusers were young girls, and there was only their own testimony to support their charges. Were the distinguished jurors who found the accused guilty themselves imbeciles? How can we understand their findings?

Finally, why, in this instance but not before or after, did the outbreak expand as it did? Earlier outbreaks in New England since 1647 had resulted in a total of only

15 executions. Those executed were local people, marginal, following the general pattern: Accuse your neighbor if he or she is powerless and likely to be suspected by others on grounds of unpleasantness. In Salem in 1692 several hundred people were accused, 150 imprisoned, and 19 executed, and the accused included the wealthiest ship owner in Salem Town and 2 of its 7 selectmen, 2 sons of a former governor, themselves prominent public figures, and even the wife of the governor! And unlike all previous outbreaks, most of the accused were people outside of Salem Village, in the nearby village of Andover (Boyer and Nissenbaum 1974, 22–30).

Evidence and Confessions

Everyone in Salem accepted that witches did exist. Satan's struggle for the souls of people was evident in the world, and misfortune always had a moral tinge to it. As the historian Perry Miller has written, Puritanism had no room for failure. When failure came, it was due to the work of Satan in the world, and among his favorite vehicles were witches.

What was the evidence of witchcraft? According to the canons of evidence of the day, several kinds were admissible (Boyer and Nissenbaum 1974; Demos 1982). One was empirical evidence, which included behavioral traits: These could be positive, such as great physical strength, or negative, such as the inability to recite the Lord's Prayer all the way through. Second was the category called "Anger followed by Mischief," that is, when after a quarrel or even a sharp look someone was stricken with illness. This evidence was eventually rejected because of the difficulty of ascertaining the empirical links between the "anger" and the "mischief." Finally and most dramatically, there was Spectral Evidence—in this case, when the afflicted girls saw figures of the accused coming toward them and harming them. This evidence could, of course, be produced at a moment's notice. Mary Warren, one of the girls, tried to recant her own accusations against previous witches when the other girls accused her master, John Proctor. The others responded to her defection by immediately seeing specters around *her*. At this threat, she retracted her recantation and returned to their side. But when "respectable" townspeople began to be accused, some of the ministers remembered that Satan was capable of creating specters and images to mislead the God-fearing, and at that point Spectral Evidence began to be doubted publicly.

Of course, many people confessed before the case could come to trial. Those who did confess were but released. From the perspective of a modern trial court, this course of action seems very odd. Why release confessed criminals and hang those who insisted on their innocence? But from the perspective of comparative witchcraft studies, this is what we would expect. As in the Azande case, the confession purged the community of tensions and, in this instance, of the deep guilt it felt for straying from the righteous path. As with the blowing out of water among the Azande, the confession gives a language for conflicts, the language of Satan and witchcraft.

Here is another way the Salem events went wrong. The first three women to be accused had confessed but after that confessions virtually ceased. Why? The historians Paul Boyer and Stephen Nissenbaum (1974) argue that a cultural change was just then occurring in New England, one that valued individual conscience and pride, such that many people were no longer willing to confess for the sake of community. But the logic of accusation and confession had not quite caught up with their new sense of obligation and responsibility. From this point of view, the events in Salem are a terrible result of uneven moral and cultural transition, away from one world view, that of the Puritan, toward another, that of the outward-oriented Great Awakening (Boyer and Nissenbaum 1974, 209–216; Miller 1956, 153–166).

We also have to explain why it was Salem village where these events happened. Boyer and Nissenbaum argue that the village suffered from particularly divisive social and economic tensions. The families who had settled in the western portion of the village found poor land with no way to expand production. Those settling the east enjoyed land better for farming, and they were also close to the road running toward Salem town. They became wealthy from mixed farming and trade. The witchcraft accusations provided an outlet for the frustrated western settlers, and in particular for the Putnam family, who took the lead in accusing people of witchcraft. Young Ann Putnam was the principal accuser. Thirty of the 32 accusers lived on western lands, whereas 18 of 25 accused witches lived along the eastern road to town.

The unusual outbreak at Salem village thus happened where it did largely because of the unusually high level of tensions that divided the village and set it against Salem town. The events happened when they did because several rising trajectories of anxiety came together at this moment and place: The social and religion tensions within the village were rising at the same time that there were fears of Indian attacks from the west and there was a crisis in Massachusetts governance. The accusations had the content they did because of the long history of ideas about witches and Satan; they died down as sharply as they did because of local doubts and debates among influential churchmen about those ideas.

As Mary Beth Norton (2003) argues, these events involved all of Essex County, Massachusetts, and not just Salem Village and Town. Indeed, one of the distinctive features of the 1691–1692 events was precisely the extent to which Salem villagers accused people living in Andover and Salem town, with whom they had had little or no contact. We might, however, draw parallels between the way in which rising levels of economic tension and anxiety in Salem created a geographically expansive pattern of witchcraft accusation, and the ways in which accusations in some African societies have reached beyond the usual range of kin and neighbors to include the rich and the powerful. In both contemporary Africa and late seventeenth-century New England, new patterns of trade, gain, and political power created new lines of worry, hostility, and resentment.

Note that at the same time that we can see parallel, powerful, psychological changes in two very different times and places, we also explain each set of changes in terms of local ideas and forces. The anthropological insistence on locally based accounts of change precludes easy recourse to vague psychological notions, such as "modernization," or political economic ones, such as "globalization," as if such concepts explained a local series of events. At the same time, the anthropological insistence on comparisons and regional analyses can lead to better understandings of the mechanisms and processes underlying social change. Earlier, we saw an example of such an analysis in the case of Bruce Knauft's studies of sorcery in South Coast New Guinea societies. Knauft first showed the particular set of events that made sorcery accusations plummet in the society he studied. He then pointed to very different trajectories in other New Guinea societies; these contrasts allowed him to point to the "differences that made a difference" for this region of New Guinea.

For Salem, Norton argues (262–265) that the trajectories of accusations and confessions depended on the specific social character of each village. Salem Village, long racked by internal dissension, produced many who denied the accusations against them, and thus led to the reliance on spectral confessions. In nearby Andover, the site of many accusations, people were accustomed to proceeding by consensus. In that town, many people, especially women and children, acceded to the demands of their male elders that they confess. For example, Mary Tyler later told Increase Mather of the series of pronouncements made to her by her brother-in-law, magistrates, and the Reverend John Emerson that she was a witch; Emerson seems to have tried to beat the devil out of her. She succumbed to these accusations and confessed. Most telling was her brother-in-law's assertion that "God would not suffer so many good men to be in such an error about it" (that is, her guilt), in other words, not to confess would be intolerable since so many prominent people had stated that she was a witch.

Conclusions

Although we often safely consign ideas of witches and sorcery to the back closets of old history and harmless pranks, in fact these ideas continue to furnish people with ways of explaining why some succeed and others fail, some stay healthy while others die. If we expand our compass a bit to include ideas that the Devil lurks among us and causes malfeasance, we might see ourselves as, sometimes, participating in these ways of thinking.

Discussion Questions

Do contemporary religious groups in North America or Europe ever engage in identifying an "enemy within" their ranks? Do we accuse people in ways that remind us of witchcraft accusations among the Azande or Salem Puritans?

Media Resources

A full-length documentary on Edward Evans-Pritchard can be used for the section on Azande witchcraft: http://www.youtube.com/watch?v=8q9HyONL_10&feature=relmfu, for about the first 24 minutes; the segment contains quotations from his writings. You can also use the full-length film *Witchcraft among the Azande*, which shows the practices discussed in this chapter and how people reconcile them with their Christianity. Many films explore the Salem trials, including the History Channel's *In Search of History: Salem Witch Trials*; you can also see a film of the play *The Crucible*. For teaching resources on the Salem trials, consult: http://www.law.umkc.edu/faculty/projects/ftrials/salem/salem.htm. For humor, I show the corresponding discussion of proof of witchery from Monty Python, available at: http://www.youtube.com/watch?v=zrzMhU_4m-g.

Worship, Hierarchy, Conflict: Focus on Hinduism

In previous chapters, we have focused on particular aspects of religion, such as death rituals, and we have taken examples from several distinct religious traditions in order to highlight certain commonalities across religions. This way of studying religious practices has its advantages: It encourages us to compare, to find similarities, and to think about why we might find such similarities. But it does have one important disadvantage in that it does not allow us to approach religious life in the way that a participant does. For a practitioner of a specific religious tradition, the tradition does not come carved up into different realms, it is rather experienced as a coherent whole. Consequently, in this chapter, we take that second point of view, and explore the ritual, intellectual, and sociopolitical dimensions of one religious tradition, that of Hindus living in India. I try to give a multidimensional portrait of one religious tradition by moving from worship rituals and ideas about deities to social hierarchies and political conflicts.

SACRIFICE, OFFERINGS, AND DEITIES

In India, sacrifice, offerings, and devotions are directed toward gods, of which there are many. About 80 percent of India's 800 million people consider themselves Hindus, and most of them, daily and in countless ways (including sacrificial ways), carry out rituals of offerings and homage to the gods (Fuller 1992, 29–56).

Hinduism refers to the many practices of worship and devotion that arose in southern Asia to seek blessings from deities, to maintain rules of purity, and to meditate on the wheel of suffering (as in Buddhism). As a label for longstanding features of Indian society, Hinduism also refers to the four classes or varnas, realized locally as caste groupings, associated with traditional occupations: Brahmins (priests), Kshatriyas (warriors and nobles), Vaishyas (farmers and merchants), and Shudras (workers), plus the non-caste classes (Dalits or "untouchables"), Muslims and others. The core of Hindu ritual is puja or worship, directed to a deity and accompanied by offerings and chanting. Hinduism has spread as South Asians have moved into parts of North America, the Pacific, and Europe.

Some gods are entirely specific to a village or district. Others may have locally specific forms, but are also manifestations of pan-Indian gods. Particularly important are Vishnu and Shiva. These two gods stand in complementary relationship to each other, Vishnu as the preserver and Shiva the destroyer, Vishnu the king and Shiva the ascetic (the renouncer of worldly pleasures), Vishnu at the center of the world and Shiva outside of it. (Brahma, not to be confused with the Brahmin caste grouping, is less prominent in worship, but is in fact the creator.) Because creation is cyclical—creation following destruction in the cycles of cosmic history—both are necessary elements in the world.

Vishnu is usually worshiped through 1 of his 10 incarnations, in particular as Rama or Krishna. The ancient epic of the Ramayana tells of Rama's life as the king of the northern realm of Ayodhya (later the site of intense conflict; see below). The epic represents his life as the model for a righteous king's conduct. The Ramayana is known throughout India (and in much of Southeast Asia) in various versions, some emphasizing Rama's divinity. It is read or viewed today in the form of sacred texts, popular stories, comic books, and shadow puppet plays, and during 1987–1988 it appeared as a hugely popular television series—a series that also raised popular enthusiasm for Hindu nationalist politics.

Krishna is portrayed as a warrior or as a mischievous child. His battles are recounted in another well-known epic, the Mahabharata. But he also transcends mere human warfare. In a section of the epic called the Bhagavad Gita, he counsels his cousin Arjuna to remain above the world even as he is forced to continue his battles. Krishna is also worshiped as a youth and remembered for his romance with the cowherdess Radha.

Shiva has many manifestations. He may be represented by a phallic linga statue, or as a human-looking image. Shiva has two sons, Skanda and Ganesha, the latter represented with an elephant head. Both Vishnu and Shiva may have different wives in different temples, although Vishnu is most often represented with the goddess of fortune, Lakshmi.

Both Vishnu and Shiva have followers, Vaishnavas and Shaivas, respectively, who worship them either by these names or in their local manifestations, often alongside other, lesser deities. Each temple in India is in principle unique, and each is dedicated to a particular, local form of a deity. For Shiva and Vishnu, this localization of worship means that they are addressed by a distinctive name. In the south Indian temple to Meenakshi, for example, Shiva is present as Sundareshwara, Meenakshi's consort. At a temple in Benares, Shiva's holiest site on the Ganges River in north India, he is addressed as Vishwanatha (Fuller 1992, 37–38).

As with the Virgin Mary, one person and yet also distinct in her many manifestations in the thousands of Marian shrines (see Chapter 8), these Shivas are many and one. Indeed, some Hindus say the same of Vishnu and Shiva, that they are one, Vishnu–Shiva. Many temples have legends explaining how Shiva or Vishnu came to occupy a spot at that particular temple—after a battle, or a great deed, or to become the consort of a local deity. The one-and-yet-many conception is thus basic to Hindu religion, but at the same time a feature that at least some Hindus find requires an explanation, usually in the form of a legend.

The same unity-and-multiplicity is found with respect to the Goddess, Devi, who exists in multiple forms. As Durga, she fights off demons; as Kali or Shakti, she is power itself and is supreme over the gods, often shown trampling on Shiva. She manifests herself as not only a consort of one of the great gods but also in local forms, where she not only brings powers of heat, and sometimes disease but also fertility—all being forms

Priest purifies the image of Shiva with water, Shiva temple at Yanaimangalam, Tamil Nadu state, India. (*Courtesy of Diane Mines*)

of her power, *shakti*. In south India each local settlement has its own tutelary goddess, known by one name throughout that region. Thus, in much of Tamil Nadu (Fuller 1992, 43) the goddess is Mariyamman: Mariyamman of this place versus Mariyamman of that place—different goddesses and yet also localized forms of the single goddess.

But Hindus also have local, lesser deities, and because Vishnu and Shiva, concerned with the cosmos, are unlikely to respond to requests for assistance in everyday matters, worshipers turn to local, lesser deities, such as the god-queen Meenakshi mentioned earlier, or still lesser deities worshiped by particular castes. These deities may be ghosts who were enshrined as a means of controlling their powers, or they may be humans, who can be especially relied on to respond to human problems. A village might have dozens of these deities, worshiped by different persons or groups, or approached for particular problems.

Thus, some Hindus identify little goddesses, matas, who occupy various places in the environment—in a thorn bush, under a three-brick "altar," in a house. They are associated with the Goddess, and their festival is on her day of Navaratri, but they are distinct from her. As with the *kami* of Japan (see Chapter 3), these deities are many and mostly unnamed. They may enter certain men and women and possess them, and through this possession heal a child or answer a vexing question posed by a fellow-villager.

At the other end of the deity scale, modern religious and political movements have adopted specific gods as symbols for their idea of an all-Hindu India. A prominent Bengali nationalist, Bankim Chandra Chatterjee, created a form of the goddess as "Mother India," Bharat Mata (Fuller 1992, 42). In her temple at Benares, she is represented not as a personage but as a map of India—a literalistic fusion of the goddess with the nation and the state!

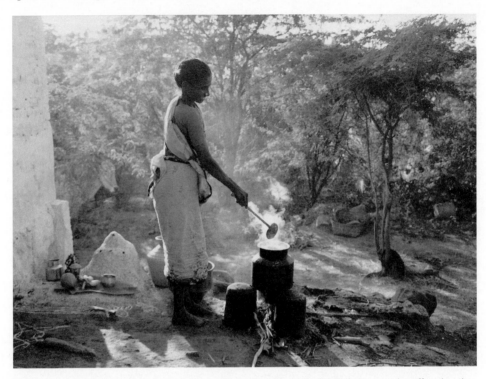

Woman cooking *pongal*, a dish cooked from "raw rice" and suitable for Brahmans, to be offered to the "backyard God" pictured to the left, at Yanaimangalam. (*Courtesy of Diane Mines*)

Do Hindus Sacrifice?

The Hindu ideology best known to the outside world is that of renouncing violence and avoiding eating meat. And yet animal sacrifice continues to be an important part of religious practice, especially, but not exclusively, in eastern and parts of southern India. Goats, pigs, fowls, and, ideally, a male buffalo are slaughtered and offered to deities—smaller animals to lesser deities and the buffalo to goddesses, and in particular to the Goddess in the form of Durga, who slew the buffalo-demon and whose victory is celebrated on Durga Puja or Navaratri (Fuller 1992, 83–105; Hiltebeitel 1985).

As in most religions where it is practiced, Hindu animal sacrifice is both a substitute for the giver and a gift to the god, a way of both honoring the god and transacting with him or her. Animals are often sacrificed to "hot" deities who bring violence, and particularly epidemic diseases such as smallpox. The offering appeases and honors them, asks for the disease to be removed, and for the deity to protect the sacrificer. The meat offering is a substitute for the sacrificer; it is offered, consumed by the goddess, and then taken back to be eaten as *prasada* ("blessed food," "grace") by those present, who thereby take in the grace of the deity. The deity is responsible for both the disease and the source of grace, and the twinned acts of sacrifice and consumption bring together these two functions.

Although in the term used to denote it, sacrifice (*bali*) is contrasted to worship with vegetable foods (*puja*), in ritual practice it often complements vegetable worship.

Animal sacrifice may conclude a sequence of worship events, or vegetables and meat may be separately offered to two complementary deities.

How can sacrificial practices continue to coexist with the principles of nonviolence? It is not as if sacrifice is a marginal practice that has somehow escaped the attention of Brahmans. Indeed, in eastern India a Brahman priest often purifies the sacrificial animal before its slaughter (which is carried out by someone else), and the offering may take place at a major temple. One Brahman in west India told the anthropologist David Pocock (1973, 72–73), when asked about the animal sacrifices he conducted on the occasions of foundation-laying for houses, that "of course it's violence (hinsa). So what? You can't have a foundation ceremony without a blood sacrifice, it's essential and that's that." Although he was never present at the actual killing of the animal, the Brahman considered these and other sacrifices to simply be a necessary way of responding to the demands of certain deities.

Buffalo sacrifice was outlawed at independence in 1947, and from time to time the police try to break up sacrificial rituals. Stories circulate (Fuller 1992, 104) as to how officers who made these attempts were rendered blind by local goddesses until they allowed the ritual to proceed.

The Vedic Roots of Indian Sacrifice

Sacrifice once served as the mainstay of Indian religion, of what is often called the Vedic religion that preceded Buddhism and modern Hinduism. Indian religious ideology shows a change from practicing animal sacrifice to renouncing meat consumption (a change that parallels—in quite different form, of course—changes in Jewish ritual practice).

Hindus have available a large number of older sacred works, including the early texts (the Rig Veda and the Upanishads) composed over the millennium 1400–400 B.C.E. and known collectively as Veda, "knowledge"; the two later epics already mentioned, the Ramayana and Mahabharata (conventionally but controversially dated between 500 B.C.E and 400 C.E.); and subsequent treatises on law, state craft, and devotions. Evidence for early sacrifice comes from the four Sanskrit texts called the Vedas. The Vedas consist chiefly of hymns for use in sacrificial ritual; the oldest, the Rig Veda, describes how the world and its institutions were created by sacrificing Purusha ("Man"). The four exemplary, male victims—horse, bull, ram, and he-goat—served as substitutes for human sacrifice, and were killed and cooked.

Agni, the god of fire, is said in these texts to be present at all sacrifices. Fire, today as well as in antiquity, is required for sacrificing even grain and milk products—recall the clarified butter placed onto the fire in household worship, and the camphor flame used at temples. In the Vedas, Agni is described as receiving the sacrifice with his tongue of flame, and carrying it up to the other deities with his smoke. The very first hymn in the Rig Veda (1.1.1) is to Agni:

> *"I pray to Agni, the household priest who is the god of the sacrifice,*
> *the one who chants and invokes and brings most treasure."*

By the sixth and fifth centuries B.C.E., the older Rig Vedic religion of sacrifice was submerged by new religious ideologies. One important break with this tradition comes with the teachings of Gautama Buddha (563–483) that one must renounce violence.

Buddhist teachings became the religion of state under Asoka (r. 268–239), who constructed a new imperial state in India. Buddhism supplanted the sacrificial religion of the Vedas. But post-Rig-Vedic texts within the Hindu tradition also appeared after 500 B.C.E (in particular, the Upanishads) that deemphasized sacrifice and instead stressed the individual's obligation to adhere to a moral code, the *dharma*, that forms part of a universal moral and physical order. In this code, every action has its consequences according to the laws of karma, such that one's deeds in this life or in a previous life shape one's present condition. Ideally, one would be able to renounce this life and pursue the goal of liberation (moksha) from the eternal cycle of suffering and rebirth (samsara).

In the first centuries of the common era (c.E.), a new "Brahmanic religious synthesis" developed, with renunciation of violence and sacrifice at its core. Sacrifice continued as a central element in Hindu life, but now as a submerged line of practice under a quite different ideology. Animal sacrifice was now conducted alongside vegetable offerings.

Today, particularly in south India, one may find two deities, side by side, in a temple. One, the dominant one after whom the temple is usually known, receives only vegetarian offerings. The other deity requires, and receives, animal sacrifice. The vegetarian deity's image may be screened from the sacrifice as a sort of insulation. The great gods do not divide into two complementary deities in this fashion; their worship is more thoroughly shaped by the Brahmanic synthesis, in which the great god, vegetarian worship, and vegetarian Brahmans are absolutely superior to all else.

Offerings and Grace

Let us focus on the more common vegetable offerings to deities, or puja. These offerings may take the form of an informal family rite or that of a village temple festival. You may perform puja to ask a favor from a deity (usually a minor deity; greater ones tend to be above that sort of thing), or when you recite sacred Sanskrit texts about the exploits of a goddess, or when you join a group in singing devotional Hindi songs to Krishna.

A relatively simple puja might be focused on the ancestors of a joint family, of parents, sons, their wives, and children (Fuller 1992, 57–82). Here is an example: In a village in Madhya Pradesh, central India, the father regularly worships his agnatic (through males) ancestors in the home. Just before noon he bathes himself, offering some of the water to his ancestors; his wife and sons' wives meanwhile prepare an elaborate meal. He takes a plate of the food, a dish of clarified butter (ghee), and a brass pot with water from the bath, and, in the kitchen, kneels before a piece of flaming cow dung. He sprinkles water around the dung and places some of the butter on the fire. Again he sprinkles water, and this time places some of the food on the fire. After a third sprinkle, he bows before the flame, his hands pressed together, touching his forehead. He then joins his family for their meal. Because some of the food has been offered to the ancestor, all the meal now contains the "grace," prasada, of the ancestors. Homes also contain altars with images of family deities and teachers; women as well as men worship there daily or occasionally.

Here is a second example: In a village temple in the southern Indian state of Tamil Nadu, a priest is ready to honor Meenakshi, the goddess-queen of an ancient kingdom, and her consort Lord Shiva, in one of his many local manifestations. Each of the deities is represented by a two-foot-high movable image, set up in the temple complex and

Worshiper receives from temple priest as prasada a garland that had been offered to Shiva, Shiva temple at Yanaimangalam. (*Courtesy of Diane Mines*)

draped with white cloth. Musicians play, and their loud drumming signals the close of each ritual stage. A chanter recites sacred formulas (mantras). The priest purifies the images by bathing them with a series of liquids, including sesame-seed oil, milk, and water that has been infused with divine power through the chanting of mantras. The gods' images are adorned with clothes, jewelry, and flowers, and their foreheads are marked with three stripes of white ash, the mark of Shiva. Food is held out to the deities while water is sprinkled around the offering. The priest waves oil lamps and a candelabra with seven camphor flames in front of the images. People attending the ritual then crowd in to place their hands over the flames and touch their fingers to their eyes, and to accept white ash from the priest to place on their foreheads.

This temple ritual may be reduced or elaborated. The images may be purified with water before the ritual, and at its conclusion butter may be poured onto a flame as a final offering. More foods may be offered, and distributed to all worshipers. Or the ritual may be reduced to a presentation of one camphor flame to the deity, with a plantain on the side as an offering. The reduced ritual is still valid (it counts as puja); the elaborations are not superfluous (they add to what is accomplished).

Forms of offering vary within India and abroad. Major Hindu communities are found in Africa, Europe, and the Americas, and Hindus make up a large proportion of the populations of some Caribbean islands, Fiji, and Bali. Men and women may worship at home or in a temple, where the deity may be an incarnation of a great god, usually Vishnu or Shiva, or a local deity. Festivals all revolve around making offerings to the gods. Festivals vary across India, including the springtime Holi, celebrated in north India to mark the burning of the demonness Holika and the start of the agricultural season, and a sequence of festivals in September and October, in particular the festival

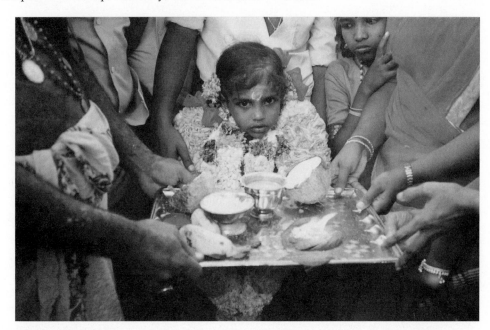

Girl with food that she has offered and received as prasada, part of an annual offering she makes to fulfill a vow, temple to Murukan, son of Shiva, Pattamadai, Tamil Nadu state, India. (*Courtesy of Diane Mines*)

of lights, Diwali, a time for welcoming, and escorting, departed ancestors. (The celebration of Diwali at my own university is one of the season's highlights, with students of all religious affiliations lining up overnight to get tickets.)

All forms of offering, simple or elaborate, involve purifying, communicating, and making offerings. Some objects are by their origin pure, such as cow products, from butter to dung to the ash of the dung, and thus can be used in rituals. You can purify something by pouring water over it, thus the importance of bathing, particularly in the Ganges, and sprinkling water at an altar.

People and deities communicate through multiple channels: chants, music, words, and gestures. One always shows respect to the gods through the gesture called namaste or pranam, holding the hands together and touching the forehead. It, too, may be succinct or elaborated: A supplicant may merely hold up the hands to the forehead, or may bow down, even touch the feet of the deity. You also indicate respect to other people by drawing on this same repertoire of gestures, and according to how they rank in the social hierarchy relative to you. Through this gesture, you honor "that bit of god which is in every person."

We also see the deities—and they see us. We exchange *darshan*, "vision," just as we exchange gestures and words. A priest can attribute this power of seeing to the statue of a deity by painting eyes onto its face. This act brings up a critical point about images in India: The image is not the same as the deity, but the deity comes to be in the image, and also, at any one moment, exists in many different images throughout India. Worshipers enhance the exchange of vision by placing a light, especially a camphor flame, by the altar.

These exchanges of vision already imply the commingling of human and divine essences, but this exchange focuses on food. Whatever we do to dress a deity, sing to it, or chant over it, we must feed it. The food may be anything that people eat, but it is always offered to the deity, taken back, and distributed to those present—family, neighbors, or temple-goers. It may simply be placed before the god, or it may be put on fire—"the flame is the tongue of the gods." The consumed food becomes the embodiment of the deity's power or "grace," the literal meaning of prasada, the food offering. Anything that has been placed in contact with the deity and then returned to humans— ash, water, food, or flowers—is prasada, and conveys that divine power to the human partakers.

We can see that puja is most importantly *transaction:* Something is given and something is received, and by this event the worshiper takes on something of the divine being.

Reform and Devotional Movements

Opposition to sacrifice was one element in broader movements for religious reform and national self-determination. Some of these movements were influenced by Western rationalist ideas about religion, but the movements also incorporated Brahmans' ideas about proper Hinduism. Brahmans had relegated sacrifice and meat-eating to non-Brahmans, but new movements for reform urged all Hindus to renounce meat-eating (Fuller 1992, 155–203).

Reform movements began in the early nineteenth century with Ram Mohan's Brahmo Samaj in Bengal, which claimed to have discovered a "rational" and monotheistic Hinduism in the Vedas and Upanishads. Indeed, Hindu reform movements share with many Islamic and Christian ones an emphasis on returning to the sacred texts, not as a way of escaping the present but, quite the contrary, in order to rationalize religious practice and purge it of undesirable traditions and superstitions. In the Hindu case, the practices to be discarded included most spectacularly the self-immolation of widows (sati) and the exclusion of untouchables. The still more influential Arya Samaj movement, which spread across north India after 1877, was less radical in its reform agenda, but it, too, called for an end to animal sacrifice as a barbaric incongruity in a religion dedicated to nonviolence. Arya Samaj was dedicated to universalizing the Hindu message and making it accessible to members of all caste groupings—and, indeed, to uniting Christians and Muslims under the banner of Vedic principles.

A different kind of reform comes from the proliferation of Agamic schools, designed to lead priests to memorize the important texts to be used for ritual, those thought to have been produced by Shiva for Shivaite temples (Fuller 2003). These schools produce priests who may be no more expert or adept at performing the physical acts of worship and offering, but who now know what to say during their physical acts. These schools promote the idea that one must learn the content of religions before learning to practice it—an element of reformism that we will find elsewhere as well (see Chapter 11).

Some reform movements have emphasized devotion, and these movements appeal particularly to middle-class Indians. Urban, middle-class associations bring people together to sing songs of bhakti ("devotion") to gods. Most popular are songs about the exemplary devotion of the cowherdess Radha for the god Krishna. The songs sung in their praise are erotic and religious. These associations provide new ways for urban dwellers to create social forms of religiosity, and in some cases also to maintain religious purity in an urban world of social intermingling—hence their appeal to some middle-class Brahmans.

These devotionalists joined nationalists and other reformers to oppose animal sacrifice. In Gujarat, west India, where Vaishnava (Vishnu-centered) devotionalist movements campaigned against sacrifice, many villagers have simply abandoned the goddesses who demand animal sacrifice. The convergent pressure of these movements has been to flatten out worship: All deities should be treated the same, as vegetarians. Mahatma Gandhi contributed to this pressure, raising his own Vaishya caste's vegetarian dietary code into a universal moral imperative that "Hindus shall not eat meat" (Fuller 1992, 103).

Within the collection of practices, teachings, and ideas called "Hinduism," a tension has persisted between a notion of religion as effective action, where an offering produces a result, and religion as obedience or devotion to transcendent deities. This tension has itself produced some of the diversity of practices observable in Hindu settings, whether in South Asia or elsewhere, and it invokes broader differences about what religious practice really is: obedience to a deity, or actions taken to obtain material or spiritual benefit?

BATHING AT BENARES

The Hindu pilgrim's goal is to enhance his temple experience through journey, to "exchange vision" (darshan) with deities many times in many places. Each site is called a "crossing place, ford" (*tirtha*) to somewhere beyond; a pilgrimage is a *tirtha-yatra*, a journey to a ford (Fuller 1992, 204–223).

The prototypical goal is Benares (Kashi, Varanasi) in north central India (Eck 1982). This "City of Light" lies alongside the Ganges, a river said to have descended from heaven to earth. Over 70 landings line its banks, some containing temples to Shiva, who makes Benares his earthly home. Benares has always been an earthly crossing, the place where the old trade route across northern India crossed the river Ganges. As with other places of pilgrimage, it is also a spiritual cross, one where earth and heaven meet. Here the dead may be assisted in crossing over the Ganges to the condition of moksha, liberation from rebirth, the ultimate goal of the Hindu. Here, too, the gods may descend from heaven to earth. Shiva lives not only in the city's many temples, but also in its ground and buildings: "The very stones of Kashi are Shiva," goes the popular saying.

The gods descend and pilgrims cross at many other fords throughout India. Of the thousands of places where Shiva, or the hero Rama, or the goddess Durga have emerged to split rocks or crushed enemies, a few cities are particularly favored. Some are associated with Rama, and in particular his capital at Ayodhya. Others, including several associated with Krishna, are on mountains; still others mark the four corners of India.

Benares is the most widely acclaimed of all, however. To many Hindus, it is the center of the universe (as is Jerusalem to some Christians, Mecca to some Muslims, and Beijing to some Chinese), and located directly under the heavens. Benares also encapsulates worship in India: Temples in other parts of India, from the Himalayas to the southern tip of the subcontinent, have replicas in Benares. One may visit these replica temples and exchange vision with their deities without leaving the city. The city has absorbed their power. And in one new temple, the devotion is of "Mother India," Bharat

Mata, represented in the form of a relief map inside the temple where the image would usually be. The map shows the major pilgrimage places, which pilgrims can view and thus "exchange vision" with all at once! But this logic of replication also goes in the reverse direction, for Benares is replicated elsewhere in hundreds of temples called "Shiva Kashi" found throughout India (Fuller 1992, 208–209). The deities are here, in this city, because gods and God, the spiritual force behind all the gods, are everywhere. One pilgrim, longing for the black stone dedicated to Shiva found near his own village, remarked: "I miss God."

Benares also attracts pilgrims to bathe in its particularly sacred waters and to cremate their dead. The pilgrim's first duty is to bathe in the river on one of its many landings. Pilgrims bathe in the Ganges to partake of its purifying powers, brown and replete with ashes and bacteria though it is. Indeed, usually they take the popular "Five Fords" trip along the riverfront, where they bathe at each of five landings (*ghat*). At each stop, the pilgrim recites a statement of intention, that he or she is undertaking this pilgrimage; and if the pilgrimage is made to fulfill a vow or with a goal in mind (which is not necessary), a statement to this effect is added, such as "I am making this pilgrimage in hope of bearing a son." Each stop has stories of kings and gods associated with it, and nearby are temples, or phallic linga statues devoted to Shiva, or even a mosque (Eck 1982, 211–251).

The last bath is taken at the landing of Manikarnika, at the center of the three-mile long waterfront. This bath is the most important. The site has a cremation ground and a large sacred well nearby. Shiva is in the temple, but Vishnu built the well as the world's very first tirtha. And a manifestation of the Goddess or Devi guards the well.

Manikarnika is called the "burning landing" because when seen from the river one sees the plumes of flames from the crematorium located among the temples. Those who die in Benares are cremated next to the Ganges and their ashes are scattered over the waters. Some who die elsewhere have their ashes brought, or even mailed, to Benares. When one's ashes lie on the Ganges, one's spirit crosses over from earth to liberation. But even failing this, pilgrims will say prayers for the dead to ensure that the ancestors will dwell in heaven. So important are these rites that when long-lost ashes from the cremation of Mohandas K. Gandhi's body were discovered nearly a half a century after the event, they were carried to the Ganges to be poured into the waters (*New York Times* January 31, 1997).

Corpses brought here are placed by the river's edge before being dipped into its waters for their final bath and then hoisted onto the funeral pyre. The eldest son circumambulates the pyre, lights it, and when the burning is finished, walks away without looking back. Members of an untouchable caste in charge of the cremation ground throw the ashes into the river, where they are gradually carried downstream.

The religious importance of seeing sacred places and images helps us understand why a rapid bus tour of a large number of sites makes religious sense. Pilgrimage is the major reason why Hindus travel, and they do so by the millions every year, traveling on foot, by bus, or by train. They value the journey itself: joining others in travel, making merit by giving alms, seeing many deities, getting away from normal routines, and experiencing another realm—both another part of the country and a glimpse into the beyond. Hardship may itself be felt as a proof that merit has been earned through the journey, even if it is not explicitly sought out.

Or, pilgrims may choose a bus tour that, without the hardship of journeying on foot, offers a greater number of chances for darshan with deities. The anthropologist

Ann Grodzins Gold (1988, 262–298) traveled by bus with a group of pilgrims from northwestern India to the eastern coast of Orissa. The pilgrims were from different castes and came from town and village settings. The villagers included Brahmans (the order or *varna* associated with the priesthood), Rajputs (traditionally a warrior caste and of the second-ranking Kshatriyas order), and people from farming, gardening, and other miscellaneous castes. The pilgrimage did not erase these distinctions; indeed, the castes stayed apart; "the fact that we were sharing a pilgrimage did not act as a leveler of rank" (Gold 1988, 269).

On the road, pilgrims sang songs about the deities Ganesha and Rama, and about the Sun King, from whom a woman in the song takes darshan each morning. They stopped at one site after another. Upon reaching a tirtha-yatra, they would bathe in the waters, view the images in the temples, make gifts to priests and beggars, and occasionally perform a short offering ritual. They traversed the country where Lord Krishna had spent his childhood and observed darshan tableaux of his babyhood. They made a whirlwind tour of Benares's many temples, which left a colorful blur in their minds. The deepest and most favorable impression was made by the sea. "These Hindus had seen countless icons in their lives," remarks Gold (1988, 284) after one pilgrim, emerging from the famed temple at Puri, said with a shrug that "Well, God is God." But, she continues, they had seen "only one sea."

What did the pilgrimage mean to them? None of Gold's fellow pilgrims thought that bathing in sacred waters would cleanse them of bad deeds. Rather, and in a more diffuse way, the entire experience of getting out of everyday routines, taking many powerful darshans of gods, enduring the hardships of the road, and giving alms to beggars would be good for the soul. Hitting the road and seeing the gods lightens the pilgrim of goods and attachments and concerns, bringing her or him nearer to "the deity within himself." Approaching one's inner divinity prepares oneself for the moment, perhaps in some future life, when one will finally attain release, *moksha*. "Sweeping the road ahead," suggested one widow.

While some pilgrims thought that pilgrimages causally improve one's chances of eventually achieving moksha, others were more skeptical. One pilgrim told Gold (1988, 288) that traveling and bathing could not effect what God determines, although He would reward giving alms: "From what does moksha come? From his own hand, God's, that's from whom. It does not come from wandering. Whatever you give, in whatever place give it. From this comes moksha. What kind of dharma is dirtying the water? But dharma is giving-and-taking."

In scholarly debates as well, Hindus are of two minds about what pilgrimages get you. On the one hand, some commentators on the classic texts assure the pilgrim that "Even if a man be a sinner or a rogue or irreligious, he becomes free from all sin if he goes to Benares." But others equally clearly say the opposite, that it is the inner self that must be purified through meditation. After all, observes one scholar, "Fish are born and die in the water (of tirthas); and *they* do not go to heaven."

MUSLIM–HINDU VIOLENCE

During the 1980s and 1990s, there took place violent conflicts and riots pitting Hindus against Muslims. The flash point for some of these was located in the northern Indian city of Ayodhya, Rama's birthplace (van der Veer 1994). Ayodhya is a holy tirtha over the holy river Sarayu and a place for the pilgrim to "cross over" from the mundane world to make contact with Rama. Many Hindus claim that Rama was born on a site in the city where the Moghul (Muslim dynasty) ruler Babar built a mosque in the sixteenth century. Moghul rulers allowed Hindus to worship on this site, even inside the mosque compound, and the subsequent Muslim dynasty endowed Hindu temples in the city.

In the twentieth century, relations between Muslims and Hindus deteriorated as in much of South Asia. Hindus launched attacks on the Babar mosque during the celebration of the Day of Sacrifice in 1912, and again in 1934. The situation heated up further after the 1947 Partition and the flight of many Muslims to Pakistan. In 1949, a statue of Rama appeared in the mosque. Hindus and Muslims naturally interpreted this event in very different ways. For the Hindus, Rama had appeared in their midst, giving them a sign to liberate his birthplace from the Muslims. For the Muslims, their mosque had been defiled. Riots ensued, and the army was called in. The government closed the mosque, and it remained closed to both Muslims and Hindus until 1984, when national politics came to a head in the city.

By the mid-1980s, there had emerged a strong Hindu nationalist party, the Bharatiya Janata Party (BJP), which garnered support from Hindu nationalist movements and in particular from the Vishva Hindu Parishad (VHP). The VHP was an attempt to create a united Hindu organization. Given India's diversity in religious practices and beliefs, creating a unified Hinduism would be a daunting task. What Hindus plausibly shared, however, was a belief in certain sacred objects and symbols. One was the sacred river the Ganges, and in 1983 the VHP organized a drive to symbolize Hindu unity based on shared water. Large trucks were sent throughout the country, each carrying enormous bronze pots with water from the Ganges. This water was given to villagers en route, and the pots were replenished with water from local sacred sources, symbolizing Hindu unity—and giving the VHP a way to firm up its local support network.

Hindu unity meant opposition to Muslims, and the VHP called for mosques to be removed from several sacred spots, including in Ayodhya. By 1989 the VHP had begun to mobilize support for building a new temple in Ayodhya. In November, just before Indian general elections, Hindus were urged to send or bring bricks for the temple, and bricks poured in—from Hindus in Europe and the United States as well as from throughout India. The VHP was eventually stopped from building the temple by the ruling Congress government, but the flames thus fanned led to massacres of Muslims, and numerous Hindu deaths as well, in northern and eastern India.

One year later, violence erupted again, this time brought on by the political party, the BJP. The BJP joined forces with the VHP in part to oppose the government's plan to reserve a greater number of jobs and positions for lower-caste people. (In its mass support and vote-getting, the BJP appeals most to urban, upper-caste people.) Despite police bans, some volunteers bent on rebuilding "Rama's temple" made it to Ayodhya, where many were killed. In December 1990, to further dramatize BJP support for the Hindu nationalist cause, the party leader L. K. Advani began a "chariot-led procession" to Ayodhya. Perhaps because the Ramayana epic had been serialized on television a few years earlier, Advani decked his party out as Rama's army. His chariot, drawn by an air-conditioned Toyota, was carved and gilded to recall Rama's chariot. He carried the bow of Rama, brandishing it to ward off his enemies. Supporters, marching alongside, were decked out in warrior garb and handed bows as well.

The procession began from a place in Gujarat, west India, widely associated with the tenth-century destruction by a Muslim ruler of Hindu temples. This choice of starting point played up anti-Muslim sentiments. The procession moved across India before being halted in the eastern state of Bihar, where Advani was arrested—an arrest which then led to the collapse of the fragile coalition government. Mass strikes and riots followed; all trains and buses that passed anywhere near Ayodhya were canceled, but nonetheless many people were killed. Then in 1992, supporters of the BJP/VHP rushed to Ayodhya and demolished the temple. The riots that ensued led to over one thousand deaths, mostly of Muslims (van der Veer 1994).

Although religious sentiments were front and center during the campaigns and riots, we would err in thinking of these conflicts as the emergence of "primordial" or traditional sentiments in opposition to the nation-state. The conflicts and riots developed out of a modern idea of a Hindu nation-state, itself with roots in colonial constructions of religious communities and postcolonial electioneering. In the nineteenth century, the British created the idea of a "Hindu majority"—and a Muslim minority—through the census. They interpreted these categories as native Hindus versus foreign Muslims. This view has had an effect on later Indian notions, promoting the idea that one's primary loyalty is as a Hindu to the "Hindu community" or as a Muslim to the "Muslim community," rather than to local communities or leaders. And it was on these notions that Advani and other Hindu nationalist leaders drew to mobilize support for Rama and anger against Muslims. Although Hindu–Muslim tensions predate colonialism and independence, the kind of violent religious nationalism exhibited in this case (and in many other places) is to a great extent a modern creation.

And for most Hindus, as for most people, anywhere, these nationalist claims have little to do with the practical bases and emotional pulls of religious practices. "Ram is supposed to dwell in our hearts, not in a temple," said one north Indian villager (quoted in Fuller 1992, 261). "We don't need to learn about our dharma from politicians seeking votes."

EXPLAINING WHERE VIOLENCE OCCURRED

If the violence just described was justified in religious terms, we still need to understand why it occurred in some places and not in others. Here we can make a more general point about how not to understand violence and how to approach an adequate account of its eruption.

All too often, when violence breaks out anywhere in the world, we look for causes in other features of those places. When, during the 1990s, Hindus and Muslims attacked each other in some cities of India, we might be tempted to say that, in general, the coexistence of Hindus and Muslims leads to conflict and violence. But in most places, most of the time, in India as elsewhere, religious and ethnic groups live side by side in relative peace. Religious or ethnic differences do not, of themselves, cause conflict (Bowen 1996; Brubaker and Laitin 1998). What we need to do, then, is to look for other features of social life that promote conflict.

Ashutosh Varshney (2002) asked precisely this question of Hindu–Muslim violence in India. Varshney begins by noting that 95 percent of the Indian population was not involved in the riots of the 1990s, that riots took place in cities, not villages, and that a handful of cities account for most of the deaths. These cities are scattered throughout

India. Rioting and deaths are thus not generally true of India or even of urban India, and not of one region rather than another. To uncover the factors accounting for violence, Varshney ingeniously paired cities of similar size and religious composition, but where one member of the pair did experience violence and the other did not. He then looked for differences that consistently occurred in these pairs, differentiating the high-violence city from the low-violence city.

It turns out that the best predictor of nonviolence in Indian cities is the degree to which stable, formal civic associations, such as trade unions, professional organizations, or political parties, brought Muslims and Hindus together on a regular basis. How did the presence of such ties lead to peace? In places with such associations, peace committees were formed at the threat of riot, and moved across communities, preventing escalations and contradicting rumors. Without them no one stopped the escalation of violence and often intra-community associations fanned the flames. Now we can understand why rural areas would be much less likely to have such conflicts: In villages, everyone already exists in a kind of civic association, with everyday encounters on a face-to-face basis and village organizations dealing with justice, farming, and politics.

Varshney's study thus emphasizes the importance of what Robert Putnam (2000) has called "bridging" social capital, meaning the networks and friendships that reach across social divisions, over "bonding" social capital, meaning networks that strengthen solidarities within social groups and which thus may harden social divisions. This analysis highlights the proximal social mechanisms that prevent or dampen down conflict between Muslims and Hindus. But one may then ask: Why did some cities develop these civic associations and others not? The answer to this question lies in a deeper history, one that refers us back to the activities of the Congress Party and other political organizations in the 1920s. Congress tried to develop such interreligious associations in India's cities, but only succeeded in those places where the major divisions in the city were along lines other than that of Hindus versus Muslims.

Let us see how these pathways developed in two cities: Calicut, a trade-oriented city in the southern state of Kerala, and Aligarh, an industrial city, known for Aligarh Muslim University, located in the northern state of Uttar Pradesh. In the early twentieth century, conflicts among Hindu castes dominated social life in Calicut, making it possible for the Congress party to create political, trade, and cultural associations that brought together Hindus and Muslims. When Hindu–Muslim violence did break out in 1921, the Malabar riots, it did not spread. In Aligarh, however, tensions between Muslims and Hindus dominated civic life and prevented the formation of civic intercommunal associations. Instead, politics replicated religious affiliations. The middle-class Hindu Arya Samaj movement developed influence within the local Congress Party, whereas the Muslim League, born of Aligarh Muslim University, championed the creation of Pakistan and thus was in opposition to Congress's ideal of pan-Indian union. During the 1990s' violence, politicians and peace committees worked across religious lines in Calicut to prevent local riots, but *within* religious communities in Aligarh to fan the flames.

The historical causal chains thus run from long-standing lines of cleavage within each city, to the political creation (or not) of crosscutting civic associations, to the contemporary activities of those associations, to the presence or absence of major Hindu–Muslim violence. One intriguing by-product of this analysis is that strong political tensions between upper-caste and lower-caste Muslims, as in Kerala, help to dampen down conflict between Muslims and Hindus. Class conflict thus promotes peace! Varshney's study reminds us that when we seek to understand conflict (or for that matter any social phenomenon), we need to look at cases where it is absent as well as those where it is present, lest we erroneously attribute causality point to a spurious variable, one that co-occurs—"innocently," we might say—with conflicts, but that also co-occurs with peace. And, to stay with our concern in this book, religious difference is one such variable. Because we often see and hear about instances of conflicts between groups of different religious affiliations, we often mistakenly think that religious difference "causes" conflict.

But if we examine a wide sample of cases for the causes of intrastate conflicts, we do not find such an association. One such analysis (Fearon and Laitin 2003) found that religious or ethnic diversity does not predict a greater likelihood of conflict. (The best explanations seem to be conditions favoring insurgency, such as rough terrain and a weak state.)

Conclusions

We have traced developments in Hindu practices, from early sacrifice, through the Axial Age transformations into a religion based on obedience to religious commands, to the complex imbrications of colonial rule, nationalism, and violence in today's India. We can usefully compare the Hindu transitions with those of Judaism discussed in Chapter 2. We can also draw on the analysis of religious violence to critically examine claims made about violence attached to other religions. Religion does not explain conflict, but religious allegiances may be a mobilizing force—an issue we will continue to explore in Chapter 12.

Discussion Questions

How does the pilgrimage to Benares resemble and differ from the Islamic hajj we discussed in Chapter 4? How would you explain the differences?

What are the conditions under which religious differences are more likely to contribute to violence? Do the lessons drawn from the India case have a bearing on conflicts elsewhere?

Media Resources

I would recommend a film on Indian pilgrimages, such as *An Indian Pilgrimage: Kashi*. I also use a film on American Hindu devotions: *Puja: Expressions of Hindu devotion*. Short clips are also available, such as the four-minute film segment at: http://www.youtube.com/watch?v=_G84pghbOS4&feature=fvw, which shows a puja to Shiva in beautfiul simplicity. To show something of the popular representations of the Ramayana, which played a crucial role in popular enthusiasm for rebuilding the temple at Ayodhya, I show a bit from the 1987–1988 television serialization of the epic, for example at: http://www.bharatmovies.com/tv/ramayan/ramanand-sagar-ramayan-part-78.htm

Imagery and Faith:
Focus on Catholicism

At least starting with Augustine of Hippo (354–430 C.E.), the Catholic Church set out to do two things that one might think near-impossible: spread throughout the world and do so all the while maintaining a strict hierarchy centered on the Pope. What follows is a very specific window into this truly transnational religion, approached here through its use of imagery in promoting faith.

RELICS AND IMAGES

Catholic imagery has been based on different types of meanings and multiple associations in the minds of worshipers. When we think of Catholicism, we usually think of elaborate representations of saints, Jesus, and Mary. But Catholic images also draw on other kinds of symbolic meanings to become powerful, multivocalic foci for worship and social life.

Catholicism is distinguished from other branches of Christianity by the authority of Rome, the importance of sacraments and the Eucharist, and the doctrine of the Trinity. Rome's authority stems from Jesus's designation of Peter as the first leader of the church and the continuous descent of authority from Peter ("apostolic succession"). The Eucharist is defined by the miracle of transubstantiation, or the direct conversion of wine and wafer into the blood and body of Christ. In similar fashion, God's grace is objectively realized through other sacraments, such as baptism and matrimony. The Trinity is the existence of God through three persons: God the Father, God the Son, and the Holy Spirit.

A famous example is the Shroud of Turin, a cloth held in Turin, Italy, since 1578 that has on its surface an image of a bearded face, said by some to be the image of Christ. The shroud is venerated by many Catholics, not just because it is a likeness of Jesus but because they think that it was produced by direct and miraculous physical contact with his face, in a fashion similar to the process that produces a photograph; we call this an "indexical" relationship between the sign and that for which it stands. This claim of direct contact generates in many pious people a sense of direct communication between the viewer and Jesus. The arguments about the Shroud's authenticity turn exclusively on this issue of contact, not on its resemblance to Jesus. In fact, the iconic qualities of the image on the Shroud, its resemblance to conventional ideas of what Jesus looked like, are precisely what skeptics point to when they claim that it is only a painting. The relative weight of iconic and indexical meanings is thus of great importance for the Shroud's religious status.

Christianity is, after all, founded on ideas of contact and physical presence, in particular the idea of incarnation, the embodiment of godliness in tangible form as Jesus Christ. The central ritual of the Church is based on the worshiper's direct contact with Christ through eating and drinking of his body. Holy Communion enacts the miracle of the Eucharist, in which ordinary bread and wine are consecrated by a priest and, at that exact moment, turned into the body and blood of Jesus. This countlessly repeated miracle parallels the sacrifice Jesus made of himself for the sake of humanity.

The idea that Christ is in the bread and wine was popularly assumed for centuries. It was finally codified in 1215, when the Fourth Lateran Council ruled that consecration does indeed convert the ordinary substances into Christ, or, in the technical language of the Church, that "transubstantiation" takes place. The Council also ruled that Christ was whole in every particle of bread and wine "under two species." This second idea, called "concomitance," responded to the concern, evidently widespread at the time, that when one dropped crumbs of the bread on the floor one was dropping bits of Christ, that chewing the bread was chewing his bones, and so forth.

The History of Relics and the Host

Relics preserve the history of religious miracles through their own history of physical contact with sacred persons or events. They make up an important part of the history of Catholic religious objects—which is also the history of Catholic politics. Religious objects have mediated between the community and the church hierarchy, between local and universal perspectives, between religion and the state, and between cultures.

The central Church ritual, communion or the Eucharist, is based on a miracle of incarnation. In the early Church, the central ritual of communion or the Eucharist was carried out in a way that was expansive and collective. The priest said "Peace be with you"; the lay worshipers responded in kind and exchanged the "kiss of peace" with each other (men with men, women with women). Worshipers then brought forward their sacrifices of bread and wine to be consecrated by the priest. Communion was thus the Church partaking of Christ and worshipers communing with each other. Christianity drew on its Jewish roots but also broadened them. Communion widened the bounds of the Jewish seder to include the entire community beyond the realm of one's family and friends. Communion, thus, modeled socially the universal ideal and ambition of the Church (Bynum 1987, 48–69; Feeley-Harnik 1981, 107–168).

Communion recreates for a brief moment what is in effect a direct physical link to Christ. But Christian churches also relied on other kinds of sacred indexes to maintain a sense of connection among churches and among worshipers. As the Church expanded in Europe and North Africa, it created a network of churches under the control of Rome. Churches were built on shrines or as shrines, sometimes near or around cemeteries located just outside city walls, where the buried remains of saints sanctified the ground of the new church. There was a practical consideration at work as well—the belief current at the time was that on the day of Resurrection, the first bodies to be taken up to heaven would be those buried near the body of a saint (Ariès 1974).

A Christian shrine or church usually contained sacred objects, an image or relic that gave the shrine its religious status. A relic was a remnant of a saint—a bone, bit of hair, or an entire corpse—or an object that had been made sacred by contact with a saint (or Jesus). It was movable, and so separate from the place itself. Except in Ireland, where the pre-Christian Celtic veneration of places continued unabated, it was the relic, not the place, that was considered sacred.

Saints' bodies, sometimes partially or wholly mummified, have been favorite relics for churches. In the early churches, they were often exhibited to worshipers and pilgrims. Today as well, the faithful consider saints' bodies to be capable of working miracles. Some bodies exude healing fluids, such as a marble sarcophagus in the French Pyrenees that accumulates clear water. Throughout the year, the water is collected by individuals and used for healing, and the remainder is pumped out each July 30 at a special ceremony. Soil may be taken from the burial place of a saint and used to heal, particularly in Ireland and the Americas. A small church near Santa Fe contains such a miraculous source of earth. Bones are also used as church relics, today usually contained in elaborately sculpted boxes or reliquaries.

The logic of sacrality through contact reaches beyond body parts and sacred soil. Paintings and statues may acquire sacred status from having once been in contact with a sacred person or object. For example, some paintings of the Virgin Mary draw their religious force from their historical ties to what is called the True Icon (*Vera Icon*) of Mary: a painting said to have been made by Saint Luke and considered to be holy because he, a holy person, painted it, and not because of a property of the representation itself. Paintings that are understood as copies of the True Icon are found in Italy, Spain, and most famously in Poland. Our Lady of Czestochowa, the national icon of Poland, is a painting of a dark Madonna, and it is housed in a fourteenth-century church in the southwestern part of the country. It is the object of the major pilgrimage for Polish Catholics. It is said to derive from the Saint Luke painting. Other paintings or statues are touched to the painting in Czestochowa, and from that contact derive a special (indexical, we would say) power. Copies of the True Icon become as effective as the original in working miracles. (At least by the sixth century c.e., we find stories of paintings carried into battle to ensure victory.)

Images versus Relics

By the late fourth century, a lively traffic in saints' remains had developed across Europe. Remains were sent as gifts, sometimes stolen from crypts in Italy. This traffic was encouraged by the idea that remains could be divided up, and the saint became present in each fragment (analogous to the idea that Christ was totally present in every fragment of the consecrated bread). As Theodoret of Cyrus proclaimed: "In the divided body the grace survives undivided and the fragments, however small, have the same efficacy as the whole body" (Bynum 1987, 48–53).

During the eighth century, a rapid rise in missionary activity led the Church to develop rules for creating new churches. In 787, the Second Council of Nicaea declared that a new church had to possess a saint's relic in order to be consecrated. The new rule further increased the demand for relics. People began to scour the Roman catacombs for bone fragments that could be attributed to early Christian martyrs, and a virtual flood of these bone fragments poured forth from Rome out into northern Europe. The hunger for relics turned major discoveries of bones into momentous cultural events. In the early ninth century, Saint James' bones were discovered in northern Spain, and the site of this discovery, known thereafter as Santiago de Compostela, became the third most important Christian pilgrimage site after Rome and Jerusalem (Nolan and Nolan 1989, 160–171).

The propagation of relics not only expanded the bounds of the Church but also provided a firm spiritual foundation for the empire created by Charlemagne. From the ninth century onward, the oath administered to witnesses was taken on saints' relics, and read: "May God and the saints whose relics these are judge me that I speak the truth" (Rothkrug 1980).

During the early years of Christian expansion, there were no official procedures for evaluating relics, or indeed for canonizing saints. A local church could declare someone to have been a saint and then build a church around him or her. The remains would be disinterred and placed on an altar within the church. If the body was found to be intact, or in the language of the times, "uncorrupt," this condition was attributed to its holy qualities, which had continued to reside in the body after death. (Note that in this tradition, intact bodies were signs of purity; by contrast in the Greek Orthodox practices, discussed in Chapter 4, total disintegration of the flesh is a sign that the soul was received into heaven.)

Many of the relics were, in fact, fakes: Countless pieces of wood from Christ's cross circulated throughout Europe, as did chalky stones from the Milk Grotto in Bethlehem said to be colored by milk Mary used to nurse Christ. The market pressures also encouraged theft: One Roman deacon named Deusdona contracted to steal the remains of Saint Peter and to supply them, broken down into small parts, to the Franks. As their authenticity was increasingly doubted, their value declined. (Compare with Gresham's Law in economics: "bad money drives out good.")

The Church responded in two ways. First, it began to exert authority over the status of holy man or saint. It carried out its first canonization of a saint in 993 and gradually gained control over that process. Second, the Church tried to substitute images for relics. Early Christian art (like Islamic art) had been largely decorative. Many people felt that the crafting of human figures would be tantamount to worshiping graven images, a fear inherited from Judaism. In the words of Saint Epiphanius in the fourth century C.E.: "When images are put up, the customs of the pagans do the rest." But popular use of imagery, pictures of saints, developed in the late fourth century and became widespread by the sixth. The Church came to encourage this trend in the interest of promoting universalism. Saints, after all, were many, and their stories often emphasized local miracles and military victories rather than the universal message of Christ that was central to the Church. Basing the legitimacy of a local church on relics underscored the local bases for worship rather than the Church's universalism. To the extent that the Church was able to refocus worshipers' attention toward paintings or statues or other images, it would be able to emphasize the universal figures of Mary and Christ, whose bodies were not available to be relics (Nolan and Nolan 1989, 160–171).

To meet popular objections that only relics were sacred—and the practical point that only relics would share in the resurrection—Church authorities encouraged the crafting of reliquaries: elaborately carved boxes, often with jewels and gold, or statues in the image of a saint that contained minute pieces of the saint's bones. These objects were both relics and images. Images such as paintings or ordinary statues were also said to have had direct contact with a sacred person, or, as in the case of the True Icon mentioned above, to have been painted by a saint, or to have been once physically touched to a painting that was painted by a saint, and so forth, along a historical chain of direct, sacred contact. These efforts drew on popular ideas about contact and sacrality but also promoted universal images.

A More Hierarchical Ritual

The Church's efforts to emphasize its universal message over local sacrality gained momentum in the eleventh, twelfth, and thirteenth centuries, a period of growth in the political power of the Church. What we often call the "age of faith," or, in reference to the great energies devoted to church crafting throughout Western Europe, the "age of cathedrals," also saw a shift in the relationship of people to the institution of the Catholic Church. Rome began to exercise more control over local churches, and in each church priests recast their role vis-à-vis lay persons in a more hierarchical or vertical way.

The eleventh century saw the growth of powerful monasteries, which resisted secular control, the struggle for priority in spiritual affairs over the kings, and the Crusades, which began in 1096. The church became "monumental" in several senses. Doctrine was systematically formulated, most notably by Thomas of Aquinas (1225–1274); the great cathedrals of northern Europe were built; and Rome was able to exert ever-greater control over the behavior of individual churches. It was the great age of pilgrimages to such sites as Santiago de Compostela in northern Spain, to England's Canterbury Cathedral, the site of Thomas à Beckett's assassination in 1170 (and the destination of the pilgrims in Chaucer's *Canterbury Tales*), and the first great Holy Year pilgrimage to Rome in 1300. Many religious orders that promoted pilgrimages—Dominicans, Franciscans, Carmelites—were founded during this period.

All these developments added to the general sense of a Christiandom united by movements of people, the mobilization of popular energies, and a central, controlling power lodged in Rome. In worship itself, these changes led to a great focus on the priest's role, as the representative of Rome, over and against that of the people. Communion and other aspects of liturgy became more centralized, more in the hands of priests and monks. Saint Thomas himself wrote that priests engage in the communion of Eucharist on behalf of others. Saints once had come from the popular ranks, even after canonization became a Church monopoly. Now male saints began to be drawn entirely from the ranks of priests (Bynum 1987, 53–69).

The ritual transformation that most evidently represented this change was the shift from *receiving* communion to *seeing* the Host. By the twelfth century, churches had begun to offer communion less frequently and instead to concentrate the attention of worshipers on Christ's presence in the bread and wine at the moment they were consecrated by the priest. Christ could be seen on the altar and adored there. Physical contact was downplayed in favor of, again, the image of Christ, albeit an image of the Host that had become Christ.

As priests emphasized the "adoration of the Host," other changes were made as well. Elaborate containers for the Host, reliquaries, were made and placed so that all could see. Holes were made in some church walls so that even horses could commune by viewing the Host. The Host began to be raised up for general view; this practice of "elevating the Host" first occurred in Paris in 1200. Fifteen years later, Pope Innocent II declared as dogma the miracle of transubstantiation, the change of bread and wine into Christ's body and blood. In 1264, a new feast day, the feast of Corpus Christi, the "body of Christ," began to be celebrated. By the fourteenth century, a new kind of vessel called a "monstrance" ("displayer") was created to display the consecrated Host. As the historian John Bossy (1983) writes, the "socially integrative powers of the Host" were transferred from the mass to the feast of Corpus Christi.

From the twelfth century onward, receiving the Host became something priests did. Already by the eleventh century only priests could take Christ in their hands; others had to receive a wafer directly in their mouths from the priest. The priest had once carried out the consecration of the Host in full view and standing facing the worshipers—after all, in the early church it had been their bread and wine that had been brought to be consecrated. But now the priest celebrated with his back to the people. He took communion for their sake with his back turned. Special "rood screens" were constructed to seal him off from view. In these churches communion became a mystery, a miracle that touched only the priest, who was sometimes venerated precisely because of his privileged contact with Christ. In the words of Saint Francis of Assisi (1181–1226): "He touches Christ with his own hands."

The "two species" of the Eucharist were now treated differently. When communion was offered to worshipers, the consecrated cup was sometimes withheld and ordinary wine substituted. The reason given was that the church feared that a careless parishioner could spill Christ's blood. The wafer now became the focus of this longed-for ritual act. It became a strongly held symbol of the unity of the church and of fears of its being desecrated. Anti-Semitism was often voiced as an accusation that someone had defiled the wafers. Stories circulated of Hosts turning to flesh and bleeding in protest against misuse (for example, by sorcerers) or in an effort to warn churchgoers against an approaching danger (Bossy 1983; Bynum 1987, 53–69).

The Host increasingly became a symbol of the church, rather than a source of redemption for the individual person. Some people protested this church control; these protests included demands to receive the Host "in both species," that is, as consecrated wine and bread. A hunger for the chalice and communion intensified, and ordinary people, particularly women, experienced religious devotions and ecstasies as sensing and eating God.

The central objects that located or founded a church also shifted from relics of saints (with the Host as one of many relics) to the general adoration of Christ and the Virgin Mary. In 1150, the pope rejected his former title, "Vicar of Saint Peter" for the new one, "Vicar of Christ," shifting his grounds for authority from the presence of Saint Peter's body in Rome (a relic), to his direct receipt of authority from Christ.

The Church also began to desacralize relics and to replace them with images of saints. It developed the idea of the saints and Mary in the "communion of saints," or "the unity under and in Christ of the faithful on the earth, the souls in purgatory, and the blessed in heaven." Dead souls were enrolled in the new brotherhoods and orders as part of this universal community. This idea of the communion of saints allowed one soul to pray for another. Helping other souls through prayer became a major activity both in church masses and at pilgrimage sites.

Christ Incarnate

The Eucharist, as it became the focus of church activity, is best seen as Christ's incarnation—it gave the worshiper direct contact with Christ. Recall that it was only in 1215 that the Church proclaimed as dogma the eucharistic miracle of transubstantiation. The elevation and adoration of the Host began about then, and Corpus Christi followed in 1264.

These steps addressed what we can think of as the problem of Christ's relics (Nolan and Nolan 1989). After all, according to the church, Christ ascended to heaven 40 days after the Resurrection, leaving no body behind to generate relics. In popular opinion, he did leave some relics behind: his blood and the earth that was touched by it; pieces of the cross and nails from the cross; garments worn during the Passion; the Shroud of Turin. The church gradually accepted the idea that his milk teeth, foreskin, and spilled blood could, in theory, have remained on the earth even though he ascended to heaven. Popular pressure was for more relics of Christ, perhaps because of the more difficult access to Christ through communion.

The steps taken by the church in the thirteenth century to promote the worship of Christ may have been responses to this pressure. The doctrine of transubstantiation not only provided an officially sanctioned opportunity for direct contact with Christ incarnate but it also allowed numerous further miracles, at least in the popular imagination.

Sometimes the Host was said to really become flesh and blood. In at least one shrine, in Lanciano, Italy, are small pellets of blood and a strip of flesh said to have been formed from consecrated bread and water during the celebration of Mass by a doubting monk in the eighth century. Bavaria has a shrine where sacramental wine, spilled on an altar cloth in 1330, formed an image of Christ. Christ could now become real, the object of worship (and sometimes even contact) within a more hierarchical church (Clark 1967, 410–434; Nolan and Nolan 1989, 216–290).

MARY IN EUROPEAN SOCIETIES

The church has also promoted the adoration of Mary as Mother of God. This "cult of Mary," which undoubtedly draws on older images and ideas of a virgin mother goddess, first appeared in Turkey in 431 and expanded across the West. At some point a popular idea developed that Mary herself was conceived in her mother, Saint Ann, free from the original sin that everyone else receives by virtue of Eve and Adam's transgression in the Garden of Eden. This idea of "immaculate conception"—conception in the womb free of original sin—spread on a popular level but was not immediately accepted by the church. In the sixteenth century, the Council of Trent declared Mary free of original sin, but only in 1854 did Pope Pius IX declare as dogma that Mary indeed had experienced an immaculate conception.

Marian worship on a widespread, dominant scale dates from about the eleventh century and is due in part to the activities of the Cistercian order, all of whose churches were dedicated to Mary. The popular idea that she was bodily assumed into heaven was officially proclaimed as Roman Catholic dogma in 1950. As with Christ, this doctrine meant that very few relics could be claimed to be available: her sash and veil, a few strands of hair, pieces of milky rock white from her breast milk—slim pickings indeed. More popular were images of Mary, usually as the Pietà, holding the body of the dead Christ.

This image of Mary drew, intentionally or not, on much older notions of a virgin mother goddess who bears a child who later dies in her arms. Inanna, the Queen of Heaven in Sumerian mythology, gives up her son Dumuz to torture and death. The Egyptian Isis nurses and mourns for her son Osiris. (And as we shall see, such pre-Christian images are found in the Americas as well.) Pietà images are especially popular in German culture (70 percent of these images are found there), probably because of the long-standing tradition of imperially founded nunneries. Around 1300, Dominican nunneries began to promote the image of a suffering Mary, a representation of their own direct, personal, at times erotic relation to Christ. The pietà image generally becomes popular during times of sadness and war, because it provides an especially apt image for suffering. For example, many new pietà statues were carved after the trauma of the Thirty Years' War in the seventeenth century, and again after the First World War in our own century (Nolan and Nolan 1989, 191–209).

The numerical analysis of to whom a shrine is dedicated shows how sharp has been the change from saints, usually based on relics, to Mary, always based on a shrine image. In the period before 700 c.e., 92 percent of the shrines formed were dedicated to a saint. That percentage dropped to 20 percent in the "high medieval" period of 1100–1400, and has remained about the same since. The percentage of shrines dedicated to Mary was only 6 percent in the early period, but 73 percent in the high medieval period, and level ever since. Shrines dedicated to Christ have remained at below 10 percent throughout the common era (Nolan and Nolan 1989, 155).

Marian Apparitions and Modern Life

Over the past 150 years, Mary has taken on a new identity in the popular imagination, less as Mother of God and more as an individual who intervenes on behalf of individuals in modern, industrialized societies. She begins to appear in the sky to troubled individuals and to offer solace and instructions. Hundreds of such apparitions have occurred in the past two centuries, but seven were approved by local bishops and gained international attention; these occurred in France, Belgium, and Portugal. These visions include the apparitions of Mary at Lourdes, France, in 1858, and in Fatima, Portugal, in 1917. Both were eventually accepted by the Church; most others were not (Zimdars-Schwartz 1991).

In 1917, in Fatima, three children reported a series of appearances of Mary. One of the three, Lucia dos Santos, later discussed in her memoirs her religious upbringing as well as the events surrounding the apparitions. Lucia took her First Communion at age 6 rather than at the usual age 10. She tells of how the priest told her to kneel before the image of the Virgin and to ask Mary to take care of her heart; when she did so, she saw the statue of the Virgin smile at her, and she heard the Virgin say she would do this for her.

Lucia was 10 when, together with her friends, she saw the Virgin appear on six separate occasions. Mary spoke to the children, saying that they had come from heaven, and that she would take them to heaven. All three children reported hearing the same words. Others came to the place where the apparitions occurred. Some of these other watchers reported seeing a small cloud appear over the tree where the children saw the Virgin and the tree's branches bend.

At the time, the children reported hearing three secrets from the Virgin. In 1941, Lucia revealed two of them. The first concerned the nature of hell. The second was a prediction of war unless the world became devoted to her Immaculate Heart. Mary further specified that her followers would need to secure the consecration of Russia to her Immaculate Heart and to convert that country's people. If such steps were not taken, she warned, the world would be annihilated. Lucia wrote the third secret down, and in 1957 her note was sent to Rome. In 1977 Pope John Paul I visited her (Zimdars-Schwartz 1991, 190–219).

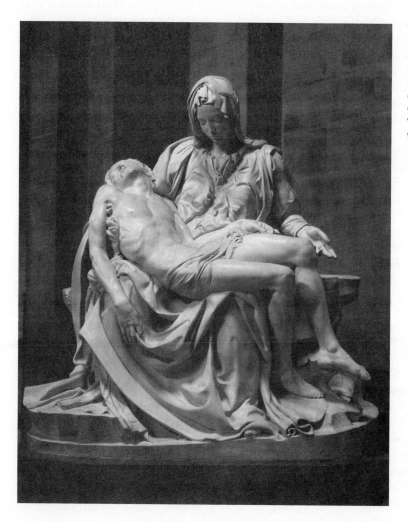

The Pieta by Michelangelo, (Italian, 475–1564). C. 1498–99, Marble. The Metropolitan Museum of Art, John T. Johnson Collection, Funds from Various Donors, 1895, 95.40.5

Other reported sightings of Mary followed in the late 1940s, and manifested the worries held by many European Catholics about the general loss of faith and the coming clash with communism (Christian 1984). Marian apparitions provided a kind of collective catharsis, a general focusing and release of these tensions, and have continued unabated into the twenty-first century.

One of the more recent apparitions has been occurring frequently on a hill just outside Medjugorje, Bosnia, since June 24, 1981. Six children saw Mary on the first day; since then more than 20 million pilgrims have come for a view. The children moved the place for their visions into the church, until the bishop ordered them out. Since then some people have reported nightly appearances of Mary (Bax 1991; Zimdars-Schwartz 1991, 220–244).

Pilgrims to the site often return with stories of personal conversions and healing. One Irish woman described her visit as at first just a "holiday." But then she saw the concrete cross that had been built on the site, and saw the sun behind it turn blood red, with a small piece of the sun missing after it had moved behind the cross. On her return home she attended a funeral mass and when the priest held up the Host she saw it as "the image of the sun at Medjugorje and I really believed in the presence of Christ—the sun had been the Host with the piece missing like when the priest breaks off a piece—and I was overcome and cried."

Medjugorje spreads. An Italian family bought a white plaster statue of Mary during a visit to the site, and in February 1995 reported that tears of blood had begun running down the statue's face. Crowds began to flock around the family's home near Rome, and the local bishop had the statue removed. CAT scans of the statue showed no hidden mechanisms; laboratory tests showed the blood to be human; DNA matches with the family's blood were proposed. In the end, the bishop became a believer in the miracle (Bohlen 1995; Warner 1996).

In the United States, an American returned home to New Jersey after a visit to Medjugorje in 1988 and reported that he had been healed of a back injury and hearing loss. Mary appeared to him in his backyard six months later, stating that she had work for him to do. In August 1992, he publicly announced when the second visit would happen, and 8,000 people came to witness the event. About the same number showed up in Cold Spring, Kentucky, when a local pastor predicted an apparition (Steinfels 1992).

The Church has been ambivalent about the apparitions. On the one hand, the apparitions encourage popular faith, and their message is in keeping with the interest of the Church. On the other hand, the apparitions occur outside Church control; they challenge the hierarchy of the Church by providing an alternative source of religious enthusiasm to worship in churches. The Church has given official recognition to the apparitions at Lourdes and Fatima, but not to Medjugorje. There, the local Franciscan fathers, who for centuries functioned as the parish priests, have encouraged people to enjoy the special grace provided by the visions. But the Bishop of Mostar, whose district includes the apparition site, has forbidden worshipers to make the pilgrimage and has called the apparitions "theatrical practices." His ruling has been part of an effort, backed by Rome, to wrest control of the parishes away from the friars, and Mary, here as elsewhere, has become a key token in that struggle (Bax 1991).

Religious sentiments in Catholic Europe have always included some resentment of the power and privileges of the clergy. For those visitors to the sites of apparitions who share these anticlerical feelings, the Church's rejection of visions makes the visions even more attractive. The apparitions are usually reported from marginal regions during times of trouble—Bosnia and southern Italy in the 1990s, economically depressed parts of the United States in the 1980s, post–war Western Europe.

Spanish Shrines

As the Church increasingly came to promote Mary as an object of worship, people have made her into a local protector as well as the symbol of Church worship. In agrarian parts of northern Spain, each valley of herders and farmers contains a number of small villages. Each village parish has its own active patron, whose image is in the village shrine and who protects the village as a whole. The shrine may be an isolated chapel at the boundary of several villages or the parish church at the village center.

In the Nansa river valley studied by the ethnographer William Christian (1989) are 14 such village parishes. Of these 14, 1 has Christ as its patron, 3 have the souls in purgatory (*Las Animas*), and 10 have a particular aspect or realization of the Virgin Mary. Thus, in one village the patron is Our Lady of the Queen's Ford; in another, Our Lady of the Light; in a third, Our Lady of the Bridge; and so forth. Each shrine, each saint, protects a particular territory, a "territory of grace," acting as patron to its inhabitants.

Some of the shrines to Mary are located at boundaries of villages or herding districts. In one district, three statues of Mary are found right at the meeting point of three villages' lands, each facing back toward "her own" village. In local stories, the Virgin is said to choose the spot where the shrine is to be built. In one case a shrine was placed at one spot, but during the next night two oxen came and moved the shrine up the hill to the place where she had desired it to be placed. The Virgin keeps the sheep at home, say local herders, and calls down divine power to protect them. William Christian calls the shrines "energy transformation stations."

One of these patron saints is Our Lady of the Queen's Ford, the patron of the village of Tudanca. The shrine is located in a chapel about five kilometers behind Tudanca. The saint's name comes from a nearby ford, but the patron is also identified as Our Lady of the Snows, an aspect of Mary recognized by Rome and given a feast day, August 5. Over the centuries, celebrations of the feast day have waxed and waned, depending both on the level of nearby economic activity and on the attitude of the parish priest toward the shrine. At present, the shrine is visited only by some Tudanca residents; in other decades, however, it has received attention from people of other villages as well. The shrines patronize and protect their own villages, but they may be appealed to by anyone, especially people from neighboring villages.

In the first week of May each year, the image is carried down from the isolated chapel to the parish church in town, where it remains for three months and is the center of church devotions. The period when the image is in the church is also the period of plowing and sowing the fields, and its presence may once have been intended to protect the crops. On the feast of Saint James, July 25, the image is carried in a procession of all the villagers, organized in the following order: children first, then lay men, priests with the image, and women. The villagers thus see themselves as a whole composed of parts. "The villagers for once in the year," writes Christian (1989, 70), "see the village as a social unit, abstracted from the buildings and the location that makes it a geographical unit."

It is the women who continue up the mountain to the shrine and re-place the image in its resting place. A woman keeps the key to the shrine, and when, on the patron's feast day of August 5, a mass is held at the mountain chapel, even the priest has to wait for her to unlock it. In other villages, too, special roles in the devotion to the patron are handed down from mother to daughter. Women are the chief worshipers at the shrines.

These patrons are firmly planted in the rural landscape. Each exists and acts on her own. Some of the names are unique, appearing nowhere else in Spain. Others do appear elsewhere, but then are given additional local tags to emphasize their individuality. A shrine to Our Lady of Carmel, for example (a common name for the Virgin Mary), will become Our Lady of Carmel of Cosio, or of another village. These shrines have existed for a long time; some may pre-date Christianity (when clearly they were known and worshiped by other names).

From the standpoint of these "localized devotions"—worship activities focused on a local manifestation of Mary or a saint—Mary appears as many distinct patrons woven together into a general community of sainthood. The Mary of the Snows is an agent distinct from the Mary of the Bridge, despite the fact that all are manifestations of the one Virgin Mary, Mother of God.

Many in One

Recall a similar feature of worship in India. In south India each local settlement has its own tutelary goddess, known by one name throughout that region. So throughout the state of Tamil Nadu, for instance, one finds Mariyamman of this place versus Mariyamman of that place, as different goddesses and yet also localized forms of the single Goddess (Fuller 1992, 43). This many-in-one is quite similar to that found in northern Spain and elsewhere in the Catholic world. Mary exists in both a highly local and a universal form at the same time in the consciousness of some Catholics, as does Mariyamman (the similarity in names is a coincidence) for Hindus.

The parallel stops at the level below Mary, however, for whereas Hindus have local, lesser deities as well as the major gods, most Catholics have only the major textually sanctioned figures to turn to—Mary, Jesus, and saints. In Catholicism the distance between God and local, reachable spiritual beings is mediated by proliferating the number of forms of Mary, and remaining entirely within a restricted pantheon.

There is an irony in the fact that the adoration of Mary was encouraged by the church as a way of unifying and centralizing devotion, but that Mary became the vehicle for differentiated devotions and representations. Of course, even in the universal language promoted by the church one has different names or "advocations" (different forms of a deity) of Mary, a variety that in part stems from the very images the church used: Mary of the Immaculate Conception, Mary the Pietà, Mary of the Assumption, and so forth. Mary is shown in different contexts, and these images become signs of different attitudes or emotions. But it may also be that relying on replicable images as the basis for Catholicism (or any other widespread religion) itself gives rise to this dual character, the "one Mary or many Marys" problem. Once the image takes on any local roots, it begins to be thought of as the image of a local individual. The very replicability of the image poses a problem: Is it one or many? If one, what are all these other objects? If many, are they different actors?

A Japanese Comparison

Just as Catholics have created "many Marys" to provide nearby, accessible images, so have Japanese men and women turned to deities called "bodhisattvas," or "Buddhas-to-be." These deities, who put off their transition to Buddha status in order to help humans, are nearer to hand when one needs help than are the distant Buddha figures.

Especially important among them is the goddess Kannon, who ensures fertility and safety in childbirth. In India, Kannon was the many-armed god Avalokitesvara, and became (via a gender change) the important Chinese goddess Kuan-Yin, and then the Japanese Kannon. The bodhisattva Kannon is capable of rescuing people from earthquakes, fires, shipwrecks, witchcraft, execution, snakes, and thunderbolts, and of giving a woman the child she wishes, son or daughter. She is sometimes depicted as associated with the waterfall because of her power; her many arms are likened to the many different streams of a fall. She also has lesser spirits called *jizo* who act as guardians of travelers and children. Travelers often set out small statues of jizos on their routes, and especially when they are embarking on a pilgrimage. But one may also set out a jizo as a concrete way to take a request to Kannon. These requests are most commonly either for forgiveness for having had an abortion or for safe delivery of a child.

Kannon is both a single goddess and many personal guardians. She can be depicted as a single protector, or as highly individuated. For example, a shrine to Kannon at Kyoto is supposed to contain "60,000" statues of Kannon, one for every face there is in the world; this way of representing her is supposed to guard all the people of the world.

A debate has arisen in Japan over the practice of buying jizo statues from a temple to atone for an abortion. Setting out the statue is thought by some to help guide the fetus across the river that separates the world of life from the world of death. These statues, called "water child jizos" (Mizuko jizo), are sold by Buddhist temples for several hundred dollars each. More than 2,000 temples now offer these statues, and temple leaflets warn that failure to appease the spirit of a dead fetus could lead to cancer, heart disease, back pain, rebellion of children against parents, and so forth—a list long enough that anyone who fails to buy the statue will surely find herself victim of the fetus's spirit. Is this service a way the temple serves people's needs or, as one magazine called it, a "business of terror"? Some women continue to visit the statues for years or even decades after the abortion, dressing them up against the cold or pouring water over them to quench their thirst (WuDunn 1996).

Generalized Devotions

Let us return to the Nansa valley of northern Spain, where shrines to Mary, each with her own distinct name, proliferate. Priests coming to Nansa have had to work with the shrines already in place, but sometimes they have tried to discourage devotions at the shrine. In most cases, devotions go dormant, reappearing a decade or more later. The priests bring with them devotional emphases of the papacy, and often of a religious order. They try to refocus the devotions of villagers on universal images of Mary and Christ, rather than on her specific manifestations, what one priest called approaching "to the main doors, not the side doors" of the church.

These "generalized devotions," in William Christian's (1989) phrase, are based on the circulation and promotion of images that are highly interchangeable. In homes

Jizo statues set out to atone for an abortion or to ask for safe delivery of a child, at the shrine to Kannon near Kamakura, Japan. *(Courtesy of John Renard)*

and in parish churches, one finds paintings, lithographs, pamphlets, calendars, and rosaries. These images could be substituted easily one for the other, or replaced with a new batch, without any loss of religious significance. The images are usually of Mary as the Madonna, and sometimes of the cross, and they are used in family devotions. They often come from Rome or from the religious orders currently in papal favor, and their propagation and use is intended to underscore the universality of the Church. For example, the Dominican brotherhoods have promoted the devotion to the Holy Rosary at home using personal rosary beads. The brotherhoods teach people that saying prayers with the beads will allow one to share in all the prayers said by all members of the brotherhood throughout the world. Other orders, including Capuchins and Passionists, have provided images of saints or Mary that correspond to their particular religious emphases.

Mary has played her part in efforts to reuniversalize worship, both through her interchangeable pictures in homes, and through her role in regional and national shrines. Many villages in the Nansa valley have been visited on trips to the regional shrine to Mary, which was approved by the Vatican in 1954, on the hundredth anniversary of the papal proclamation of the Immaculate Conception.

Jesus, Mary, and the Nation–State

Of particular importance in changing local worship practices has been the devotion to the Sacred Heart of Jesus, begun in 1673 when a nun in Paris had visions of Jesus Christ in which he urged her to devote herself to his heart as a symbol of his love for humankind. But it was not entered as general feast of the church until 1856, when it quickly became an image, to which popes and rulers tried to rally the faithful. In 1899, Pope Leo XIII consecrated the world to the Sacred Heart of Jesus, and King Alfonso of Spain did the same for Spain in 1919, with the backing of a conservative government. Images of the Sacred Heart entered the Nansa valley about that time as well (Christian 1989, 84–85).

Because of its association with the political right, in the 1930s statues commemorating the Sacred Heart became symbols of the Nationalist forces, the right wing fighting under Franco to topple the government. The national monument to the Sacred Heart was frequently "executed" by the Loyalists, and pictures of the ruined monument were circulated by Franco's side to rally Catholic support.

Elsewhere too, the Sacred Heart of Jesus became a symbol of conservative governments. In late-nineteenth-century France, the relation of a largely Catholic people to a secular state (and largely secular capital city) was a continuing source of tension. In 1871, many Parisians rose up against the Thiers government, in part because of the state's capitulation to Prussian forces. The government, which had fled to Versailles, brutally suppressed the uprising, known as the *Commune,* and regained control of the city. Shortly thereafter, in an attempt to underscore the central place of the church in French life, the government constructed the magnificent church on the hills of Montmartre called Sacre Coeur—Sacred Heart. Although much loved by tourists (and many Parisians), the association between the building and the suppression lives on in the minds of many on the left. (I happened to be living in Paris in 1971, the year of the Commune's centennial, and I witnessed Sacre Coeur being pelted with tomatoes and stones.)

At the same time, images of Mary surface as symbols of national resistance. In communist Poland, the national shrine of Polish Catholicism dedicated to Our Lady of Czestochowa has for centuries been associated with national resistance against foreign conquerors. The Polish Primate under communist rule, Cardinal Wysynski, mobilized the nation around the shrine image, beginning with the rededication of the nation to this "Queen of Poland" in 1956, and following with hugely successful annual pilgrimages of the shrine to every single town in Poland.

The state's use of religious imagery underscores the changes in how the Church represents itself. In the ninth century, a person was sworn in on relics as the clear chain of direct contact to local sources of sacrality. By the late nineteenth century, the state was staking its claim to loyalty on images of and devotions to Mary or, in particular, to Christ. Christ seems more immune to the differentiation process that has made Mary many. Indeed, the role of Mary in Catholicism as an emblem for emphasizing local identity goes far beyond Spain, as we shall see.

Conclusions

We have traced the changing religious and political roles of saints, Christ, and Mary in Europe from the beginning to now. On the one hand we have the idea of the unchanging and centralized message of the Catholic Church and on the other the changing em- phases in worship and images, and conflicts between the hierarchy and local worshipers. In the next chapter, we extend the analysis to the transatlantic world, linking both Europe and Africa to the Americas.

Discussion Questions

In North America and Europe, we often discuss religion as a matter of individual choice, but for most of Catholic history (and in different ways for other religions) priests have seen obedience as an obligation. Moreover, most churchgoing parents have not left the choice of religion up to their children, but taught them so that they will follow the same faith. To what degree can and should ideas of choice play a key role in religious lives, vis-à-vis ideas of obedience and discipline? How do you see this issue in your own religious traditions; what are the moments of choice and what are the moments where choice is not available? Recall the critique by Talal Asad of Clifford Geertz's approach to religion, discussed in Chapter 2. How would each approach produce differing analyses of Catholic images and ritual?

Media Resources

There are treatments of Catholic pilgrimages, not discussed here, that could be presented in counterpart to those in Islam and Hinduism discussed earlier. In Poland, the image of Mary called "Our Lady of Czestochowa" is a national shrine, and associated with St. Luke; a brief video clip on the shrine can be seen at: http://www.youtube.com/watch?v=J1PYwQjnxpc. For Lourdes, a short clip follows English pilgrims at: http://www.youtube.com/watch?v=OVZ49YitUwc.

For Medjugorje, a video attesting to one woman's apparitions is at: http://www.youtube.com/watch?v=Fbhhqs3uuTU. If usually play the first minute or so.

Transatlantic Religion

Although we often speak of "globalization" as a late-twentieth-century process, in fact people have been moving across long distances for centuries, carrying new ideas with them—as we saw when we discussed the Axial Age.

The history of religious innovation across the Atlantic is an important case of these often neglected trans-state socio-religious networks. Catholics in Mesoamerica appropriated the symbols of the Church into their own cultural frameworks and political struggles. Africans forcibly brought to the Americas as slaves developed new images and religious practices based on West African religions, but in the guise of Catholicism. But these peoples in turn shaped later developments of religions in Europe and Africa, just as Africans today are reshaping older churches in Europe. By looking at these phenomena as elements in a field of "transatlantic religion," we can see that religions cannot be studied only within the nation-state context.

MARY IN MESOAMERICA

The nurturing and tragic image of Mary has served as a particularly powerful figure in translating Catholicism into other cultures. Not only are there universal resonances with her story, but one also finds very specifically similar stories about a sacred and virgin birth or an assumption to heaven in other cultures.

The story of Mary in the Americas exemplifies the logic of religious syncretism, or the blending of two or more traditions. Syncretism occurs when people adopt a new religion but attempt to make it fit with older ideas and practices. The process usually involves changes in both or all of the traditions. As we saw in Chapter 3, Japanese religious history is virtually defined by syncretism, as Japanese have combined elements from Chinese Confucian political ideology, Buddhist teachings and practices, Christian ceremonies, and the older practices called Shinto. As we have seen in Chapter 8, places already sacred before Christianity became the sites of shrines to Mary. When this happened, the meanings of these sacred places changed, because now they no longer were simply local sacred spots but places that tied local worship to the broader Catholic religious tradition. In the Spanish case, for example, images of Mary in the shrines were carried to the common parish church for feast-day worship. But the meaning of Mary was also changed, in that she became locally specific and concerned with rendering assistance in local affairs, and not just a remote semi-deity. (More examples of these changes in the meaning of Mary are offered later.)

The Virgin of Guadalupe

In Mesoamerica, today's Mexico and Guatemala, the Mary of Guadalupe has served as a symbol of nation and people, sometimes in opposition to foreign rule. During Spanish conquest and rule, beginning in the mid-sixteenth century, native Mayan people of eastern Mesoamerica organized rebellions. These rebellions soon incorporated the symbols of Catholicism, reworked in Indian terms. The insurgent movements often included figures anointed as Christ or king. In some cases, villagers were visited by the Virgin Mary, who then instructed them to start a new church organization. She would leave proof of her visit in the form of an image that she created either on cloth or as a statue (Lafaye 1976; Wolf 1958).

In the two most influential cases, both from the sixteenth century, the Virgin revealed her image to a peasant (in both cases he was named Juan Diego). The first apparition, in which Mary left her figure on a cloak, took place in 1531 in Tepeyac near Mexico City and became known as the Virgin of Guadalupe; the second, known as the Virgin of Ocotlan, occurred about 10 years later in Tlaxcala state, when Mary imprinted herself on an *ocote* tree.

The Virgin of Guadalupe was to become the master symbol of Mexico. The Mexican War of Independence was fought under her banner, and her shrine at Tepeyac became the major Mexican shrine. In the official story of the events, the Virgin addressed a Christianized Indian, Juan Diego, 10 years after the Spanish conquest of the area. The Virgin commanded him to go to the archbishop of Mexico and tell him that she wished a church built in her honor on Tepeyac Hill. Juan Diego tried twice to win the archbishop's approval, but was unsuccessful. Mary then performed a miracle. She told Juan Diego to gather roses in a dry spot where roses never grew, and then to present them to the archbishop. He did so, but when, standing before the archbishop, he unfolded his cloak, there appeared from inside, not roses, but the image of the Virgin miraculously imprinted on the cloak. The bishop immediately acknowledged the miracle, so the story goes, and ordered a shrine built on the spot where she had appeared.

This particular spot was not, however, a random choice. It had once been the site of a temple to the goddess of fertility Tonantzin. Tonantzin, Our Lady Mother, is associated with the moon, as is Guadalupe's image. Indeed, for at least the next 50 years worshipers called her Tonantzin as well as Guadalupe, and this still is the case in parts of Mexico. Stories about Tonantzin continue to be told in Mexico: In one, she intervened when God wanted to punish his children, by challenging him to try to produce milk so that she could nourish her children.

These associations or "syncretism" are not unique to the New World, of course. In Spain, there probably were pre-Christian deities where now there are shrines. In Ireland, statues of the Virgin are often erected in spots formerly considered sacred because of an unusually shaped rock formation or a sacred grove. And in the Church of

Saint Germain in Paris, a black image of the Egyptian goddess Isis was displayed as the Madonna until 1514.

Guadalupe and Mexican Resistance to Spain

In later centuries, rebellions against Spanish control frequently formed around cults of the Virgin Mary. In 1721 in Cancuc (Chiapas), the Virgin appeared to a young girl and asked her to place a cross in her hamlet, build a chapel around it, and offer incense. A local Mayan leader then claimed to have ascended to heaven where he spoke with the Virgin Mary, Jesus Christ, and St. Peter, and was told that the people were to appoint their own officials and no longer needed the Spanish. This man, Sebastian Gomez, then appointed bishops and priests, all using the symbols of the Catholic Church.

Devotions in the local church had already become "localized" in the sense in which we used the word earlier: Worship focused on locally specific images of the Virgin that were understood as protecting the village. Services consisted of giving offerings and prayers to these advocations of Mary and to other localized saints, rather than addressing prayers to God. Gomez and his followers now renamed Cancuc "Jerusalem" and referred to the Spaniards as "the Jews who persecuted the Virgin Mary." Although the movement was suppressed, it illustrates the ways in which local opposition to Spanish rule was elaborated in what were once the conqueror's own images, the sacred images of Catholicism itself. By choosing Mary and the saints as key images, those local movements that did not reach the stage of open rebellion managed to insulate themselves (and popular religious practice generally) against charges of heresy. The Spanish Inquisition investigated these religious movements and looked for evidence of idolatry, in particular prayers said to images that asked them to directly heal illnesses. The Indians whom the inquisitors interrogated denied that they acted in this way, claiming that they merely appealed to the patron saints and to the Virgin Mary for help. Because the Spanish Church accepted as legitimate both the cult of the patron saint and the possibility of visitations by the Virgin, the inquisitors were unable to find solid ground to prosecute Indian religious leaders (Lafaye 1976).

Why was it the Virgin Mary (and not Christ) who became Mexico's national symbol? The answer is in part due to the way the Church itself portrays Mary and Christ, and perhaps in part due to local family dynamics. The Virgin is associated with struggle and life in Mexico, while Christ is associated with defeat and death. On the religious plane, these distinct associations stem from the crucifixion of Christ, on the one hand, and the nurturing role of the Virgin, on the other. The anthropologist Eric Wolf (1958) argues that on the family plane, the associations grow out of the distinct sentiments the child forms toward his or her mother and father, in both Indian and Mexican families. The child experiences a paradise of closeness to his or her mother, and sides with the mother in her struggle against domination by the father. Mary thus brings out a wealth of early pleasant memories; Christ, the object of struggle. Sentiments formed in the family are expressed in the culture through the symbols of the Virgin and Christ.

On the plane of politics, the Virgin Mary, in the specific form of the Virgin of Guadalupe, is associated with the struggle against Spanish military and religious colonization. Many Mexicans interpreted Guadalupe as the goddess Tonantzin who has returned to liberate Mexico. This interpretation follows an indigenous logic of cyclical history, in which gods depart only to return later. Mexico appears as a new paradise, to which came the Virgin to herald independence. In a seventeenth-century text, the Virgin of Guadalupe is linked to the woman portrayed in the Revelation of John, "arrayed with the sun, and the moon under her feet, and upon her head a crown of twelve stars," and who is to realize the prophecies of Deuteronomy. Not coincidentally, the image of the Virgin of Guadalupe in the shrine today is adorned with a sun and moon and the 12 stars.

The Virgin of Guadalupe thus links family (mother), politics (liberation), and religion (salvation). Against the background of these linkages, we can understand how it was that in 1810 the patriot Father Miguel Hidalgo y Castilla began the revolution for Independence with the cry: "Long Live the Virgin of Guadalupe and down with bad government." The political and religious associations have continued in full force into this century. In the early twentieth century, the church, trying to render more uniform the devotions of the faithful, attempted to replace the Virgin of Guadalupe with the Sacred Heart of Jesus from Rome. This attempt was perceived in Mexico as an effort to supplant a Mexican figure with a European one, and it was strongly, and successfully, resisted. And in 1996, the Bishop of Guadalupe, speaking to a reporter in Italy, declared that he considered the peasant Juan Diego to have been a mythical figure (*St. Louis Post-Dispatch,* September 7, 1996). The remark led to his immediate removal from office!

AFRICA AND BRAZIL ACROSS THE ATLANTIC

The example of Guadalupe and Tonantzin suggests that religious imagery can be effective in translating a new religion into an older cultural and religious context: Mary made sense to Mayans who already venerated Tonantzin. Sometimes this process involves a literal translation across deities. Such is the case for religions found in the Americas but derived from West African religions. In Brazil, Cuba, Haiti, and elsewhere, Catholic deities provided useful cover for slaves who wished to continue to practice their own religions, but had been forbidden to do so. As this need for subterfuge decreased, Americans have been free to explore both the African roots of the traditions and the appeal these traditions have to a wide range of Americans, including those of European descent. Known now by the names *Umbanda, Candomblé, Santeria,* and *Voudun,* these Afro-American traditions have formed a distinct religious stream alongside, though at times intermingling with, Catholicism (Murphy 1994).

Yoruba religious ideas and practices, in particular, shaped the development of Candomblé religion in Brazil, with its center at Salvador de Bahia, but Yoruba religion itself was shaped by people returning from Brazil (Matory 2005). The case of the Black Atlantic shows us that even as African images and ideas became the basis for New World religious creation, there also emerged a transatlantic network of men and women who shaped developments on both continents.

The slave trade brought large numbers of African people to the southern and central portions of the Americas as well as to the colonies in North America. Slavery lasted longer in the southern regions; until 1888 in Brazil. Many of the Africans were taken from what is today Nigeria and Bénin. In particular, Yoruba people were brought to Brazil and Cuba, and Fon people were brought to Haiti. Slave traders and slave owners tried to wipe out cultural traditions and mixed slaves from different regions, as an effort to prevent Africans from organizing rebellions (Walker 1990).

Because slave-owners prohibited the practice of African religions, some Africans translated ideas and deities of West African religions into the images and language of Catholicism. Slavers thought that they were imposing Catholicism; Africans understood that they were preserving older traditions. In Brazil, these traditions today are called Umbanda and Macumba in Rio de Janeiro and Candomblé in the northeast region of Bahia. They combine, in different proportions, African qualities, especially in Bahia, and Brazilian innovations, especially in Rio, with Catholic imagery and ideas from a Euro-Brazilian movement called Spiritism.

In Rio, a woman presides over services in a small storefront center called the Spiritist Tent of Granny Maria Antonia of the Congo, one of many places to which people come to worship and seek help from the spirits (Guillermoprieto 1990). In this center, as in many others, there is a particular "patron" spirit, Granny Maria Antonia. She is understood to be a woman who was born in Africa and was brought as a slave to Brazil, where she died. She is of a recognizable type of Afro-Brazilian spirit, the "Old Black Woman." Also exhibited at the center are statues of Christian figures: the Virgin Mary, Jesus, St. George (of dragon-slaying fame), and others. Each resembles corresponding statues in, say, European Catholic churches. But each also corresponds to an Umbanda deity called an Orisha, and can be traced back to its original in Yoruba society, West Africa. Today people freely offer the Orisha as well as the Catholic name for each image; a century ago any but the Catholic identity would have been strongly denied to outsiders.

In this schema of cross-religious translation, God is Olorun, the creator of the world. The image of Jesus is also identified as Oshala, the creator of human life. Saint George, depicted slaying a dragon, corresponds to Oshossi, the hunter god, and St. Lazarus, protector of lepers, to Omolu, a deity governing disease. Mary is identified with Yemanja, the mother of some of the other Orishas. Furthermore, and here note the parallel with our Spanish valley, other Orishas who are mothers are also identified as manifestations of Mary. These maternal deities are associated with the water and sea as well.

The lifting of the veil surrounding this momentous project of religious translation was not followed by the crafting of new, original statues. In Yoruba and Umbanda thought, the Orishas have no concrete form; they are forces and principles rather than personages. Thus, the process of rendering African deities in Catholic form added a new visual and individuating dimension to worship, and the Catholic images remain as foci for Umbanda worship. The identification extends to ritual occasions as well. People observe the Catholic feast days that apply to their "translated" deities, but do so in a way that corresponds to the Afro-Brazilian meaning of the deity. For example, Yemanja (Mary) is identified with the sea, so people flock to the sea on the Catholic feast days for Mary and once there, they offer gifts to Yemanja, wading out into the water and letting the sea carry them away.

Umbanda and Candomblé in fact bring together three religious traditions. Alongside of Catholic and Yoruba religions is the doctrine of Spiritism or Kardecism, popular among the elite in Europe and Brazil in the late nineteenth century and today adhered to by millions in Brazil, either as part of Umbanda and Candomblé or on its own. Spiritism provides a means of healing people from physical and mental afflictions. The doctrine attributes a wide range of events in the material world to the desires and actions of spirits. Sometimes spirits possess people, and when they do, they can cause the person to suffer illness. Specialists can communicate directly with these spirits, ask what their wishes are, and restore the person to health.

Afro-Brazilian Trances

In Brazil today, healers draw on these Afro-Brazilian religion traditions to carry out their art. In Macumba sessions (Richeport 1985), trance is employed in varied settings to aid in healing. In sessions involving "professional mediums," specialists sit in a separate, cordoned-off part of a room. They are dressed in white and are already in a trance. They each have special "spirit familiars" with whom they communicate. Patients deliver to the staff slips of paper containing their questions; usually the questions are about their own illnesses. The mediums then ask for answers from their spirit familiars and relay these answers back through the staff. These sessions are calm, although sometimes a supplicant will slip into trance, and in such cases he or she may be approached about becoming a medium. A second type of session involves mass trances. Dozens or hundreds of people gather together for evenings of trance, dancing and music, and consultation. These large-scale sessions also employ mediums, but they walk and dance around on the floor, mingling with other people who wish to attend. Rather than having personal spirit familiars, all the mediums cycle together through several standard spirit types during the evening. Each type represents both a familiar cultural figure of the Brazilian environment and a kind of emotion. When the mediums are possessed by the "old black slave" spirit, they sit, smoking pipes, and dispense this old man's wisdom to those attending (who are often relatives or friends). When they take on the flashily dressed woman called *Pomba Gira*, they are seductive and loose, enjoying this break from normal behavioral restrictions. When they are a child, they scamper about eating candy. (There is also an Amazonian equivalent of these sessions, in which Indians act the role of whites, drink champagne, and act terribly refined.) Use is also made of trances at clinics for the mentally ill. Patients are encouraged to enter a trance state and act out their emotions and frustrations; often they, too, take on stereotyped roles such as those mentioned previously.

Umbanda in Rio

Umbanda was in fact born as a revolt against the elitism of Spiritism in Rio (Brown 1986). By the 1920s, Spiritism had become a highly intellectualized and European-oriented set of practices. Lighter-skinned Brazilians (Brazilian color coding of individuals contains many categories, from very dark to very light, rather than a simple black/white dichotomy) controlled the séances. They were speaking with the likes of Voltaire and Plato. If an Indian spirit appeared, possessing one of their own, they would refuse to allow him to speak.

In 1920, a middle-class Rio man, Zelio de Moraes, suffered an illness that left him partially paralyzed. His father, a real estate agent, was a Spiritist and took him to his group for healing. There he was visited by the spirit of a Jesuit priest, who revealed that the illness was spiritual, and that he had a mission, which was to found a truly Brazilian religion that would be dedicated to the worship and propitiation of Brazilian spirits. These spirits included *caboclos*, spirits of Brazilian Indians, and *pretos velhos*, spirits of Africans enslaved in Brazil.

Zelio received additional messages from other spirits. The "Indian of the Seven Crossroads" told him the new religion would be called Umbanda. Zelio then did as he was told, and founded the first Umbanda center, today called the "Mother House." This center, the Spirits' Center of Our Lady of Piety, attracted a largely white and middle-class clientele. But the spirits that spoke through the participants were those of Indians and Africans, giving them the voice denied them by the Spiritists. The movement grew rapidly, attracting a diverse range of participants.

The social and political role of these movements has changed dramatically in this century. At first tolerated, it was repressed as heretical in the 1930–1950s by the Catholic Church, with support from the Brazilian state. State repressions began to loosen in the 1960s, and since 1970 people have enjoyed relative freedom to worship openly. The initial reason for this tolerance was political, as politicians seeking office sought support from the large communities of Umbanda-Candomblé followers. But the change has also been motivated by social and cultural changes (Walker 1990). In the past 30 years, many Brazilians have sought their "roots," and some, including many of lighter skin color, have found them in the links back to Africa. Many of these people, mostly of the middle class, have found these links through the experience of possession by an African spirit. In doing so, they have moved away from the Catholicism that once was virtually required of those seeking high social status. Being known as follower of Umbanda or Candomblé is no handicap to political office, and participation in the movements can be combined with a range of political and social doctrines. The Brazilian Secretary of Public Works in the 1980s, for example, called himself a "Marxist-Spiritist," believing in both reincarnation and Marxist-Leninism.

These movements have also become part of a broader popular culture in Brazil. On New Year's Day, the major newspapers in Rio run the Umbanda seers' forecasts for the next year. In Bahia state, the home of Candomblé, pop singing groups have risen to the top of the charts with songs based in Candomblé; new wave filmmakers have drawn on the Orishas for their subjects, as in the popular film *The Amulet of Ogun*. The Orisha named Esu, who controls roads and pathways, was adopted as the patron deity of all communications facilities, and a statue to him stands in front of the post office in Salvador, Bahia's capital (Murphy 1994). The urban poor are drawn to these movements. Many of Rio's poor people live in squatter settlements called *favelas*. For them, "survival calls for imaginative solutions, and Umbanda is nothing if not the triumph of imaginative thought," writes the reporter Alma Guillermoprieto (1990).

Let us return to the Granny Maria Antonia center mentioned earlier. The center is located in a two-story house located in a lower middle-class neighborhood in central Rio. A black woman named Stella Soares runs the center. Stella, a former nurse, insists that all who attend don white uniforms; this measure makes everyone more nearly equal, she says. Certain specific spirits visit the center and possess those who attend its services. They are the spirits of individual Indian and African people rather than Orishas. They include the Indian of the Seven Crossroads, the Indian of the Coral Cobra, and the "Indian who tears up tree stumps with his bare hands." They speak, they embody the local identity of black and Indian Brazilians, and through the experience of being possessed, the worshipers can experience several identities, several sides of themselves. Her clientele includes not only dozens of mainly white, middle-class initiates, who go into trance, but also many very poor black clients. "Once they have changed into their white clothes," she says, "you cannot tell the difference."

Are these religions part of Catholicism? Catholic priests call on people to abandon Umbanda, claiming that it has nothing to do with Catholicism, and some practitioners (probably an increasing number) consider themselves to be followers of Umbanda and not, or no longer, Catholics. But many other Umbanda followers claim status as Catholics. They point to a number of close relationships between Umbanda practices and Catholicism. The images in worship are all Catholic. Some Candomblé priests require initiates to be baptized Catholics before they can join in the rituals. The story of how the first center was founded also underscores the connection with Catholicism—it was, after all, the spirit of a Jesuit priest who commanded Zelio to open up his center. Catholic feast days are observed, and many Umbanda practices reinforce the link to the Catholic Church. For example, on August 16, the feast day for Saint Lazarus, Umbanda priestesses drive by churches where the mass is held and sprinkle popcorn on all so that they will receive benefits from Omolu, the deity associated with the saint.

As we saw earlier, Catholic images, and especially the image of the Virgin Mary, have served to mediate translations of religion across vast social and cultural divides, first within Europe, and then out across seas with the expansion of the Church. But the very capacity of the image to carry multiple meanings—what we have called the multivocality of the image—has allowed subordinate groups to contest the dominant meanings. Spanish villagers insist on their own Mary's capacity to protect and nurture; Mexicans, of the Virgin of Guadalupe's role as a national symbol; Brazilians, of Yemanja/Mary's powers over the sea; Christians throughout the world, on Mary's willingness to appear to them and to deliver messages of hope and struggle. Each set of claims to Mary is asserted over and against official counterclaims that underscore the unity of Mary and Christ and the single authoritative voice of Rome.

In this example, transnational Catholicism appears not as a single set of ideas and practices, but as a set of contested images, and, in the case of Afro-Brazilian religions, as part of a contested legacy of religious survival and creativity.

The Black Atlantic

But in the nineteenth and twentieth centuries, Brazilian-born men and women traveled to West Africa and helped shape the development of religious practices in Nigeria (Matory 2005, 46–72). Following uprisings in Brazil in the mid-nineteenth century, thousands of people were able to return to West Africa, and most of them gravitated to the now bustling seaport of Lagos. The British encouraged the immigration of these and other people into West Africa, and there they began to build up a new sense of Yoruba identity. The cultural nationalism that developed in Yorubaland at that time included a sense of the superiority of Yoruba religions, and this sense was then carried over to Brazil in the late nineteenth century. Thus, what some had thought to be "survivals" of West African ideas in Brazil in fact were brought to Brazil as part of a continual traffic across the Atlantic by African Brazilian men and women.

The Brazilians developed a notion of religious purity that was absent from the Yoruba side of the Atlantic. Matory (2005) chronicles how by the 1930s traders working the route between Lagos and Bahia were nourishing a Brazilian appreciation for "pure African" goods (good for trade) and religion (good for prestige, and thus for trade). Afro-Brazilians began to "purify" Candomblé of what they saw as accretions from Catholic or other influences. In particular, the head of a Bahia Candomblé temple, Mãe

Aninha, was able to successfully claim that her knowledge of African practices made her version of Candomblé more pure and authentic. She was able to jump to the top of the Bahia hierarchy through these claims. (A second wave of "purification" of religion came in the 1980s when Nigerian religious experts visited Bahia.)

Because of this new concern with purity, Candomblé incorporated into its central practices a concern with ritual cleansing that is not central to Yoruba practices. Contemporary Yoruba practices emphasize maintaining health through restoring the balance of elements within the body. Candomblé healing, by contrast, emphasizes expelling polluting elements from the body (Matory 2005, 128–133). The deity Esu may have been adopted as the patron saint of communications, given his position at crossroads and thresholds, as mentioned above, and he is the guardian of the centers, but because of his liminal position he is also responsible for introducing disorder, and can be bribed into bringing disease and misfortune. Cleansing an afflicted person of these misfortunes requires using products thought of as "pure African" such as kola nuts. Thus, the transatlantic production of notions of African purity has reshaped the practice of healing.

The same logic has been at the heart of ideas that link Brazilian identity to Africa. Celebration of the African roots of Candomblé was a way for Brazilian cultural leaders to oppose the dominance of the United States. And beginning in the 1980s, increased, and often state-financed, trips by Brazilian Candomblé priests to Nigeria and reciprocal visits by Nigerian priests have led to a movement to recognize the independence of Candomblé from Catholicism and its place in a transatlantic network and history of religions. As Matory (2005, 152–181) shows, these transatlantic affiliations by no means diminish attachments to nations and to territories. Brazilian nationalism increasingly is based on transatlantic memories and connections. Conversely, the houses (or "nations") of Candomblé are rooted in specific parcels of land in Brazil.

Indeed, Matory's (2005, 177) affirmation that "diaspora is therefore better described as a *pluralization* of territorial identities than as an abandonment of them" serves well in examining other transnational projects as well. In Chapter 13, I focus on Muslims in Europe, where far from developing a deterritorialized or new sort of transnational citizenship, one sees men and women developing citizenship projects in two or more countries.

BLACK CARIB RELIGION IN HONDURAS AND NEW YORK CITY

Now let us follow another story of movement, diaspora, and transformation of African religions across the Atlantic, this time centered in the Caribbean, on the Antillean island of St. Vincent (Johnson 2007). This story concerns the people now known as Garifuna, historically as Black Caribs. During the 1500s and 1600s, Africans arrived by many means on this island: some surviving shipwrecks, others fleeing slavery elsewhere in Caribbean. St. Vincent had native peoples on it already, and these "Yellow Caribs," as they were called in Western accounts, fought with and to some extent mixed with the newcomers, the "Black Caribs." The latter developed lucrative tobacco and sugar trade with French and British settlements elsewhere and resisted enslavement and colonization from either power. They fought with British forces for control over the lucrative plantation lands, but by 1800 had been defeated and deported to an island off

Honduras. Spreading along the coast, they lived alongside native groups and settlements of Africans who had arrived by way of other Caribbean islands. During the first part of the twentieth century, the expanding banana economy provided work for many Garifuna, but by the 1960s, with the decline of banana production and the opening up of immigration to the United States, tens of thousands of Garifuna left the Honduras, many migrating to New York City.

Garifuna in Honduras and in New York engage in religious practices that draw in varying mixtures from Africa and the Caribbean. In Honduras, ritual focuses on fulfilling obligations to deceased members of the community. Shamans (*buyei*) lead people through a hierarchy of such rituals, starting with a burial ritual, and followed by a mass a year later (but only if the ancestral spirit requests it), the more elaborate *chugu* later on, and, only if required, a large ritual called the *dügü*, which even far-away relatives must attend. Shamans engage in divination to determine whether any or all of these higher-level rituals need to be carried out. As more and more Garifuna emigrate to the United States, *dügü*s are held more and more often, probably because they provide the best way to bring the dispersed family together.

As the ethnographer Paul Johnson (2007) points out, the Garifuna think of themselves as located in a diaspora—but with "diasporic horizons" depending on where they live. Honduran Garifuna think of St. Vincent as their origin point, and this perspective orients toward a shared sense of being Caribbean people, with much in common with other native American peoples and a memory of their struggles against the British. The thousands of Garifuna living in New York think about Honduras but they think even more about Africa as their homeland, and they find more in common with others who see themselves as of African origin.

Honduran shamans draw on a range of saint and spirit figures that resemble those we discussed for Brazil. Against the malevolent spirits they seek the aid of Catholic saints, including the Virgin Mary. But the local spirits are never thought of as coming from Africa; they are more likely to come from St. Vincent. The shamans feature figures of ships on their altars, and rest on hammocks during the major rituals—both ships and hammocks bring to mind the peaceful conditions once enjoyed on St. Vincent, by contrast to the sufferings of the deportation. Africa is absent from this repertoire of symbols. Shamans diagnose lingering illness that does not respond to other treatments as indicative of possession by ancestors, and curable only by holding a large-scale ritual, usually a dügü.

New York shamans have developed their craft in a different direction: as one member of a family of Caribbean religions that include Candomblé, Santeria, Voudun, and Cuban Palo Monte. Shamans have fit into a new semiotic niche, one in which Afro-Caribbean spirits rule the roost. Some of the Cuban or Brazilian spirits are very useful. As one Garifuna shaman in New York told Johnson (2007, 129): "The Garifuna ancestors, they're family, but they can be slow; the muertos [of Cuban Palo Monte], you have to watch out, because they eat *everything*, but they work fast." The New York shaman sees his "family" as one part of a much larger clan, all members of which are available to help out. This makes these men and women conscious of a shared African identity, which links them to others who have arrived in the United States by way of Brazil, Cuba, or Haiti. Indeed, some may become initiated into one or more of the other Afro-Caribbean traditions, and always have one or more helper spirits from Africa: Kongo, or Yoruba, or even African American spirits.

These identifications take Garifuna in two directions. First, they borrow particularly from the Santería set of Afro-Caribbean ritual practices associated with Cuba. But they learn these practices mainly from Puerto Rican practitioners of Santería, mainly because there are many more Puerto Ricans living in New York City than there are other Caribbean peoples. So, much of what the Garifuna learn about African deities and rituals comes by way of Cuba, and then by way of New York Puerto Ricans!

Second, Garifuna have become black; that is, they identify with others of African descent as well as being labeled as "black" by white Americans. African identity movements in the United States have highlighted Yoruba religious traditions and in particular their deities, or Orishas. The Orishas figure in most Garifuna shamans' altars as they do in those of Cuban and Puerto Rican shamans working in New York. Now, all this might simply mean that these groups identify with the Yoruba, or with western African societies more generally, not that they identify themselves by a racial term such as "black." And yet it is very difficult for dark-skinned immigrants to the United States to avoid being classified as "black" by whites: Race works as the overarching way of categorizing other peoples. Sometimes Garifuna will foreground other horizons of their identities, as when they joined 1992 protests against celebrating Columbus's arrival, and did so as Amerindians, or when they joined electoral coalitions in New York City politics as Hispanics. But on a religious plan, shamans assert their specifically Garifuna identity by highlighting their African ties, not those of Amerindian or Hispanic heritage. What the shamans emphasize is the African diaspora that joins them to Haitians, Puerto Ricans, and Cubans, but this emphasis then leads them to self-identify as black, not as Hispanic or Amerindian (or Honduran). In other words, a religious means to emphasize distinction highlights African ties, which in the race-over-all American identity framework means that they are black.

Conclusions

In this chapter, we concentrated on one transnational space and some of the religious movements and practices found therein. The Atlantic turns out to be a pretty complex space: for the Garifuna living in New York, the relevant horizons for thinking through religion and healing are a changing diasporic network involving Africa and the several major sources of religion in the Caribbean. For many Brazilians, those horizons include native peoples, Africans, and Europeans. For many Mexican Catholics, they include both Mexican history and global Catholic networks and institutions

Discussion Questions

Can you think of other transnational spaces constituted by a religious diaspora? How are they like or unlike the one discussed here? How do ties change between counties of origin and counties of settlement: Consider people who have ties to India, Israel, Somalia, and Italy and live in the United States. Break into groups and discuss each case, looking at reasons for emigration, activities in the United States, and continuing ties to the country of reference or origin.

Media Resources

The forthcoming film on the Virgin of Guadalupe by Joe Eszterhas promises to be controversial; in the meantime there is Santiago Parra's *Guadalupe*. A, somewhat melodramatic dramatization of the story is at: http://www.youtube.com/watch?v=cs80bzYGol8. A two-minute clip (low-quality) on visitors to the shrine in Mexico City is at: http://www.youtube.com/watch?v=fKEGdZo9kaw.

Several films chronicle the healing associated with Afro-Brazilian religions; I have used *Macumba: Trance and Spirit Healing*. The film *Legacy of the Spirits* traces religion and healing from Africa to Haiti to New York, and would complement well the study of the Garifuna in this chapter. There are shorter resources, such as the radio report with images available at: http://www.youtube.com/watch?v=CD1ywfmy_ew.

For those who read Paul Christopher Johnson's book, cited in the text, clips of Garifuna dances in the Honduras are easily found, such as at: http://www.youtube.com/watch?v=V5xOup3YaGo&feature=results_main&playnext=1&list=PL852435782CC9DD3E.

Boundaries and Selves in Orthodox Judaism

Many religions stipulate not just things people should do, such as sacrificing and worshipping, but also things they should not do: eating certain foods, wearing certain clothes, coming into contact with people of other religions or of lower status, and so forth. Prohibitions or "taboos" are some of the most striking features of religions, in part because they distinguish, and often socially separate, people of different religions. They most strikingly bring religious affiliation into everyday social life, shaping social interactions.

TABOOS AND COMMUNITY IN JUDAISM

All religious rules involve a degree of conformity; they lead practitioners to behave in certain ways that mark them off from other people. In his definition of religion, the sociologist Emile Durkheim argued that rules prohibiting to you certain objects or actions—in short, taboos—serve to define the community of practitioners:

> A religion is a unified system of beliefs and practices relative to sacred things, that is to say, things set apart and forbidden—beliefs and practices which unite into one single moral community called a Church, all those who adhere to them. (Durkheim 1995, 44).

Durkheim is saying two things: that there is a moral community of adherents, and that their focus or center is a set of things that are classified as sacred (as opposed to profane), as outside of normal society and as forbidden, dangerous, powerful. Durkheim found this association between tabooed objects and religious community in many societies. He thought that he saw it most clearly in the use of totems, sacred objects, to define social groups in Australia and native North America. The group shares a totem—a kangaroo, or a sacred place, or a dream—that enhances their sense of being alike, and being different from others. This turn-of-the-century fascination with totem and taboo led some writers to theorize about the origins of religion, including Sigmund Freud in his speculative book *Totem and Taboo*. Although these analysts went far beyond the evidence, they were right in pointing to the powerfully society-shaping role played by taboos and other laws regulating the behavior of members of a religious community.

Taboos are preeminently about keeping distinct and apart people and things deemed to be importantly different: men and women, impure people (menstruating women, unclean men) and pure people, high and low status people, meat and milk products, and so on. These rules are sometimes just about keeping one's distance, but they also often involve rules about eating. Rules about food—what to eat, when to eat it, with whom to eat it—as well as beliefs about food's special powers seem to be important in many religions. Indeed, it appears that just about everywhere in the world, rules about what you may eat (particularly, whether you may eat animals or not, and, if so, which ones) are of great social and moral importance. So are rules about how you eat: with whom, using what hands or implements, at what times of the day, with foods arranged in what order of consumption, and so on.

In the several religions of Middle Eastern origin (Judaism, Christianity, Islam), meals serve as key symbols of religious affiliation and as practical rituals through which religious acts are carried out. Consider the Passover seder, for which one must rid the household of all leaven; the Islamic month of fasting, followed by a great feast; the strict adherence to dietary rules by many Muslims and Jews; and the importance of the Last Supper as a central image in Christian traditions. (The Eucharist, celebration of Christ's sacrifice through the transformation of bread and wine into his body and blood—or symbols of them—is the single most disputed ritual of this tradition.)

Elsewhere in the world, food and eating appear as ritually and religiously very important. In rites of passage, for instance, people are often denied those highly valued foods that would identify them as full members of the society. Or individuals may deny food to themselves as a means of seeking a higher level of religious experience. Eating together is a primary means of achieving peace everywhere. But eating together, or even receiving food, is completely impossible between members of certain castes in India, where, according to beliefs about caste and gifts, food is seen as a primary carrier of pollution. In many New Guinea societies, competitive feasting is an important way of creating, validating, or changing relationships between groups; people "fight with food," seeking to outdo each other in the ability to host a feast.

Eating is, of course, also a central element in secular culture. We tend to emphasize the right of people to eat what they want and where they wish, but consider the popularity of books on "eating to win," where steak means power, fish means wimpiness, and so forth, or how in the 1960s the refusal of lunch-counter owners in parts of the U.S. South to serve black people became a key symbol of the civil rights struggle.

Rules about food may be especially characteristic of those religions that have spread out over wide areas of the world—in particular, Judaism, Christianity, Islam, Hinduism, and Buddhism—because of the concern for defining the boundaries of the religious community that accompanies this spread. Wearing special clothing is another such boundary marker, as we shall see later in this chapter. Food taboos are a way of maintaining a degree of uniformity in practice as a religious community moves out from a center, and disperses among those of other religions. If this is so, we would expect to find the development of such taboos occurring at historical moments of dispersion or expansion, and by and large we do, and in this chapter we shall examine the case of Judaism more carefully.

For some religious communities, food taboos primarily mark the boundaries between adherents to the religion and everyone else. The precise definition of these boundaries—how to tell "us" from "them"—is of more concern for some religions than others. Buddhism, for example, does not have salient markers of this boundary. Someone can claim to be a Buddhist, and have this claim accepted, without having the claim cleared by authorities or undergoing special rites of conversion. The reasons for these "fuzzy boundaries" were set out in Chapter 3: Buddhism, like many other religions, is not based on allegiance to a single creed or book, nor is it limited to a particular ethnic or tribal group.

By contrast, both Judaism and Islam have shown special concern for maintaining external boundaries. Both are defined around obedience to a set of laws; Judaism also is historically associated with ideas of descent from original tribes.

The Prohibitions of Leviticus

Not surprisingly, then, food taboos are particularly salient markers of membership in the Jewish and Muslim communities. For many Jews and Muslims, the foods that should not be eaten serve as daily reminders of religious obligation and distinctiveness. For Judaism, a list of prohibited foods is found in the Bible, in Deuteronomy 14, Leviticus 11, and elsewhere. We find proscriptions on the eating of certain animals: camels, rabbits, mice, crocodiles, and pigs, among many others. The puzzle is: Why this particular assortment of animals? Leviticus begins as instruction about the right and the wrong ways to offer sacrifices to God, and then proceeds to list in detail the things and conditions considered pure and impure. The transition is at Leviticus 11, which begins as follows:

> And the Lord said to Moses and Aaron, "Say to the people of Israel, These are the living things which you may eat among all the beasts that are on the earth. Whatever parts the hoof and is cloven-footed and chews the cud, among the animals, you may eat. Nevertheless among those that chew the cud or part the hoof, you shall not eat these: The camel, because it chews the cud but does not part the hoof, is unclean to you. And the rock badger, because it chews the cud but does not part the hoof, is unclean to you. And the hare, because it chews the cud but does not part the hoof, is unclean to you. And the swine, because it parts the hoof and is cloven-footed, but does not chew the cud, is unclean to you. Of their flesh you shall not eat, and their carcasses you shall not touch; they are unclean to you."

The passage continues, prohibiting things in the water that do not have fins and scales; a long list of birds: eagle, osprey, falcon, sea gull, owl; all winged insects that go on all fours, excepting those which have legs above their feet (thus, locust, cricket, and grasshopper); any "swarming thing that swarms upon the earth," thus reptiles, but also the mouse and weasel.

Many Jews continue to follow these proscriptions, along with other dietary rules (*kashrut*) developed by the rabbis, most notably the rules for slaughtering in a way that minimizes pain, and separating all dairy and meat products. In the city of St. Louis, for example, an Orthodox "council of the city" has the authority to decide whether any food or food product produced in the region judge is permitted or forbidden. Their jurisdiction extends to any materials used in making food, such as a chemical release agent made locally for worldwide production of candies or cereals.

Muslims follow a similar set of rules. Early in his prophetic career (622 C.E.), Muhammad, his life endangered in Mecca, fled to the nearby city of Medina. There he was accepted by Jews and non-Muslim Arabs as their leader, and adopted several ritual practices from the Jews, including food taboos. Even after the breakdown of the Muslim alliance with the Jews, certain of these rules were preserved, including the prohibition against eating pig, blood and carcasses, and the requirement of ritually slaughtering animals. Today, Muslims consider observing these dietary rules, in particular avoiding pork, to be one of the most important signs of being a Muslim.

As we saw in Chapter 2, the shift from sacrifice to taboos in Judaism was part of a massive transformation in the Jews' conditions of living. Dispersion to diaspora made sacrifice at the Temple impossible, and favored a renewed emphasis on each household's obedience of the sacred law. But we still may ask why the law took this form: Why was this particular set of foods proscribed for Jews, and later for Muslims? Scholars in these religions have asked this question for centuries, and have produced a wide variety of explanations. Some have said that it is the very arbitrary nature of the taboos that is important: Because the taboos make no immediate sense, following them teaches discipline. Others speculated that the animals tabooed were allegories of virtues and vices: for example, the mouse is particularly destructive, so prohibiting its consumption leads us to ponder that particular vice.

These accounts have died out, but many people continue to find convincing the notion that some taboos were motivated by health concerns. Early Jews may have known, through simple association, that improperly cooked pork can transmit trichinosis and other diseases, and that shellfish can concentrate impurities, as do mud-burrowing fish. (The observation about fish is recorded from the twelfth century C.E.) One weakness of this explanation is that anthrax and other diseases were commonly carried by cattle, not pigs, and were much more dangerous at the time.

Moreover, if banning pigs and shellfish was important, why the complicated set of taboos set out in the Bible? Mary Douglas (1966), drawing on Durkheim's theory about taboos and community, argues that prohibiting certain foods was a way of carving up the natural world into the pure and the impure, and thereby creating a model for thinking about the purity of the Divine. Indeed, many other prohibitions in the Bible are of things that are partial, maimed, or blemished. Animals offered in sacrifice must not have a blemish; no one who has a physical defect may become a priest; even fields should be sown with only one kind of seed.

For Douglas, the food prohibitions are an instance of a drive toward order within the theology of the times. Certain animals with which people were most familiar served as model of the divine order to be found in nature and to be instituted in social life. Cattle were the typical livestock animal, and people took the fact that cattle have cloven hooves and chew the cud as part of their orderliness, as a "natural" combination of attributes. Animals with only one of these two attributes were judged disorderly. The pig, among other animals, is impure because it is incomplete: It has the cloven hoof but does not chew the cud.

Douglas's account has the virtue of corresponding to the explanation that the Bible gives of the rules. It also is supported by studies in psychology of how we use prototypes to carve up the world perceptually. We think about the category "birds" not in terms of all possible birds, but by imagining a prototype that is something like a robin or a bluebird, not like a pheasant. The ancient Jews, goes this argument, thought about livestock by using the prototype of a cow, not a pig. The pig is marginal, conceptually "dirty," and thus unfit for consumption.

Other prohibitions also have to do with species which fall outside of three main categories of animals: those that fly in the air with wings, those that swim in the water with fins and scales, and those that walk or hop on the land with four legs. The mouse, weasel, and crocodile appear on the list because their feet bear an uncanny resemblance to hands. "Swarming" creatures are inedible because they use a different mode of propulsion entirely. Hare and rock badger seem to chew the cud. The Biblical focus on order, writes Douglas (1966, 57), makes the dietary rules "like signs which at every turn inspired meditation on the oneness, purity, and completeness of God." Moreover, because pork was highly valued food for non-Jews, its prohibition also reinforced rules against intermarriage and helped preserve the cohesiveness of the group.

Jewish Ritual Life

Jewish ritual life today contains many references to those historical events of dispersal and survival that transformed ways of worship. The history of Pesach, or Passover, with its central meal, the seder, illustrates how Jewish ritual life was moved from public sacrifice to domestic celebration and observance of taboos (Bokser 1984). Pesach began as two spring festivals. Shepherds would sacrifice a lamb or kid from their flock on the full moon during the month when the animals were born. The lamb (the *pesach*) would be roasted whole and eaten completely during the night. At about the same time farmers would celebrate their early spring harvest by offering unleavened bread, to symbolize the separation of the old grain (in the form of fermented dough used to leaven bread) from the new, harvested grain. (Two other agricultural festivals—Shavuot (weeks) and Sukkot (harvesting booths)—celebrated the later harvests.)

At some point in early Jewish history, these celebrations of harvest and birth were merged into one ritual and were given a new meaning, the celebration of the Jews' deliverance from Egypt. The unleavened breads, in the form of matzohs, now became signs of the haste of flight: Not enough time was available to leaven the bread before leaving Egypt. And in celebration of this event, the book of Exodus (12:19) orders Jews that for this day "No leaven shall be in your houses"—leaven defined for these purposes as contact between grain and water for more than 18 minutes. Sacrifice was still carried out, first at altars throughout Judea, and then, after Josiah in 621 B.C.E forbade all sacrifices in "high places," at a single gathering at the Temple in Jerusalem. Each family brought a lamb to be sacrificed in commemoration of the lamb sacrificed in Egypt. They killed the lambs around the Temple, and gave some of the blood to the priests to be thrown at the base of the altar, then roasted them and ate them with unleavened bread.

After 70 C.E. Temple sacrifice could no longer be made, and the rabbis replaced the earlier focus on sacrifice and harvest with an exclusive focus on the covenant with God and its document, the Torah. Passover was now solely a commemoration of the flight from Egypt, and it was held at home (not at the synagogue, perhaps to avoid implying that the synagogue had replaced the Temple). The matzoh replaced the sacrifice as the main element of the meal, although a piece of meat on a bone remains as a reminder of the now-lost practice of sacrifice of the pesach itself.

Jewish lives today combine feast-day commemorations of past events with everyday observance of religious laws. At Passover celebrations today, families read the Exodus tale from a liturgy called the Haggadah. Although brought out in numerous editions with new material, all Haggadah texts recite the story of the persecution of the Jews in Egypt and their deliverance by God. A cup of wine is left for Elijah, whose arrival is supposed to herald the Messiah. And many also celebrate the survival of the Jewish people and the birth of the modern state of Israel as additional holidays.

On other holidays, too, different stories make the same general point, that through their covenant with God the Jews, despite their persecution, were delivered from evil. Purim, a times of games and merry-making, nonetheless commemorates the hanging of Haman and the slaughter of the other enemies of the Jews of Persia through the intervention of Esther. Hannukah, a celebration of freedom, observes the victory of the Maccabees. Sukkot, once, like Passover, a harvest feast, became a period to recall the long journey out of servitude (Schauss 1938).

Jewish festivals have changed over the years to reflect shifting concerns. The fasts and the agricultural festivals of Sukkot and Shavuot have receded in importance, and new holidays, such as those commemorating the Holocaust and Israel's Independence, have come into being. And yet ritual preserves a common element, of linking the current generation to key events in the past, some of them disastrous events for the Jewish community that nonetheless point toward that community's Covenant with God.

But this history may be interpreted in widely varying ways, and these variations return us to the central issue of boundaries and identity. The Passover Haggadah reminds Jews that "in every generation they rise to annilihate us," and the story of Esther can be read at Purim as chiefly saying one must slaughter one's enemies before they do you. In 1996, between Purim and Passover there occurred terrible suicide bombings in Tel Aviv and Jerusalem, and some Israelis drew on those possible readings of history to argue that continued war was inevitable, peace impossible. And yet others argued that Purim was chiefly about resisting oppression; Passover, about faith in deliverance, and that reacting to the bombings with oppression and lack of faith was in effect giving in to terrorism.

Central to these debates is both history and the Covenant, which is embodied in the Torah, the first five books of the Bible (Genesis, Exodus, Levicitus, Numbers, and Deuteronomy) given to Moses as the Law. At a boy's major rite of passage, when he becomes a "son of the commandments" or bar mitzvah, he shows his ability to read from Torah. Recently, as we saw in Chapter 3, some Jews have added a ritual for girls, the bat mitzvah. For many Jews, prayer in Hebrew and reading of Torah remain daily rituals. In daily prescribed prayers, the worshipper praises God, and petitions Him for the restoration of the Temple. Orthodox and Conservative Jews pray in Hebrew; Reform Jews often use their vernacular language. On the head and left arm, the worshiper may wear the tefillin, boxes containing Biblical quotations to remind the wearer of his religious duties. Although many events take place in the synagogue, home is the center of ritual life. The threshold of many Jewish homes is marked by a small box on the door post, the mezuzah , which contains a biblical passage proclaiming God's unity: "Here O Israel, the Lord is our God, the Lord is One." (Deuteronomy 6:4).

Jews have always felt that correctly applying Torah to daily life required further writings. Out of a consensus within the Jewish community on the correct understanding of scripture in the second century c.e. came the Mishna, a collection of rules and spiritual teachings. Scholars then wrote further commentaries on the Mishna, and these commentaries, called gemara, were joined to the Mishna to form the Talmud—in fact, two Talmuds, coming from scholars in Babylonia and Palestine.

Let us take an example of how scholars explicated the Law. The Torah gives as the fourth commandment:

"six days shall you labor and do all manner of work;
but the seventh day is for the Lord, your God;
you shall not do on it any manner of work"

(Exodus 20:9–10)

But the Torah does not tell its readers how to apply this commandment. Questions arise, and arose to Jews trying to observe the Law, and rabbis attempted to arrive at answers. What is "work," and does it depend on where you are? Scholars specified that carrying heavy objects on the sabbath was permitted in private—that was not work—but not in public places. When in the day does the Sabbath begin and end? Days begin in the evening, and scholars gradually pushed back the exact moment of its beginning. When may one break these rules? Health reasons were listed.

Some scholars have pointed out the resemblance between the multiple cross-references and layers of commentary in these texts and the hyperlinks across computer sites available on the World Wide Web, and there exist today texts and commentaries in hypertext format.

Movable Boundaries

Strict observance of religious laws may require ways to modify the ways those laws are carried out. For example, on the Sabbath one may not carry anything except within one's private domain. "Carrying" has been defined to include carrying an infant, or pushing a wheelchair. But what if an invalid needs to attend services, or an infant needs to be carried to the synagogue? One can, decided the rabbis, create a cooperative private domain, called an *eruv*, which might include the houses of a Jewish community and its synagogue. The eruv must be enclosed in some way, for example with posts and wires, as are, often unbeknownst to most residents, parts of some U.S. cities (including an area around the Congress and White House).

Often unobtrusive, eruvs have surfaced in at least one public debate in London over whether public, non-Anglican, religious objects were appropriate—and in particular religious objects that defined boundaries (Trillin 1994). Orthodox Jewish residents of a northern London neighborhood proposed to construct an eruv around their six-and-a-half-square-mile area, using 20-foot posts connected by fishing line, and mainly along existing roadways or rail lines. In the ensuing debate, opponents of the eruv, including some in the older generation of Jews, argued that England's cohesion depended on religious differences remaining private affairs (in a context where the Anglican Church remains the Church of State, headed by the Queen). A younger generation of Jews, and in particular several Orthodox groups, argued that their religious freedom depended on building the eruv (see further discussion in Chapter 12).

ULTRA-ORTHODOX JEWISH COMMUNITIES

Devoting their lives to the Law, some Jewish "pietist" movements place special emphasis on correctly observing the many commandments (*mitzvot*) from God—said by some to be 613 in all, positive and negative. Centuries of persecution, especially in eastern and central Europe, have intensified the desire to maintain internal cultural order through following the commandments. The pietists called Hasidim, who grew in the late eighteenth century under the tutelage of holy men in the Ukraine and eastern Europe, hold that obeying these rules brings the entire cosmos closer to light and goodness. In the remainder of this chapter, we look at two such communities, both with large populations in Brooklyn—the Lubavitchers and the Bobovers.

The Lubavitchers of Brooklyn

The most important Hasidic group today is probably the Lubavitchers, whose head-quarters since 1940 has been in Brooklyn. The Lubavitchers venerate their leader or Rebbe, the holy man (*zaddik*) who mediates between God and the world. The Rebbe is specially blessed by God and that blessedness is passed on genealogically. All seven generations of Rebbes have been descendants of the movement's founder, Schneur Zalman (b. 1745), each a son, or son-in-law (and usually also cousin because of close intermarriage) of his predecessor.

Recent Rebbes have had strong influence in Israel. Lubavitchers, along with some other Orthodox groups, argue that non-Orthodox rabbis (Reform and Conservative) have no standing, and the marriages and conversion they perform are worthless. They also hold that only Orthodox Jews, those who maintain the laws of purity and agree that the Torah remains fully active as Law, have the right to return to Israel under the Law of Return, and in 1988 they nearly succeeded in making their view into the official Israeli position. In the 1980s and 1990s, the Orthodox religious parties, which often held the balance of power in the Israeli Parliament, the Knesset, would from time to time call the Rebbe in Brooklyn to check the propriety of their positions on religious matters.

Many Lubavitchers were certain that the seventh Rebbe, the Paris-educated Menachem Mendel Schneerson (1902–1994), was the Messiah, at whose coming the Temple would be rebuilt. Some flew to Israel at his death to await what they called "the ultimate retribution" for centuries of persecution. In September 1996, two years after the death of Rebbe Schneerson, the new Israeli Prime Minister, Benjamin Netanyahu made a special trip to Queens, New York, to say prayers at the Rebbe's grave (on a trip where he did not meet with the leaders of American Jewish organizations).

In her book *Holy Days*, Lis Harris (1985) describes everyday life for one Brooklyn household that belongs to the Lubavitchers. Harris underscores the meaningfulness that the women of the household find in living a life of restrictions and rules. The enforced rest on the Sabbath, when no cooking, not even turning on a light, may be done, gives them leisure and freedom from working for others—an important theme in the context of historical persecution of Jews. "No one is master of any Jew on the Sabbath," states Sheina, who had married into the community. Such rules "force me to think about the sanctity of the ordinary facts of my existence" (Harris 1985, 125).

Sheina had grown up in an Orthodox home, but a personal tragedy and chance meetings with Lubavitchers had led her to join the community. She had agreed to a marriage arranged by a rabbi, and had come to joyfully embrace the many rituals and commandments of the Hasidic life. Of the purifying bath in the communal bathing-place, the *mikvah*, not used by most Jews, she said that a community is supposed to build a bath even before a synagogue, so important is maintaining purity. For Sheina, rules that prohibit sexual intercourse between husband and wife for two weeks each month (during and after menstruation), and a ritual bath at the end of the period, make sex more passionate, "like a new bride every month" (Harris 1985, 140).

A similar passion for obeying the Law pervades Sheina's weeks of work before Passover to rid her house of the least bit of leavened food—grain that has come into contact with water for more than 18 minutes. Exodus (12:19) commands that "no leaven shall be found in your houses," and Hasidic housewives labor hard to comply. Sheina cleans her house from top to bottom, replaces the stove top with a special Passover cook top, and brings out an entire set of Passover cook ware that is sure to be free of leaven. Her matzohs come from a nearby bakery, where bakers race from kneading the dough to scoring it to baking the matzoh—all in nine minutes, well within the limit! Sheina and her husband also sell all leavened goods—packaged foods and whiskey (made from grain), for example—to a non-Jew, and then buy it back after Passover. The goods remain in their house, locked away, but the transaction means that the Law has been obeyed, because the goods are not theirs.

Sheina's Passover meal, like most such meals, featured the foods symbolic of exile and suffering: the meat, of that eaten before leaving Egypt, the egg dipped in salt water and the bitter herbs, of sadness and suffering. But the meal followed hours of discussion about the truth of exile as the Jews' present condition. All those present agreed that the state of exile was permanent until the Messiah should come, and that all attempts at assimilation to the larger world were futile.

What Is the "Jewish Community"?

The Lubavitcher Jews set themselves off from others on the basis of God's command: "I am the Lord your God who has set you apart from the nations." Yiddish continues to be the first language for many, and many avoid what they consider to be unnecessary contact with non-Jews in their midst. But this effort at seclusion also has contributed to tensions in the Brooklyn neighborhood of Crown Heights where many Lubavitchers live alongside others, especially African Americans. Jewish citizens' patrols called the Maccabees, after the leaders of a successful revolt in second century B.C.E. Judea, were accused of harassing local black residents; in 1991 black residents rioted after a black child was killed by a Lubavitcher-driven car, and some Lubavitchers denounced the Mayor of anti-Semitism (Remnick 1992).

Lively debates within the Orthodox Jewish movement turn on whether separating oneself from the cultural mainstream is necessary for purity and survival, or a denial of the changing, larger world. Lubavitcher rabbis, through their 1,350 yeshiva schools worldwide, their Chabad houses in many cities, and their active outreach programs, seek to convince other Jews that as "the chosen" they are unique, and will never be fully accepted by non-Jews.

Other Jewish leaders, heirs of the nineteenth-century Reformed movement toward cultural assimilation, stress that Jews are also citizens of the countries in which they live and part of modern world culture. German and eastern European immigrants to the U.S. in the nineteenth century found a world where no religion was enforced—religion was a matter of individual choice. Whether Reform or Conservative (the latter being more concerned with keeping the Law), synagogues built in the suburbs during the religious revival of the 1940s and 1950s were dedicated to preserving the tradition or civilization of Judaism even for those who did not practice many of the rituals. Some features of ritual were borrowed from the dominant Protestant churches—organ music, men and women sitting together—and social clubs, libraries, and youth groups became at least as important to many Jews as worship. As Riv-Ellen Prell (1989) has argued, as adults became less and less drawn to the synagogue by the obligations of religious law or the force of community, the synagogue focused more and more of its activities on teaching children "how to be a Jew."

In the 1970s, some of these children developed "countercultural" religious institutions, in particular new prayer communities (*havurot*). They did so in an effort to infuse their lives with a stronger religiosity, to recapture a lost totality—nostalgically located in the eastern European Jewish town, the shtetel. And yet they created these new forms within American culture. Membership in the prayer groups was as an associational community, of free choice. Cultural values of gender equality and democracy suffused their activities. Women as well as men were counted toward making up the minimum of 10 worshipers for a prayer group (*minyan*). Prayer sessions involved sharing of roles and discussions of proper prayers (Prell 1989).

Mainstream U.S. Judaism and its further offshoots thus developed in distinction to the emphases on maintaining boundaries through strict observance of the law found among some Orthodox Jews today, including the Lubavitchers. American cultural ideals of democracy and expressive individualism make a law-centered religious life difficult. Of course, this very difficulty reinforces the notion of being in "permanent exile" that animates Lubavitcher life.

And yet the centrality of law to Orthodox Jewish self-definition, and the monopoly of Orthodox rabbis over Jewish legal institutions in Israel, means that the question of "Who is a Jew?" continues unresolved. The approximately 10,000 conversions to Judaism made each year in the United States are generally performed by Reform rabbis and are not recognized by Orthodox authorities. Nor do Orthodox rabbis recognize marriages conducted under Reform auspices, or civil divorces not accompanied by a religious court's divorce declaration, the *get*. Although these cleavages disturb many in the United States and have given rise to calls for an American religious court, they are of particular importance in Israel, where they bring to the fore not only the issue of Jewish identity but also of Israeli identity.

GROWING UP ORTHODOX

Let us now look more closely into ways in which Orthodox women and men learn to dress, speak, and generally behave so as to maintain the distinctiveness of their religious community. We saw how Sheina adapted to her new community among the

Lubavitchers. Ayala Fader (2009) has examined the ways young women in the Boro Park neighborhood of Brooklyn position themselves in the world. She argues that they develop "non-liberal" selves, meaning a concept of the self that is appropriately responding to strong religious norms and boundaries. If "liberal" in the philosophical sense implies that an individual seeks to rationally revise basic value commitments at all times (nothing is ever settled), "non-liberal" implies accepting *ab initio* certain limits to such revisions. One's goals then include living within the tradition as faithfully as possible. (Recall Talal Asad's stance on power and belief mentioned in Chapter 2.) A number of new anthropologies of religion, in particular Saba Mahmood's (2005) study of pious Muslim women in Cairo, explore the conceptions of agency and selfhood implied in these attitudes.

In Boro Park, young women grow into a role that both preserves boundaries and prepares them to engage with modern urban life. If men prepare for relatively isolated careers of religious study, women take on the tasks of negotiating with the wider world.

Judaism claims a continuous line of descent from the Prophets and the transmission of God's covenant with the Children of Israel. The Hebrew Bible (Tanakh), and in particular the first five books called the Torah, along with the rabbinic commentaries, provide the basis for Jewish law. The different ways Jews combine legal and ritual life have given rise to several distinct religious categories. About half of the 18 million people considering themselves Jewish live in North America; most of the remainder live in Israel, Europe, and Russia; Jews in each of these places generally regard themselves as either Orthodox, Conservative, or Reform. Orthodox Jews (a category including Hasidic movements) stress observance of legal rules; they hold that the Torah and the commandments are God's word as revealed at Sinai and continue to be binding on all Jews. Conservative (or Historic) Jews also recognize the validity of the Torah, but emphasize the historical continuity of the Jewish people and the capacity of the people to change law and practice. Reform Jews (along with the smaller Reconstructionist movement) focus on the spiritual essence of Judaism rather than the idea of a ethnically based nation, and have been more willing to abandon older rituals and laws.

In the conception of this Hasidic group, called the Bobover, every individual is endowed at birth with a set of personality characteristics, *mides*, and it is then up to her or him to work on these so as to adapt them to the community. Young women learn to emulate past Jewish women, including exemplary figures from Biblical times or their own European ancestors, to counter the wave of secular modernity. They also learn not to make important decisions on their own, even if these decisions are to act in a more religious fashion. They learn not to overly question authority.

Within this learning environment, young Bobover women learn distinct ways of speaking and dressing. Let us first look at speaking. These women (and their male counterparts) draw on three linguistic sources to create distinctive linguistic registers, or speech styles that carry social and religious meanings. The Hebrew that is considered to be God's language in the Torah is called *loshn-koydesh*; it is mixed into everyday speech to raise the religious value of speaking. Yiddish and English also are used, and elements from one often introduced into the other. The resulting three-way interaction or "triglossia" is developed in different ways by men and women.

Although boys and girls start peaking Yiddish in the home, by early primary school they follow divergent paths. The Bobover boys are destined to remain within the community and speak mainly a form of Yiddish that incorporates elements of English and loshn-koydesh, which they call "Hasidic Yiddish." The girls use mainly English among themselves, but a form of English that incorporates elements of the other two languages. This linguistic trajectory will allow them to speak with those living outside the Hasidic community as well as with each other.

Let us look more closely at the religious reasons young Bobover women learn to speak in this particular register. In Fader's analysis (2009, 87–117), using Yiddish and Biblical elements transforms English, otherwise a secular vernacular, into a holy way of speaking that adds light to the universe. But because it is English, it provides a tool for engaging with modernity, for venturing into non-Hasidic domains of New York.

The formal features of Hasidic English include a rising-falling intonation, derived most likely from the melodic forms of Torah recitation developed in New York City and recognizable even when all other features of a sentence are in standard English. It also includes adopting Yiddish grammar into English, such as in the sentence:

"If I would be an anthropologist I would look like her."

This sentence reflects a Yiddish grammatical construction. In standard English it would be:

"If I were an anthropologist I would look like her."

The same logic shapes the ways in which boys and men speak Yiddish: When using English words, as inevitably happens, they try to pronounce them in Yiddish fashion, so as to "religiously uplift" the English words. So one might pronounce the English word "wire" as "vire"; this sort of transformation is sufficient to make English Jewish. As one writer has stated (quoted in Fader 2009, 96), "the goal of the Yiddish language is to separate us from Gentiles."

But these Hasidic girls use their linguistic repertoires to navigate a careful middle path between what they see as two extremes: the overly Hasidic women whose English is not good enough to successfully engage with the modern world, and those overly modern women who do not distinguish themselves sufficiently from the Gentiles. They also can adjust their Hasidic English to be more or less Yiddish, depending on their interlocutors. They characterize the "just right" practices as "with it but not modern."

Similarly, these young women develop ways of being modest that mark a middle ground between too Hasidic and too modern. Very Hasidic girls wear dark stockings with seams and shave their heads at marriage, wearing a kerchief. The "middle way" is to choose knee socks or sheer stocking, and to cover one's real hair after marriage. The semiotic codes are complex. Fader (2009, 152) mentions an instance where a girl's father approved of her new skirt because it was dark and long. Her mother, however, noted that the skirt was made of denim, which, as she then explained to the father, was too modern a fabric.

Dressed up, with stylish wigs, and able to speak a standard English, these girls and women are able to maintain their sense of following the rules and of maintaining their Jewishness, but also of being able to move among the Gentiles, to be with it and yet also un-modern.

Conclusions

We have looked at the importance of prohibitions and rules governing everyday behavior through the case of Judaism and in particular its Ultra-Orthodox variants. Other variants of Judaism draw on Torah and the traditions in their own, distinctive ways. Eating, dressing, and speaking provide domains in which religious actors can develop semiotic codes, which allow members of one religiously defined community to position themselves vis-à-vis members of other, alternative communities. Some of the distinctions may seem very minor, but these can work to maintain distinctions under a broader umbrella.

Discussion Questions

Are there other religious communities in North America who draw on these semiotic codes (dress, food, manner of speaking) to maintain boundaries? Do all religious communities do this? Discuss the corresponding sets of rules or taboos for your own religious tradition: Why do they exist?

Media Resources

A documentary called *A Life Apart: Hasidism in America*, is available on YouTube; the first part at: http://www.youtube.com/watch?v=3L9cxOCm1gI gives images and comments from people living around the Hasidim (and is narrated by Leonard Nimoy and Sarah Jessica Parker). Either of the two books cited in the text, by Ayala Fader and Lis Harris, works well as texts: Fader more detailed, Harris more biographical. For a longer film (just over one hour) that looks at Jewish people in the twentieth century, you could view *Faith and Fate*, available at: http://www.youtube.com/watch?v=S58ivjU9PeE.

Speech and Grace in Protestantism

It is hard to think of a religion in which set ways of speaking—spells, prayers, recitations, and so on—do not play central roles. Humans are talking animals, and we use our powers of speech to understand and shape events in both the visible and invisible worlds. Most rituals we have examined so far have had certain speech forms at their center: invocations of ancestral spirits (in Africa, Sumatra, or New Guinea), stories and spells that heal (in Japan, Panama, or the United States), and pronouncements that channel the meaning of images (in the Catholic mass).

Some religious traditions place particular emphasis on the centrality of the spoken word to religious practice. In Chapter 5, we saw that the Navajos of the American Southwest consider that the world was brought into being by the Gods when they spoke and sang it into existence. In Hindu, Buddhist, and Islamic traditions, the word that is spoken and heard has primacy over that which is written and read. It is not only in the European traditions of Moses, Plato, and Jesus that writing has been understood as secondary to speech (mistakenly so, argues the philosopher Jacques Derrida), but in other religions, of greater and smaller scale, as well. Written scripture may play an important role in these traditions—"scripture," after all, means "writing"—but it does so as the written record of what was originally an act of speech.

Certain religious movements portray their own distinctiveness by contrasting their emphasis on the spoken word to the mistaken reliance of competing faiths on images. In seventh-century Arabia, Muhammad and his followers contrasted the Word of God, which they followed, to the images of polytheists, which they condemned. Moses responding to Aaron's setting up of the golden calf, or Joseph Smith and Brigham Young leading the Mormons across the United States: both condemned the worship of "graven images" and urged their followers to focus on the Word of God. Luther chastised the Christians of his time for following the Church rather than scripture, and the "letter of the Bible" has been the watchword for Protestant movements of reform ever since. Each of these leaders has accused other faiths of forgetting or ignoring God's words.

But how can we tell if certain words come from God or some other supernatural agent, rather than from a human, or the Devil, or one's own anxieties? It could be that the speech itself is wonderful in some way, or that other signs of the divine source present themselves. When Augustine of Hippo heard commands coming from the other side of a wall to "take and read," he could understand them to be God's commands to pick up Scripture. Muhammad's illiteracy made his reports of receiving complex, poetic revelations from God all the more believable. Sometimes revelations are received in written form so as to attest to their divine quality, as with Moses and the tablets, and Joseph Smith and his tablets.

But speech, like images, can be meaningful in more than one way. When we speak, we refer to concepts and through them to things in the world. We also call up associations in the minds of our hearers, associations linked to their memories of hearing such words before, or to the style, rhythm, or voice tone of the speaker. Thus, the *way* in which a sermon is delivered or a hymn sung can be as meaningful to worshipers as the manifest content of the sermon or hymn. We also understand some speech as directly accomplishing something, as having force as well as meaning: A marriage vow seals a pact; a spell compels a spirit to act. Within a religious tradition, people often discuss and debate how best to understand their own speech. Is a sermon better if it is carefully crafted beforehand (as clearly a human product), or is it better if it is spontaneous (allowing the Holy Ghost to offer direct inspiration)? Can a prayer, a mass, or the recitation of a verse work directly on the universe, or is it only a request to a deity or god?

In this chapter, we consider the relationship between ways of speaking and divine powers in Protestant religions, in which God reveals his word through scripture and spontaneous, inspired speaking. In Chapter 13, we look at comparable features in Islam.

THE LETTER AND THE SPIRIT OF SCRIPTURE

Protestants introduced the idea that everyday speech by ordinary people can, when accompanied by God's grace, be divinely inspired.

Protestantism in its many variants grew out of "protests" against certain practices of the Church, beginning with Martin Luther (1483–1546) and John Calvin (1509–1564), who gave rise to the Lutheran churches and to a line of "reformed" churches including Presbyterians. Against the Catholic emphasis on the objective and necessary role of the Church for salvation, the Protestants argued that God bestowed grace without Episcopal mediation, requiring only faith based on the direct study of Scripture. Certain streams emphasize the availability of grace to all, hence "universalism" and including many Baptists, Methodists, Evangelicals, and Lutherans. Others, following Calvin, emphasized God's pre-determination of who would (and who would not) be saved. Evangelical and the more recent Pentecostal movements have emphasized conversion, piety, and experience, and spread rapidly in parts of the Americas, Africa, and the Pacific.

In the sixteenth century, several Christian scholars, notably Martin Luther (1483–1546) in Germany and John Calvin (1509–1564) in Geneva, protested against certain Church teachings, thus giving their worship movements the name "Protestant."

Although differing strongly among themselves, these movements shared the dual conviction that, first, people could be saved only through their faith and by the grace of God and, second, that scripture, not human institutions, was the ultimate source of religious authority. As the billboard outside a Lutheran Church near my home in St. Louis has proclaimed: "Only by Grace; Only by Faith; Only by Scripture."

Protestants make the claim that faith and grace connect individuals directly to God in conscious opposition to the Catholic claim that the Church, through its sacraments, creates that connection. For the Catholic, the miracle of the Eucharist means that Christ is produced in the bread and water of the Mass. For most Protestants (and, from at least the ninth century onward, for some Catholics), the objects of a mass are signs of, not the substance of, Christ. Moreover, for Protestants the ritual of the Eucharist does not automatically confer merit or salvation or grace on the individual worshiper. Nor do chants said on behalf of the dead aid the dead in their struggle through purgatory to heaven. The individual has free and direct access to God, and God may bestow grace on anyone—or may refuse to do so. The gift of the Word of God thus may reach anyone at any time and place and in unpredictable ways. Faith is all that is required (Clark 1967, 99–115).

In the wide array of movements and churches that followed Luther's break with Rome—Methodists, Baptists, Lutherans, and so on—this emphasis on universal access to God's grace and revelation of grace through speech and hearing led people to develop many different ways of worship. Quakers and some Baptists have stressed the universal nature of the minister's role, that anyone may be visited by the Holy Ghost and moved to preach. Charismatic and Pentecostal churches (and certain movements within Lutheranism) have encouraged worshipers to let the Holy Ghost visit them and lead them to speak in tongues, as did the apostles after the death of Jesus. But other movements denied the universal access of people to grace and salvation. John Calvin argued that God has predetermined who is to receive his grace and be saved, and who is to be condemned to hell. This doctrine of *predestination,* held by the Puritans in early North America as well as Calvin's followers in Europe, implied that one's good works had no bearing on one's fate after death.

The ultimate authority on all religious matters for Protestants is scripture, and not the teachings of a church or pope. But what is "scripture"? One interpretation of the Protestant slogan "only scripture" (*sola scriptura*) is that the written text is paramount. Luther was indeed an outstanding biblical scholar, learned in Greek, Latin, and Hebrew, and did argue for the importance of the scholarly interpretation of the text as written. Early Protestant preaching never strayed far from the text of the Bible. What came to be called "Fundamentalist" movements, but might more correctly be called "literalist" emphases on the literal meaning of the text, follow from this focus on the written word.

For some Fundamentalist churchgoers in the United States today, literal truth resides in the 1611 King James Version of the Bible. Some of these Christians call modern translations "perversions." KJV is the Bible "as it is written" (Ammerman 1987, 53). Rather than considering the Bible as a whole, and worrying about contradictions between various parts, Fundamentalists (along with many other Christians) tend to refer to a verse or a phrase, on which they then elaborate, both in sermons and in discussing everyday life. People turn to individual verses that they have memorized, and they also use the language of some of those verses in everyday conversations. They may speak of their sicknesses as "suffering in beds of affliction" or having "a thorn in the flesh" (Ammerman 1987, 87). This literalism can lead some Fundamentalists to a point at which they are nearly using the Bible for divination, as in the case of a man who decided to order a tent from Sears and Roebuck Company because he found listed among the permitted foods in 14 Deuteronomy the "roebuck" (Ammerman 1987, 54).

This interpretation of scripture can, of course, be used to underwrite claims of special authority grounded in learning. But these claims are often countered within the tradition of Luther and Calvin by appeal to a second understanding of scripture. Luther, Calvin, and other reformers looked beyond the text to the divine message it conveyed (Graham 1987, 141–154). They placed no special value on the original languages of the Hebrew Bible or the Greek Gospels, and indeed Protestant reformers have encouraged translation as the best way to spread God's word. In this respect, they differ from Muslims, for whom there can be only one Qur'ân, the Arabic-language speech of God. (Indeed, most Muslims consider it impossible to "translate" the Qur'ân; English and other versions are usually called "interpretations" or "renderings.")

For the Protestant reformers, then, speech and writing was best thought of as a window to God's word, transparent to its referent. Holiness lies in the Word, not the particular words and letters. The Bible as preached, translated, interpreted, and witnessed in one's life is the key to the proper understanding of God, not the scholastic analysis of the Hebrew or Greek constructions. The Word of God, thus understood, can take different forms, including the presence of Christ himself in the world, as the Word made flesh. God can communicate his word in very different ways. Luther underscored the importance of inner communication with God, communication that did not depend on learning. He wrote that "no one can understand God or God's word rightly unless he receives it directly [literally, 'without mediation'] from the Holy Spirit." And Calvin wrote that "all of scripture is to be read as if God were speaking," and that the spirit of scripture was more important than the letter of scripture. In their view, God can communicate with ordinary people through many media: the revelations recorded in scripture, the embodiment of the divine in Christ, and the visiting upon any of us of the Holy Ghost (Graham 1987, 143, 147).

Because these inner modes of communication—hearing with help from the Holy Spirit—must accompany the reading of the Bible, Luther linked speech and hearing to the central value of faith: "If you ask a Christian what work renders him worthy of the name Christian, he will not be able to give any answer at all except the hearing of the word of God, that is, faith. Therefore the ears alone are the organs of the Christian person, who is justified and judged a Christian not by the works of any member, but through faith" (Graham 1987, 141).

The writings of Luther and others thus could be taken to give to individuals the right to hear God's word, no matter what statements were made by the authorities of a church. This radical giving of spiritual rights to individuals surfaces time and again in subsequent history.

Election and Signs

Most Protestant Christians would agree that God bestows his grace where he sees fit. But how and when does he see fit? Can our actions bring on grace?

The struggles over this issue within Christianity trace back to the very roots of the religion. On the one hand, Christianity drew from Judaism. It began, after all, as a sect within Judaism, where obedience to the Law determined the fate of individuals and, indeed, that of the universe. The idea that good works redeemed one's soul was developed by the Church into elaborate doctrines of penance, masses, and salvation. Many Protestant traditions also incorporated such a notion, Methodism among them.

But Christianity became, not a sect within Judaism, but a new religion, and did so in large part by adopting ideas from Hellenism, the world view that pervaded the Mediterranean world (Jaeger 1961). Hellenism included the idea of divine grace that is visited upon humans rather than achieved by them. This concept accorded well with the idea of an all-powerful God, and indeed with the unpredictability of the God of the Hebrew Bible. After all, if God does not need humans, he will dispense grace in ways that fit his plans, and not simply respond to our works.

The idea that God's grace is entirely independent of human actions finds its most eloquent exposition in Paul's letter to the Romans, in a section where Paul is distinguishing between the older idea of the Jewish "chosen people" and the Christian idea that God chooses, or elects, some people (and not others) both from among the Jews and from among the Gentiles:

> [W]hen Rebecca had conceived children by one man, our forefather Isaac, though they were not yet born and had done nothing either good or bad, in order that God's purpose of election might continue, not because of works but because of his call, she was told, "the elder will serve the younger." As it is written, "Jacob I loved, but Esau I hated."
>
> What shall we say then? Is there injustice on God's part? By no means! For he says to Moses: "I will have mercy on whom I have mercy, and I will have compassion on whom I have compassion." So it depends not upon man's will or exertion, but upon God's mercy. For the scripture says to Pharaoh: "I have raised you up for the very purpose of showing my power in you, so that my name may be proclaimed in all the earth." So then he has mercy upon whomever he wills, and he hardens the heart of whomever he wills.
>
> You will say to me then, "Why does he still find fault? For, who can resist his will?" But who are you, a man, to answer back to God? Will what is molded say to its molder, "Why have you made me thus?" Has the potter no right over the clay, to make out of the same lump one vessel for beauty and another for menial use?
>
> (Romans 9, 10–21)

Just as the potter may select some pots for greatness, and others for quick destruction, without the pots having the right to answer back, how can we, God's creations, question the will of God, our Creator?

The doctrine of election formed a central part of the teachings of (Saint) Augustine of Hippo in the fifth century (Burns 1994). Because original sin cost humans their free will, he wrote, all our fortune, good or ill, is due to God's grace. In the sixteenth century, John Calvin developed this argument into the idea of predestination, which became founding doctrine for the Presbyterian Church. As inscribed in the Westminster Confession of 1647, which the English Parliament accepted the following year, the doctrine was stated in the form that "some men and angels are predestined unto everlasting life, and others foreordained to everlasting death" (Weber 1958, 98–101).

This doctrine left its adherents with a radical uncertainty about their future. Calvin taught that no one can know whether he is saved (although Calvin apparently thought he was), because the damned can have all the mental states possessed by the saved except for the final state of trust in God. So, although a strong feeling of faith in God is necessary for salvation, it is insufficient as a source of reassurance about salvation.

This uncertainty has one loophole, contained in the "doctrine of signs," that even if we cannot know with certainty about our salvation, we can see signs of it. These signs could be in one's ability to succeed in the world. Some Protestant theologians argued that one had a duty to assume that one was saved and act accordingly. Individual psychology led believers in the doctrine toward intense worldly activity in the hope that leading a rational, systematic life for the greater glory of God on earth would itself be a sign that one has been called to serve God, and therefore has been elected. Some added an additional tenet that helped close the logical circle: that only the elect had faith strong enough to keep them hewing to this path. Thus, success and profit are themselves signs of election.

Although this line of thinking brought even Calvin's heirs back to a position, in which good works counted for something on the religious plane, it was not a return to Catholic doctrine. The Calvinist still has no possibility of absolution; if he is damned, there is still nothing he can do about it. Furthermore, in the idea that a life spent for God was a sign of election, it was the whole life that mattered, and not the individual work, as in the Catholic calculus of sin and absolution.

Max Weber (1958) drew on these religious responses to develop his theory that what he called the "Protestant ethic" provided a psychological push for the development of modern capitalism in Europe. He noted that the pioneers of modern capitalism in Europe were mainly Protestant rather than Catholic, despite the fact that Protestant theologians were far more restrictive regarding what we might call the modern business necessities of interest and competitive pricing than were their Catholic counterparts. Luther, for example, wrote that "the greatest misfortune of the German nation is easily the traffic in interest. . . . The devil invented it, and the pope, by giving his sanction to it, has done untold evil throughout the world."

Weber's idea was that Protestantism spurred on the development of capitalism, not directly through its doctrine but through the psychological consequences of that doctrine. Men tormented by the unknowability of election were spurred on to succeed in the world, to build edifices of successful businesses as monuments to their worldly success. Weber called this cast of mind "worldly asceticism": denying pleasure to oneself but doing so in a life very much devoted to this world. The capitalist experienced loneliness, since no one could save him and God was distant; had a hatred of material, sensuous life, since it had no positive religious role and tempted people to idolatry; and threw himself into a social life that was solely work for the glory of God.

Weber advanced his thesis by studying the sermons and diaries of Calvinist theologians in the seventeenth and eighteenth centuries. Richard Baxter, for example, served in Cromwell's government as well as in the Puritan Church. He preached hard, methodical work as a religious labor (and opposed sports). The divine quality of work will be "known by its fruits," he wrote. As a consequence of this idea, these men preferred specialization and the division of labor because of the greater returns to labor they brought, and thus the greater indication of their own personal election they conveyed.

The doctrine of election—or "particular election" as it came to be called—was by no means universally accepted by Protestants. An especially widely effective treatise written by Jacobus Arminius in 1608 and called *Declaration of Sentiments* argued that God wishes all people to be saved and gives them the means to do so. Living the good life, stated Arminius, can bring one to God's grace. This position (often called "Arminianism") implied that humans are "perfectible." This argument was taken up in the eighteenth century by John Wesley. The movement he founded was named Methodism for the methodical life he urged Christians to lead. Methodists and other movements accentuated the emotional work required to bring about certainty of salvation and to lead the person into the state of grace.

Baptists gained their distinctive position within the array of Protestant churches through their argument that only those who had gained their faith should be baptized into the church. They thus rejected infant baptism. But Baptists themselves split over the issue of election, with some teaching that Jesus died for everyone; others, that he died only for the elect. Those who held the first view were called "General Baptists" and included the group that left England for Holland in 1607, some of whom then journeyed to Plymouth, Massachusetts, in 1620, and whom we know as the Pilgrims. Those people holding the second view, called "Particular Baptists," founded churches in England and also sent groups to America. Today, some Presbyterian and Reformed churches in Europe and the United States advocate the doctrine, but may place more or less emphasis on it.

SINGING AND CERTAINTY AMONG U.S. PRIMITIVE BAPTISTS

One group of churches that has attempted to remain faithful to Calvin (and thus are "Particular Baptists") call themselves "Primitive Baptists." Their churches are scattered throughout the Appalachian mountains; I draw here on a study conducted in the early 1980s by James Peacock and Ruel Tyson (1989) in the Blue Ridge mountains straddling North Carolina and Virginia. In this sparsely populated region, both elders and other worshipers travel from church to church to worship, often staying Saturday nights with friends. Services include hymn singing, one or more sermons preached by elders, and large meals spread out on communal tables. The churches belong to the Mountain District Association.

The Primitive Baptists adhere to the Westminster Confession (see above), and they actively wrestle with the difficulties the doctrine presents. They attempt to uphold election and reject the idea that we can earn our salvation or have certain knowledge of it. As one preacher put it, "every time you feel inspired, it didn't necessarily come from the Lord." But they also hold to the idea of signs of salvation that one can sense in the world. These signs include the experience of community attained through fellowship and church services, "a sweet meeting," such as one preacher recollected in a sermon in the early 1980s. "Oh, my friends, sometimes we've sung songs here that've lifted us up," he reminds them. And the beauty of their singing is a sign, a foretaste of heaven: "Beyond the little foretastes of experience now, ah, in heaven's pure world today there are angels that sing" (Peacock and Tyson 1989, 112).

"Hymns are small sermons," notes one church elder. Peacock and Tyson describe how, concerned with not overstepping the boundary between faith in their salvation and (mistaken) assurance about it, they choose their songs carefully: "Amazing Grace" and "Guide Me O Thy Great Jehovah" affirm God's absolute sovereignty and "In Sharon's Lovely Rose" expresses hope of reaching heaven, but "Blessed Assurance, Jesus Is Mine" is unacceptable because it presumptuously claims assurance of salvation. In their style, too, they express resignation and modest hope, but avoid the joy that could dangerously approach certainty. Upbeat tempos and complex harmonies are avoided; unison singing in a dignified cadence is preferred. Peacock and Tyson recall the tears running down the cheeks of the congregation while singing; their participation in the service is no less emotional than that of their more animated Pentecostal brethren, but it bespeaks a resigned, stoic attitude in the face of God's great and unknowable will (Peacock and Tyson 1989, 114–118).

Sermons pose two related dilemmas for the preacher. Does one prepare an elaborate sermon and risk the sin of pride, or wait for the Spirit to emerge inside one, and risk incoherence? Does one urge people to perform their duties as Christians and risk strengthening the erroneous idea that doing their duties will win them salvation, or refrain from any exhortations and miss the opportunity to guide them along a righteous path? Preachers do not, in fact, preach from outlines or notes. To do so would be to insult the "Spirit that bloweth where it listeth." Sermons come from the heart. "If I can't feel that power, I ain't preaching the Gospel. I may stand up there and quote scripture and so on, but it ain't the Gospel," remarked one preacher. For, as Luther and Calvin proclaimed, the Bible is the inspired word that emerges in and through humans, not the dead letter of the written book. It was the Word of God that produced the Bible and inspires people today as well. Or does not: An elder may rise to preach and after quoting scripture, sit down when he finds he has nothing to say (Peacock and Tyson 1989, 118–126).

In their sermons, preachers strive to avoid implying that religious experience is evidence of salvation or that good works can lead one to salvation. Elder Bradley used a sermon he preached in a North Carolina church to trace his own path. His experience preaching and "saving souls" had led him to think that preaching could bring a person to salvation. He realized his error after revisiting the passage in the Letter to the Romans on election. His sermon reminds us how what appears to be an obvious reason for preaching is indeed in error from the perspective of the doctrine of election, and also how the apparent gloominess of this perspective can be in fact the basis for joy:

> Finally came to the conclusion that this which I'd been taught, that salvation was dependent upon men hearing the gospel, repenting of his sins and believing on Jesus, that God was using this the preacher to reach the dead sinner, that this was totally contrary to that which was taught in the word of God, but that this salvation depended upon God's own sovereign pleasure and that he made choice of a people in a covenant before time began. And, oh what a joyful sound it was, and how beautiful it was for me then to

see things in that order! To see that God planned this salvation, and if God planned something you can rest assured it's not going to come to naught. That which God has planned will be executed. God declared this salvation before men ever had being in himself. (Peacock and Tyson 1989, 122)

The "sweet meeting" that comforts the soul depends on community: Preaching, singing, and eating together makes up what these Baptists call "the visible church." But here enters a difficulty: If your group consists of both the damned and the elect, how can you construct a solid community? Two ideas of community have emerged in the Mountain District, roughly corresponding to the contrast between North Carolina and Virginia churches, and these two ideas have consequences for practices of speaking, singing, and gathering in fellowship.

Two Models of Church Authority

For reasons of topography and modes of livelihood, the churches in North Carolina are dispersed in fields and hills, whereas those in Virginia are located in villages (Peacock and Tyson 1989, 87–117). The North Carolina churches are less well attended than the latter group, and worshipers are more likely to live individualistic lives, usually as independent farmers. Charisma, or direct divine inspiration, governs the lives of the elders, and it appears in their sermons, which often recount personal experiences. Songs of stoic resignation, sermons about doctrine, moods of individualism, and antibureaucracy sentiments characterize the North Carolina churches. In contrast to this individualistic structure and attitude, the Virginia churches have created some degree of bureaucracy, and their elders emphasize organization over charisma. The lives of those attending services are more likely to involve work in government civil service or small businesses (although here, too, many farm). Sermons are more likely to dwell on duty. Singing has changed in some Virginia churches, evolving in the direction of mainline Protestant church singing, with major keys predominating and harmonies explored.

Peacock and Tyson recount how the two groups of churches have come into conflict over their differing ideas of authority and community. The North Carolina churches have favored allowing individual churches and members to go their own ways, as the Spirit moves them. Charisma, the gift of grace from God, dominates. Those in Virginia have stressed the importance of following rules and obeying duly constituted authority.

The contrast surfaced in a dispute during the 1980s about the right of a church to exclude some of its members (Peacock and Tyson 1989, 71–85). Churches do exclude members, and members cannot join other churches. Because members and elders rotate where they worship, they can effectively keep out the excluded. In this case, one church excluded a majority of its worshipers on grounds that they had associated with a sinner. They had shown themselves not to be of the elect and so had to be thrown out of the church—much as did the Puritan churches of seventeenth-century New England that we read about earlier. The church is responsible for community as a whole, and must exclude sinners.

But the excluded members then formed their own church and asked to be recognized by the Mountain District. The rule-following Virginia churches supported the exclusions and refused to recognize the new church, because doing so would contradict the righteous authority of the church that had thrown them out. The North Carolina churches supported the right of the members to form a new church. They felt called to do so, and who can say they are mistaken in their calling?

At issue was not just who makes the rules, but who has access to the Word of God. If the Word of God is given to anyone and everyone, at any time and place and in unpredictable ways, then the worship and preaching of anyone should be recognized and attended to. If an individual is called by God, his or her subsequent actions should be respected. But if the right to provide an authoritative interpretation of scripture is held by those persons capable of correctly reading it, then all others should obey that authority. Here the North Carolina churches stood in favor of the availability of God's word to anyone; the Virginia churches, of the importance of a duly constituted hierarchy based on knowledge and the consent of the community acting as a whole.

This tension about authority and community plagues all Christian movements that attempt to structure themselves around the ultimately unknowable grace of God. The Virginia churches have moved toward hierarchy and a "routinized" authority. The North Carolina churches have resisted this pull. Here we see encapsulated in this tension a basic dilemma of Protestant forms of Christianity: Who gets to say where the Spirit is to be found?

CHARISMATIC AND PENTECOSTAL CHURCHES

Other Christian churches in the same part of the United States have maintained an independent stance but have taken different positions on the question of whether we can perceive and experience signs of our own election or salvation.

Many Fundamentalists, such as those in the Northeast U.S. church studied by Nancy Ammerman (1987), doubt that everyone who claims to be saved is in fact saved, and they look for signs of salvation, most importantly some outward, noticeable change in the person's life. They should have given up smoking and drinking. They should show confidence in the Lord; constant worries are signs they have not yet been saved.

Throughout much of the South, Holiness churches are scattered in hills and towns much as are the Primitive Baptists. Preachers and ordinary people often travel long distances to worship. The focus of worship is on the relationship between the individual and God, as in all the movements we have considered so far. But here the role of rather dramatic signs is paramount, for snake-handling is often part of the service. Surviving snakebite, or a drink of poison, or an electric shock is a sign of God's grace. The women and men who have been bitten sit together in services as the "true believers," or the "true saints." These saints, having survived, have themselves become signs, or "charismata" that are given by the Holy Ghost. They are proofs of Jesus' power to save them; cups of strychnine are called "salvation cocktails" (Covington 1995; La Barre 1964).

One church name says it all: "The Church of Jesus Christ with Signs Following." The phrase is in reference to 16 Mark, a key chapter for worshipers at Holiness churches and for many other churchgoers throughout the South—just as the Primitive Baptists and other believers in particular election take their cue from 9 Romans. In 16 Mark, Jesus appears to his apostles and upbraids them for not believing those who said they saw him risen. He then commands them to go into the world and preach the Gospel, and says:

> *He who believes and is baptized will be saved;*
> *but he who does not believe will be condemned.*
> *And these signs will accompany those who believe:*
> *in my name they will cast out demons;*
> *they will speak in new tongues;*
> *they will pick up serpents, and if they drink any deadly thing,*
> *it will not hurt them;*
> *they will lay their hands on the sick,*
> *and they will recover.*

Mark continues to relate that these apostles did indeed go forth and do the work of the Lord, and the Lord confirmed the message "by the signs that attended it" or, in the King James Version, "with signs following." Here ends Mark, and from here derives the name of the Holiness church mentioned above.

The relation of speaking in tongues to salvation is further evidenced in 2 Acts, the second key text for Pentecostal and Charismatic churches. It relates, speaking of the apostles:

> *When the day of Pentecost had come,*
> *they were all together in one place.*
> *And suddenly a sound came from heaven like the rush of a mighty wind,*
> *and it filled all the house where they were sitting.*
> *And there appeared to them tongues as of fire,*
> *distributed and resting on each one of them.*
> *And they were all filled with the Holy Spirit and began to speak in other tongues,*
> *as the Spirit gave them utterance.*

Because these events took place on the Pentecost (the Greek name for the Jewish Feast of Weeks), religious movements that seek to experience what the apostles did are called Pentecostal, or they are called Charismatic because of the adherents' desire to receive the charismata, the gifts of grace visited upon them by the Holy Spirit. Participants in these movements believe that their own speaking in tongues and ecstatic experiences are signs that they are saved. They have renounced the doubt that plagues those who adhere to the doctrine of particular election, and they embrace the idea that anyone may be saved—and yet these signs of salvation are still required.

Perhaps it is the strong need to overcome strong doubt that explains the great lengths to which some worshipers go to prove their salvation to themselves and their fellow worshipers. Some handle snakes; others swallow poison. Snakes may have been chosen precisely for the shock the handling delivers to outsiders. "Spread the Word! We're coming down from the mountains!" announced one preacher. The snake-handling Holiness churches date from about 1900. As with the Primitive Baptists, these churches value their independence. They are usually scattered throughout rural areas and are visited by a series of preachers. They first practiced snake handling in 1909, in Tennessee. Apparently it was not until 1918 that someone died from snakebite, and he was denounced as a backslider, someone who had lost his faith, when he died (La Barre 1964).

Snakes are typically brought out in their cages partway through the service, after a sermon and singing have taken place. Sometimes music continues, usually on a guitar, and worshipers begin to dance and enter trance states, at which time someone may pick up a snake and handle it before dropping it back into the cage or passing it on to someone else. The handling may take place in a more subdued setting, the snake passed from one person to another. Women and men handle the snakes. Perhaps 20 or more people are known to have died from snakebites in Holiness meetings; some state governments have responded by forbidding the use of poisonous snakes.

The Church of Jesus Christ with Signs Following in Alabama received national attention in 1992, when the church's preacher, Glenn Summerford, was accused of attempting to murder his wife by forcing her to put her hand in a case filled with poisonous rattlesnakes. She claimed he was trying to kill her because he could not divorce her and retain his position in the church. He claimed he did it to prove her innocence and that the snake bit her because she was backsliding. He was convicted and sent to jail, and his church, lacking any institutions for succession, disbanded. Other preachers soon began to hold outdoor snake-handling services, however (Covington 1995, 1–63).

The height of the service is the moment of "anointing," when the Spirit descends upon the worshipper and moves him toward taking up a serpent. Participants describe a diminished sense of the external world at that moment: "It's kind of on your peripheral vision" (Hood and Williamson 2008, 146–151). They feel "peace" and "protection" from danger, and empowered by God. They are also aware when these feelings start to ebb, and then they are careful to put down the serpents. The experience is always available to the consciousnesses of participants, so to describe it as "trance" does not capture its specific experiential quality.

Efforts to capture physiological correlates of these experiences also indicate that they are specific to these services and differ from other practices where participants also experience some degree of dissociation (see Chapter 5). The few studies that have measured brain states at the moment of anointing report handlers moved into a state close to meditation before the moment when they experienced anointing, and that they enjoyed endorphin highs during the experience. The former correlates with their experience of reduced awareness of the external world; the latter to the lack of fear and the reports that pain was not felt, for those who also engaged in fire-walking.

But snake handling is just the most spectacular of a wide range of practices intended to bear witness to the divine presence within oneself. It is itself the most visible sign of the powerful need to bear witness in a striking and public way to God's grace, to the presence of the Holy Spirit in oneself.

Much more widespread than snake handling are practices of speaking in tongues. Even the relatively staid Lutheran churches of suburban St. Paul, Minnesota (near where I grew up), have begun to encourage members to speak in tongues. Some report a sense of release and of grace as the incomprehensible words flow out of them. They do not speak of the experience as like a trance, but as an experience over which they have some control. Charismatic movements are growing within Roman Catholicism as well, and in 1981 John Paul II met with Charismatic church leaders and gave his approval to their movement. Worldwide perhaps 120 million Catholics can be considered to be

Charismatic. And Pentecostal churches are growing rapidly throughout the world, particularly in South America and Southeast Asia. In Brazil, where Umbanda and Macumba had become popular as supplements or alternatives to Catholicism, many are finding that Charismatic churches that focus worship on God but offer the opportunity to speak in tongues combine the best of both worlds.

All these movements are seen by participants as bringing the divine into themselves through the mediation of the Holy Ghost. The religious experience provides a material sign that God has accepted the worshiper and that he or she can hope or know of salvation. This particular emphasis on the individual's avenue to grace through personal experience—often spoken experience—is a key characteristic of Protestantism. The individual's relation to God through the inspirited Word is markedly different from the idea that contact with God is through the miracle of the Eucharist, itself mediated by the priest. Protestantism relocated God's miracles, his charismata, signs of grace, from communion and the icons of Mary and Jesus, to the individual's ways of speaking. Doing so made possible new forms of community and authority based on those ways of speaking, of which the churches discussed here are but a few instances.

ENCOUNTERS AND CONVERSIONS

Most anthropological studies of Protestantism in small-scale societies start from the question of conversion from an earlier religious system to some Protestant denomination. As Fenella Cannell (2006) notes, the serious anthropological turn to studying Protestant faiths occurred rather recently, for a number of reasons. Many anthropologists have held in disfavor the sort of hybrid cultures that sometimes result from conversion, considering them adulterated forms of more "authentic" cultures. Others have (partly for this reason) seen any forms of resistance to conversion and to the Western influences that accompany conversion as a good thing, perhaps as part of a general ethical preference for cultural self-determination over cultural affiliation to broader networks.

Whatever the causes of this relative tardiness, Protestant forms of Christianity recently have become a central topic for anthropology. Anthropologists have highlighted the processes of adaptation and change as people living in small-scale societies convert to Pentecostal and evangelical churches, often as a result of missionary activity (Comaroff 1985; Keane 2007) but also for quite different reasons (Robbins 2004). Robbins (2004) argues that anthropologists have been particularly likely to take seriously these forms of Christianity because they have been forced to. The smaller-scale societies we often study are more likely to have "adopted" these forms of Christianity in a full-scale way, to have taken on a wide range of cultural meaning from the new religion, rather than to have selectively borrowed from Christianity. Anthropologists therefore could not very easily ignore the cultural content of these forms of Christianity. We can also add that evangelical missionaries have been especially active in the regions of Africa and Asia where many anthropologists work.

A South African Standoff

Let us consider three cases of these encounters and conversions. Jean Comaroff and John Comaroff (1986, 1991, 1997) have studied the British colonial project of converting "natives" in South Africa to Christianity and creating a socially modern and disciplined colonial society. They describe how Protestant evangelical missionaries failed to realize their dreams of constructing a unified black Protestant church but succeeded in reshaping the way Africans carried out their lives. Their study focuses on the lives of the Tswana people of South Africa and Botswana and on the activities of the Methodist London Missionary Society, beginning in the 1820s.

The Comaroffs point out that Methodist missionaries (and, in varying ways, other Christian missionaries) measured their effectiveness not merely by obtaining formal conversions, but by their success in changing natives' ways of behaving. South African Methodists were bent on teaching the Tswana the "arts of civilization," which included the arts of cultivation. Missionaries urged the adoption of the plow, which, because only men tended cattle, had the effect of raising the value of male labor relative to female labor. They also taught that natives should live in monogamous households arranged in rows and squares rather than in circles and arcs. The church clock and the church calendar now regulated social life. And as the hourly base for figuring wages, time was now used to measure the value of an individual's labor. But the Methodist message contained the seeds of destruction for the colonial project. Central to the Wesleyan idea of self-perfection preached in the churches was the equality of people and their freedom to perfect their natures. This message was blatantly contradicted by the realities of mining labor in the nineteenth and twentieth centuries. It also gave ammunition to those within particular churches who would resist any kind of central control, leading to the subsequent proliferation of churches, as dissatisfied factions set out to found new denominations (Comaroff 1985).

The Comaroffs present the encounters between missionaries and Tswana as part of an ongoing conversation. Each side incorporated the other's messages into its own way of thinking, and yet also changed its religious practices slightly as a result of the encounter. The control of water was a matter of survival, for example, but also a political and cosmic matter (Comaroff and Comaroff 1991, 206–213). It was the ruler who brought on rains, and the rainmaking rituals, carried out at his direction, that ensured the rains' arrival. The missionaries regarded these rituals as the height of superstition and thought they should be eradicated. But they themselves were caught in a contradiction, proclaiming that rain was a matter of nature and scientific meteorological detection, while saying that rain was ultimately in God's hands. The Tswana concluded from this missionary double-talk that their scientific instruments were merely their version of rainmaking devices, which worked through their deity.

Consider how the Tswana people's firm grasp of missionary logic shaped the following dialogue between a mission medical doctor (MD) and the rain doctor (RD).

MD: . . . you cannot charm the clouds by medicines. You wait till you see the clouds come, then you use your medicines, and take credit that belongs to God only.

RD: I use my medicines and you employ yours; we are both doctors, and doctors are not deceivers. You give a patient medicine. Sometimes God is pleased to heal him by means of your medicine; sometimes not—he dies. When he is cured, you take the credit for what God does. I do the same.

The rain doctor is here calling the medical doctor's bluff: If he really believes, as the missionaries did indeed claim, that all is in the hands of God, then how could he or any other European claim that his human science had cured someone or predicted rains? The Tswana version of how rain arrives was in fact fairly complex. Rainmaking rituals did not work in some automatic, mechanical way; they required that the community be in a state of "moral rectitude, of 'coolness' (*tsididi*)" (Comaroff and Comaroff 1991, 210). Therefore, the ritual expert's primary task was to remove social pollution that might be preventing the heavens from unleashing the rain. It was thus fully within Tswana logic when they later blamed the presence of the Europeans for the failure of rainmaking rituals. For their part, Europeans began to include rain services in the church calendar, the more effectively to combat the natives' view. The conversion effort thus became an extended exchange of and change in the views of both sides. At stake was how to read signs of God's intentions and powers.

Calvinist Purification in Sumba

Calvinist missionaries working in Sumba, eastern Indonesia, focused on replacing indigenous ritual conceptions with properly Protestant ones. Webb Keane (2007) draws from the work of Bruno Latour (1993) the idea that modernity has required purifying our social worlds of intrinsic connection to material things. He employs that idea to understand the work of Calvinist missionaries in Sumba. As is true for most Protestants, Calvin emphasized the sincere intentions of the Christian in prayer and in action, and the grace given by God to that Christian, or withheld by Him. Calvin objected to Martin Luther's acceptance of the Catholic idea of transubstantiation, whereby the body and blood of Christ exist in the wafer and wine given at Communion. For Calvin, we only employ such symbols as the bread and wine because we, weak humans, are so incapable of directly grasping the will and nature of God.

This way of stating the Protestant impulse emphasizes its self-demarcations from the contemporary practices of the Catholic Church. But more generally, Protestantism stresses the value of faith and belief of the Christian and the grace of God over the value of ritual practices or material objects. The religious condition of a practitioner is not affected by a ritual performed by a priest; it follows from his or her individual beliefs and commitments. Communion is symbolic of something already taken as a certainty, not a miracle that transforms wafer and wine into the body and blood of Christ.

Keane argues that this emphasis led to a cycle of reactions against the inevitable routinization of practices and the creation of material objects—statues, churches, robes. He makes the broader argument that reform of religion, from this perspective, is shared across faiths, including Judaism and Islam, and is part of a modern striving to "purify" our human world of domination by things, to make ourselves free to act as we wish, unburdened by material constraints. Keane argues that the religious ideas of the immediacy of meaning in human intention gave a historical push to purification.

When Dutch Calvinist missionaries came to eastern Indonesia to convert the people on Sumba, they brought their ideas about meaning with them. They took local practices and expressions to be ways of talking about religious concepts, which then could be allied with, or translated into, Christian concepts. So the blessing with "cool water" that was part of local ritual was rendered as a metaphor: The water stands for God's blessing, and so can be replaced by it (Keane 2007, 111). The material form, in this case flowing water, was immaterial, so to speak, to reaching the higher goal of realizing God's purpose. In similar fashion, missionaries scoured the world for evidence of God's revelations, degraded though they might now seem. Ideas of a "high God," or of salvation, all were read for their deep, ultimately Christian meaning.

But even if there are traces of revelation in local "pagan" religions, some saw conversion as requiring a sharp break with the past. Ironically, in Sumba, when Dutch missionaries urged Sumbanese converts to preserve the songs and gongs from their traditional culture in their Protestant liturgy, the converts refused to do so lest these tokens of the past bring older deities back to mind (Keane 2007, 134). They believed that keeping key terms of the new religion, and in particular the name for God, in a foreign tongue could prevent people from mistakenly resist assimilating the new God to an old deity.

The Sumbanese case presents a generic dilemma in cases of conversion. On the one hand, translation across conceptual systems can encourage people to convert, as they then can see something familiar in the new faith. On the other hand, if the old and the new seem to similar, then people can question the necessity of converting at all, or commit theological error by using an older theo-logic to understand the terms of the new religion.

When a local Sumbanese notable converted to Calvinism, he tried to solve the problem of continuity vis-à-vis rupture by delivering a ritual speech about his conversion. Sumbanese ritual speech highlights ancestral pathways in order to legitimate actions; these paths link today's people back to original centers. The speech forms use ritual couplets, which mark the speech as having special powers to communicate with the ancestors. This notable placed himself in the pathways set out by the ancestors, even as he began a new pathway, to the future as a Christian. But he refused to carry out the ritual sacrifices that normally provide the material support for such speeches, permitting the speaker to communicate with ancestral spirits, and so he left himself open for attacks, which did indeed follow.

The attacks pin-pointed the contrast in how Calvinists and the traditional ritual practitioners communicate with spirits: The Calvinist claims to have immediate contact with God by virtue of speaking, whereas the traditional practitioner uses the ritual couplets provided by the ancestor. These couplets are themselves the material of religious ritual. The contrast and debate that took place about religion in Sumba mirrors that between Calvinist and Catholic theories of communication: directly with God through faith and belief, or mediated by the priest and his objectively efficacious rituals.

Conversion also makes the individual the lone agent of worship. The structure of the church emphasizes individuality. One aristocratic Sumbanese woman told Keane that she feels embarrassment when she attends church, which she does every Sunday, because she finds herself among strangers. Social life in this society is for the most part among those you know. Conversion thrusts you as an individual not only before God but also among other people with whom you share nothing but a presumed common faith.

Urapmin Ethical Labors

Deep inside many new forms of Christianity are projects of ethical reflection and self-fashioning. Working among one of the many small-scale societies in Papua New

Guinea, the Urapmin, Joel Robbins (2004) found that conversion took place without extensive missionizing. The Urapmin found themselves relegated to a marginal position in their regional ritual system, largely because they were bypassed by colonial institutions. Some men reacted to this sense of marginalization by studying at a mission school elsewhere in the highlands. In the late 1970s, these individuals began to preach to local groups, saying that people needed to let God into their lives. At that point there began a Christian revival. The entire community became Christian as they attended meetings and felt the Holy Spirit enter them, felt "kicked" by it.

Without a tradition of possession, the Urapmin sought out a new vocabulary for their experience. The few men educated in the Bible were called on to interpret these new experiences to the people having them. For some of these pastors, it was only at that moment felt that they truly could read the Bible. Robbins (2004, 132–134) proposes two accounts of what happened: Pastors developed their reading skills to the point where meaning jumped out at them, or they now could interpret Urapmin life in terms of the book. Words and experience now "clicked." In either case, they felt that the Holy Spirit was intervening to guide their reading. Both senses of what it means to read Scripture that we found in Luther also come through in the Urapmin experience: They could now understand the text, and they felt that the Spirit spoke to them through the text.

A new social category appeared at this moment: "Spirit women" who would enter into a trance state, speak in tongues, and then later, out of trance, tell others what their inspiration meant, what action should be taken, all guided by the Spirit. They could divine where lost objects could be found, or they could determine the causes of illness. Illness might be caused by local spirits, and in the case the women would ask God to banish the spirits. Or it might be that anger in the community was causing illness. These new activities assured women a prominent role in local Christianity, and linked Christianity to everyday concerns. (In this respect we can contrast the Urapmin case with what happened in Zande society, in central Africa, where the Catholic Church came to occupy a place outside the domain of sorcery and healing; see Chapter 6.)

Adopting Christianity challenged the older Urapmin sense of ethics. Urapmin had placed a great deal of emphasis on the importance of regulating the will and preventing negative emotions, principally anger. But they also followed a set of taboos regarding their everyday conduct: what they could eat, where could garden, etc. Adopting Christianity meant liberating themselves from the rules of observing taboos, but it also meant that they now felt themselves too willful, bereft of the rules that previously had governed their actions and reigned in overly active willfulness.

In their sermons, Urapmin pastors urged people to cultivate an appropriate Christian response to this sense of vulnerability by cultivating a "peaceful heart." The Holy Spirit aids people in doing this; furthermore, by cultivating peace and calm, you allow the Spirit to enter and further aid you: a feedback loop, then, between cultivating one's proper self and effectively inviting in God—not unlike that between God's grace and one's own faith for many Protestants in other societies.

The Urapmin way to carry out this task of cultivating peace, the "technology of the self" one employs (Foucault 1997, 223–251), consists largely in moral self-reflection and confession in church. Urapmin confessions reveal the ways ordinary people reflect on their social lives in ways that give the greatest importance to maintaining a peaceful heart. Robbins recorded Jenny's confessions, which involve the misdeeds of others regarding the distribution of goods. But Jenny does not blame them for those misdeeds, only herself for having had a feeling of anger. She insists that the only topic of the confession is her own sin. To do otherwise would be to completely misunderstand the purpose of confession: calming the heart, not assigning blame. Urapmin Christianity directs moral reflection toward the ideal of following God's will and dampening down one's own. Only then are dangerous and disruptive emotions kept from arising in one's heart.

And yet following this path leaves Urapmin men and women without the ability to engage in the actions of sociability-building that are necessary for everyday life, such as building a village and negotiating the bride price for a marriage. Their Christianity has not given them a template for positive social action. And precisely because their morality condemns exercising the will, people are always looking for such willfulness in others, much as the early Puritans looked for the sin-revealing missteps of their fellow villagers. This focus on willfulness exacerbates the problem.

This tension sets up a deep dilemma for Urapmin society and ethical thought. It is addressed through Christian ritual. Ritual begins with prayer and sermons in church services. Sermons state that all present are sinner, and that they must submit to God. This submission includes preventing the will from doing anything other than listening to the sermon: People are warned against such distractions as looking at their neighbors, or thinking of tasks to be completed later on. Doing these things replicates the sins of anger committed in everyday life.

Healing ritual carried out right after the service also begins with the afflicted person confessing instances of harboring anger, presumed to be at the root of the illness. This concern with anger has motivated the Urapmin to carry over an older, pre-Christian ritual of anger-removal, carried out through exchanges, and to see it as a sin-removal ritual, within the conceptual framework of Christianity. It does the double duty of removing anger and the sin that results from it, the sin that is the Christian (negative) value of anger. The prayer that is read out over the sinner, by a deacon, speaks only of sin, not of anger, placing it squarely within the Christian framework, and it mentions the sinful act that the person committed. Only when the sin has been dealt with, and if need be the earthly penalties paid at court, can the person go to confession.

But the final step in spiritual transformation comes through the spirit possession dances, *spirit disko*. These dances are intended to remove sins from the person. Sins accumulate inside you and make you "heavy." At the disko, men and women dance and sing. The songs use traditional melodies and the lyrics speak of being with Jesus in heaven; they concern redemption. During the dance, the Holy Spirit will enter the person and throw out the sins. Possessed, the dancer flails wildly and bumps into church walls and other people—and if those bumped feel anger they quickly seek out a deacon to confess. The possession over, the person falls, limp, to the floor; the ritual is over.

Now, the spirit disko poses a problem in terms of ethical reflection, because it performs willfulness—all this flailing and bumping. For Robbins (2004, 287), the dance is redemptive because it portrays willfulness, showing what would happen if people did not act in a Christian manner, and yet transcends willfulness, pulling out sin from people and leaving them limp.

Ritual shows the problem but it does not overcome it. Willfulness remains both at the root of sin and a necessary component of social life. The Urapmin continue to live with this contradiction.

Conclusions

Across these varied cases of Protestant theories and practices, the problem of language stands out clearly. Language is material, and it is human, but somehow it also can tell us something about God's intent. How we work out that "somehow," how we talk about it, and how we act on it: These are the key questions that have driven debates and disputes among Protestants. What is it to read Scripture? Does it require the presence of the Holy Spirit, and what signs attest with certainty to that Spirits presence? Here inner feelings strive to align with outer signs: the anointing and the snakes, the certainty of election and success in the world, the Urapmin feeling of anger and sin with acts intended to transcend those feelings.

Across many religious traditions an idea emerges that sacred speech, in its utterance, places the speaker in contact with the divine. Reciting the Qur'ân is repeating God's own words and can confer power on the speaker. Chanting Blessingway reenacts the events of creation that accompanied the first chanting by the First People. For some Protestants, a true worship service requires speaking in a holy way—in tongues, or when called by the Holy Spirit to preach, or when reading from the Bible in a state of inspiration. This inspirited speaking is in some respects the equivalent of other worshipers' contact with an image—the drawing in of power through an "exchange of vision" with a Hindu statue is probably the closest equivalent.

Catholic, Hindu, Japanese, and other traditions also rely on prayer for worship, of course. But Protestants (and Muslims, as we shall see in Chapter 13) have taken the spoken element of worship and made it into the privileged element. When this is done—and it is done in different ways in different branches and steams—the subjective state of the individual also becomes a matter of increased concern. If an object is the center of worship, its objective qualities—its separation from the worshiper—give the process of worship an air if not a doctrine of objectivity: The worship succeeds if certain steps are taken. The Catholic mass is objectively efficacious even if the priest or the worshipers have their minds elsewhere. But once the words uttered by the worshiper become the whole of worship, those daydreamings endanger the very idea of worship. "Thought is the inner form of speech," say the Navajo; "no actions are effective without the correct intention," echo Muslims. Speech is close to thought, or ought to be, and words uttered must be accompanied by the proper state of mind if they are to reach their destination. Subjectivity now takes center stage.

Discussion Questions

Those who have experience in Protestant faith might look into the doctrinal statements of that church about salvation and action, and reflect on the way those questions are dealt with in sermons. Indeed, group discussions of different sermon traditions could reveal different ideas about who has the right to speak and in what ways, as would sharing experiences with communion. What songs tend to be sung most frequently and what messages do they convey?

Media Resources

A short clip shows instances where worshippers or a pastor speaks in tongues, at: https://www.youtube.com/watch?v=whpHwKIM_8M. Singing is a rich source of emotions but also a way to understand how particular ideas about salvation are put into liturgical practice. There are clips of different styles of singing "Amazing Grace"; one at http://www.youtube.com/watch?v=ckvzvFXtdic&NR=1 shows the simplicity of shape note singing, allied spiritually to attitudes of humility. And a "Primitive Baptist" church of the sort discussed in the chapter sings the same sing at: http://www.youtube.com/watch?v=jByWbxIg7OI.

As for snake handling, a number of short clips give the idea, such as this 1994 report: http://www.youtube.com/watch?v=ObhvOeNCKhs. An older film, from 1967, *Holy Ghost People*, is easily available, with excerpts online, such as, for speaking in tongues as well: http://www.youtube.com/watch?v=c5KjNH3AAkU&feature=related. (I use this last clip.)

New Religious Movements

Although there are a wide variety of religious organizations, here we turn to the rise of New Religious movements, for they bring up a set of specific questions: What leads people to follow a particular new call and leader? How do movements recruit (if they do)? What leads some movements toward violence? In Chapter 5, we already studied one of Japan's "New Religions," the Mahikari healing movement. Here we look at a range of such movements.

REVITALIZATION MOVEMENTS

Many prophets hold out the promise of a "new heaven, new earth," a new kind of world in which the trials and problems of this one are replaced with a just and perfect order. Their promises sometimes lead to movements of people seeking to overturn the present order, or converting others to their beliefs, or simply awaiting the promised transformation. They may not only develop and grow particularly in times of rapid social change and perceived threats to older ways of life, but also offer innovations, not just reactions to change.

We find such movements throughout time and throughout the world, being called by many labels. Judaism, Islam, and Christianity are all built on such a promise of a future redemption and the return of a messiah. This hoping for a future redeemer can be called "messianism" and such movements "messianic." In the histories of Judaism, Christianity, and Islam, there have been other persons claiming to be messiahs or perceived as such by followers, such as Joseph Smith, the founder of Mormonism; the Lubavitcher Rebbe; and the Imam Mahdi of the Sudan. These figures and followers fit squarely within the tradition of messiah-beliefs.

More generally, we can use the relatively neutral term "revitalization movements," taken from Anthony Wallace (1956, 265). Wallace defines such a movement as "a deliberate, organized, conscious effort by members of a society to construct a more satisfying culture." Although his definition imputes a singular psychology to such movements, it aptly emphasizes that such movements are creative and aim toward social and cultural improvement.

Many Christians have belonged to a specific version of such a movement, animated by the belief that Christ will return to the earth and reign for a "millennium" or 1,000 years before the Last Judgment. The belief is called "millenarianism," and it is based on a passage in the book of Revelation (20:1–10) describing the imprisonment of Satan and the "first resurrection" of righteous souls during this period, a great battle with Satan, the Judgment of all souls, and then the creation of a "new Jerusalem," a new heaven and earth. Many early Christians expected the Second Coming in their lifetimes, and millenarian movements flourished in western Europe in the medieval and early modern periods (Cohn 1970).

Today as well, some Christians consider the millennium to be near. Believers hold one of two ideas about the millennium, however, and the difference between the two ideas, fine as it might seem on paper, has important implications for the role of the believer in the world. Since the 1940s, the two ideas have defined two different groups of U.S. churches (Casanova 1994, 135–145; Wuthnow 1989). One group, which includes Seventh-Day Adventists and most groups calling themselves Fundamentalists, follows the idea of "premillennialism," that Jesus will return to reign before the millennium. Before he arrives, the world will grow increasingly corrupt, until finally those who are truly saved will be taken up to heaven in the "rapture," leaving the others to face a time of tribulations. These groups keep separate from the sinful world, building their own schools and universities for their children.

The tendency of Fundamentalists to separate from the world was challenged in the 1970s, when the Moral Majority movement led by Jerry Falwell urged Fundamentalists to work to change the world. José Casanova (1994, 156) argues that Falwell and others realized that fundamentalism "cannot survive in a world devoid of shared moral meanings and standards, in a postmodern world in which it would become just another quaint subculture, like that of the native Indians or the Amish, to be added to the 'gorgeous mosaic' of American cultural pluralism."

By contrast, "postmillennialists" hold that Jesus will come after the world has experienced a millennium of harmonious existence. For most people in this group, which includes many Evangelical Christian denominations, the task at hand is converting as many people as possible to Christianity, in order to prepare the world for Jesus. Once led by Billy Graham and now by his successors, and emphasizing conversion, large rallies involve healing and speaking in tongues and worldwide crusades. In Brazil, the work of U.S. evangelists has led to millions of conversions from Catholicism or Afro-Brazilian religions to an Evangelical church.

Millenarian movements in Christianity and in other religions promise a total social transformation at a particular, world-shattering moment to come in the near future. Such movements have particular appeal to those people who believe that the entire society needs to be changed, and that some great event is needed to accomplish these changes. Contemporary U.S. society produces such figures and their followers at near-regular intervals—David Koresh, or Jim Jones, for example. But so do other modern societies: Mahdis or Imams in Islamic societies, or spiritual healers in Japan. Millenarian movements developed in one context often spread to others, as when the Zion church of Chicago became a basis for a "countercultural" church in colonial South Africa (Comaroff 1985). Other examples of these movements include modern

Melanesian "cargo cults," movements based on expectations of social transformation when native peoples acquire the same wealth or "cargo" as owned by Europeans, and the Chinese T'ai-ping Rebellion, a late nineteenth-century rebellion against the Ch'ing dynasty that was inspired by the vision of a new Heavenly Kingdom close at hand. The Ghost Dance movement began with Paiute Native American prophets and then spread across the North American Plains, promising a more peaceful future, and eventually inspiring Sitting Bull's effort to resist white rule.

LAND, WEALTH, AND RELIGIOUS VISIONS

Even where something short of a millennium was prophesied, a wide variety of revitalization movements arising in colonized parts of Asia and Africa have drawn on the imagery and language of the book of Revelations, often associating it with the power and wealth of the colonizers (Burridge 1969; Trompf 1995). Throughout the Pacific islands, colonization brought rapid and often radical changes to local ways of life. Three transformations stand out. Colonists seized lands that had belonged to local people. Missionaries built schools and hospitals, and through conversion created new divisions among people. Europeans also brought new manufactured goods, and encouraged or demanded of locals that they grow cash crops and purchase these goods.

> Native North America contained and contains a wide variety of beliefs and practices about the relations of humans and spirits, difficult to summarize. Most share concern with the land and with the development of the individual human being in a broader environment. The Diné or Navajo people emphasize ways of restoring balance to the world and to a person as the basis for healing, as do the Zuni people of the Pueblos. The peoples living on the Great Plains focused on their relations to spirits and especially the Great Spirit. Young people in many of these societies went on quests for a guardian spirit, through dreams or a journey; these peoples developed a more individualistic emphasis to their conceptions of spiritual order than did peoples in the Southwest.

Local responses to these dislocations highlighted the three issues of land, trade goods, and religious innovation. Their particular emphases were shaped by specific local conditions, but they generally featured creative combinations of European and local ideas and practices. Some responses drew on Christian paradigms; others blamed their own neglect of their gods as responsible for their current troubles, and emphasized the revival of customs or rituals. One variety of these Oceanic revitalization movements was based on the premise that if local people engaged in some European religious practices, they would receive European trade goods. These movements came to be called "cargo cults," from "cargo," the neo-Melanesian word for trade goods.

"Cargo Cults" in Samoa and New Guinea

A movement in Samoa during the 1830s and 1840s was primarily motivated by the desire to possess the power and control that Samoans associated with European trade goods. Here emerged a "cargo cult," intended to produce new material wealth, but also based on a new combination of religious ideas. Siovili, the leader of the movement that bore his name, was an early convert to Christianity, and traveled widely on European ships, visiting Tahiti and Australia among other places. He was also subject to trances and traditional forms of spirit possession (Burridge 1969, 22–27).

Upon his return to Samoa, Siovili began to claim that Jehovah and Jesus Christ spoke through him. Some of his followers thought he was Christ. He stated that those who joined him in following these religious practices of the Europeans would share in the European goods. But his movement was also religious, one of many cults found in Samoa in this period that emerged out of the various missionary teachings and immigrants from other islands. Chiefs competed for the power that the new religious ideas might bring them. Other Samoans joined churches and cults for a mixture of motives.

Siovili's followers built churches, brought various books to service, and recited words over them, in the hope that these acts would bring Jesus with his material gifts (Trompf 1995, 174–175). One of his followers claimed that she had become possessed by Jesus Christ and announced that Christ was about to revisit the earth, at which time the dead would arise from their graves. She ordered other Samoans to throw out the crops growing in their gardens, walk down to the sea, and there await Christ's arrival. Christ would cause abundant food and goods to fall from the sky. This woman's followers did wait on the beach for three days, after which time they returned to their gardens to see if they could rescue any remaining food (Burridge 1969, 15–27).

"Cargo cults" are especially common in Melanesia, the area that includes New Guinea and Fiji, perhaps because of the importance of prestige goods in these societies. Political leadership and social prestige in many Melanesian societies result from success in accumulating and redistributing food and other goods. But the revitalization movements in Melanesia were also religious movements, inspired by new religious ideas and practices.

One Melanesian movement that attracted a particular degree of foreign attention was called the "Vailala Madness," a series of events occurring among the Elema people along the Vailala River in New Guinea from 1919 to 1922 (Worsley 1968, 75–92). As in the cases described above, the "Vailala Madness" grew out of a particular conjuncture of resistance to colonial land control, religious innovation, and the desire for new material wealth. Just prior to the "madness," the Anglo-Persian Oil Company had begun drilling for oil in the region; both this company and plantation owners took Elema men away as indentured laborers. Many of these workers died of dysentery. In addition, European authorities were trying to extract agricultural revenue from the district, and to do so they had ordered the Elema to pay a head-tax and to grow rice for sale. Elema had no desire to do either.

The local mission church authorities, from the London Missionary Society, supported the colonial cause but also urged Elema churchgoers to transform their lives through spiritual experience. These Elema did just that: They began to speak in tongues and became possessed by the Holy Spirit. Although church authorities interpreted their behavior as spiritual growth and enthusiasm, colonial authorities came to view the behavior as a dangerous "madness." (Recall our discussion in Chapter 6 of the differing interpretations Puritans made of girls' speaking in tongue, and the role of such speaking in Pentecostal movements, in Chapter 11.) One observer described local people as "taking a few quick steps in front of them, and would then stand, jabber and gesticu-late, at the same time swaying the head from side to side; also bending the body from side to side from the hips" (Worsley 1968, 75). People so possessed said they had been given special powers by the ancestors to divine and to cure.

The leaders of the movement were men who had traveled out of the district; many had been pressed into service in the oil fields or the plantations. They abolished traditional practices, burning sacred objects and substituted their own prophecies. The prophet Evara foretold the coming of a new order without the colonizers. Ships would bring back the spirits of dead ancestors (including those who had died while laboring for the Europeans) and considerable "cargo," material goods. He and other leaders told their followers to engage in actions that would bring back the spirits. Tables were set up in the villages, with flowers on them, around which the relatives of dead per-sons would sit, dressed in European style. Some leaders contacted ancestors through the village flagpoles, perhaps on the model of Oil Company wireless (Worsley 1968, 85). Leaders ordered strict moral codes to be observed, including observing Sunday as a day of rest.

Although after many years the movement gradually died down, some living in the area remembered it as having produced real miracles: Messages had indeed been re-ceived via the flagpoles; the steamers of the ancestors had indeed arrived; "the ground shook and the trees swayed" (Worsley 1968, 90–91).

The Ghost Dance in North America

Similar to the Oceanic movements was the Ghost Dance that was begun by Paiute Native American prophets and then spread across the North American Plains. Born in condi-tions of repression and starvation, the dance has continued its existence as part of a politi-cal and cultural heritage for some Native Americans, though with a changing message.

First introduced in 1870, the dance was revived and its message spread widely by a Paiute prophet in western Nevada, Wovoka (c. 1856–1932). During a solar eclipse in 1889, Wovoka fell into a trance, during which, as he later reported, he rose to the other world, where he saw God. God instructed him to remain on peaceful terms with white people and to dance a special circle dance that would place dancers in contact with the spirit world; hence its name. Dancing the dance would hasten the time when the people would be reunited with the dead, he taught. Euro-Americans would be wiped out, and Native Americans would return to their earlier state of plenty. (European-manufactured goods would remain behind for Native American use.)

Wovoka's prophecy was spread both by word of mouth and by delegations sent to see him from other Native American groups. Some delegates returned reporting that Wovoka, as "the messiah," had done wondrous things: made animals talk, descended from heaven on a cloud, and conjured up a vision of the spirit world.

As the message spread into new areas, with different cultural backgrounds and different relationships to the Euro-Americans, it was transformed. In Wovoka's mes-sage, the destruction of Euro-Americans was to happen automatically, and less as a punishment than as a means for Native Americans to regain their earlier ascendancy. His prophecy stood in a tradition in this part of North America of myths about the dead returning to life and inaugurating an age of plenty.

In Dakota Territory, however, the Lakota Sioux interpreted the teachings in a different context. The culture as well as the economy of the Sioux had revolved around the buffalo: buffalo furnished food and materials for houses and bedding and were the objects of many rituals. The art of hunting was a central part of life. All this was lost when Europeans wiped out the buffalo herds. During the 1870s and 1880s, the Sioux were confined to smaller and smaller territories until, in 1890, they occupied a particularly barren part of the Dakota territory, where, deprived of buffalo, they were supposed to live from crops, cattle, and government rations. In 1888 the cattle were destroyed by disease, and the following year the crops failed, followed by epidemics of measles and whooping cough. In 1890 came another crop failure and a reduction in government rations.

In March 1890, Sioux delegates returned from seeing the messiah, Wovoka. Within a few months, most Sioux had begun to practice the Ghost Dance. In their version of the message, the Spirit had sent the Euro-Americans to punish them for their sins but had now returned to their side and had made European bullets powerless against them. To prepare for the coming catastrophe, Sioux must rid themselves of European things, they said. No metal of any kind was allowed in the Sioux dances, and people began to wear "ghost shirts" of buckskin or cloth. Nor was any weapon carried in the dance. (The ghost shirt was not part of the Paiute dance and was disavowed by Wovoka.)

In October 1890, Sitting Bull began to practice the dance at his camp, claiming that he had received a direct message from the spirit world that he should do so. He urged all Sioux to gather in one place and dance, in order to advance the coming of the great change. Although he did not urge the dancers toward violence, publicity about the Ghost Dance movement exacerbated Euro-American fears of renewed fighting with the Sioux. Government soldiers were sent to arrest Sitting Bull, and they killed him in his camp. Shortly after that there occurred the massacre of a band of Sioux at Wounded Knee. Some Sioux killed at Wounded Knee wore the ghost shirts, believing them to be impenetrable by bullets.

After these events, and the failure of the expected resurrection to take place, Wovoka, in Nevada, began to alter his message, stressing the importance of proper living. Other groups picked up the dance and the messages, now shorn of the predictions of a coming apocalypse. In Wyoming, the Shoshone combined the Ghost Dance with a ceremony of thanks to God. During the ritual, shamans would report visions of the dead waiting in heaven to return to earth. The Ghost Dance occupied a place in subsequent Native American religious and political life. Later, Christian converts among the Sioux reinterpreted the messiah proclaimed in the Ghost Dance as Christ. In the 1970s, as Wounded Knee became, for some Native Americans, a symbol of U.S. repression, the American Indian Movement revived the dance.

CULTS, RECRUITMENT, AND VIOLENCE

Revitalization sounds good; it is about renewal after all; but some such movements can take on violent characteristics toward their own members or toward others. But few begin this way. Why do some movements "tip" into violence? And what attracts people to already violent movements?

Aum Shinrikyo

The Japanese movement Aum Shinrikyo at first resembled many other Japanese New Religions in promoting meditation and ascetic practices under the leadership of a charismatic person, in this case the blind Asahara Shoko (Reader 2000). Asahara had earlier joined a religion called Agonshu, whose adherents practiced yoga and meditation, and sought special psychic powers. Like many others in Japan, Asahara was attracted by the movement's teaching that the world was threatened by environmental or nuclear disaster. He left to form his own group in 1984, which began by setting out goals and ideas that were similar to those of other Japanese religious movements (Davis 1980). Members sought greater psychic powers, perhaps through contacts with ancestors, in order to purify themselves or to solve their everyday problems. Like other such religions, Asahara saw people as being reborn according to their karma, and most people as falling into undesirable rebirths.

Starting in the mid-1980s, Asahara began to preach a coming conflict between good and evil, but at first he saw his mission as purifying the world to avoid conflict. He urged followers to form *sanghas*, using the word for Buddhist monasteries. His demands were strict: Those who would join the sanghas had to break off all ties with their families and friends. Even under these conditions, over 1,000 people did join a sangha, and perhaps 8,000 more joined the movement. As with other Japanese New Religions, many of the recruits were educated young professionals. Asahara offered them the chance to engage in research, much of it aimed at giving them superhuman powers; some of it consisting of fabricating amphetamines and hallucinogens along with poisons and explosives. The recruits practiced ascetic regimes and meditation along a path set out by Asahara. Disciples could purchase containers of what was supposed to be the guru's bathwater, or vials of his blood, which would give them his special DNA (and which probably produced effects through the addition of hallucinogenic drugs). They had to rent a helmet that would connect them with the guru's brain waves and enable them to reach his state of meditation (Hall, Schuyler, and Trinh 2000, 76–110).

The stated purposes of these practices changed over time. At first they were supposed to give practitioners personal powers and thereby enable them to save humanity. But as Asahara failed to reach his own goals of massive recruitment, his disillusionment led him to turn toward a more dramatic form of apocalyptic preaching, in which he said that mass destruction was coming and only a few people on earth would be saved. In itself, this doctrine is not so different from that adhered to by many Christians in North America who believe that at the coming moment of Rapture only a few saved souls will be brought up to heaven to avoid the destruction that will follow on earth. But (as readers will be quick to add) doctrine does not determine people's ideas or practices. In this case, Asahara responded violently to his failure, blaming the world for what had happened. He turned inward, demanding complete obedience from his followers, and set an example by having his wife beaten until she complied with his demands to lead an ascetic life. He had others beaten and forced to follow regimes involving near-starvation or other extreme practices, and in 1988 one of his followers died after a regimen involving repeated immersion in baths. Asahara was waiting for legal recognition of his movement as a religion and covered up the death; worse, he ordered the killing of a follower who was about to defect and tell the authorities of the death. The murder changed Asahara's writings and preaching; now he warned of Satan corrupting some in his movement, a logic akin to that of the Salem witchcraft accusations.

The violence escalated, as did opposition from families of those who had cut their ties to the outside world in order to join one of Aum's sanghas and from some disillusioned adherents. Asahara ordered the murder of an opposition group's lawyer and his family. His entry into electoral politics in 1990 failed miserably, adding to his humiliation and leading to a decision to destroy large numbers of his opponents. He may have ordered as many as 50 people killed. His efforts to develop weapons of mass destruction culminated in the sarin gas attack on the Tokyo subway in 1995, which killed 12 people and injured thousands, leading to the arrest of Asahara and many of his followers.

Order of the Solar Temple

The Order, or OTS in its French version, came to the world's attention in 1994, when police investigating the burning of vacation villas in Switzerland and Québec found that they contained bodies neatly arranged on the floors and killed with bullets to the head. The dead turned out to be successful men and women from Switzerland, France, and Belgium—a nuclear engineer, a mayor, and wealthy businesspeople. A year later, more people died in the same manner near Grenoble, France. Letters sent out the day of the 1994 deaths explained that those who died were in fact in "Transit" to another world. It turned out that some had killed themselves, while others had been "assisted" in their journey. Some dissidents had been outright murdered.

The Solar Temple Order developed in the 1970s from the partnership of Joseph Di Mambro, a French former member of Templar and Rosicrucian orders, and the Belgian homeopathic doctor Luc Jouret. Di Mambro had earlier joined a movement in France that saw itself as the successors to the medieval Knights Templar, and some survivors of the massacre-suicides compared the fate of the Order to that of the Knights (Hall, Schuyler, and Trinh 2000; Introvigne and Mayer 2002). The Knights were formed during the Crusades in the twelfth century in order to protect Jerusalem. Their order was chartered directly by the Pope. During the twelfth and thirteenth centuries, they succeeded brilliantly both in combat and in amassing and investing wealth from donations. They established parallel lay organizations that functioned as shadow Churches with their own rituals. Their secrecy, success, and activities in the financial world aroused envy and suspicion; and once they failed on the battlefield, the Church and the king of France, Philip the Fair, moved together against them. In 1310, Philip had 54 Knights burned at the stake for heresy.

The mystique of the Knights has propelled them into literature (most recently in *The Da Vinci Code*) and into the popular imagination. The red (or "rosy") cross they wore gave the name to the Rosicrucian order, and Masonic orders claimed descent from both Templars and the Rosicrucians. Hundreds of such "neo-Templar" and Rosicrucian orders have formed over the past two centuries, each combining mysticism, chivalry, secrecy, and promise of delivery from death. The Vatican II reforms that lessened the sense of mystery and tradition associated with the Catholic Mass gave a further boost to the creation of such orders (and to New Age movements generally).

It was out of this cauldron of movements and mysticism that the Solar Order emerged, based on ideas about a "Solar Christ" and the existence of "Ascended Masters" who move in and out of historical existence. Jouret had been ordained as a priest by a dissident Roman Catholic priest, and became the Grand Master of the Solar Order. Drawing on his homeopathic medical background, Jouret lectured throughout the French-speaking world, linking health concerns to the Order's ideas, and selling cassettes, books, and lecture tickets in health-food stores and New Age bookstores. Jouret's lectures were by all accounts spellbinding, and he had clubs for people to join—on nutrition, gardening, music, and so forth. His message was that a vital essence in ourselves was troubled when we felt sick, and that the same essence in our environment was troubled, a line of thought leading him to predict ecological apocalypse. His appeal was in his ability to link together a number of New Age themes: astrology, health and environmental consciousness, a mixing of science and faith, and to tie these to the mystical countercultural Catholic traditions, in which francophone Catholics disaffected by the liberal reforms of Vatican II could rediscover history and mystery.

Even as he was predicting that humans would find it difficult to make the crossover from this age to the Age of Aquarius, Jouret came under suspicion in France, where active anticult organizations watch out for such movements. He developed a new center in Québec, where the Order's initiation ceremony happened to be videotaped by a member. The tape shows how the internal structure of the Order worked in a ritual. The Order was governed by an inner group, below which were three degrees of initiation, each with three internal ranks. In the videotaped ritual, initiated members wearing white robes with red crosses enter an outer room, line up, and raise swords toward the light emanating from a single candle. A priest blesses a new member, at which point Jouret emerges from behind a door to bless the group. Behind that door was the inner sanctuary where a few initiates would be admitted to witness images, which probably were holographic projections but were experienced by the initiates as visitations by Ascended Masters. They saw apostles of Christ, grand Templar masters, Moses, and other world figures. Di Mambro himself was considered to be the reincarnation of the Pharoah Akhnaton, Osiris, and Moses. The Order demanded the members donate money and sought a high degree of control over their lives, to the point of rearranging marriages in order to produce "cosmic children" who would create a New Age. Some rebelled at these measures, and dissidence increased when it became known that the spectral appearances of Ascended Masters were the result of technologically sophisticated image projections. By the early 1990s, police and anticult groups had begun to investigate the Order. In 1993, Québec police raided an Order building, found weapons, and arrested Jouret and others; they were eventually convicted of weapons charges. The trial added to the group's negative publicity and built up their feeling that the outside world had conspired against them.

The group's leaders responded by declaring that cosmic messages indicated the need to make a "Transit" out of this world and into another (specifically, to the star Sirius). They then took the steps that led to the murder-suicides of 1994 and 1995 in Switzerland, France, and Québec. Would the massacres have taken place had there been no outside intervention against the group? It is hard to say, and it did not take much to push the leaders over the edge, but letters sent by the group pointed to police raids and arrests as the reason for their decision to embark on the Transit at the moment they did so. French and French-speaking authorities were quick to apply the standard analytical framework used in these countries to denounce "cults" (*les sectes*): The members were gullible people, marginal to their societies, who had been brainwashed by dangerous leaders. However, most followers of the Order were solid, middle-class citizens. Why, then, did this group march toward destruction, and why did many of its members willingly commit suicide?

As with Aum Shinrikyo, the best account of the group's "success" focuses both on their internal social and psychological dynamics and on the effects of external pressures on the group. Even by the late 1980s, the group's message of apocalypse considered the end of the world to be part of a long-term cycle of birth and death, the idea of 6,000-year cycles found in Hinduism. These events would develop naturally, without any need for the group to take action. In this respect, the Order resembled Aum Shinrokyo at a similar, early stage of development. The group amassed money and arms for survival in face of a coming catastrophe, not in order to kill others, and in that respect resembled the mainly peaceful activities of survivalist groups in western parts of North America. Apocalyptic beliefs thus do not appear themselves to be a sufficient cause of violence.

It was a combination of perceived threats and fears that they were losing their hold on their followers that led the leaders to move to a new stage of killings and suicides. By the early 1990s, Di Mambro and Jouret had begun to express desires to leave this earth. At the same time, police investigations of Order finances and firearms procurement combined with dissent within the movement to create a sense of external threat in the minds of the leaders. Of course, that they responded by killing dissidents requires a further psychological explanation. The members' reasons for maintaining their involvement also are unclear, but most likely had to do with that enjoyment of being in on a secret, being one of the few to know what really is going to happen, that adds strength to secret societies around the world, whether in Masonic temples or New Guinea societies. If we can believe the letters sent out just before the mass suicides and killings, the members of the Solar Order saw themselves as leaving a sullied world for a purer one. Whether they would have followed through with the Transit even without outside opposition is difficult to say, but surely their drive to do so came initially from within themselves, through a conviction nourished by age-old narratives of Christian martyrdom, mysticism, and dispensed salvation, maintained through rituals of access to wisdom, and reinforced by contemporary concerns for psychological and environmental purity.

The series of events that led to the destruction of the Order appear in a number of other cases of small apocalyptic groups, such as Heaven's Gate, whose adherents committed suicide near San Diego in 1997, and the Peoples Temple of Jim Jones, living in its communal settlement in Guyana, South America, where 918 people died in 1978. All three groups believed that they had come from, and would return to, another world. They felt persecuted, and were particularly threatened by defectors and dissidents. Attacks on some of these groups added to this sense of persecution: The fate of the Branch Davidians at the 1993 Waco shootout convinced many cult leaders that they were next in line to be destroyed. In their efforts to restore authority, reclaim charisma, and remove themselves from their persecutors, they took violent action against themselves and others. These actions were also statements to the world. The Order and

Heaven's Gate sent out press releases before destroying themselves. Jim Jones said: "We've got to be in the history books."

These and other groups that ended in violence had apocalyptic expectations about the soon-to-arrive end of human history. Their expectations led them to engage in practices intended to deliver them from catastrophe, but that had the indirect effects of promoting strong norms of internal solidarity and loyalty. In the society at large, they were confronted by a strong group of cult detractors whose efforts to expose, oppose, and sometime destroy cults reinforce their feelings of persecution.

Persecution does not in itself lead to violence, of course. Scientologists have been subjected to more governmental scrutiny and harassment than was the Order of the Solar Temple; and although Scientologists may have carried out revenge actions against dissidents, there has been nothing approaching the behavior described earlier. The difference lies in part in the internal ideas: Even though Scientology does demand secrecy and conformity from adherents, it does not (as far as we know) organize its activities around the idea of an impending apocalypse.

But then again, the beliefs in an apocalypse do not necessarily lead to violence either, as is evidenced by the millions of (relatively) peaceful churchgoers in the United States who believe that the end of the world is near, the "dispensational premillenarianists." One could believe that the world will end and draw a wide range of consequences from that belief: that one should better the world to attract a savior, that one should lead an ethically correct life so as to achieve salvation, or that one should convince others to do so as well in order to save the largest number of people. For a movement to move from apocalyptic beliefs to violence demands additional internal elements as well as a perception of external repression. Movements such as those described in this chapter moved from a simple belief that the world would terminate in an apocalypse to a drive to either to flee the world or bring about its end. This turn toward world-ending or world-fleeing action was led by a small number of individuals, whose charisma and paranoia allowed and drove them to carry it off.

WHY DO PEOPLE JOIN VIOLENT MOVEMENTS?

Even if we understand how people might call on religion to justify killing others, we still do not understand how it is that a small number of people join terrorist groups or bring themselves to kill other people. What roles do religious beliefs and practices play in recruitment and killing itself?

We might begin by looking at terrorist acts and asking to what extent religions play a role. We might suppose that over the past decade, Islam has been behind terrorism in some respect. But we might do so because of the small number of spectacular events, particularly the attack on the World Trade Towers on September 11, 2001, and because terrorism associated with Islam is a relatively recent phenomenon.

Fortunately, a 2007 study of terrorist attacks in Europe provides some sense of the relative magnitude of different types of terrorism. The EU report (Europol 2007) found 498 attacks during 2006 that it (and the member states) counted as terrorist, or involving violence within the state intended to destabilize the political order. Of those attacks, one involved Islam (in Germany), and 424, thus the vast majority, were separatist, mainly in Corsica, directed against the French government, and in Spanish Basque country. Most of the remainder came from left-wing groups operating in Greece, Germany, Italy, and Spain. Now, about one-half of all arrests made in cases of terrorism were of Muslims; but even more importantly, over half (342 out of 706) of all terrorism arrests made in the EU in 2006 were made in France, with the majority targeting Corsican separatists. Of course, attacks in 2004 in Madrid and in 2005 in London caused a large number of casualties, and those years look different than does 2006, but then again in still earlier years it was Catholic-Protestant conflicts in Northern Ireland that caused a great number of attacks.

Since 2001, a number of social scientists have studied the pathways that lead ordinary Muslims to join any one of a number of small or large groups that stand apart from mainstream Muslim organizations. Most of these have peaceful objectives. The Tablighi Jema'at, for example, aims at reaching Muslims who have become lax in their daily religious duties of prayer and piety, and it recruits them to spread this message to others. Tablighi members often stand out in their societies for their choice of long beards and "Islamic" dress, the men wearing long white robes. Although a few Muslims move from Tablighi membership to more militant, or even violent organizations, others move in a different direction to higher education or electoral politics. In its missionary "call" for Muslims to become better Muslims, it resembles the work of orthodox Jewish Chabad organizations, which make a similar plea to Jews.

Quite different in its objectives is the Hizb ut-Tahrir, which is overtly political and often appears radical in its demands, which include the creation of an Islamic state and, in the meantime, the disengagement of Muslims from civic participation in non-Muslim states. They tend to dress like other well-educated and articulate members of the society where they live, despite their call for a distinct Muslim society. In these respects, they resemble the U.S. conservative Protestant groups, led by Jerry Falwell, Pat Robertson, and others, who have called for the restoration of God's dominion on earth as part of the preparation of the return of Christ.

Although we may consider the Tablighi Jema'at and the Hizb ut-Tahrir to be "radical" because they stand out from more mainstream Sunni Muslim organizations, their doctrines and practices are no more so than are the corresponding Jewish and Protestant organizations mentioned earlier. Some Muslims in Britain call for governance by scripture, but so do some Protestants in the United States!

Other movements adopt a militant and sometimes violent stand against the governments of their own countries, and call for new regimes that would follow Islam. Muslims have fought or are fighting in Kashmir against Indian control, in Chechnya against Russian rule, in Bosnia against the Serbs, in Algeria against the military-backed regime, and in the case of Hamas for the liberation of Palestine. One may be before or against these local jihads—the United States aided the jihad against the Soviets, and many in Europe and North America supported the Bosnian struggle—but their character is akin to other internal wars that do not include an Islamic ideology, even if fought mainly by Muslims. For example, the PLO includes Christians and its goals historically were primarily secular; the GAM rebel movement in Aceh, Indonesia, although Muslim, did not have an Islamic dimension to its demands. Quite different again is the global jihadist movement, what Marc Sageman (2004) calls the "global Salafi jihad," and which targets the "far enemy," meaning non-Muslim nations removed from areas of conflict. These people, who are linked in one way or another to al-Qaeda, differ in important ways from men and women fighting for the liberation of a particular territory, such as Palestine or Kashmir, and from people fighting on religious grounds against their own government, as in Algeria or Central Asia. The global Salafi jihad aims to create an Islamic state, and it sees the West as standing in the way of that aim. Those jihadists who turn to terrorism differ importantly with other movements, such as the Hizb ut-Tahrir, who work toward the creation of a worldwide Islamic state but do not engage in terrorism to do so.

The profile of these *mujahîdîn* contrasts with certain popular images. They are, relative to others in the countries from where they come, well educated, usually in secular subjects. Other than the Indonesians, who did often attend religious schools, these terrorists come from technical faculties, and approach Islam in a manner similar to the way they approached those secular subjects: as a set of propositions to be learned directly from scripture, and not mediated by traditional disciplines of jurisprudence. The counterterrorism expert Marc Sageman writes (2008, 58–60) that most terrorists had little religious education and so were unable to critically evaluate the simplistic jihadist arguments—"it follows that more religious education for these young men might have been beneficial."

Why did they join the movement (al-Qaeda or an affiliate)? Most did so away from home: Egyptians and Saudis while in exile in the Sudan in the early 1990s, Indonesians while in Malaysia, and many from North Africa and elsewhere while in Europe. "Lonely people looking for companionship" (Sageman 2004, 93) met new friends at a mosque, and sometimes these new friends brought them into contact with someone urging a global *jihad*. They may not have been particularly devout, but they translated their personal alienation into a wholesale condemnation of the West and of the regimes it supported. They may have begun their violent activities in the late-1980s anti-Soviet jihad in Afghanistan, where they were trained by Pakistanis (working from CIA financial aid), but more likely if they had a jihad experience it was much later in Afghanistan or in Bosnia. These jihadists were not recruited and certainly not brainwashed by senior al-Qaeda personnel. Theirs was a pathway that began as social and led gradually to incorporation into a tight friendship group in which radical Islamic ideas became the stuff of their everyday lives. They eventually joined the jihad as a group rather than as individuals (Sageman 2004, 110). In other circumstances, those ideas would have been those of left-wing terrorist groups in Europe preaching the virtues of Maoism, or right-wing groups spouting anarchist ideas. Or they would have been nonviolent ideas that also would have given them the sense of order and purpose they craved: perhaps the structure of a political party, or a social movement, or a more mainstream religious group.

Sageman (2004, 111) makes an important methodological point in his study: If you interview people already in a religious movement, they will tend to say that they joined it because of its ideas, because at that point they have bought into the group's ideology. But studies that draw on data about preexisting social networks and activities find that friendship, casual social contacts, and kinship play important roles in recruitment. But there remains a leap from joining an organization to sacrificing yourself for the cause. What adds this dimension of radical commitment? Clearly religious belief plays a part. The jihadi terrorists met others at mosques, and they spent time listening to sermons and watching videos about the jihad in various parts of the world. They internalized a script that explained why bad things were happening to good Muslims, and in which the role of the West was paramount. But the exposure to these ideas is far from sufficient to explain why someone becomes a terrorist. As Sagemen (2004, 119) points out, al-Qaeda has recruited virtually no one from places where its headquarters have been located or where it has held training camps, in Afghanistan, Pakistan, and Sudan, and where presumably exposure to their ideas has been greatest. Those people who join al-Qaeda are living temporarily away from home, and they join in part to find a home. Joining a movement accentuates the sense of separateness from everyday life: You dress differently and commit your life to the organization. Here we can recall the Japanese Mahikari movement we examined in Chapter 5. The appeal of the movement depended in part on the script that explained current ills suffered by patients and also set that explanation in the broader context of a mythic Japanese history. People who already experienced tensions and wished to find religious solutions found the movement enticing.

But most people who meet this description do not join any particular movement. Recent work in the sociology of religion (Lofland and Stark 1965; Stark and Finke 2000) adds an additional social dimension to the analysis of the general question. People who end up joining a religious movement are likely to have recently moved away from their previous social ties, and, after initially encountering the new doctrine, to form positive social bonds with one or more members of the new group. In other words, there may be cognitive reasons why a group's script is attractive, but one also needs the socioemotional dimension—initial detachment from a former group, subsequent reattachment to the new group—to account for joining. This general pattern has held for studies of the Reverend Sun Myung Moon's Unification Church, as well as the Egyptian Islamic movements' influence by Sayid Qutb's writings, the Islamic Liberation Organization, and the Jamaat al-Muslimin (Sageman 2004, 126–135).

Conclusions

New Religious movements draw adherents because of their capacity to reframe experience in new terms. In his Mahikari study, Davis speaks about the "salvation syndrome" particular to any one such movement: their narrative that explains why things aren't going so well in the world, and their answer: following a Savior, waiting for a Messiah, or killing those who are oppressing you. People find their way to such movements for a variety of reasons; it is usually once they have joined up that they take on the movement's ideology, not beforehand. Most such movements offer new kinds of meaning to adherents and cause very little trouble to others, but a few move toward violent acts—which leads us to the issue for debate.

Discussion Questions

What is it that leads some people to commit violence in the name of religion? How much does religious doctrine have to do with it, and how much is it social or psychological factors?

Media Resources

A short, good clip on cargo cults is at: http://www.youtube.com/watch?v=c7RA4UnEuQO. On the Lakota Sioux Ghost Dance, there are documentaries on Sitting Bull, such as the 44-minute documentary at: http://www.youtube.com/watch?v=vz7R9m2CYVE. You can view a recording of the Ghost Dance made in Thomas Edison's studio in 1894 at: http://www.youtube.com/watch?v=ewwEzfKnfwU.

A short documentary on Aum Shinrikyo just after the sarin gas attack in Tokyo covers the essentials of the cult: http://www.youtube.com/watch?v=kZ3prE4sG3E. The film simply called *Islam and War* features interviews with key Muslim leaders on jihad.

Revelation and Authority in Islam

Islam should be the ideal religion for the "standard model" of a religion, with a book, a prophet, and a set of globally accepted teachings. But precisely for that reason, Islam provides a great case study in how difficult it is to define religion—and how the standard model fails to capture much of Muslim religious practice.

We often hear statements to the effect that Islam concerns all of life. And, indeed, Muslims consider that God set out a way or path, the shari'a, which should guide all people in all that they do. As humans have engaged in interpreting God's revealed signs, they have constructed a set of norms or rules to guide people along that path. These rules cover two broad domains. One is the set of rituals that fit pretty well with the Enlightenment notion of religion, and that include the "five pillars" of Islam: testifying to one's faith, carrying out daily prayer, giving alms, fasting during Ramadan, and making the pilgrimage to Mecca. These acts Muslims perform for the sake of God, and are called the *'ibâdât* (from the root `-b-d, "servant," here, of God). The second domain is a set of acts that concern relations among humans and are for their welfare; these are the *mu'âmalât*.

Although this distinction is important, its meaning is hotly contested. Many Muslims would deny that it separates religious acts from secular or mundane ones, because such everyday activities as running a business, greeting a neighbor, or eating lunch also should be guided by the principles given by God—and they can cite verses of the Qur'ân and statements or exemplary acts by the Prophet Muhammad that bear on each of these activities. Many of these Muslims, indeed, would extend the meaning of 'ibâdât to take in all activities that may be carried out with God in mind. Other Muslims cite a *hadîth* from the Prophet to the effect that Muslims should follow him with regard to worship and service to God, and follow their own learning in the pursuit of their other affairs. This major disagreement—actually a whole nest of debates about the various ways one should or should not draw lines between "religion" and the rest of life—runs throughout the topics we discuss here and concerns the very nature of a modern Muslim society and individual.

These debates have important consequences for modern Muslim movements. Some of those Muslims who think that there is a divine precept and a Prophetic example for every action in life also believe that they should work toward creating an Islamic state. The Hizb ut-Tahrir (which flourishes in London, Indonesia, and some other countries but is banned in most of the Muslim world), for example, preaches this line and criticizes all efforts to work within any Western—or any non-Islamic—political system. I recall a major meeting held west of London at which some of the thousands in attendance asked if they might work for parliamentary candidates and were told that doing so was forbidden (*harâm*), because "the Prophet Muhammad did not hold elections." Other Muslims following this general line of thought hold that Muslims should marry in the manner followed by Muhammad and ignore the requirements of civil law.

By contrast, Muslims who hold to a separation between domains where scripture is to be followed and domains where Muslims should look to other kinds of authority—scientific or cultural—work to create ways to live fully Islamic lives in Western countries. They argue that Muslims should look to the purpose of the tenets of scripture, and then ask how best to reach those objectives in the lands where they now live. For example, Muslim teachers in France and the United States argue that Muslims should consider that marrying and divorcing in civil courts already counts as Islamic. If the purpose of religious marriage in Muslim lands is to guarantee that the marriage is carried out with the consent of the husband and the wife, and that it lasts, these purposes are met in Western lands through the laws and procedures enforced by courts. By this logic, a civil marriage is already a religious one, because it does what Islam set out to do.

Muslims disagree, then, over where the boundaries of religion lie: Is a civil marriage religious? Should politics be religious? They also disagree over whether some practices are part of Islam or are superstitions, or magic, or in fact sinful efforts to worship a being other than God (as I mentioned in Chapter 1).

This rather open pluralism of religious knowledge can be puzzling to those on the outside (and often for Muslims as well). After the 9/11 attacks, many who knew nothing of Islam wanted to know what "Islam says" about war, violence, Christians and Jews, and all manner of other topics, as if there was a single set of answers somewhere, perhaps in the Qur'ân. There is no such set. Instead, those who looked for answers on the news saw, often one after the other, calls by terrorists to kill Americans in the name of Islam and statements by venerable gentlemen saying "Islam is a religion of peace." Now, nearly all Muslims would (and do) say that the former is a perversion of Islam. But the second fails to convince anyone: How could this be true at the same time that some Muslims fight for their religion? The platitudes—Islam is for peace; the Qur'ân says you shall not take a life—fail to take account of the rich and complex structures of interpretation that characterize Islam.

THE QUR'ÂN AS RECITATION OF GOD'S SPEECH

For Muslims, speech is sacred and powerful because God made known his commandments by speaking them, and because Muslims can obey those commandments through various ways of speaking. Muslims' sacred book is the Qur'ân, a word that comes from the Arabic root meaning "to recite." The Qur'ân is the collection of verses spoken to Muhammad by the angel Gabriel, who conveyed them from God. The revelation of these verses took place between 610 and 632 in Mecca and Medina, in Arabia. Muslims believe that the Qur'ân preexisted these revelations, that it already was God's speech, probably for eternity, before it was revealed (Graham 1987, 79–115).

These revelations were handed down orally before they were first written down, and even today Muslims consider it important to memorize and recite these words of God. In its written form, the Qur'ân is arranged as 114 chapters, each divided into verses, and arranged not in the order in which they were spoken to Muhammad but, by convention, from the longest to the shortest.

Unlike the Hebrew Bible or Christian Gospels, the Qur'ân is not a collection of long narratives. It contains brief parables and stories but mainly consists of directives and exhortations to Muhammad and his people. Muslims learn the fuller stories of the prophets and of Muhammad's life from other narratives, not from the Qur'ân itself. Much of the Qur'ân concerns about how Muslims ought to live: It sets out values, social norms, and what we generally call "law." These guidelines for living are called shari'a, "the way." (Law in the narrower sense of enforceable jurisprudence is designated by the term *fiqh*.)

The Qur'ân is God's major gift to humans, analogous to the presence of Jesus among humans in Christian understanding. It is an exact replica of the words spoken to Muhammad; therefore, the forms of the spoken and written words themselves take on sacred value. It is also evidence of direct historical contact between God and Muhammad. This direct contact is crucial to Islam's religious foundation, and explains two areas of study within Islam: one that proves that Muhammad was illiterate and could not possibly have created the Qur'ân, and the other that shows the Qur'ân to be inimitable in grammar and rhetoric. These lines of investigation, taken together, prove that the Qur'ân is from God. (Contrast the lack of importance to most Christians of the original sound and shape of the Greek words in the Gospels.)

Let us consider an example, the very short chapter of the Qur'ân called Sûra al-Ikhlâs. This *sûra* or chapter comes toward the end of the Qur'ân, as Chapter 112—precisely because of its length. As I noted earlier, when the revelations were first collected, they were placed in order from the longest to the shortest, placing this *sûra* or chapter near the end of the Qur'ân (although it was one of the earliest to be revealed). It reads:

Qul hu wallâhu ahad	*Say, He is God, one,*
allâhu samad	*God the everlasting refuge,*
lam yalid wa lam yûlad	*Neither begetting nor begotten,*
wa lam yakul lahu kufuwan ahad	*and having as an equal none.*

The sûra affirms the single most important value of Islam, the unity (*tawhîd*) of God. In a few short lines, it unpacks the dimensions of this unity. God is eternal as well as an indestructible refuge (the word *samad* predicated of God has both senses), and He is prior to all things, the Creator of all. He created all but is not a father, and here the verse underscores the monotheism of Islam in contrast to Christian ideas of God the Father and of the Trinity. God is without equal. This proposition places Islam in clear opposition to polytheism (*shirk*), the act of attributing divine attributes to a being other than God. Polytheism is one of the gravest sins in Islam.

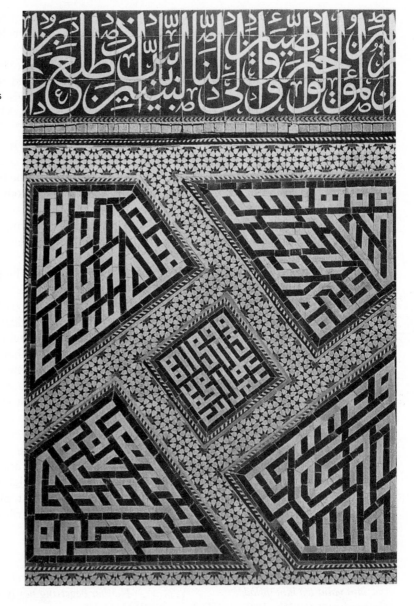

Islamic calligraphy in the Congregational Mosque in Isfahan, Iran. The inlaid tile design shows both cursive and geometric styles; the inscriptions include Qur'ânic passages and, in this Shi'i setting, invocations of both Muhammad and 'Ali. *(Courtesy of John Renard).*

The sûra begins by commanding the reciter: "Say" (*Qul*). Just as Muhammad began his career as Messenger by hearing the order to "Recite," so the worshiper begins this recitation by quoting God ordering us all to restate the fundamental truths contained in the chapter. The sûra is thus a kind of *da`wa*, a call or an outreach to other Muslims, reminding them of the bases of their religion. The title of the chapter, "Sincerity" (*ikhlâs*), adds an additional value to its message, that of sincerity, humility, and authenticity, the appropriate attitude of the worshiper before God.

Because it is one of the shortest chapters, children will learn to memorize it early in their lives as they begin to assemble their repertoires for worship (*salât*). They will also hear it explained countless times—by parents, in school, at a lesson held after morning or afternoon prayer, and sometimes with the statement that because it sums up so many key ideas, it encapsulates the entire Qur'ân. Children also hear adults in their community chant it aloud during congregational prayer, either on Fridays or on any occasion when two or more people pray together. In my own experience, they will hear it chanted in a straightforward way, with little embellishment. Hearing these repeated chants gives the child a basic idea about the melody, timbre, and rhythm (through paying attention to long and short vowels) to be used in reciting from the Qur'ân.

Children also hear the very different rhythm of the *adhan*, the call to prayer that is performed prior to each prayer time. In singing out the call to prayer, whether in a field, a mosque, or over a loudspeaker to all in an urban neighborhood, the reciter typically draws out some vowels to great lengths and pronounces others quickly. He begins with repeated cries of "God is great" (*Allâhu akbar*): twice pronounced very quickly, in a rising intonation, to grab attention (and, in the morning, to wake up sleeping Muslims), and then twice with the long vowel in Allâh drawn out.

The Sûra al-Ikhlâs is recited on other occasions as well, for meditation or to achieve a practical end. And here we move from general features of Islam to observations from anthropological fieldwork, beginning with my own. When in the 1980s I lived in the highlands of the Sumatran village of Isak with my many Gayo-speaking friends and neighbors, I heard the chapter recited repeatedly after Friday worship as a way of meditating following the genre of repeated chanting called *dhikr*. I also heard it recited at ritual meals held in conjunction with Islamic feast days, or to help the spirit of the recently deceased navigate through the trials and tribulations that occur after death. (Muslims in other parts of the world chant scripture in similar ways and for similar purposes.)

Indeed, the all-night sessions of chanting verses that follow a death in that community are called *samadiyah*, from the last word in the chapter's second line: *samad*. In the sessions I attended, men and women, seated in the home of the deceased, chanted the chapter 40 or 60 times, first quickly and then slowly. (They said it more times if fewer people were present, so that the total amount of merit generated would be about the same for every deceased person.) Many of my acquaintances stated that because the chapter contained so many of the truths in the Qur'ân, it had the value of one-third of the entire Qur'ân. The assembled villagers chanted many other verses, both short, complete chapters, and segments from longer chapters, including portions of the second chapter, al-Baqarah. Verse 255 of this chapter is called the "throne verse" for its invocations of God's majesty, reminding us in part: "His Throne encompasses the heavens and the earth, and their preservation does not burden Him. He is the Most High, the Most Great." Recitations have a long history of use for power: During the revolution against the Dutch, the Gayo men would chant the Sûra al-Ikhlâs as a way of keeping bullets away from themselves; others still recite it as part of charms or spells.

The average adult in a simple Sumatran village thus has at her or his command a great deal of scripture, and knows when and how to recite it. Not everyone agrees that all of those uses are appropriate. Many Muslims find the very idea of chanting verses for the dead, a practice found across Muslim-majority societies, to contradict the reliable report (*hadîth sahîh*) that the Prophet Muhammad once said:

> Three things accompany the deceased [to the grave]: his family, his wealth, and his deeds. Two return and one remains: his family and wealth return; his deeds remain.

In other words, after death you only benefit or suffer from what you have done during life; your family cannot help you, and your wealth is for naught. When relatives gather to chant for your benefit, they are at best deceiving themselves, and at worst contravening God's explicit commands.

In the Gayo highlands, especially in the 1920s and 1930s, Muslim teachers who wished to alert people to the impropriety of many of their practices wrote and sung poems—indeed, they invented a new genre of poetry just for this purpose of religious education and correction. These poems often began with a verse from the Qur'ân or with a report from the Prophet Muhammad, and then developed the idea in the Gayo language. To discourage people from chanting for the deceased, for example, they would recite the hadîth quoted above and then expand on its meaning, concluding with the message:

> If you die and your relatives give alms (*sedekah*), the merit does not reach you.
>   Did you not hear the words of God, "a person shall have only as s/he has labored?"

By beginning with a statement attributed to the Prophet, and ending with a verse from the Qur'ân (the part in quotations, recited in Arabic), these change-oriented teachers secured their message with scriptural proofs (*dalil*). By singing Gayo-language poetry in between the hadîth and the Qur'ânic verse, they appealed to ordinary people.

Note how much ground we have covered by beginning with this small unit of knowledge, the short Qur'ânic chapter "Sincerity," and then tracing the diverse ways in which Muslims understand and use it. It functions in everyday life as a unit in worship and rituals, and as a summary of basic Islamic teachings, suitable for expanding for teaching and discussion. Its repeated recitation in the *dhikr*-chanting sessions (dhikr means "remembrance," here of God) brings men and women to a state of transcendence and nearness to God. Some people believe that the reciting transmits spiritual merit to other people, or that it converts God's blessings into bodily protection. Others disagree. Its very range of uses gives rise to further citations of verses and hadîth in commentary and debate about the proper uses of verses. Knowledge may begin with learning how to recite a small snippet of revelation, but it quickly expands to a wealth of religious and ritual activities and to a set of debates about the power and limits of religious acts.

Learning religion begins, then, in mastering the many ways to draw on God's revelations. Revelations tell you how to pray, how to carry out the pilgrimage to Mecca, and how to perform the many ordinary acts of everyday life that could be seen as having a religious dimension: how to enter and leave a mosque, how to greet other people, how to dress and eat properly (and to say the "Bismillah" before starting to eat). This knowledge is practical knowledge. Of course, there are also basic tenets to learn—the five pillars of faith, the required beliefs, and so on—but these are the easier elements of basic knowledge. God's major gift to humans is scripture; humans' major obligation to God is to follow His commands. Humans must thus begin by mastering scripture and learning how to follow those commands, before delving into the subtleties of theology, ethics, or jurisprudence. And indeed, such is how schooling progresses, from knowing how to, eventually, knowing about.

Islamic history, too, is above all a history of revelation (*tanzil*). Two methodological points follow. First, the facts of where and when God chose to send down a revelation may have theological and thus normative relevance for Muslims. When Muslims turn to the historicity of the Qur'ân, it is not to debunk it (although some non-Muslim historians have tried that) but to ask whether it makes a difference that, say, the verse permitting men to take more than one wife was revealed after wars had left a number of widows and orphans. Do these circumstances of revelation mean that polygamy is only permitted under such conditions of demographic imbalance? Or do they mean that such was an opportune moment to make believers aware of an option always available to them?

But the precise historicity of revelation also gives a high degree of religious value to the exact words used by God, through Gabriel, to speak to Muhammad. Revelation was aural, and transmission has continued to take place in an aural/oral mode. Writing was never absent (a point to which I return below), and Muslims recognize as legitimate a number of slightly differing written forms of the Qur'ân. But today, just as centuries ago, Muslims use written scriptural texts in order to learn to recite them. The precise form of recitation continues to refer back to the moment of revelation, the presence of the spoken word.

The sounds of revelation share in this value of originality. Throughout the world of Muslim-majority societies, many boys and girls, and men and women, learn not only to recite the Qur'ân but also to recite it melodically, using certain rules of pronunciation (*tajwîd*). Far from Arabic-speaking regions, Indonesians enthusiastically enter local, national, and international contests (and do quite well), and they often raise the question: Can we not use Indonesian melodies? The authoritative response has been: no, because the Qur'ân was revealed to Arabic speakers—and indeed, some Indonesian reciters practice sounds from Arabic music in order to become habituated to Arabic singing styles.

This epistemology of revelation—valuing the precise act of aural revelation and repeating the act of oral transmission—derives from the ideology of absolute and unmediated *presence* that founds the religion. Gabriel appeared and spoke directly to Muhammad, and he to others, and so on. Muhammad did not interpret the words, and as an illiterate man he could not have created them; he is a vessel of God's message.

But Muslims debate among themselves about what the implications of the Qur'ân's divine source are for everyday life. Many Gayo Muslims, for example, consider prayers (*do'a*) that include Qur'ânic verses to be directly effective in healing, or giving one invulnerability, or harming one's enemy. One of my friends, for instance, used a passage from Chapter 61 of the Qur'ân as the beginning of an invulnerability spell:

> *And He will give you another blessing which you love:*
> *help from God and present victory.*
> *Give good tidings, O Muhammad*
> *to believers.*

To which he would append a plea ending in the lines:

> Let my blanket be from God,
> my cloak from God,
> my shawl from God.

My friend thought that when he uttered the prayer, God gave him a cloak and shawl, as the material realization of God's promise to give "help from God and a present victory." In his own memory, these divine gifts had served him well during battles fought in the 1950s, making bullets and knives skip off his clothes as he fought. But in the 1980s, others pointed out to him that the Qur'ânic passage had been revealed to Muhammad as a message of peace, to stop fighting. One scholar objected to my friend that reciting the Qur'ân could not automatically confer any power on the reciter; that all power came from God and that He knew all that happened in the world anyway and would do as He pleased, regardless of what mumbo-jumbo ordinary men and women chose to recite. All that we can do, he said, is to live good lives and worship God, and then perhaps He will choose to reward us.

AUTHORITY

Islam was born against a background of polytheism, and the statement most often pronounced by a Muslim, called the confession of faith, begins with the dictum: "there is no other deity but God." Islam began in the desert central area of the Arabian Peninsula in the seventh century C.E. Trade and social life were organized by tribes, without central authorities. Power resided in one's lineage connections. Arabs also worshiped many deities, although trade with Syria had also brought the monotheistic ideas of Judaism and Christianity.

Muhammad's own tribe, the Quraysh, dominated the city of Mecca by its control of the caravan trade. Mecca became a religious as well as a trade center; people came to the city on pilgrimages to its shrines, which included the Ka'ba. Several verses of the Qur'ân berate the Meccans for worshiping many gods, and for letting the Ka'ba, built by the prophet Abraham, degenerate into a site of pagan worship. Monotheism remains one of the central emphases in Islam. This emphasis makes especially sensitive the appeals routinely made by many Muslims to other entities (spirits, saints, or prophets) that they intercede with God. These appeals are often branded as polytheism by other Muslims, who cite the Qur'ânic texts originally directed at the merchants of Mecca.

The second part of the confession of faith reads: "and Muhammad is his Messenger." Muhammad was born about 570 C.E. and was orphaned early in his life. He married an older woman, a trader, and managed her caravan. He began to receive revelations when he was 40, in 610 (Peters 1994). The first verse of the Qur'ân to be revealed reached Muhammad when he was in a cave. The archangel Gabriel appeared to him and said: "Recite, in the name of the Lord who created, created man from a clot." (The first word of this verse is sometimes translated as "read," and quoted as evidence that God intends people to educate themselves.)

Muhammad then began to warn the Meccan people of the errors of their polytheistic ways. A few men followed him; most threatened him, and in 622 he fled or made the emigration, *hijra*, to the nearby city of Medina. The emigration marks the beginning of the (lunar) Islamic calendar. In Medina, Muhammad became the leader of the community through his skill in arbitrating between its several populations. He joined with the Jews of the city in praying in the direction of Jerusalem; verses revealed during this time stress the similarity of the two religions. (These verses include the dietary laws, for example.) Muhammad's growing group of followers engaged the Meccans in several battles, most notably those of Badr and Uhud, and his victories finally won him the right to make the pilgrimage to Mecca. He died after making the pilgrimage, in 632.

The place of Muhammad in Islam is both as the Messenger of God and as the Seal of the Prophets. As Messenger of God, Rasulullah, he brought a new collection of God's revealed word to humankind. Other messengers in the past had brought other books: Moses, the Torah; David, the Psalms; and Jesus, the Gospels. This lineage of revelation makes Jews and Christians, along with Muslims, "people of the book." (Hindus were later included in this category because of their use of sacred texts.) Because of their special status, members of these two religious communities were accorded special, protected treatment in Muslim-held territories.

As a prophet, *nabi*, Muhammad is the last in a long series of prophets, including the earlier Messengers. Among the prophets mentioned in the Qur'ân are Abraham, Noah, Hud, Salih, Lot, and Shu'ayb. Hud, Salih, and Shu'ayb do not figure in the Hebrew Bible, but appear in various stories, often as specifically Middle Eastern personages. Shu'ayb warns his people against dishonest business practices, as did Moses warn the Pharaoh against preventing the Israelites from going free.

Muhammad was thus human, a normal human being granted the role of God's mouthpiece. What is sent are words, and not Muhammad himself. Because all messengers are said to have this status, Muslims strongly deny the claim that Jesus was the son of God. Nonetheless, many Western commentators on Islam continue to make the error of presuming that the place of Muhammad in Islam is analogous to that of Jesus in Christianity. (Islam once was called "Muhammadanism" in the West.) It would be more accurate to draw an analogy between Jesus in Christianity, and the Qur'ân in Islam, in that each is held by the religion's adherent to be God's major gift to humans. Similarly, the Gospels, the accounts of the life and statements of Jesus, are best compared not to the Qur'ân but to the hadîth, the record of Muhammad's life and statements.

Who Rules after Muhammad?

Muhammad's authority in the early Muslim community came from his direct ties to God. He was a prophet, but would have to be succeeded by someone who was not a prophet. Who was to rule after his death? On what principle should he be chosen? Or in terms introduced by Max Weber (1978) in his writings on authority and religion, how was Muhammad's charismatic authority to be converted into a routine mechanism for selecting leaders?

Muhammad had neither designated a successor nor suggested a way of doing so. He had no male heir, but even had there been one, it is not clear that this person would have succeeded him. As it happens, upon Muhammad's death in 632, his closest followers in Medina gathered and chose one among them, Abu Bakr, to be the first caliph (*khalîfa*), "deputy" of the Prophet. He was succeeded by another close follower,

'Umar, under whose able rule Muslim armies conquered the rest of Arabia and moved on to Egypt. 'Umar realized the need to create a regular procedure for choosing rulers, and convened a council, *shûra*, to select a new caliph. This action legitimated the idea of reaching decisions by council, and the process continues to be followed in the Muslim world. 'Umar's committee chose a weak candidate, 'Uthmân, an early convert to Islam, who was assassinated in his own house by dissident soldiers.

Shi'ites and Sufis

The next caliph was 'Alî, one of the key figures in Islamic history. 'Alî was the son-in-law of the Prophet and also his cousin, and had a great deal of support because of his kin ties to Muhammad. He was the closest to an heir available to the community. But he failed to punish 'Uthmân's assassins, and he revoked some of his decrees, and thereby provoked the ire of 'Uthmân's own kinsmen, a powerful Meccan aristocratic clan called the Umayyads. Their own leader, Mu'âwiya, challenged 'Alî's leadership. He called for a new council to select a caliph, and met 'Alî in battle (the dispute was arbitrated). 'Alî's rule began to crumble and he was assassinated in 661. His son Hasan abdicated in favor of Mu'âwiya, who began a new period of Umayyad dominance. But 'Alî's other son, Husayn, grandson of the Prophet, became the champion of dissident Muslims who began to see themselves as the "party of 'Alî." In 680, there occurred an event that was to mark the Muslim world forever after: en route to the Iraqi city of Kûfa, Husayn was ambushed and his entire company massacred by Umayyad forces at a place called Karbala. His head was taken as proof of the defeat.

The Karbala massacre became the pivotal event in the emergence and identity of the "party of 'Alî." Now known as the Shî'î, "party," this group conceived of legitimate authority as being forever charismatic. The spiritual and temporal authority of the Prophet was handed down through his grandchildren to a succession of spiritually perfect leaders called *imâms*. Born in opposition to the regime in power, the Shî'îs or Shi'ites have continued to stress the chasm between political realities and a longed for truly Islamic world. Shiite populations, most importantly in Iran, Iraq, and Lebanon, formed communities of teaching and learning divorced from the regimes under whose control they had to live. The date of the Karbala massacre, the 10th of the month of Muharram, 680, is commemorated annually in ta'ziyas, "martyr plays" that feature the assassination of Husayn. Sometimes the events include processions of men striking themselves with chains to participate in the pain and sadness that characterize the Shiite community's historical self-understanding (Momen 1985).

By contrast, the Umayyads and their successors saw themselves as the majority party and the continuers of the Prophet's ways, calling themselves Sunnîs, after sunna, referring to the Prophet's "custom" or usual practices. Sunni conceptions of authority return to the first council that chose the caliph. The entire Muslim community or *umma* inherits political authority, which they then bestow on a leader through a council. This way of routinizing authority drew on Arab tribal ideas of succession and loyalty, and was also effective in incorporating new peoples as part of the umma.

A third type of Islamic authority, alongside those of the council and kinship, is that which binds disciples to Sufi masters. Sufi orders offer paths to greater spiritual awareness and closeness to God, through prayer, chanting, and poetry. Each such order offers a specific *tarîqa*, "way" or "method." The current teacher or master in the order traces his authority back along a spiritual lineage to his teacher, that teacher's teacher, and so forth, often back to one of the immediate followers of the Prophet Muhammad (Eickelman 1976).

The first Sufi order was founded by the Persian scholar Abdul Qâdir al-Jîlânî (1078–1166). Abdul Qâdir's influence as a preacher grew so large that followers established a special retreat for him, where people came to study and listen. He taught that to approach God, people would first need to divest themselves of worldly goods; that these goods acted as veils that came between them and God. As in other Sufi orders, he urged people to practice dhikr: "remembrance" of God by chanting phrases either aloud or in one's heart. Dhikr chants vary from one order to the next, but often include multiple recitations of "there is no deity but God," the first half of the confession of faith, and of praise phrases such as "glory be to God." These activities of remembrance may also be enhanced by music and dance, such as those performed by members of a Turkish order called the Mevlevi (dedicated to the Persian poet Rûmî), and known in the West as "whirling dervishes" (Schimmel 1973).

After Abdul Qâdir's death, people began to ascribe miracles to him, and to consider him a saint. His sons, and their sons, and so on, succeeded him as heads of the Qâdirî order. As the order spread throughout Asia and North Africa, it gave rise to suborders, each linking back to the founder. These orders were an effective way of converting people to Islam, offering as they did spiritual activities and a well-organized religious structure. Each present-day local order has its own spiritual genealogy, detailing the transmission of knowledge back to Abdul Qâdir. These spiritual genealogies connect Muslims in South and Southeast Asia, the Middle East, northern and western Africa, and Europe into an international network of Sufi practice and worship.

INTERPRETATIONS OF SACRIFICE

Given the particular distribution of Islamic authority, over numerous scholars and leaders living in different parts of the world, the interpretation of a particular part of Scripture, or of a particular topic, will vary from one scholar to another, and will be shaped in part by regional traditions and practical challenges. Let us consider an example: the command to sacrifice on a feat day each year.

Across the world, many Muslims sacrifice an animal on the Feast of Sacrifice, the Id al-Adha (`Îd al-Adhâ), which occurs on the 10th day of the last month of the Islamic calendar. This day falls in the middle of the pilgrimage period, and pilgrims perform the act in the city of Mina near Mecca, while other Muslims carry out the sacrifice wherever they reside. The explicit command to sacrifice at this moment has a clear scriptural base, but how Muslims interpret it brings in varying and changing ideas about how best to carry it out.

Moroccan Gender Roles

Let me contrast one set of practices I observed in Gayo society in Indonesia with those described for Morocco; in the next chapter, we will draw on this example again to see how some of these same Moroccans rethink how to respond to this command when they move to cities in Europe. In the 1980s, the anthropologist Abdellah Hammoudi (1993) studied sacrificial rituals in a village of Berber-speaking Muslims in southern

Morocco, near Marrakech. The sacrifice performed during the pilgrimage month was similar to that performed elsewhere, but it was accompanied by a masquerade. For days beforehand, men and women prepared special foods and chose the sacrificial victim with care. Those who could afford it killed a sheep. The animal had to be without defect (ideally a non-castrated male) to be a suitably complete offering to God.

On the morning of the feast day, the men proceeded to a spot marked off for the prayer, an outdoor area indicated only by a pile of whitewashed stones. As they assembled, they chanted praises to God, and, when all the village men had arrived, an imam led them in two cycles of *salat*. (Unlike the ordinary Friday worship, the sermon comes after the salat.) In the first part of the sermon, the imam reminded his listeners of the perils of the grave, the tests to which they would be put after death, and their only hope: adhering to the rules of Islam. After a brief rest, he then celebrated the feast day and described its rules at length: The victim must be an edible domestic animal in good condition, and the killing must take place during the next three days. Sermons delivered in other years placed more stress on Abraham's exemplary willingness to sacrifice his son as the feast day's central message.

From the place of worship the men proceeded to the mosque, where they held a meeting about the mosque's finances and auctioned off that year's walnut crop to pay for the mosque's upkeep. Each man then returned home, where he slaughtered the victim or had it done by someone else. Women prepared the animal, sometimes outlining its eyes in black (underscoring the role of the animal as a substitute for humans). Men laid the animal on its side, facing Mecca, and one man, dedicating the animal to God, quickly cut its throat with a large knife. The women caught the spurting blood and preserved it for use in warding off harm and curing illness. The meat was prepared for eating, then or later, and the skin was dried to be sold, given away, or used in the masquerade to follow, days later, when an unmarried man would don the skin of a victim, prepared in such a way that "everything on him is topsy turvy," with the animal's testicles hanging over the player's rear. Other young men played the roles of Jews, workers, or women in the carnivalesque procession that flaunted sexuality and reversed social hierarchies.

The separation of men and women, their complementary roles, and the carnival-like masquerade are characteristic of this part of North Africa. As we shall see later, in other societies the Feast of Sacrifice appears quite different. But in many respects—the sermon, the choice of victim, the method of killing—this rural Moroccan sacrifice resembles those in Indonesia, Iran, or Los Angeles.

In urban Morocco, other political messages are layered onto the social and religious one. Elaine Combs-Schilling (1989) describes how the rulers of Morocco use the sacrificial ritual to publicly reaffirm their claims to be the direct descendants of the prophet Muhammad. Each year on the day of sacrifice, the king publicly plunges a dagger into a ram's throat, reenacting his ascendant Muhammad's own commemorative sacrifice in the seventh century. In Combs-Schilling's account, the sacrifice also reaffirms patriarchal power in the family and embodies a notion of male fertility. In many urban households, the patriarch follows the ruler's lead by publicly killing a ram. The size and virility of the ram is taken as a measure of the man's own virility. The men of the household stand erect to witness the sacrifice; women and children are either absent or in the background, seated. Women play only the role of passive observers to the sacrifice; after the killing, they may dab some of the victim's blood on their faces to "share in the power of sacrifice" (1989:231).

Already we can see that men and women play different roles in different Moroccan contexts. Hammoudi's account from the Berber village shows how the public role of the married men is complemented by the ritually crucial activities of women in preparing the victim for slaughter. Women purify the victim with henna, thereby transforming it from ordinary animal to sacrificially appropriate victim, and they gather the victim's blood for use in guarding the home and in combating illnesses. Other anthropologists working in Morocco add to the picture of variation by noting that often the head of household has someone else kill the victim, and that the victim may be a sheep or goat.

Even looking at one country, then, we quickly realize that with the ritual of sacrifice we have both a core set of practices and ideas, and a good deal of room for variation. In the next chapter, we ask what some of those Moroccans do when they and others from North Africa move elsewhere: What do they preserve and what do they leave behind? We will not be surprised if there are vigorous debates among Muslim migrants over these questions.

Indonesian Contrasts

If we move to Indonesia we can see, first, distinctions among Indonesian Muslims that stem from their broader theological debates and, second, an overarching Indonesia-wide pattern that contrasts with the overall Moroccan one and that has to do with broad cultural contrasts between the two regions.

As I mentioned earlier, for years I lived in the largely traditionalist village community of Isak in the Gayo highlands of Aceh. There, households sacrificed various kinds of animals: chickens, ducks, sheep, goats, or water buffalo. Nearly all Isak households performed a sacrifice on the feast day. At the very least, a household would kill one of its chickens or ducks, or buy a chicken or duck from another household. If times were very bad, two households might jointly hold a feast and share a duck. As long as the throat can be cut and the meat eaten, I was told, the sacrifice meets the demands of God. (In principle, said some, half-jokingly, even a grasshopper would do as a sacrifice.)

Just prior to cutting the victim's throat, the sacrificer dedicated the animal to one or more living or deceased relatives. In 1978 my neighbor Abang Das sacrificed a buffalo for the benefit of his parents and grandparents. Just prior to cutting the animal's throat, he pronounced the Bismillah ("In the name of God, the Merciful, the Compassionate") and the confession of faith ("I attest that there is no deity but God and that Muhammad is his Messenger"), and then dedicated the buffalo to his father, mother, and their families, followed by his own name.

In contrast to the Morocco case, most of these sacrificial events were carried out in the back of the house, with no more ceremony than the quiet utterance of the dedication. Who actually cut the throat was not of great importance; a man might delegate the job to someone else. Nor was the event interpreted in patriarchal terms. The sacrifice was carried out for the household as a unit: Women as well as men spoke of "their" sacrifice, and couples decided jointly on a list of people who would receive its spiritual benefit. In the case of a buffalo, the beneficiaries usually included parents of the husband and the wife, and daughters as well as sons. Widows also carried out sacrifice (without being socially redefined as men); and when a wealthy female trader in Isak sacrificed a buffalo, everyone spoke of it as her sacrifice, not as her husband's (who was also part of the household). This set of features alone makes the Gayo case markedly different from Moroccan public forms, where, as we saw, the physical act of throat-cutting iconically signifies the virility, power, and self-sufficiency of the male as opposed to the female.

In Isak, the throat-cutting is not the most publicly salient moment of the ritual, nor are the Moroccan patriarchal messages communicated. The focus of social attention is instead on transmitting benefit to one's relatives by means of the sacrifice and, especially, at the ritual meals (*kenduri*) held afterwards. The kenduris held on the Feast of Sacrifice varied considerably in their size and form. If a family killed just a chicken or duck, then they would eat it with little fuss. At most, the household head or a learned relative recited a short prayer. If they sacrificed a sheep, then they would be likely to invite neighbors and relatives to share the feast. If a buffalo was killed, then everyone in the village was invited to eat together. Guests brought raw foods (milled rice, coconuts, and sugar), which the hosting household and their close relatives prepared for eating, and they could then take home a bit of the raw meat from the sacrificed animal.

At feasts where a buffalo or sheep was eaten, a religiously learned man would lead a group recitation of short Qur'ânic verses, recite a long petitionary prayer (punctuated by choruses of "*âmîn*"), and, for good measure, repeat, for God's hearing, the names of the beneficiaries of the just-completed sacrifice. These recitations play an instrumental role in securing the benefit of the sacrifice; they also reaffirm relations of sociability among the participants.

Some ritual meals were attended by more than one hundred people. These large meals featured night-long recitation sessions (*samadiyah*). The learned man who led the guests in chanting would have been given a list of the people to whom the merit should be transmitted; he then embedded these names in a long prayer (sometimes saying the names very softly), thereby directing the evening's merit to the intended beneficiaries.

In Isak, for each of the four years when I was present for the Feast of Sacrifice, three or four households each sacrificed a buffalo, sponsored a village-wide feast, and held an all-night recitation session. They held the feasts at different times so that men or women with ties to more than one village would be able to satisfy their multiple obligations. These major feasts were occasions for relatives who had moved away from Isak to return and join in transmitting merit to those who had died before them. The sponsors whom I knew well spoke to me about the dead who were to benefit from the night's sessions; these days were times for reflection and remembrance as well as for contributing to the welfare of relatives and neighbors.

These events of transmission (at the moment of killing, the afternoon *kenduris*, and the nighttime *samadiyah*) are central to most Isak villagers' ideas about sacrifice. Indeed, they generally reserve the Gayo phrase "to sacrifice" (*gelé qurbën*, lit. "to cut the throat of a sacrificial animal") for occasions when a goat or buffalo is killed and served at a kenduri. Kenduris are a general framework for ritual in Gayo society (and elsewhere in the Malay-Indonesian archipelago). Most kenduris combine the recitation of prayers with the burning of incense and the offering of special foods; both incense and foodstuffs help to transmit the message of the meal to the intended spiritual recipient. Kenduris are held on Muslim calendrical holidays and for a wide variety of practical purposes: to fulfill a vow, to request help from ancestors in healing a sick person, or to call on God to ensure the safe passage of a deceased person's spirit into the next world. By making the Feast of Sacrifice into a kind of kenduri, Isak Gayo have configured it as an event of transaction and communication.

The sacrifice also provides a specific, future material benefit, for on Judgment Day the persons named as sacrificial beneficiaries will be able to ride on the animal to the place of judgment. Only one person can ride a goat or sheep, but seven can ride on a buffalo. A buffalo sacrifice thus provides the opportunity to bring together parents, children, and grandchildren on the back of the afterlife vehicle, and if they had the resources most Isak households would stage a buffalo feast sometime during their lives.

Isak couples shaped their sacrificial strategies with afterlife sociability in mind. Each couple tried to provide a vehicle for themselves, their children, and, if possible, their parents and grandparents. Parents felt a particularly strong obligation to provide a vehicle for a child who died young, as did children for those parents and grandparents who did not have the resources to make a sacrifice in their own name. I heard stories about children who would not acknowledge their parents on Judgment Day, because they had not bothered to sacrifice for them. "Without a sacrifice there is no tie between parents and children," said one woman. The prospect of future abandonment by one's children horrified most people and provided further encouragement to perform the sacrifice. It also led people to include in their dedications even those parents or children who already had a vehicle provided for them, in order to ensure that family ties would be preserved during the harsh times of judgment. I was told that in the past, just before a sheep was sacrificed all the close relatives of the beneficiary would grasp its tether rope, thereby strengthening their ties in the afterlife.

Isak transactions and images contrast sharply with the centralized dynastic meanings and father-son pairs of Morocco. Gayo and Moroccans conceive of the events in Islamic terms. Both views are articulated through the performance of the Feast of Sacrifice and through the rich imagery of the past (Abraham's sacrifice) and the future (Judgment Day). Isak Gayo project that imagery out from the ritual event to the family's fate in the afterlife; Moroccans concentrate that imagery on the immediate structure of domination in the kingdom, the community, and the family.

Conclusions

As a religion founded in prophetic authority, Islam both continually refers back to prophecy and has had to create new structures of authority following the death of the Prophet. That death opened up divergent pathways to locating authority, and this divergence is reflected in the Muslim world today.

As a tradition, with its scriptural basis, Islam creates a sense of universality. Any Muslim, anywhere in the world, can and does refer back to Muhammad and to revelation. But Muslims also refer to centuries-long regional traditions of interpretation, such that practices differ from one part of the Muslim world to another. It will therefore not be surprising when we see in the next chapter even more divergences when Muslims begin to settle in large numbers in new places.

Discussion Questions

It can be very useful to examine ways in which writers refer to Islam, to Shariah, and to Islamic leaders in newspapers and magazines. Elsewhere (Bowen 2012) I have tried to correct common false claims about Muslims in the West.

Media Resources

On Islam, a number of films trace Muhammad's life; *The Message* (starring Anthony Quinn) is interesting because it is widely showed by Muslims. *Beyond the Veil*, though somewhat dated, is still a superb film on how women in Cairo think about veiling, while *Divorce, Iranian Style* shows how a divorce court really works in Teheran.

Migration and Adaptation: Focus on Muslims in Europe

In this chapter, we focus on the ways in which Muslims have adapted to new countries of residence in Europe and at the same time have continued to participate in transnational religious networks. We will see how their histories of migration have shaped how they and other Europeans have come to see themselves and each other.

As with Catholicism and Buddhism, Islam always was transnational in its conception, in the sense of having a global reach. Sunnis and Shi'is alike envisioned the Islamic state as transcending preexisting boundaries that were ethnic (or "national" in today's sense) so as to include all Muslims. In that sense, many Muslims saw the ideal political arrangement as one in which all Muslims would be in one state, with one ruler. Even today, some Muslims envision a future time when a single Muslim state or caliphate will unify all Muslims.

Muslims established a presence in Europe early in Islamic history. They expanded into Europe from two directions: from northern Africa into Spain (and for a brief period into southern France), and, later on, into the Balkan Peninsula. The former left a rich Islamic heritage, which many in Spain claim today; the latter created Muslim majority societies in today's Albania, Bosnia (and, of course, in Turkey).

In the remainder of Europe, the presence of Muslims is due to the colonization of Muslim-majority lands in Asia and Africa. France, Britain, the Netherlands, and Italy all had colonies with Muslim populations. France invaded Algeria in 1830 and by the century's end had made it part of French territory. By the turn of the twentieth century, France was recruiting male laborers from northern and western parts of Africa, as well as from elsewhere in Europe, to work in its factories, and these patterns of "circular labor migration" continued to develop during the first half of the century. The Dutch ruled today's Indonesia and Suriname, and the British today's India, Pakistan, Bangladesh, and Malaysia. Some Muslims from those Asian regions moved to the Netherlands and Britain. Italy's ventures in northern and eastern Africa led to some migration later from those areas to Italy.

MIGRATION AND TRANSNATIONAL TIES

Large-scale movement of Muslims to Europe only began after the Second World War, however, when the demand for unskilled labor to rebuild Europe far outstripped the European supply. Muslims from Kashmir and what is today Bangladesh came to Britain, benefiting from policies that allowed free movement within the Commonwealth. The unrest and uncertainty produced by the Algerian War (1954–1962) led many French Algerians to settle in the metropolis with their families. By the late 1960s, Moroccans and Turks were moving into the Netherlands and the Scandinavian counties. Worldwide recession in 1973–1974 led European countries to limit labor migration, however. Since that time, most Muslims arriving in Europe have come to join a close family member already enjoying legal residence, to claim asylum on grounds of conflict or persecution, or as an illegal entrant. In those areas of Europe that had experienced relatively little earlier labor immigration, including the Scandinavian countries and Italy, asylum seekers make up a relatively large proportion of the Muslim population. Elsewhere the older patterns of labor migration continue to shape today's immigration patterns.

In the 1980s, the Europe-born children of the major wave of Muslim immigration came of age and began to demand public recognition of their religion. They wanted to have mosques, halal food, and to be allowed to dress in a recognizably Islamic fashion. They did so at the very moment when the rise of what came to be called "political Islam" elsewhere in the world—Khomeini in Iran, new political movements in North Africa and the Middle East—stoked fears about Islam in Europe. Debates about the character of European Islam thus began at about the same time as the rise of a strong anti-immigrant trend in many countries and the rise of anti-Islamic sentiment.

The distinct trajectories of Muslim migration have produced widely differing profiles of Muslims in each European country. France and Britain stand out in this regard because most of their Muslim residents (or their parents) came from former colonies, giving them some knowledge of the host country's language and customs and thus facilitating integration. Although the Netherlands colonized the world's largest Muslim population in Indonesia, most Dutch Muslims today are from Morocco and Turkey, without prior knowledge of Dutch. Turkish Muslims arriving in Germany may have known some German language because of the long history of labor migration from Turkey to Germany, but Moroccans, say, traveling to the Netherlands or to Norway, or Senegalese arriving in Italy, are unlikely to arrive with more than a smattering of words in their new country of residence, and their hosts are, in turn, unlikely to know much about Morocco or Senegal.

Adding to these differences were variations in migration patterns across Europe. In some countries, immigrants have tended to live and socialize mainly with others from the same country of origin, and such ethnic concentration has made integration and understanding across religious lines more difficult. Today we see the sharpest conflicts on religious grounds precisely in those counties where Muslims live apart from others.

South Asians in Localized Britain

We can see these processes and mechanisms more clearly if we focus on several cases. Let us first look at Britain. British Muslims tend to come from a small number of places. About one-half of the Muslims in Britain are from Pakistan; Bangladesh and India provide the next largest numbers. Many of these Muslims come from just two districts in South Asia, Mirpur in Pakistan and Sylhet in Bangladesh. About 60 percent of U.K.-resident Pakistanis are from Mirpur, and in some cities with large Pakistani populations this percentage is higher (Lewis 2002, 216). New migrants sought out those they knew from home districts, and once further immigration was restricted in 1962, new residents came under the rubric of family reunification, which favored residents of districts already overrepresented in Britain.

Pakistanis have been the most active and visible in British Muslim affairs and organizations, adding to the effect of this concentration on non-Muslim British perceptions of Islam in Britain. Muslims are also overwhelmingly perceived as non-English looking; of the relatively small number of converts, most are black British or Caribbean.

Furthermore, Muslims tend to live in a small number of places in Britain. Nearly half live in the London area; others have settled in Bradford, Birmingham, and a few other large industrial cities. These concentrations magnify those of origin to the extent that people from the same origins settled together: Half of all Bangladeshis live in East London, and the Mirpur migrants have concentrated in a few cities in the West Midlands and the north.

Subsequent developments in Britain added to the strength of transnational ties to specific places of origin. As Muslim populations grew in each city, mosques tended more and more to attend to people from one origin district and often who followed one particular South Asian school of Islamic thought. Many parents have sought spouses for their children from their own districts of origin; these intercontinental marriages continue to be organized in new generations.

Philip Lewis's (2002) study of Bradford provides an excellent picture of this organization. Early Muslim migration was by single men, who made few demands in the religious sphere and settled together regardless of origins. It was when families began to settle in the city in the late 1960s that fission began, following lines of community of origin (Lewis 2002, 56). Groups from different countries or districts within countries tended to settle together. Mosques were major agents of fission, because they were headed by religious officials, imams, who held allegiance to a specific South Asian movement, such as the Deobandi school or the Barelvis.

Bradford Muslims tended to form local associations specific to an ethnic or regional identity, such as the Azad Kashmir Muslim Association, the Gujar Khan burial society, or the Pukhtoon Cultural Society, all of which provided communication and mutual aid. Public funds were available to organizations that identified themselves as representing ethnic or racial minorities. Reinforcing these ties to South Asian localities was the practice of organizing support for Bradford political candidates around what had been local caste groups, *biradari*, in Pakistan. Pakistani political parties also shaped allegiances for Bradford elections, as when Islami Jamhoori Ittihad, the Pakistan coalition opposed to the Pakistan People's Party, brought together the same component groups within Bradford that they had assembled in Pakistan (Lewis 2002, 74).

The role played by mosques has grown in Bradford. Once Muslim families began to immigrate to Britain in the 1960s, more and more mosques appeared and became centers for spiritual development and religious teaching. They also began to make demands to local authorities on religious grounds, in contrast to the demands based on racial or ethnic discrimination claims made by the state-subsidized associations. In Birmingham, it was in the mid-1980s that the rise of mosque influence coincided with a greater receptivity on the part of city authorities to considering the interests of Muslims to produce new guidelines for school policies toward Muslims on dress, provision of halal meat, and so forth.

Although Pakistanis have claimed an Islamic public identity, that identity continues to have a strong Punjabi cultural content (Werbner 2003). Urdu remains both an important link to Pakistan and a vehicle for religious instruction. In that sense, it maintains an ethnic or regional consciousness in a way that knowledge of classical Arabic does not. Arabic can be understood as a vehicle for Islamic knowledge that transcends place; Urdu inevitably retains its Asian association. The enclave existence of some Pakistanis also facilitates and is reproduced by the transcontinental marriage, which Lewis (2002, 217) states accounts for over half the marriages in cities with high Muslim concentrations.

The concentration effects of the migration process also lend a particular texture to discussions within Islamic communities about religion and culture. For example, Katy Gardner's (2002) study of burial practices by Bangladeshis living in East London considers their decision to bury a deceased relative in Britain or to send the corpse back to Bangladesh for burial. The Muslim undertaker she consulted estimated that 60–70 percent of Bengali corpses were sent to Bangladesh (and specifically to Sylhet district) for burial. And yet sending corpses requires embalming, a practice these Muslims consider to be forbidden. It also violates the hadîth known to them, commanding Muslims to bury soon after death. The major reasons given to Gardner for sending back the corpses despite these rules are that the deceased's close relatives need to visit the grave regularly in order to pray for the soul, a necessary practice to ensure that it reaches heaven. Because there are no Islamic burial grounds near the Tower Hamlets area where they live in London, these visits would be difficult to carry out in Britain. Sylhet people also view their homeland as particularly holy because their spiritual leader (*pir*) Shah Jalal was buried there.

North Africans in Centralized France

In Britain, then, how Muslims migrated has reinforced their transnational ties to their origin places. In France, by contrast, the political culture of secularity (*laïcité*) and explicit government policy produce a marked split between official and unofficial practices of category politics. Officially, individuals are treated as citizens and they are not assigned to ethnic or religious categories, a refusal that makes the work of demonstrating ethnic or racial discrimination particularly difficult. However, in everyday life, both public actors and ordinary people are engaged in a process of assigning others to such categories, most notably that of *maghrébin* (North African), based on various features of appearance, a process of everyday racialization that can produce comic results when, as in my own experience, some, but not other, children of a "native family" are suspected of being North African because of their slightly dark hair or features.

The demographic character of Muslim immigration to France differs in a number of ways from that in Britain. About 60–70 percent of Muslim immigrants to France have come from three countries of North Africa. Algerians and Moroccans have contributed the largest numbers, followed by Tunisians. Turks and West Africans form the next largest groups. The dominance of North African Muslims in the public sphere is even greater than these numbers might suggest, for a number of reasons. The North African countries had historically close colonial ties to France, and Algeria was part of France until 1962. North African immigration in the 1960s and 1970s was massive and concentrated in industrial cities. If "black British" immigrants set the tone in Britain, it was North African Muslims who did so in France, thereby making Islam identified with one region.

Men who came to France in order to work in the 1960s and 1970s were usually housed in large public housing units (HLM) where they were mixed together. Thus, immigration did not begin with origin-specific neighborhoods, as in some British cities. In any one neighborhood in the poorer suburbs of Paris or Lyon, or in the center of Marseille, one finds Moroccans, Malians, and poorer French families living together. People from one country surely seek out one another, but this is less the case for their children, who are more likely to identify with other Muslims, or other "Maghreb people" (a category that is itself the product of immigration), or people of similar socioeconomic situation. Certain ties can reinforce country allegiances, as when an association or a mosque is predominantly associated with one country, or a Sufi order preserves ties to a particular saint. But even those mosques, religious schools, or associations sponsored by Muslims from a particular country rarely are exclusivist, because they usually do not seek to reproduce a particular theological or ritual tendency. For many in the generation of Muslims born in France, it is the experience of being discriminated against as "Maghrebin" or "Arab" that creates their sense of "ethnicity" (Cesari 1998).

The common Arabic language has facilitated some degree of cooperation across the three North African communities, as has a relatively shared degree of religious jurisprudential reasoning (following the Mâliki *madhhab* or legal school) and religious practices. This cooperation exists both at the national level, for example, in the activities of the largest national organization, the Union of French Islamic Organizations (*Union des Organisations Islamiques de France (UOIF)*), and usually at the local level in the forms of shared worship in mosques. In cities or neighborhoods where cross-ethnic cooperation is high, the shared Arabic language facilitates common participation by North Africans (but not others) in congregational prayers. Indeed, the growing distinction, and sometimes tension, is between the older generation's preference for sermons in Arabic and younger Muslims' preference for French.

By contrast, Turks have not had the same historical ties to France, and they more often settled together in neighborhoods in eastern France and around major cities. Many of the Senegalese and Mali immigrants have distinct forms of religious practice and social organization, in particular the Sufi orders focused on a specific teacher in West Africa (Soares 2003). Other Muslims, from the West Indies or the Indian Ocean islands, for example, have organized into ethnically specific associations and formed a grab-bag national organization to represent their interests as "non-Maghrebins."

Within the North African category, although Algerians are numerically dominant (one-half of North Africans, one-third of all Muslim immigrants) and they control the important Paris mosque, Tunisians and Moroccans play important leadership roles in a number of national organizations, and Tunisians, in particular, despite being a "minority's minority," only one-fifth as many as the Algerians, have taken on major roles as leaders of religious schools, particularly around Paris. Moroccans, for their part, make up 40 percent of all imams (sermon-givers at Friday prayers) in France.

Thus, in France no one country group is predominant across categories (in the way that Pakistanis dominate in Britain), and the Arabic language serves as a (potentially) uniting element across the most politically active groups. Furthermore, whereas differences in religious affiliations (and lineage ties) in South Asia were replicated in British cities, the same is not true for France. Pakistan is severely divided into religious movements, each defined vis-à-vis the other and each associated with a set of transnational organizations (the Tablighi Jama'a, Deoband-affiliated schools, the Barelvis, and so on). The demographic concentration of emigrants from one Pakistani region facilitated the replication of these oppositions in Britain. This competition of religious associations is less intense in North Africa, and the emigrants come from a wider range of districts in Algeria, Morocco, and Tunisia. The Tablighis are present in France as in Britain, but they do not have a set of opposed Pakistani organizations next to them in, say, Paris, as they do in London. The divisions that one does see tend to be by country of origin rather than by any religious orientation: thus, Algerians versus Moroccans vying for control of a mosque, or each, along with Comorians and others, having their own mosque and associations.

The associations that attract the most enthusiasm from young people in France are based in neighborhoods and usually with a nonreligious central activity: sports, employment, music, and so on. It is here that the strongest identifications form, and these are not necessarily inflected by ethnicity in a specific sense or by religious affiliation, but by a perception that they are perceived by others as North Africans or as Arabs.

This specific context for the deployment of ethnic, religious, and other processes of self-identification has meant that younger French Muslims tend to reflect on distinctions between Islam qua religion, on the one hand, and the tradition or culture of their parents and the "country of origin," on the other. (This emphasis contrasts with the British case, where many younger Muslims continue to identify themselves in terms of an integrally linked package of a specific ethnicity and Islam.) As one young French Muslim woman told a sociologist, "I became a practicing Muslim thanks to France, because it provides structures so that we might learn Arabic and our religion. I am glad to have come to know my religion, true Islam, because, 'back there,' it is too traditional and troublesome" (Venel 1999, 71).

Further Variations

In other countries we find other, specific sets of transnational ties between those Muslims with a foreign origin or ancestry and their countries of origin. Spanish Muslims, for example, come overwhelmingly from neighboring Morocco and maintain close ties with their home country; Spain even owns two cities located in northern Morocco. Patterns of Muslim migration to the Netherlands resemble those in Britain to the extent that immigrants remained separated into country groupings, except that they came from a wider array of countries. Each large Dutch city is likely to have several mosques, each allied to a different transnational community and each with a preference for its own language. Utrecht, for example, has two Turkish mosques, two Moroccan ones, and one for Surinamese Muslims. Languages for sermons are correspondingly different: Turkish, Arabic, Urdu for South Asian-origin Surinamese, and Dutch for Indonesians and Javanese-speaking Surinamese (Landman 2002). Like Britain, the Netherlands encouraged each immigrant community to develop its own institutions, in the Dutch case reflecting an older, and now largely abandoned, way of organizing society around the major religious and political "pillars."

Although Germany has a broad policy of recognizing and supporting (through taxation) religious organizations as public entities, divisions among Muslims are sharp and are reproduced in mosques. Schiffauer (1996) traces the history of mosques in the southern city of Augsburg and shows that the current proliferation of mosques is the result of a series of fissions, which were the direct product of competing loyalties to Turkish political organizations: the official Turkish Islamic office of the Diyanet, the fascist Grey Wolves, the major Turkish Islamic party (called the AKP by the 2000s), and the Islamic association Milli Görüs. Until recently, all these groups considered Germany to be a country of *hijra,* of temporary immigration, and they were more interested in promoting political and religious positions important in Turkey than in constructing a Muslim society in Germany itself. As one indication of this contrast in social focus, Schiffauer (1996, 162) reports that in the 1990s he could find not one sermon among all those available on cassettes in the bookstores that discussed problems of Muslims in Germany—in contrast to France, where this is the topic of nearly all of the many cassettes for sale!

ADAPTING SACRIFICE TO FRANCE

With the great amount of attention paid to radical Islam in Europe, less noticed have been the creative efforts by European Muslims to adapt religious practices to new social surroundings. Sacrifice has been one focus of those efforts for a number of reasons: It offers possibilities for creating new kinds of social relations, and it raises all sorts of questions and problems, from the very practical issues of hygiene and transport to cultural debates about how to treat animals.

We already saw that Moroccans generally carry out their sacrifice within the family, with the father often killing the animal, at or near home, before the family proceeds to join in collective worship. The same is true of other North Africans, Algerians and Tunisians. But French law, and indeed European law, forbids the slaughter of animals anywhere but in an abattoir, and then only by someone who has been certified by the state. Therefore, it is illegal to carry out a sacrifice in a house, farm, garage, or even in a municipal space designated for that purpose. Those families who own their own house might be able to kill their animal at home without being troubled by the long arm of the law, but most Muslim families live in urban environments and often in housing projects. The degree to which families have been able to sacrifice at home despite the Europe-wide ban on such practices depends on the attitudes of each country's (and each locale's) authorities, and also on the spatial dynamics of immigration. For example, in Belgium many immigrants live in pavilions, where it is easier to carry out the killing in private, and local authorities have felt the pressure from Belgian ranchers to allow this lucrative trade in sacrificial animals to continue. In Britain, certain urban areas are mainly Pakistani, and thus few non-Muslims witness the sacrifices.

Nothing in principle prevents people from arranging for sacrifice at an abattoir as the law requires. But practical problems arise: The majority of Muslims live near or in large cities, far from abattoirs; and when many properly sacrificed animals are required on the same day, the demand becomes difficult to meet. Since 2008, French supermarket chains have tried to provide properly prepared meat, and these efforts have begun to meet the demand. French law did require animals to be stunned before slaughter; a 1981 law made an exception for religious slaughter, but annual human rights campaigns protested this "loophole."

Even in the 2000s, the majority of Muslim household heads living in France were born elsewhere. Their thoughts about whether and how to sacrifice frequently refer back to practices in their countries of origin. One Algerian worker told ethnographers about the poverty his family suffered when he was growing up. His father would manage to buy a chicken to sacrifice, but this did not count for them, as he later said, "As God is my witness, with the best of intentions we could not sacrifice. Today, I would not be forgiven if I did not sacrifice" (Brisebarre 1998, 64–65). To sacrifice means to kill a ram or sheep, and to do so at home: "There are those who do so at the farm, but normally it should be done at home." The memory of what his father wished to do but could not shapes this worker's sense of what must be done.

A Moroccan worker living near Paris stated more forcefully that he never would go to the abattoir—he would stop sacrificing first: "It is `âda, custom, because the Prophet himself sacrificed at home. If you kill anywhere else, it is not the `Îd; you might as well just buy the meat directly from the butcher!" (Brisebarre 1998, 68). And yet things may change; this man's eldest son rejects the practice entirely, even as, respecting his religious obligation, he intends, when he becomes the head of his own household, to give the value of a sheep to a poor person.

If in North Africa, some men and women were able to fashion a close tie to the sacrificial animal, taking it into their houses, and speaking to it at the moment of sacrifice, an industrial production of sacrifice, even if it meets the scriptural tests, breaks that sense of personal tie, the identification of the person and the sacrificed animal that is at the base of a logic of sacrifice. In 2004, I followed one of the new experiments in sacrifice near Paris. A mobile slaughter unit had been set up by a private enterprise working with the regional authorities. The day before the feast-day I went to talk with the young man herding the sheep and taking orders from area Muslims for the sacrifice, to be carried out the next day. Abdel explained that Islam requires the sheep to be at least six months old and goats one year old to be eligible for sacrifice. They expected to slaughter one thousand sheep.

> **JRB:** "So it is going well, you are selling lots of sheep?"
>
> **Abdel:** No, people don't want to do it this way, they would rather cut the sheep's throat themselves."
>
> **JRB:** "Is this a matter of religion?"
>
> **Abdel:** "Yes, religion; it is not about the meat but about having your children and wife there, and cutting the sheep's throat in the name of your mother and other relatives. Now how could we keep track of who each person wants the animal sacrificed for? So people would rather do it themselves, but that is forbidden; you may not take the animal out, and there are barriers so you cannot do that. Years ago people could go to places west of Paris and buy an animal and sacrifice right there, and that is what I did, and then there were abattoirs set up near here, that Muslims ran. But the government did away with them. This abattoir: the

French run it with a veterinarian, and there is a woman there now guarding it, that is why it is permitted.""I myself do not sacrifice, because I would rather send money to Palestine; if you send 200 or 300 Euros they can buy five sheep. Here we do not need meat, we eat it every day, but there they do need it."

JRB: "If you were allowed to do it yourself, as in past years, would you sacrifice or still send money?"

Abdel: "I would still send the money but I don't know about others. After all, you cannot eat all the meat yourself and indeed you are supposed to share it with poor people but who is poor in France? There aren't any poor people. So better to send it where there are poor people.

On the next day, families were waiting for their sheep to be processed and the meat to be handed to them. Each purchaser had been given a ticket with a number on it and told when to return for the sheep. The chain was about two hours behind the schedule; it was, after all, the first time. Others were congregating at the slaughtering end, including those whose sheep was being slaughtered. After approaching a woman in charge, I was allowed to walk around the back near the point where the sheep entered the processing unit. A man in his forties stood there with his two children. In previous years, they had sacrificed by taking their "camping car" into the country and finding a farm where they could sacrifice. He stopped doing that because he was concerned about the health of the animals, with all the diseases. Somehow he, too, had talked his way to the entry-point to the assembly line, and with his sons by his side could look at their sheep as it was about to be killed and say the Bismillah out loud to the sheep.

Others managed to go back and pet and speak to their sheep at some point well upstream from the entry-point but were kept from the sacrifice place and could only watch through the windows in the mobile buildings. "Many people are disappointed," explained a woman in charge, "because they would like to read out a list of names for the sacrifice and say the Bismillah, but it would slow down the chain if we let them do that." At one point too many people had managed to get back to where the sheep were, and she made an announcement over the loudspeaker telling everyone to stay out of the area of sacrifice and wait where the sheep were being delivered, because it was slowing down the assembly line.

CAN EUROPEAN SOCIETIES BE MUSLIM?

Life in Europe raises long-standing questions about whether Muslims' obligations to God change when they move to lands not ruled by Muslims. In the early centuries of Islam, scholars developed a distinction between two realms, the *dâr al-islâm* or abode of Islam, versus the *dâr al-harb* or abode of war (Abou El Fadl 1994). The former included the countries ruled under Islamic principles; the latter referred to all other places, where, presumably, Muslims would not be free to worship. Today, many Muslims find discomfort in this way of viewing the world. How is one to define "Muslim societies," the dâr al-Islam? Does one look to the correctness of the government, the piety of the people, or simply the fact that most people living in the country profess Islam as their religion? Is a majority-Muslim country whose government represses its people and prevents the free expression of religious ideas to be considered part of dâr al-islâm? Conversely, why should countries not governed by Islamic laws but where Muslims are free to worship be considered as belonging to an "abode of war?" As many Muslims in Europe began to think about religion in terms of the essentials of worship and spirituality, this category seemed increasingly out of date.

Some Muslims have proposed alternatives. Referring to the protection given to religious minorities by international law, some scholars have proposed *dâr al-'ahd*, "abode of treaty," while others have proposed *dâr al-da'wa*, "abode of predication" or *dâr ash-shahâda*, "abode of witness," emphasizing the possibilities open to Muslims in these lands. For many Muslims in Europe, the key issues are not labels—Muslim world versus non-Muslim lands—but of the social and cultural conditions for Muslims to live fully satisfying lives as Muslims. Two categories of Muslims would not accept this proposition. Some consider religion a private matter not in need of new institutions, and hence see no particular challenge to living in Europe. Others consider it provisional to live anywhere but an Islamic state, a category that includes neither European nor most Muslim-majority countries.

The practical significance of this question emerged most recently regarding bank interest. One of the more pressing questions for Muslims who are planning to reside permanently in Europe is whether they may take out loans at interest to purchase homes. The Islamic prohibition against lending or borrowing at interest would seem to prevent them from so doing, but in the late 1990s some Muslims living in Europe put the question to the European Council for Fatwa and Research, a collection of jurists of various nationalities who now reside in Europe. The council is led by the highly influential Egyptian jurist, Sheikh Yûsuf al-Qardâwî, who lives in Qatar. In 1999, the council responded to the question in the form of a *fatwâ*, a nonbinding legal opinion issued by a qualified person or group. The jurists stressed that the prohibition on usury does mean that Muslims everywhere should take steps to avoid borrowing from banks that charge interest, and should devise alternative ways of financing homes, such as paying more than the stated price but in installments. However, if Muslims in Europe could not practice such alternatives, then they could take out a mortgage for a first house (Conseil européen 2002).

In their argument, the jurists cited two considerations. First, the doctrine of extreme necessity (*darûrat*) allows Muslims to do what otherwise is forbidden under compulsion or necessity. Why is it a necessity to own a house? Renting keeps the Muslim in a state of uncertainty and financial insecurity, stated the council. Owning a house allows Muslims to settle in close proximity to a mosque and to modify their house to accommodate religious needs. Moreover, Muslims living in Europe had reported to the council that mortgage payments were equal to or lower than rents. Second, the jurists argued that while living in non-Muslim countries, Muslims may make contracts that violate Islamic law. Past jurists belonging to two of the traditional schools of Sunni legal interpretation, the Hanafî and the Hanbalî, had made this argument, they said. Muslims cannot change the institutions that dominate life in their host countries, and thus they are not responsible for the existence of an interest-based financial system. If they were forbidden to benefit from banking institutions, then Islam would have weakened them, a result that would contradict the principle that Islam should benefit Muslims.

The ruling did not change the traditional prohibition of lending at interest, but exempted Muslims living in Europe from the prohibition because of a combination of empirical circumstances: the importance of owning a house, the high level of rents, and the absence of viable alternatives. These circumstances allow the jurists to apply the principles that necessity allows for exemption, and that Muslims may use otherwise invalid financial instruments when they live in "non-Islamic countries."

As noted earlier, in the late 1980s, many Muslims in Europe shifted from seeing themselves, and being seen by others, mainly as immigrants, to taking on identities mainly as Muslims. Some, at least, Muslims and non-Muslims began to see religious commitments and practices as distinct from ethnic particularities and immigration histories. This shift has had a number of repercussions that have played themselves out over time and at different rhythms in different countries, but I think that we can best understand these changes as the creation of a number of new possibilities in self-identifications and in treatment by others. These new possibilities do not resolve to one single trend, such as "individualization," but engender new tensions.

For Muslims, the shift has made possible different ways of thinking about what it means to be a Muslim in Europe. For some, being a Muslim becomes a matter of faith and private religious practice, along the lines of older forms of European Protestantism. For others, it becomes a tradition to which they can refer, but to which they do not feel bound or obligated. Such, for example, is the position taken by self-styled "secular Muslims" in France. The opposite is equally possible; many Muslims have to come to see Islam as a set of norms and constraints that are detached from any one time or place and opposed to the traditions of various home countries. Muslims may see Islam in this last way and become highly involved in European public life, or, to the contrary, they can withdraw from public life on grounds that one can best live as a Muslim if one remains detached. These possibilities are all well represented among European Muslims today.

The "secular Muslim" approach is most present in France because the secularist media find this approach closest to proper French attitudes. Writers such as Malik Chebel promote in their books and through frequent television appearances an "enlightened Islam" that would consist of philosophy and spirituality, but eschew the legal and institutional aspects, which, he writes, do not fit well in Europe. *Self Islam* was the French title of a recent popular book that brings together the notions of religion as mainly and properly individual and internal. Several socio-political movements use the phrase "secular Muslims" (*Musulmans laïques*) and call for keeping Islam out of the public sphere, and eradicating beliefs and practices deemed inimical to the republic. In this approach, individuality, privacy, laïcité, and European values are bundled.

What could be called the "public Islam" approach argues that this bundle must be untied, and that the public presentation of Islam does not conflict with European values. The Swiss intellectual Tariq Ramadan (2002), for example, argues that at the level of values, one can find a convergence between Islamic norms and those of Europe and that to do this one need not abandon the ideal of a visible, public Islamic presence. (Ramadan also argues for a geopolitical strategy of encouraging this convergence within each distinct cultural or religious tradition.) The "young Muslim" movements once associated with Ramadan seek to change political life as coalitions of Muslims, rather than as coalitions of secular citizens. If the "secular

Muslim" approach grows out of French secularism, the "public Islam" accords best with countries supporting a multicultural recognition of ethnic differences such as Britain.

Opposed to both these stances are separatists, either those who simply keep to themselves, such as the Tablighi Jama'at, or those that promote the eventual recreation of an Islamic state, such as the Hizb ut-Tahrir or its more radical offshoots. Muslims who are attracted to one of these movements make the same distinction between "religion" and "tradition" as do those who see themselves as "secularists" or as "publicly Muslim." But whereas a figure such as Tariq Ramadan sees a way to adapt Islamic norms to Europe, on condition that Europe accepts Muslims' public presence, the Hizb ut-Tahrir does not.

For non-Muslims, the shift in frames, from immigrants to Muslims, can also produce diverse effects. By and large, European governments have moved toward recognizing Islam as a legitimate faith, deserving of the same recognition and resources as are accorded to forms of Christianity and Judaism. At the same time, however, highlighting the religion of a certain segment of the population emphasizes an element that separates them from the majority population, religion, and places into the background crosscutting elements that form the basis for allegiances and solidarity, such as occupations, political allegiances, or cultural interests.

As a result of these differences in migration histories, Muslims differ markedly across Europe in their own sense of identification. A 2006 Pew Global Attitudes Project survey (2006) asked Muslims in different countries around the world to choose between religion and nationality as their primary identity. While 42 percent of French Muslims said they were French first and Muslim second, only 7 percent of British Muslims and 3 percent of Spanish Muslims put nationality first. (Pew reports that American Christians choose between religious and national identities in almost exactly the same proportion as do French Muslims.) These same differences also show up for the population of each country as a whole. When asked if there is a conflict between being a devout Muslim and living in a modern society, 74 percent of all French people said there was none, about twice as high a figure as that for other Europeans or Americans. Indeed, French people are more positive about modern Islam than are people in Indonesia, Jordan, or Egypt!

The distinctive feature of the French experience within Europe is that there, and there alone, both colonial history and current policies push in the same direction, toward integration. Today's French Muslims, or their parents or grandparents, came from former French territories in North or West Africa, where they learned that they were now part of the grand story of France, albeit in second-class roles. French Muslims today are demanding long-denied equal status and respect, as did African Americans in the United States. Their experience is quite unlike that of, say, Moroccans arriving in Denmark, where no common pasts, languages, or experiences prepare their way, or, for that matter, South Asians in Britain, who never were told that they could become English—and many of whom today demand a distinct mode of governance under sharî'a law.

Nor do French Muslims live in ethnic enclaves. The housing projects around Paris contain people from different parts of Asia, Africa, and Europe, and stand in stark contrast to all-Turkish neighborhoods in Belgium and or all-Pakistani parts of British cities. Young Muslims who emerge from this mixed environment speak only French, demand

French-language sermons in their mosques (and increasingly get them), and they flock to French-medium Islamic schools and institutes.

French policies also push toward integration, with a mix of carrots and sticks. Headscarves are out at school, but some enlightened mayors are giving land for mosques. The state gives newly arrived men and women hundreds of free hours of French language lessons, in an effort to make them more competitive for employment. Contrast recent Dutch policies (applied mainly to poorer counties) that require would-be immigrants, even the spouses of Dutch residents, to prove that they already speak good Dutch *before* arrival, but provide no help in learning the language.

Whether Muslims living in Europe come to consider their countries of residence as part of the "Muslim World" may depend less on whether Islamic law ever gains official recognition, or Islamic private schools grow and flourish, than on whether they find themselves recognized as equal citizens. Or perhaps they will rephrase the question, and suggest that there are no more Muslim and non-Muslim worlds or countries, but places where one is more or less respected for one's quality as a Muslim man or woman.

Conclusions

Muslims have come to Europe recently and in great numbers, but their stories are different depending on where they have come from and how their new country fits them in. We featured the France–Britain contrast to illustrate this point. The story of British Muslims involves social groups moving from Pakistan and Bangladesh to new neighborhoods in British cities, where they continue to function as communities—today often with sharî'a councils handling local disputes. The story of French Muslims involves a mixing of people from across North and West Africa in ring cities and housing projects, where discrimination and unemployment present problems, but where there is little ethnic residential concentration. We can then compare these stories with those of Muslims in the United States, where there are roughly equal numbers of African Americans, Arabs, and South Asians. Do they look more like British Muslims, with Muslim community institutions, or like French Muslims?

Discussion Questions

England now has perhaps 10 sharî'a councils, to which Muslim women can come to request a religious divorce (for more details, consult Bowen 2009a); they still have to get their legal divorce at a civil court. Some of these councils act as arbitration tribunals as well, alongside secular arbitration tribunals, and hear disputes arising from a marriage (including matters of domestic violence), over the control of a mosque, or even about a commercial contract, sometimes involving non-Muslims. Some might say that it is proper for Muslims to create such councils, as they already exist for Orthodox Jews and after all arbitration is a good thing as it saves time and money. Others might say that society is better off when everyone uses the same legal institutions and that social pressure might lead Muslims to use these sharî'a councils when they would be better off going to court. What do you think?

Media Resources

We do not yet have a good number of films on the topics; you can see the series of films called *America at a Crossroads* exploring issues regarding Muslims and the United States, emphasizing security issues. But there are television documentaries available on the Internet, particularly Britain's Channel 4, on Muslims in Britain; see the one called *Divorce, Sharî'a Style*. You can find another good documentary on the Shariah Council at: http://www.youtube.com/watch?v=Ctyr5FaZJtl&feature=fvst.

Virtual Religion

Since the early 1990s, religious groups have been among the more avid users of the Internet and the World Wide Web. Thousands of Web sites are now dedicated to advancing or discussing religious beliefs and practices. E-mail lists and chat rooms facilitate long-term debates about religion and society. Virtual spaces allow collective worship. And the trend toward religion accelerates: If in 1998, 25 percent of American Internet users did so for "religious purposes" (Leibovich 2000), by 2003, 64 percent did so. Most of these users were looking for information, or were sending or receiving religious e-mails. (You can read the recent study at http://www.pewinternet.org/Reports/2004/Faith-Online.aspx.)

WHAT CAN YOU DO ONLINE?

Although it is difficult to find out what we would really like to know, that is, how people use these sites and what their *practices* are, we can, nonetheless, infer something about these practices by looking at how, and for whom, religious Web sites present themselves. Some provide ways to carry out virtual prayer or worship. For instance, Belief.net allows users to create virtual prayer circles. When Judy Spiegal's father died in 2000, she started such a circle. On the first day, a dozen people of different faiths posted prayers on the site (Leibovich 2000). In Tamil Nadu, India, a site (http://www.prarthana.com) is dedicated to the deity Vinayaka (another name for Ganesha, elephant-headed son of Shiva), which offers Hindus ways to worship a range of other deities as well, and all without leaving their living rooms. They can ask local agents to present offerings to their choice of deity at an Indian temple and receive by return post a package of the food offering, blessed by the deity. Alternatively, they can click on a virtual temple page and worship the deity on-screen. (They can also download a "very divine Screen Saver of Lord Vinayaka himself.")

These two examples can be used to suggest something of the different characteristics of the target audiences—multireligious America, the Hindu diaspora—but they share the basic feature of allowing worship at a distance, anonymously if so desired.

219

They can create a sense of a network, or a "community" of those who use the service. Much of Ms. Spiegal's comfort came from the sense that people out there were supporting her. One of the effects of the Hindu temple site is to create a sense of a community of worshipers, wherever they are located in the world.

Virtual communities may be broader or narrower, and they may change their message over time. In 2000, the site of the Cathedral of Hope in Dallas (http://www.cathedralofhope.com/), a member of the United Church of Christ, advertised itself as the "world's largest gay and lesbian church," which it can be precisely because of online participation. By 2009, the site had changed its message to one of "radical inclusion" and featured pictures of heterosexual couples as well as single people, along with recent endorsements by Texas newspapers. They had moved toward the mainstream. And by 2012, they had five campuses and were once again highlighting "Homosexuality and Christianity," perhaps as part of developing a pan-Texas church niche.

We can already see some of the dimensions along which religious sites vary and evolve. Web sites can address or invite individuals (as in the prayer circle) into a relationship with an established faith community (as in the virtual temple and the church). They can differ in the kind of audience they target, from "narrowband" to "broadband," and they can broaden their target audience over time either thematically or geographically, as did the Cathedral of Hope on both dimensions. Some sites are cyber-extensions of local churches, temples, or mosques and are intended mainly to provide a service (in two senses) for current, potential, or virtual worshipers. Even here there is a good bit of variation, between the site that is merely a convenience for those who physically attend anyway, and the virtual religious site intended to attract those who never visit the bricks-and-mortar church. (The Cathedral of Hope is probably halfway between these two points.)

Broadband sites often construct a home page that celebrates all religions together, which at times takes on a synthetic "world" characteristic (as in World Sacred Music, a musical sampler available as a download). On Belief.net, the many links on the home page take you to religion-specific sections, some of which are intended to be acceptable to practitioners of each religion. In the early 2000s, a Belief.net question-and-answer section featured a spokesman for each of several religions: Father Ted informs fellow Orthodox Christians how to fast; Rabbi David Wolpe urges the Jew who seeks to follow the Law not to lose sight of people; and so forth.

Most sites have transformed their interactive features as new technologies or habits have appeared. Belief.net used to feature letters from users connected to each page; by 2009 it featured a metablog page. The range of these blogs highlights the site's ecumenical character. The blog "City of Brass" is written by a Muslim who mixes narrow and more broadband messages: In mid-2009, one theme was hypocrisy regarding the healthcare reform debates. The "Angels on your shoulder" blog is, well, about talking with angels. But the center panel on the metablog presents a carefully chosen array of writers on political issues, identified by either religious or political affiliations, such as reformed Jewish, Catholic, Progressive, and conservative. Belief.net now links to nearly everything: film reviews, diet formulas, photos of puppies, and so on.

Beliefnet.com has used its broad ecumenical approach to offer a range of quizzes to users about their beliefs. In 2000, it allowed users to identify their religion and then answer a series of diagnostic questions about beliefs, observance, and behavior, which placed them at a specific point on the relevant doctrinal spectrum. The site told

Muslims whether they were Secular Muslims, Spiritual Seekers, Progressive Muslims, or Traditional Muslims. The reader who is classified as a Traditional Muslim learns that "the Qur'ân plays a role in your daily life as a Muslim" while the Progressive Muslim learns that "you probably interpret Islam historically and might believe that ijtihâd (individual interpretation of scripture) should be reopened." Among the practices that would classify you as Traditional are: fasting and praying during Ramadan, considering killing Salman Rushdie (the author whose life was famously threatened in the late 1980s for his book *Satanic Verses*), saving sex for marriage, and planning to marry a Muslim.

One has no idea who thought up these typologies. The idea that *ijtihâd* and everyday use of the Qur'ân would be associated with distinct types of Muslims has little relationship to the social lives of Muslims I know. But perhaps of greater interest is the sense of audience implied by this site. Who would take this quiz? It might be a Muslim student in a non-Muslim land who feels a need to identify who he is through one of these available labels. (It surely would not be a fellow who threatens Rushdie in a dark alley.) The quiz also suggests books appropriate for each of the four categories (oddly, the Traditionalist is sent to read a book decrying the influence of "Islamists" in Cairo; perhaps the real intent of the list is to subvert the categories!).

Several years later, one finds on the same site the "Belief-O-Matic," now aimed at assigning users to religions, rather than discerning your tendency within a pregiven religion. "Even if YOU don't know what faith you are, Belief-O-Matic™ knows," it reassures us. To assign users to a religion, Belief-O-Matic asks a series of questions— how many Gods? Should you confess sins?—and how much weight users place on each answer. I took the quiz, and the Belief-O-Matic was right on: It said I agreed 100 percent of the time with Unitarian Universalism (which is in fact where my family attends church), and then ranked 26 other denominations in order of agreement with my answers (Jehovah's Witnesses were at the bottom). By 2012 Belief-O-Matic was said to "assume no legal liability for the ultimate fate of your soul."

If Belief.net sorts its users into traditional categories, other sites seek to blur the boundaries. In the early 2000s, SpiritChannel (now defunct) bombarded those who opened the site with a heavy-beat song about "there's only one religion." (This was not surprising when you learned that the site's founder was Isaac Burton Tigrett, who created the Hard Rock Cafe and the House of Blues.) SpiritChannel pronounced itself a "for-profit" site, marketing "information, data, guidance, entertainment, products, and services related to spirituality and health—all via the Internet, traditional media and in three-dimensional locations."

Creole Spaces

So much for how the sites are presented. But if we think of them as existing in real space and time, then we can profit from Jon Anderson's (1999, 43–44) characterization of many religious Web sites as "creole" spaces. Anderson means the following: Just as populations in the New World mixed Spanish or French with local languages to produce creole languages, these Web sites also mediate between broadly based religious networks and local societies. They respond to the needs, fears, and hopes of a particular group of local users and creators of sites, and at the same time have a global, electronic spatial reach.

The anthropologists Daniel Miller and Don Slater (2000) give us an example of this "creole" character of some sites in their study of Internet use in Trinidad. They found that religious sites were not only highly local in their concerns but they also sought to do what they call "expand back" (2000, 178) into a larger realm. What do they mean by this? For the religions they studied, adherents see themselves as part of a much larger community than the Trinidadian one. Trinidad Catholics see their Church as universal, but they also think that the common experience of residents of the Caribbean made desirable a regional Catholic theology, something now much more likely to develop through region-wide electronic communication. Hindus on Trinidad see themselves as part of a global network of Hindus, including not only those in South Asia but also Hindus living in North America, Europe, the Pacific, and Africa. The Internet makes communication among members of that global network vastly easier.

These sites are shaped by very specific, locally grounded networks of communication and influence. The Trinidad Hindu site is maintained by Sanathan Dharma Maha Sabha, the major Hindu organization in Trinidad. On the site and in real life, this organization depicts Hindus as under threat from Christians, through such links from the Web site's home page to texts such as "Jesus Lived in India" and "Hinduism under Attack." Miller and Slater (2000, 175–176) point out that militant Hindu nationalists, mainly in their North American branches, have been active users of the Internet to alert Trinidadians of negative stories about Hinduism that they can then negate on their own Trinidad Web site. Internet communication has also instructed Trinidadian Hindus about the differences between their forms of religious life and those found in India, through the decline of caste and the influence of Christianity in the Caribbean. Thus, the site is dynamically located in both the network of global Hindu nationalism and Trinidadian social activism.

"Creole sites," then, link broad, often global spaces to local concerns. But they can also link religious concerns to broad-based consumer interests as well as targeting a specific user community. Jon Anderson mentions MyQuran.com (http://www.myquran.com), an Indonesian site for Muslims with an English title and English phrases that operated in the mid-2000s as part of a MuslimNet Ring (grouping of sites with links to each other). The main presentation of the site was universalistic: One could hear an entire chapter of the Qur'ân and follow links to other chapters, and search the entire Qur'ân in any one of 15 languages (although some of my attempts reached nonworking sites). I could download a call to prayer on Real Audio and have a choice among calls from Mecca, or Medina, one by the late Shaykh Muhmmad Rifat of Egypt, or the call broadcast from the Istiqlal mosque in Jakarta. The site's "eMuamalah" ("e-social affairs") section contained Islamic e-cards and an Islamic bookstore maintained in association with Amazon.com. That's all pretty universal in appeal, but it also built in areas of particular interest to Indonesians, particularly in the music section, where I was offered the chance to download about 50 songs by various religious-oriented Indonesian groups, plus the latest songs by Yusuf Islam (the former Cat Stevens), and links to other Islamic music collections. Each hit on the site also pops up a Hypermart window with an ad unrelated to Islam (during my visit, they were for free e-mail, Amex cards, and the latest U2 song).

This site and others like it are extremely user-friendly in more than one way. They have a modern, secular, even consumerist feel to them. They indicate nothing about a particular religious message or orientation. They serve as a portal in a theological as well as a technical sense. They communicate a meaning about tolerance toward religion through their very form. They also preserve something of a local character but highly downplayed relative to Islam's universalistic message.

INFORMATION, COMMUNICATION, AND PERFORMANCE

To what extent do these new electronic possibilities substitute a virtual religious environment for a "real" one? I think we should take account of the great differences in the kinds of communication that different sites promote. Let's try out a typology: Some sites mainly distribute *information*, some facilitate *communication* among users, while some allow users to participate in religious *performances.*

Sites that are mainly *sources of information* are like books, only unusually versatile sorts of books, with drop-down menus and hypertext links. They are not interactive in the sense of the user provoking or eliciting a response, only in the much more limited sense that the user does something that triggers a preprogrammed response, such as selecting a category or choosing an FAQ. Of course, such sites can be technically elaborate, with music, videos, and so on, but the interaction is human–machine.

But some sites of course allow for vertical communication with an authority— a religious authority in our case. Such sites are similar to the automatic, FAQ type in that they reproduce the sense of precedence, in time and in knowledge, that structures "source of information" sites: Someone knowledgeable, perhaps a religious authority, collects information and makes it available to the user. A question-and-answer site is different only in that there may be a human who receives the message and then responds. Some religions long have had these patterns of interactions between ordinary practitioners and authorities; Islam, for example, always has featured "question–answer" (su'al-ja-wab) interactions with religious scholars. Muslims may turn to any recognized authority for information, and scholars and others routinely ask each other for opinions on thorny issues. Correspondingly, one finds these exchanges featured prominently in many sites, across the entire doctrinal array of Islamic schools and opinion. By contrast, in theory, at least, the Catholic Church functions on a top-down basis, and one should seek guidance from one's priest, in one's parish. The Vatican's site contains many links to doctrinal statements, but nothing resembling a question-and-answer page.

Now, we know little about how people use such sites, but clearly there is a continuum from reliance on a single site as the source of authority to the "site shopping" intended to find sites whose opinions agree with one's own, or that meet one's own needs. Of course, Muslims are more likely to do the latter than are Catholics because of the older patterns of asking several authorities for knowledge. Among Christians, people who already attend a real-world church probably site shop less often than do others. And although we sometimes consider the Internet as a way to break out of older patterns, people may use it in ways that reinforce traditional patterns of authority, by multiplying the media through which they receive the same message. In these cases, using the Web has effects that, far from revolutionary, are highly conservative.

Communication Sites

Let's now turn to the second category of Web sites that have already been proposed, those that promote *horizontal communication* among users. This category concerns practices, not a type of technology, and includes formats that span a wide range of technological development, from simple chat rooms to simulation sites such as Second Life. All these sites promote horizontal communication, but some add pictures and sound. Users jointly produce knowledge, find a solution to a problem, share sorrows, dance together (on the 3D sites), or simply pass the time. They may thereby jointly create a sense that there are multiple communities or heretofore unknown interests within a particular religious tradition. For example, many gay and lesbian Muslims have come to know of others' existence and concerns in part through the Web sites that speak about their issues, from Muslim WakeUp's section called "Sex & the Ummah" (now defunct) to Irshad Manji's site (http://www.irshadmanji.com), which promotes a highly critical view of Islam. The UCC Church of Hope mentioned above probably did the same for gay and lesbian practicing Christians.

Many religious sites have bulletin boards, mentioned earlier; some also have chat rooms, and those on Facebook of course can become centers for exchange. But many religious-minded users also enter into protracted and sometimes heated exchanges about how best to understand their religions. I came upon one such exchange (among many) during my work on marriage and divorce among Muslims in Europe. Islamic Web sites offering information in the form of fatwâs abound in Arabic, French, and English, but many young Muslims, like young people in general, look for horizontal forms of exchange rather than authoritative replies (Roy 2002, 165–183). They might also wish to explain their particular situation in detail, and encourage others to ask relevant questions, something not possible on other types of sites. Many Muslims in Europe see their obedience to Islamic norms or law to be a set of individual commitments, not blanket obedience to a single teacher, and they seek to compare opinions with others.

Web forums are well suited to this sort of communication and knowledge seeking, and they may be attractive for these reasons, even if the participants may not be well versed in religious matters. Let me refer to one long Web exchange (appearing as a thread), which began when a woman living in France asked how she might divorce her husband in Islamic fashion. She had married Islamically, with an imam presiding, but not in a civil ceremony, so the marriage had no legal force. (The exchange took place on the site http://www.bladi.net/forum/61455-rompre-hallal/index4.html, accessed June 24, 2007.)

The respondents began to ask for details about her marriage, and a troubling fact began to emerge. At her marriage (in France), she saw no imams (though someone led prayers in an adjoining room); she had no male guardians; and there were no witnesses other than her husband's family members. No marriage gift (*mahar*) was exchanged ("but he paid for my dress and rings"); no piece of paper attests to the event. But according to most views in Islam, there must be witnesses and the bride's guardian at the wedding, and the husband must give a gift designated as the *mahar*.

The responders are nervous, pretty sure that in the eyes of God she never married because of the absence of a guardian and the lack of witnesses and, as she had consummated the marriage, that she was not operating wholly within the rules. Some respondents offered solutions as to how to divorce. "Is it not the case that one or the other of you says three times 'I divorce you'?" comments one reader (erroneously, as only the husband can bring about a divorce in this way). This is a group effort; everyone chipping in with their ideas. Several cite books of Islamic jurisprudence, *fiqh*; others bring up the amount of the marriage gifts paid by the Prophet. Each is drawing from the exchange a bit more knowledge of Islamic norms, whether correct or not, thanks to the questioner's unfortunate experience.

At this point, two of the discussants start debating whether or not one should have a civil marriage at all, and the discussants left the situation of this woman behind. But the anecdote illustrates the way people, especially younger people with little background in religion, turn to the Internet to share advice with others.

Performance and Efficacy

The third category of site is a relatively new one and consists of sites that are set up to facilitate religious *performance*: perhaps allowing the worshiper to accomplish a religious act, to experience something akin to what he or she would experience offline, or to join with others in a religious service of some sort. Let me consider three dimensions of this rather broad type of site: the promise of *efficacy*, either as a particular act of devotion or meeting of an obligation; the possibility of experiencing a *virtual analogue* to an already-practiced religious activity, such as a pilgrimage or a worship service; and the more specific experience of a *shared religious practice* by users. This last dimension is important in that many faiths consider the lived, shared, real-world performance of an act, particularly an act of collective worship, to be central to proper religious lives.

The distinction between the first two categories of site (information and communication) and the third one (performance) is related to the distinction made by some who write about these matters between "religion online," where information is conveyed, and "online religion," where users create religious communities. "Online religion" raises much more interesting anthropological questions than does "religion online," in that much stronger claims are being made or at least implied by the former. We might ask in what ways participants derive social benefits from online involvement: Do they feel solidarity with others, an accomplishment of a religious act, or heightened piety? What do various participants think is accomplished religiously? Does an avatar's prayer "count"? What does that mean?

The last question brings up the important notion of "performatives": statements and other actions that change the social status of someone, which could mean his or her religious or legal status. When a duly appointed agent of the state says to a couple, "I now pronounce you man and wife," we take it that the couple is married; that the agent (a judge, or perhaps a minister) has "performed" the marriage, rather than just celebrating it. Of course, the success of the performance is subject to certain conditions, sometimes called "felicity conditions," such as that the two people concerned are not close blood relatives and that they are not currently married to someone else. Often, what we take to be the performative act is not the real one: It is signing a document that makes a marriage legal, for example.

Now back to the online world. Many cases involving such performative acts online raise no special problems. For example, the first online wedding was held in May 1996, on AlphaWorld, a site claiming to be the oldest interactive world on the Internet (Jenkins 2008, 99). The online wedding had invited guests, invitations, and "crowd control" for the many expected online onlookers. Afterwards the groom drove 3,100 miles to be with his bride in a real-world way. The legal marriage was accomplished, in our terms "performed," by signing the documents required by the state in question. In other words, the sense of accomplishing the celebration of marriage was fulfilled online, but the performative—the legally binding act—was carried out in the real world.

Some religious sites offer a version of a ritual that has a performative character off-line but not online: an online Islamic pilgrimage that is intended to show people how it is done, or an online Catholic service. When someone conducted a Catholic Mass in Second Life in 2004, he left out the sacrament of communion so as to underscore the message that he was not trying to challenge Papal authority but wanted to show people what a Catholic Mass was like. This event and others like it led the Roman Catholic Church the following year to explicitly state that online communion would not perform the "incarnational reality of the sacraments and the liturgy," where "incarnation" is the presence of God in Christ, and of Christ in the instruments of communion. Physical copresence, of the priest and of communicants, is required for the miracle of transubstantiation to occur. But in the same document, the Church did welcome Internet communities as complements to real services, but with no performative, or sacramental, value. The Church thus approves online religion, but notes that it has no performative value: No sacraments occur.

Grafting cyberspace onto traditional rituals, with their own notions of effectiveness, poses new problems of theology and sociology. Consider the Cyber-Seder, which is held somewhere IRL ("in real life") and simulcast on a Web site. In 1998, the "real life" event was held in Lincoln Center in New York City and cybercast on http://www.jewmu.com/cyberseder/. Now, the seder has a formal structure that also allows for variation. In retelling the story of Exodus, participants ask and receive answers about the meaning of the foods served and the events celebrated. The 1998 Cyber-Seder was enlarged to include readings of poetry by Allen Ginsberg, a reading by Lou Reed, and a shofar and clarinet duo (Brasher 2001, 74). Most interesting was the chat room activity that proceeded before, during, and after the seder. Those logged on exchanged tips as to how best to obtain good sound and video feeds, and debated whether they were participants at the seder or merely onlookers. They forwarded the question to the ritual's organizer, who was unable to decide.

Ashley, a Christian engaged to a Jewish man, logged on to the seder in 1998 to learn more about Judaism (Brasher 2001, 72–78). She used the name Sarah in the chat room, implicitly identifying herself as a Jewish woman. She found the cyber-ritual at the same time broadly reaching out to engage non-Jews, through the use of nontraditional (and non-"Jewish") material, and at times excluding, as when some on the chat room slipped into Hebrew to discuss the ritual in greater detail. Six months later, she converted to Judaism.

Comparing Performativities

Do some religions lend themselves more easily than others to the idea of carrying out a religiously efficacious act online? Hinduism appears to offer more such possibilities than does Catholicism or Islam, for example. On the site http://www.prarthana.com, the Hindu worshiper can charge to her credit card a puja, a religious offering to a deity. She can ask that an offering for good health or job success be given to a specific temple chosen from a selection of hundreds. In return, she will receive in the mail a package of the food that had been offered to the deity and blessed by him. She can also experience a bit more of the puja by clicking on a rather elementary site, which brings her face-to-face with her deity of choice while a priest (or someone performing that role) chants the appropriate recitations. Other Hindu sites offer similar possibilities. Makalipuja.com requires worshipers to send in checks, and then worship is carried out at the Kalighat Temple, Kolkata. The site http://www.eprarthana. com "offers poojas to most of the deities." Puja packages assemble several different temples, constituting the five elements—earth, wind, fire, water, and sky or air. Pujas may be ordered for specific desires. To win cases in court, one offers at one of two temples (each costing US$9.00); to remove sins acquired during a previous birth, one temple in Tamil Nadu is recommended. You get the blessed food items mailed to you. But as with other sites, you can also carry out what the site calls "virtual pujas" while facing a 2D image of the deity you have chosen to worship rather than a quasi 3D temple. (The Indian sites also routinely offer matrimonial search services, a common element in South Asian sites of all sorts.)

Long before the Internet, religions differed in the degree and the location of performativity. One can say that the great debate within Christianity in the early modern period, and perhaps ever since, concerns performativity. Calvin, Zwingli, and others created new theories of the communion, as no longer effecting a change in substance (transubstantiation) when carried out by the priest, but as a symbolic way of focusing the attention of the churchgoer on Christ and God. Indeed, Calvin directed ministers to make this shift clear in the moment before the distribution of the wafer and wine, by saying that these elements are "signs and witnesses" and not material containers of God. The focus of the service then becomes the preaching, the Word and not the Flesh.

This divide, between a Catholicism of ritual performativity and efficacy and Protestant faiths of, well, faith and grace, has profound implications for the religious status of virtual acts. It is not a challenge to Methodist theology for a person of faith to pursue inspiration through the Internet, as what counts is to strengthen the faith through the study of the Word. It certainly would be a challenge to Catholic theology if a worshiper partook of communion in a virtual world, for what then would it mean for the priest to perform the miracle? It is thus not surprising that the Church produced an explicit ban on such pseudo-performative practices.

We often focus on the issue of Papal authority and the challenges to it from Catholic Web sites. But this second element of Catholic theology, the monopoly of performative efficacy, may be equally central, and certainly has profound implications for virtual religions. Online Catholicism must restrain the claims it can make, in order to preserve the Church's monopoly of authority and the priest's key role in administering to the faithful. If you go to the official site of the Vatican, you find an impressive wealth of information, much like a Papal library, with many links to doctrinal statements. But the flow of action is one way: You may search for the single authoritative document, but not choose among alternative answers or pose questions.

Note the contrast with the United Methodist Church's official Web site (http://www.umc.org), which, as with many Protestant sites, features an assortment of local, national, and global news. It links stories about Church efforts, such as fighting malaria, to actions the user can take, such as donating online with a credit card, downloading pdfs or video clips for use in a local antimalaria campaign, and getting ideas for local fund-raising activities. Back on the home page, you can reach a prayer request site and leave an intercessory prayer for someone (a prayer that God intercede on behalf of someone). Here we enter the realm of performativity. People are stationed at the Living Prayer Center 24/7 to take the requests by telephone or from the Web site. They then forward the request to one of the 300 prayer groups around the United States. (All this can be done in Spanish as well.) Children can do exactly the same through their own page, called "Pockets," which has its own "prayer wall" for posting their prayers. ("Pockets" also has children's games, poems, jokes, and thoughts for the day.) Both pages invite adults or children to pray with the person who initiated the intercessory prayer request, that is, to add their efficacy to that of the initiator.

The UMC site is particularly loaded with links to church activities and to ways of tailoring the broad message to your individual opinions, activities, and needs. You can assess your spiritual gifts by taking a quiz, which directs you toward the best approach to spiritual growth. The "MethoPedia" allows you to start from a personal concern and then find church doctrine and various interpretations of that doctrine. You may ask about AIDS, baptism, or death and dying, and thereby learn what the church says. But you are then directed to practical resources. From "death and dying," for example, you can link to a list of hymns appropriate for a funeral, or to answers to such questions as what happens after death (no clear doctrine here), or what one may do with one's organs (nor here). The UMC plays up links to outside sites. On its Facebook page, for instance, you find a long list of news stories, complete with the readers' comments, often scurrilous, that were attached to the original stories on news sites.

EXPERIENCE AND COMMUNITY

So far we have mainly explored the dimension of efficacy for this third type of site, those that foreground performance. But two other dimensions also are central to the attractiveness of these sites: the possibility of experiencing something of real-world religious activity (or perhaps something beyond it?) and that of entering or generating a religious community. How should we think about these two dimensions? Could a virtual pilgrimage carry something of the quality of a real-world one? Does worship with other online avatars resemble that in a bricks-and-mortar temple, or church, or mosque?

One of the more popular and complex sites is Second Life. Second Life is a multiuser virtual environment (MUVE), downloadable at no cost, and open for anyone to wander and talk in the form of an on-screen character or *avatar*. The term, intriguingly, has an older meaning of the concrete form a god takes on when descending to earth. You can make your avatar look as you wish: different age or gender from you? Why not? You can choose its clothing and purchase add-ons. It is easy to search for any kind of place or event you wish (beach, rave, mosque, or all three together), teleport to that place, and walk or fly around. When you meet other avatars, you can chat with them on your keyboard and use a small number of preprogrammed gestures. You can also use your real-world money to buy Linden dollars (from the site's host Linden Labs), with which you can build a house, church, sex shop, or political party booth. People do, indeed, buy all these things.

You can find both standard religious buildings (churches, temples, mosques, etc.) on Second Life and religion-like sites (Moroccan getaway, coven-like meeting house, etc.). The largest Islamic presence is due to IslamOnline, the organization best known and most used for its fatwa bank, for which they draw on leading scholars throughout the world. On Second Life, they have built a large Islamic complex, which includes a simulation of the pilgrimage (more below), a Palestine Holocaust Memorial, and many information boards.

Pilgrimages offer intriguing contexts for considering the relationships between technology and experience. Let's think of online religion as only one of several ways in which pilgrims have used technology to change the nature of their experience over the years. Most pilgrimages take a lot less time to complete than they did, say, 50 or 100 years ago. Pilgrims now can fly to Jerusalem, or Mecca, or Lourdes rather than walking or traveling by boat. They can take buses within the holy site, which can be particularly important for pilgrimages that are spread out over a large area, such as in the case of the Islamic pilgrimage, or pilgrimages to the Holy Land for the three Abrahamic faiths.

These speedups in transportation have changed the way people treat the pilgrimage in question. For Indonesian Muslims, the pilgrimage to Mecca once was treated as if the pilgrim were journeying off to death, because so many older pilgrims did indeed die at Mecca, and if they did it was considered to be a blessed event. Nowadays, even in the small highlands village where I lived in Aceh, Indonesia, a good dozen men and women had carried out the hajj by the 1980s, and several had made the journey more than once. Returning pilgrims have a new social status, that of hajji or hajjah, and a few use that status to succeed in business. From being a step toward death, the pilgrimage has become increasingly linked to one's career.

The hajj is like other pilgrimages in that it replicates a series of steps taken by a key religious figure. When Muslims travel from Mecca to Muzdalifah and Mina, they are following in the footsteps of the Prophet Muhammad. On the Japanese island of Shikoku, pilgrims who circumambulate the island and stop at its 88 Buddhist temples are following the practice of the eighth-century monk Kukai, founder of the Shingon school of Buddhism. Whereas they once made the entire journey around the island on foot, they now have the option of traveling by car or motorcycle, or alternating walking with riding. There also are miniature versions of the pilgrimage elsewhere in Japan (Statler 1984).

For Christians, the most famous journey may be the one undertaken by Jesus Christ, bearing his cross to the place of crucifixion. Pilgrims to Jerusalem often sought out these places, and at least by the fifteenth century began to regularly trace out these steps as a pilgrimage within the pilgrimage, akin to that performed by Muslims within the confines of the holy cities in Arabia. Franciscan monks soon began to build replicas of these pilgrimages in various places in Europe. The series of images of stops on this dolorous journey are called the Stations of the Cross, and today you can find them reproduced in many forms around the world. In what now is considered their traditional form, there are 14 such stations, ending with Jesus in his tomb; some argue that the series ought to end with his resurrection. But for our purposes, it is the fact that the stations can be reproduced in many ways and in many places that is crucial, for what is the difference between virtual images and those built out of stone or painted on canvas? In both cases, the worshiper is supposed to meditate on Jesus' suffering, in different ways at each station. Technology changed worship and veneration almost from the beginning.

Such a series of stations indeed occupy a prominent place in one Catholic church on Second Life. The Basilica of the Most Sacred Heart of Jesus presents the visitor with a familiar and fairly elaborate church setting. As you enter, to the left are a set of wall posters that allow you to touch and receive (as "greeting cards") a biography of Pope Benedict XVI or a detailed account of each of the seven Sacraments. Lining both sides of the church are paintings of the Stations of the Cross alternating with statues of saints. Touching a statue gives you the saint's biography and a long list of the people for whom that saint serves as patron. St Christopher's list is understandably long, including the city of Barga (Italy), bus drivers, and all who would keep away pestilence. There is a chapel to Our Lady of Fatima, and another, facing it across the nave, to the Sacred Heart of Jesus. Before leaving, one wall has direct links to sites devoted to the Virgin Mary. (By the way, there is no flying allowed in church.) Although the environment around the church is anything but religious—a neon Hard Rock Café sign looms across the street—within the church the Stations provide the possibility of hours of meditative devotions. Each offers an accessible card that contains a particular devotion written by a Catholic author. The experience is textually richer than most would be in real life, and you will have to judge for yourselves whether the 3D visual experience comes close to what you would take away from visiting a Stations site in a real-world church or an outside environment.

A second church on Second Life offers a religion-oriented natural environment. The Catholic Church of St. George is a German-language church surrounded by pillars with the Stations of the Cross; touching them provides brief descriptions, but the setting allows you to have a pleasant, meditative, second-life meander. Next door is Walsingham chapel, modeled on a chapel in Houston, Texas, dedicated to persuading Anglicans to convert to Catholicism, and with famous Anglican converts in its graveyard (the Second Life graveyard, not that in Houston). In the fields nearby, one finds a statue of Mary with Jesus, and, near the sea, several expensive homes (you are almost always next to the sea on Second Life, because it is built from islands, a little like Stockholm).

But if technology allows people to carry out these real-world pilgrimages with greater ease, it does not dramatically undermine their religious value. Such is not the case for a virtual hajj, which is fundamentally different from the real thing. As I mentioned above, IslamOnline has built a virtual pilgrimage site on Second Life, which you can reach by the usual means, by teleporting to the site. You arrive at the IslamOnline. net Virtual Airport, apparently in Mecca. You pick up a free tote bag with items for the hajj, including, for men, the ihram (white seamless garments to be worn during the pilgrimage), a tent, scissors for the required haircutting, and bald head to replace your own with to show that you've done the haircutting! You can choose to wear the ihram garments immediately and proceed toward Mecca's Great Mosque. Around a nearby mockup of the Kabah are green arrows pointing the way for your circumambulations, with information posts that give you step-by-step instructions for completing the pilgrimage.

The virtual hajj site seems to be one of the more popular places for Muslims to gather—at least it is the only place where I regularly find people present. (Contrary to what you might think, Second Life is rather underpopulated most of the time.) On August 20, 2009, the day before Ramadan began, I visited the site around the time for the Friday prayer. No prayer was happening, but a list of Ramadan activities had been posted, and several Muslims were engaged in a trilingual (Arabic, French, and English) conversation. A Moroccan man explained to me that no amount of circumambulating the virtual site counted as a pilgrimage, not even as an *umra*, which is a "little hajj" that one can perform (in Mecca) at any time during the year. An Arabian man joined in the discussion, as did a third Muslim man who spoke only English. A woman from Egypt joined us. She was dressed in tight-fitting clothing, and the Arabian man immediately said: "If you are a Muslim, then you should put on hijab," referring to modest, or Islamic, dress. We had no common language, but relied on Arabic with translations into French or English.

We can see a direct parallel with the Catholic mass: In both the cases, an online version can be welcomed as showing people how a religion is practiced, but it does not replace the real-world act; it has no performative value. Differences nonetheless exist between the two cases. A major Islamic organization funded the virtual hajj as a way for Muslims to familiarize themselves with the steps in the pilgrimage and to have a Muslim-friendly space on the Internet. It is supposed to match the real hajj as closely as possible. The Catholic Church has played no role in creating online religion, even if it has information sites, in part because it does not wish to suggest that an online liturgy could replace a real-world one. And to have online communion would surely risk the wrath of some at the Holy See.

But elsewhere among Christian churches, online religion has been very active. One of the more interesting experiments has been a series of sites and practices that at one point was called the Church of Fools. In the 1970s, some Methodist lay people ran a print magazine called the *Ship of Fools*, and in 1998 they created an online version with the possibility of bulletin board postings and of course real-world follow-ups. When one member was diagnosed with terminal cancer, she kept a diary on the bulletin board, and was deluged with flowers and cards at her hospital; after three months of near-continual postings, she died. At that point, the people running the site decided to keep it as a magazine, because they could not re-create the kind of sacred space online that would allow them to hold virtual services. But they took a step toward the bolder idea in 2003 when they created a game called The Ark, in which 12 people (chosen from over 1,000 applicants) played Biblical roles aboard a virtual Ark for 40 days and 40 nights, figuring out both theological questions and "whose turn it was to muck out the gorillas" (Jenkins 2008).

The Ark had a chapel where people gathered for services, and this experience led the group to design a new site that would be an online church. The new site, called Church of Fools, received sponsorship from the Methodist Church and the Bishop of London. It featured a chapel with an interactive Stations of the Cross. Even today in its reduced form, you can enter the church anytime and make an organ play a hymn, and sing along. During its full 3D period, up to 30 people, or rather avatars, could attend the scheduled services. They would file in and sit, and you could see the speech of the "warden" conducting the service as a bubble over her/his head. Talk by others appeared in a lower-left section. In the services I have witnessed, these off-sermon conversations could be very irreverent: "church is for fags," or repetitions of "apple pie" or "zzzzzzz," during the sermon. People got up and left. Avatars could hold up their hands in a style more common to a Pentecostal church—a gesture programmed in to make the range of gestures seem "ecumenical." Although only 30 people could be in the church at any one time as solid avatars, anyone could come as a "ghost" and remain invisible to others, although you could see yourself as a ghost and make the range of gestures. The site organizers added an element to the service of greeting the ghosts by shaking hands in mid-air, to extend the sense of community beyond what was visible to them. Real preachers gave sermons, beginning with the Anglican Bishop of London at the 2004 opening service.

Does such a site create "community"? The site's organizer, Simon Jenkins (2008), singles out the way that the Lord's Prayer became central to service, because it allowed for a participatory element. Everyone could follow along in any language, and these responses to the preacher's recitation of each line scrolled up at the bottom left; responders used English, Gaelic, French, and Latin. Thousands visited the church every week. A few "trolls" came to disrupt, but church wardens had the power to "smite" them, make them disappear from the environment. A survey they conducted showed that 40 percent of those who attended to pray did not regularly visit a real-world church; the online version gave them an alternative they could accept.

When two anthropologists (Kluver and Chen 2008) undertook an ethnography of the Church of Fools, they wanted to find out whether we should consider the online worship "real." How could one possibly answer this question? Well, they rather sensibly said that because the Methodist Church sponsored the Church of Fools, they would take that church's ideas about worship as a yardstick for measuring whether this particular online religious worship was "real," and what that would mean. For John Wesley, the founder of Methodism, worshipers employ "means of grace" both as a way of indicating that they had received God's grace and as a means whereby they received that grace from God. The main "means of grace" are prayer, Bible reading, and communion. Unlike the Catholic Church, Wesley understood "communion" to mean that taking bread and wine was a means to lead worshipers to remember Jesus and the miraculous transubstantiation of those substances into the body and blood of Christ. Now, both prayer and Bible reflections occurred at the Church of Fools, sometimes in environments where you or your avatar was participating alongside others. To that extent, we can reasonably say that worshipers were able to employ, in congregations, the "means of grace" indicated by Wesley. Only communion was missing, and it need not have been omitted if it was intended to be only the material means to induce remembrance of Christ's sacrifice.

The Church of Fools mixed genres in new ways. The 3D chapel had sacred art on the walls, and touching it gave you serious commentaries. The sermons were real, some preached by real bishops. But the organizers also wanted to attract church-phobic people and so maintained a current of playfulness. One of the video clips of the Church they have maintained on the ongoing site shows people worshiping the vending machines installed in the downstairs crypt. Did this diminish religious experience? You might compare these efforts to break down barriers between sacred and profane with those experiments in Catholic churches after Vatican II, where guitars sometimes became the musical accompaniment to worship.

Now, after several months the organizers took the Church of Fools down and substituted a 2D site, St. Pixels, which as of 2010 was active and attractive. St. Pixels continued to promote the "means of grace" of prayer and Bible reading, with an actively used page for posting requests for intercessory prayer, and responses by people saying "we're praying with you." The 2D church also has daily worship services, and worshipers participate through their 2D avatars.

Let us take away a methodological point from this case. We were able to make our questions about the Church of Fools more specific and useful by referring back to the doctrinal bases of the religion, and ask: in Wesley's terms, how should we understand what happens online? Of course, we would be in a much better position were we able to talk with Internet users about their experiences, but here research has only just begun.

COMPARATIVE COMMUNITIES

The second and third kinds of religious site—horizontal communication and religious performance—both raise an important question: Does joint Web usage create "communities," and in this case, "religious communities"? We often say so, but we do not often enough ask ourselves what we mean by "community." Efforts to create worshiping communities are good cases to think through this broader issue.

Efforts by social scientists to arrive at a more precise definition of "community" have focused on the face-to-face communication that fits images of small town life, front-porch greetings, and everyone knowing everyone else's business. Robert Putnam (2000) famously argued that membership in social groups—the real, meeting-every-week kind, not the joining-by-mail kind—was the building block of a healthy political society, because in such groups people interact in ways not limited to functionally specific routines. You may only talk office-talk with your office-mates, but in your bowling league or your Little League you talk about everything. Michael Taylor (1982) worked this last idea into the more formal concept of "multistranded ties" as part of the definition of community: that you know and interact with other people on more than one register, not just as your baker but also as a fellow parent of a schoolchild or just fellow frequenter of the same neighborhood park.

In a religious vein, these arguments would favor the parish ice cream social or the mosque-based school over an only-on-Sundays/Fridays/Saturdays sort of religious life. The latter might fail the idea of "community" entirely. What about online communities, then: Do they retain any meaning whatsoever, or is the use of "community" empty?

One way to proceed may be to ask what ideas of community are found within each of several religious traditions, and then ask whether anything of those ideas are preserved online. We have already done that somewhat for the online Methodist church; let's suggest a couple of other examples that would seem to be the most resistant to the idea of cybercommunities.

Buddhism

Within Buddhism, the community, *sangha*, is one of the Three Jewels, along with the Buddha and the Dharma. The sangha has been considered to include monks, nuns, and laypeople, and in the Theravada tradition to be structured by the passage of young men through the temples, begging by monks, and the active work by nuns and monks for the religious merit of the laypeople. What can online religion do for or to these ideas of sangha? In some cases, a traditional sangha has a cyber extension. For example, one Honolulu site is structured as a type 1 site, using our three-way classification, a top-down site to impart information from those who know to those who do not. The site is maintained by a real-world sangha; its cyber extension, http://www.shindharmanet. com/cyber, is intended to allow postings and dialogue; although as of 2009, it had little evidence of interactions. Here we can provisionally say that Buddhist notions of community are so anchored in specific real-world work that they could not be imported onto the Internet.

Wicca

In the Wiccan tradition, covens have been small, face-to-face communities, with intense and frequent participation in rituals creating a sense of belonging. For that reason, some Wiccan ventures into religion online, such as Lisa McSherry's cyber-coven site (http://www.cybercoven.org), also maintain traditional covens, and add to these practices information about covens worldwide, bulletin boards, and writings on "cutting edge magickal theory." Her JaguarMoon CyberCoven is, however, an effort to create an online religious community, a "virtual teaching coven following the path of American Eclectic Wicca." The base is an online class in ritual, which follows the same steps and degrees that a face-to-face coven would follow. Other cybercovens encourage group spells to protect members (for example, on www.witchforum.com); some build 3D worlds through the tools provided on Activeworlds (related to AlphaWorld, described above). Second Life has a Wiccan coven area, where you can join the Sacred Cauldron Group, and you run into Covensteaders, people who may also be vampires, or shapes-shifters (the women I met were) and who meet at certain agreed-on times.

Islam

We find Islamic sites corresponding to all the varieties of site we have already discussed. Some of the best-known Islamic Web sites feature articles by noted scholars. These sites thus represent different ways to find information that one might otherwise find in a bookstore: one-way, authoritative treatises on various topics, sometimes with the advantage of availability in multiple languages. Other Islamic sites (for example, http://maison-islam.com) are edited by Muslims probably unknown to most of those who consult the site, but provide clear opinions on a wide range of important topics, from family life to work issues to matters of spirituality.

Different in form but also seeking to establish an aura of authority are sites structured around the traditional format of the question-and-answer. Fatwas historically have been generated in this way, as an answer to a specific question, and some of the sites mentioned earlier may include fatwa sections having this structure. Other sites feature such sections, structured as answers to specific questions; one of the best known is http://islamonline.com, with its links to the European Council for Fatwa and Research and to the Islamic Society of North America (ISNA).

But these two types of sites offer what they frame as definitive answers, sometimes from distant lands. As we saw earlier, many young Muslims look for horizontal forms of exchange; they might wish to explain their particular situation in detail, and encourage others to ask relevant questions, something not possible on other types of sites.

Conclusions

Virtual religion is fast-changing, but for the moment I have found it useful to pull out from the myriad of sites three kinds of practices they embody: sending information from authorities to students, promoting communication among followers, and carrying out worship or other efficacious acts. In the latter case, it will be particularly exciting to follow debates among religious actors about the degree to which online practices "count," or have "performativity." You can easily carry on this line of research by asking online: What can you do at this site? Does it have a religious sense or objective?

Discussion Questions

What are the effects of the Internet on religious authority? On the one hand, anyone can promote alternative versions of a religion through the Web, and connect to others, without having to start up a new bricks-and-mortar religion. On the other hand, persons or institutions already recognized as "authoritative" could increase their reach and their effect through a Web presence.

Do participants in online religion enjoy a sense of "community"? What augments or diminishes such a sense? On the one hand, participants are likely sitting by themselves somewhere on a computer; on the other, they interact, albeit at one remove, with others.

Media Resources

For this chapter, the best idea is to view the sites themselves, many of which are mentioned here.

Secularisms and Religions
in Modern States

We have said a lot about religions so far in this volume, but less to say about all that is not religious, what we often refer to as "the secular": a secular state, way of life, or a set of beliefs. Here people often plunge into confusion. The United States is based on a "wall of separation between church and state," so we might wish to hold it up as an example of a secular state. But presidents of the United States hold prayer breakfasts; they say, "God bless America" and the like in official speeches, and it is difficult to imagine a successful candidate for the office who does not say that he or she believes in God—and we expect reporters to pose the question! What then distinguishes the United States from, say, India, Germany, or Egypt on this issue? What is a secular state, and what do we mean by secularism?

HOW TO THINK ABOUT "SECULAR STATES"

In fact, despite deep differences in history, political ideology, and religious conviction across contemporary nation–states, most of them overlap considerably on the question of the state's involvement in religious life, or so runs the argument of this final chapter. I focus here on large-scale religions in modern history. Two similarities appear again and again across modern states: Political authorities claim, and usually wield, authority over religious leaders; and states apply doctrines of "evenhandedness," that inevitably involve some involvement in religious life. I will explain these two claims here, but they will become clearer as we explore several cases.

First, in nearly all countries, the state asserts its own political priority over religious authorities, meaning that state authorities, whether they be judges or elected officials, have the right to determine matters of public policy, not religious leaders. Of course they differ in how they do this. France tries to keep religion out of political discourse entirely, as does Britain (despite the Anglican Church's capacity as the "established church"). The United States makes no such refusal, and legislators often justify votes by saying God so directs them. In India, judges refer to religious texts when faced with cases concerning marriage or divorce, as they do in Israel and Indonesia.

But in all these countries, a civil political body has the ultimate say in policy matters, and legislators will follow deliberative rules and procedures that are not religious in nature. In the United States, a law is enacted and a judicial decision taken as the result of deliberations and voting that are not subject to religious bodies or authorities, and no religious text has direct legal force. India, Israel, and Indonesia, though they apply religious law in their courts, all assert the capacity of their parliaments to stipulate what counts as religious law. Egypt admits only God's Word as a legitimate source of law, at least in theory, but in practice, judges work from the basis of a corpus of legal rulings. All these states could thus be said to be "secular" to the extent that religion is legally subordinated to the state, though not in the sense that law has no religious content.

Second, most states (though not all) proclaim neutrality or evenhandedness toward religions. This evenhandedness usually involves some degree of involvement in defining what counts as a religion. Some states support religious bodies even though they remain resolutely secular in their political philosophy. No one is more explicit about secularity as a constitutional principle than France, but the French state pays the salaries of religious-school teachers and finds ways to aid religious groups to build places of worship. With the United States, we might expect that the "free exercise" clause of the Bill of Rights would give religious groups legal advantages over other kinds of groups, but as we shall see later, religious groups win legal cases when they argue for equal treatment and not when they claim special rights qua religion. We will make similar arguments below for some states that apply Islamic law.

Three Meanings of "Secular"

In what follows, I will insist on distinguishing three meanings of the secular: legal structure, social processes, and individual orientations. Or rather, these three phrases designate distinct levels of analysis: the political and legal, the historical and sociological, and the psychological and phenomenological.

Secularism is perhaps most appropriately used to talk about how, in their constitutions and political philosophies, modern states define and regulate the place of religious bodies and religious discourse in political processes. States decide whether and how to recognize a particular body as a religion, set out its rights and duties, and formulate overall policies and philosophies of governance. Some of these philosophies or ideologies may be secularist, in that they proclaim the evacuation of religion from the sphere of public policy. Thus, France proclaims itself to be a secularist or "laic" state, the U.S. Bill of Rights prevents the government from "establishing" a religion, the Indian constitution proclaims the state to be secular, and so forth.

When we look at the long-term social processes that characterize many modern societies, we often talk about the *secularization* of society, by which we mean the effects that the division of labor has had on separations among social institutions. As work became relegated to a separate sphere, the state came to see itself as distinct from religion, and the family became a specialized sphere of socialization, each domain took on its own norms. Norms of family life and work may have been strongly shaped by religious belief, but gradually we came to see each domain as governed by its own rules, properly distinct from each other. This process has been long and is by no means simple. For example, even as marriage and divorce began to be regulated primarily by state bodies, many have continued to see them as mainly religious in nature, whether as a sacrament, as in Catholicism, or as a contract governed by revealed norms, as in Islam. Secularization does not imply a loss of faith and is compatible with a religious perspective on all domains of one's life; it does mean that each of the social institutions in which one participates has its own set of norms.

Finally, we may mean by secularization the *decline of religion* in some sense, if we believe that individuals become less likely to view matters of social life or even ultimate concerns in religious terms. Sometimes we speak of this decline to mean that individuals lose their faith in the existence of religious truths or their beliefs in the existence of religious beings. Sometimes, however, we mean that, whatever the nature of their beliefs, individuals have less to do with organized religions. Some, particularly European scholars, speak of the "privatization" of religion in this second sense.

Although social scientists once assumed that secularization processes entailed the loss of faith, because religion was destined to shrink into a private sphere and eventually to disappear, this idea of an inevitable link between these two levels now clearly is mistaken (Casanova 1994). Secularist political-legal structures and the secularization of society by no means always lead to a decline in participation in organized religion or to a loss of faith. Or, to put it positively, one may have a society where the majority of people retain a high degree of religious commitment and yet the society is highly secularized, and the state exercises little direct action on religions—the United States is an excellent example of this combination.

RELIGION AND PUBLIC LIFE IN THE UNITED STATES

U.S. history on religion, nation, and state is more complex than the phrase "separation of church and state" might imply. Running through the history of debates and laws in the United States about religion and public life are two contradictory but strong lines of argument. One stresses the constitutionally mandated separation of church and state and the dangers to freedom posed by government entanglement in religious affairs. The second stresses the historically dominant role played in U.S. public life by Christianity—or more narrowly Protestant Christianity, or more broadly a Judeo-Christian tradition.

The first argument stresses rights and laws. The second argument stresses historical tradition and shared values. Each has its claims to an antique lineage: the first, to Christian suspicion of government as inevitably corrupting (a view held by Saint Augustine, for example); the second, to the tradition of civic republicanism, where the state ensures that the community follows a set of moral, including religious, norms (Taylor 1990).

The rights argument for separating religion and state is based on the first 16 words of the Bill of Rights, which reads: "Congress shall make no law respecting an establishment of religion, or prohibiting the free exercise thereof." Many heated debates in our recent history—by the courts, in legislatures, among ordinary citizens—turn on how these 16 words are to be interpreted. Does the first clause, the establishment clause, prohibit all federal or state aid to religious schools, or all public displays in government buildings of religious symbols? Or does it more narrowly prohibit only laws that give special privileges or powers to a particular church? Does the second, the free exercise clause, protect the rights of schools to set aside a moment for silent prayer? Or does this practice run afoul of the first clause? What rights do parents have to further their children's exercise of religion? To what extent may Christian Scientist parents legally withhold medical aid from their children on religious grounds? May religious communities withdraw their children from school before the legal minimum age? Certain of these issues, such as the right to withdraw children from school, involve finding the right balance between the Constitution and the legislative power of the states. Other issues, such as silent prayer in schools, may be seen as requiring a weighing of the two clauses against each other.

Religion in the Early Centuries

The emphasis on limiting the powers of government over religion was motivated by the colonists' experience of religious persecution (Berman 1990). This persecution occurred not only in Europe but also in the colonies. The same religious groups that fled persecution abroad soon practiced it in their new homes. Authorities in New York and Massachusetts expelled Lutherans and Quakers along with Catholics and Jews. Even the relatively tolerant colony established by William Penn forbade deists to live in the colony and kept Jews from holding office.

The main purpose of the establishment clause was thus to prevent that kind of intolerance from developing at the federal level. The strongest advocates of the clause, James Madison and Thomas Jefferson, were fresh from their struggle to disestablish the Anglican Church in their home state of Virginia. Few other churches had universal pretensions; most were organized along *congregational* lines, meaning they were governed by the local congregation for the local congregation, and did not aim to become a universal church. Indeed, most residents of the colonies were Puritans, whose religious leaders were far more concerned with reserving church membership for the saved than they were with expanding their roles.

The framers of the Constitution went further, preventing the federal government from supporting all Christian churches equally through taxation. As James Madison argued in 1785, "Who does not see that the same authority which can establish Christianity, in exclusion of all other Religions, may establish with the same ease any particular set of Christians, in exclusion of all other Sects?" (quoted in Frankel 1994, 27). This sentiment lay behind Thomas Jefferson's famous phrase that there should be "a wall of separation between church and state" (Berman 1990, 40).

There was, however, no single state and no single church in the United States, then as now. Rather, there were many different governments and many different ways in which people pursued religious beliefs. The Constitution only affected the powers of the federal government, and prevented it only from passing laws that would infringe upon the free exercise of religion or that would establish a church. It did not forbid officials from acting on their religious beliefs in passing other laws, nor did it keep them from effectively making one set of religions dominant in public discourse.

Nor did the Constitution say that religion was a matter for individuals to decide. As the legal historian Harold Berman argues (1990), for Americans of the 1780s and 1790s, free exercise of religion meant the freedom of religious communities to regulate family and social life, not the freedom of the individual to do as he or she pleased. Such was clearly true for the majority of American Puritans, for whom religious membership was seen as a binding social covenant, but true as well for denominations we now think of as highly individualistic, such as the Unitarians. One Salem Unitarian church even records that in the seventeenth century it flogged and sold into slavery some Quakers who refused to contribute to a new church building! In the late seventeenth and early eighteenth centuries, states aided parochial schools and all public schooling was explicitly intended to further Christianity. Well into the twentieth century, marriage was considered to be religious, and divorce law was derived from English ecclesiastical law (Berman 1990). The authority of the community, embodied in its church, was taken for granted by most citizens of the early Republic, and it is this set of experiences that those arguing for maintaining public religious tradition cite.

Balancing Rights and Tradition in a Pluralistic Nation

In the two centuries since independence, the United States has changed from a nation dominated by Protestant, and particularly Puritan, Christians to a nation of diverse major religions, including Catholicism, Judaism, and Islam, and of many citizens not affiliated to a major religion. From a nation where most people thought of religion in terms of community norms as well as private faith, the United States has become a nation where most people think of religion in terms of individual beliefs alone.

In 1800, nearly everyone in the United States belonged to a Protestant denomination; Catholics, Jews, and other faiths taken together amounted to perhaps 2 percent of the population (Hunter 1990). Then came the enormous migrations of European Catholics at the mid-nineteenth century and again at the turn of the twentieth century, along with migrations of Jews and Asians of various religions. By the early 2000s, Catholics constituted about 25 percent of the population, and Jews and Mormons each less than 2 percent. Protestants of various denominations made up about half of U.S. residents. And within each of these large categories are more religious-based diversities than before. Whereas once the major divisions among Catholics were their countries of origin (especially among Irish, Italians, and Germans), today the major divisions concern the stands taken on doctrinal issues and on the authority of the pope. The severe cleavages today among fundamentalists, evangelicals, and others within the many Protestant denominations as well as between these denominations are paralleled in the nineteenth century only by the hostility exhibited by most Protestants against Mormons and Adventists. Nor was there an explicit "secular humanism" such as is professed by many today.

The relation between governments and religions has changed as well, but arguments for rights and those for tradition continue to have their strong supporters. Only in the 1940s did the Supreme Court explicitly hold that the Fourteenth Amendment prevented states from enacting laws establishing religion or preventing free exercise. In a 1947 case, *Everson v. Board of Education of Ewing Township,* the Court emphasized Jefferson's "wall of separation between church and state," and stated that states as well as the United States could not favor one religion over another. (Ironically, this broad doctrine was declared in a case in which the Court upheld a state law that gave state aid for buses used to take children to parochial schools.) The Court distinguished between aid to children and aid to schools, approving the former. In subsequent decisions, the Court has upheld laws aimed at granting children equal opportunity, for example, the right for a deaf child to have a sign language interpreter in a parochial school when that right is already granted to public school students. But the Court struck down as illegitimately "advancing religion" state permission for a Hasidic Jewish group to form a public school district that included only their own adherents (Frankel 1994, 96–107).

Despite these decisions, to some degree law and public discourse in the United States continue to give special status to Christian religions. Christian prayers in the White House and Congress are a reminder of the tendency to mix Christian symbols into public life. They cross party lines. In 1997, the second inauguration of President Clinton began with a prayer by the evangelical Christian minister Billy Graham; in 2009 Barack Obama asked evangelical minister Rick Warren to deliver a prayer.

Public prayer continues to be fought over in the courts. The current law of the land is that school-sponsored prayers violate the establishment clause. But this apparent consensus is tenuous, based as it is on a series of close decisions. For example, in the 1992 case, *Lee v. Weisman,* the Supreme Court decided five to four that prayer delivered by a rabbi at a public school graduation was unconstitutional. The majority opinion stressed that any school-sponsored prayer, whether in the classroom or at an assembly, engendered social pressure on those not subscribing to the majority faith. But the dissent argued that graduation prayers were a tradition, the idea of coercive social pressure was fabricated, and that Americans have always thanked God for his blessings.

Some recent decisions have emphasized the argument from historical traditions. A 1984 case, *Lynch v. Donnelly,* upheld the right of a city to display a nativity scene, and in 1983, in *Marsh v. Chambers,* the Supreme Court upheld the right of the Nebraska legislature to pay a chaplain to open sessions with public prayer.

Although today a majority Court opinion would probably not state that "this is a Christian nation," as one did in 1892; nonetheless, judges and politicians from time to time continue to refer to the United States as a Christian nation or Judeo-Christian nation. Moreover, apparently neutral laws, such as laws mandating a "moment of silence" in schools, may be seen as discriminating in practice by stigmatizing students who do not adopt prayerful attitudes or who find the dominant model of "silent prayer" to be in fact a Christian model. Muslims, for example, carry out obligatory worship or ritual prayer (salat) at specific times of the day and in doing so stand, bow, and prostrate themselves—none of which actions can be performed during the "moment of silence." The Supreme Court recognizes this problem in general; in the *Yoder* case (406 U.S. 220) discussed below, the majority stated: "A regulation neutral on its face, in its application nonetheless offends the constitutional requirement for governmental neutrality if it unduly burdens the free exercise of religion."

One contested area concerns whether only beliefs, or beliefs and practices, are protected by the free exercise clause. In 1879, in a decision (*Reynolds v. U.S.*) that upheld a law against the Mormon practice of polygamy, the Court held that religious practices were not themselves protected: While laws "cannot interfere with mere religious belief and opinions, they may with practices" (98 U.S. 166).

But in 1972, in the landmark case *Wisconsin v. Yoder,* the Supreme Court ruled that a state had to prove a compelling interest before it could constitutionally compel a community to obey a state law that conflicted with its religious practices. In that case, an Amish parent had been sued by the State of Wisconsin for violating a law requiring school attendance until age 16. The parent had removed his child from school after finishing eighth grade and claimed that continuing in school would unduly subject the child to the influence of the secular world and would thereby endanger her salvation. The Court found that the state did not show the required compelling interest in this case. Spending the years after eighth grade at home, learning the skills that would serve children best on the farm, was not obviously inferior to continuing on in school. Compelling school attendance would infringe on the Amish religious way of life, so the Court ruled that the law violated the free exercise clause.

Justice Douglas dissented in *Yoder*, noting that the Court did not know the wishes of the children, and that many children do leave the Amish community and are disadvantaged if they do not have the years of high school education required by the state.

Equal Treatment versus Special Religious Rights

Under debate in these and in more recent cases is the extent to which claims based on religious belief or practices merit special judicial consideration. As Rogers Smith (1998, 2007) has argued, these claims have not fared well in recent U.S. Supreme Court decisions. The Christian Right has advanced its arguments for a greater public presence through claims for equal treatment, not special rights.

Two issues galvanized the Christian Right at two stages of its organization: equal access to the radio airwaves in the 1940s and 1950s, and equal tax treatment for private Christian universities (the Bob Jones University case) in the 1970s. In both cases, litigants advanced claims that they deserved the same privileges as enjoyed by other groups: privileges enjoyed by liberal Protestant groups to broadcast their religious messages over the public airwaves, and privileges enjoyed by other private colleges to be free of tax obligations. In the 1970 *Walz* decision, the Supreme Court ruled that churches did not have tax exemptions as religious institutions per se, but as part of a broad class of institutions that served the public interest and that included hospitals, libraries, and professional organizations. Furthermore, the nonestablishment clause could be invoked when it appeared that the state was unduly aiding religious groups per se. A series of cases from the 1970s on struck down aid to parochial schools as involving "excessive entanglement" of the state in religious affairs (*Lemon v. Kurzman* 1971), and that "Lemon test" was invoked in subsequent cases as well.

The Christian Right strategy since that time has been to ask only for equal access to services, and equal rights of free speech, and often they have won their cases: for access to school facilities, for example (*Lamb's Chapel* 1993; *Rosenberger* 1995), or for equal opportunities to provide federally commissioned social services, the "charitable choice" argument.

THREE EUROPEAN VARIANTS

In European societies, states have developed a mixture of evenhanded regulation of all religions, nominal precedence (or "establishment") of one church, and preferences for or principles of secularist public policy deliberation. These mixtures usually achieve practical evenhandedness and general avoidance of religious claims in public. Britain may have an established Church (the Church of England, of course), but politicians generally avoid public discussion of private religious beliefs, and similar statements could be made of the Lutheran-heritage Scandinavian societies. France proclaims itself to be secularist, but actively aids religious private schools by giving them teachers' salaries. Germany, Belgium, Italy, and Spain have mechanisms for publicly recognizing certain religions, but each has developed nonreligious political discourse.

The particular features of each of these mixtures become most easily visible when pushed or tried by minority religions. Let us consider what has happened in three of these states.

French Secularism Takes on Headscarves in Schools

France has made state secularism a part of its legal framework. Throughout the nineteenth century, Republican and Catholic factions struggled for control of the schools—and through them, control of the hearts and minds of French children. From that struggle came strong laws preventing the state from granting official recognition to any religion and laws guaranteeing public, secular education to all French children. The French legal doctrine of *laïcité,* perhaps best understood as keeping religion out of public affairs and keeping public officials from displaying their religion, has generally been understood to constrain the state and its employees, but not citizens in their private capacity (Bowen 2007).

French laïcité also has a broader sociopolitical meaning, however, which transcends this legal doctrine. Many French teachers and public officials, particularly on the political left, have inherited a tradition of strong anti-Catholic sentiment that sometimes also is an antireligious sentiment. For them, the French Republic depends on a public sphere that is free of religious messages. French citizens become complete political individuals by being socialized in public institutions, and they retain their citizenship qualities by continuing to interact in such institutions qua citizens—and not as Muslims, Protestants, or Scientologists. They recognize each other as equivalent citizens, indistinguishable on the dimension of their participation in French public life.

The norm of public laïcité leads some teachers and principals of secondary schools to expel girls who come to class wearing headscarves, or some employers in private industry to demand that employees not wear "clearly Islamic" dress. When Muslim schoolgirls began to wear headscarves to school in the late 1980s, some teachers and principals resented the girls' public display of difference, and a number of prominent French intellectuals publicly cried out that the Republic was endangered. Within a few years the highest administrative law body, the Conseil d'État, had arrived at what would be its consistent ruling that nothing in French law prevents schoolchildren from expressing their religious beliefs by wearing garments that imply a religious affiliation, as long as such garments are not "ostentatious" and the children in question neither "proselytize" nor disturb "public order." Indeed, the Conseil d'État ruled that they had the right to engage in religious self-expression in school, and that the law restricted the apparel and the conduct only of teachers and other state employees.

Teachers and principals have continued to expel or isolate children wearing headscarves and sometimes they have declared strikes to dramatize their position. One such incident occurred in 2002–2003, when the teachers in a high school near Lyon threatened to strike if one female student was not expelled. In Lyon and elsewhere, some teachers and principals claimed that the presence of the headscarves was divisive, that it brought broader social tensions, and even the war in Palestine, into the schools. The headscarf issue surfaced in the media again in April 2003, when Muslims attending the annual assembly sponsored by the large Muslim association Union des Organisations Islamiques de France (UOIF) booed the call by the Minister of the Interior to enforce the law requiring women to bare their heads for their identity photos. Newspaper articles in April and May 2003 replayed the arguments first heard in the 1980s, according to which the headscarf was a sign of female submission and a direct attack on the principle of laïcité. In March 2004, after public hearings by two governmental commissions and a continued media campaign against the scarves, France passed a law preventing the wearing of any clothing or signs that clearly displayed the religious affiliation of a student in public school.

Ironically, some women consider wearing the headscarf to be part of breaking with immigrant culture, a way of distinguishing between an Islam learned in France and the insufficiently Islamic traditions of the "old country." As many French observers have noted, when young women choose to wear a head covering, misleadingly called *le voile* ("the veil"), it often signifies a moment of personal growth and transition—such as graduating from school, traveling to another country, beginning work, or making a break with the social norms of their family. Wearing a headscarf rarely is a mark of continuity in family dress but rather a mark of discovery and self-identification as an individual.

France is fast becoming an openly multicultural and multireligious country, but at this point has chosen to reaffirm its tradition of public laïcité in an effort to bring people together under the umbrella of French values and customs. It continues to find measures intended to send this message. In 2010, the French Parliament is considering a ban on wearing the *niqab*, a garment that covers women's bodies, leaving only a slit for the eyes, in all public places, or at least in public transport. It is too early to know whether these legal restrictions will have the desired effect.

The National Church in Britain

In the European context, France is an unusual case. Most other members of the European Union make available some state funding for religious organizations. In some European countries, political parties have links to particular religious denominations.

Britain, for example, has an established church, the Anglican or Episcopal Church, in which all state weddings and funerals take place. Other churches and religious organizations are allowed, and some even receive state support, but they take second place to the Anglican Church.

Some Britons have recently urged that the Church be disestablished, deprived of its official status. Non-Anglicans, including many Muslims and Jews, argue that for all British citizens to enjoy full citizenship, they all must enjoy an equal capacity to shape the public culture. Such an equality implies that the public culture cannot favor one religion over another, as it currently does.

However, some Jewish and Muslim leaders have come out publicly in support of the continuing establishment of the Anglican Church (Modood 1994). They argue that when there is a national religion, the followers of that religion feel comfortable about their place in the society and, therefore, exert less pressure on minority groups to convert or conform. They also argue that Anglicanism is less threatening than secularism to Muslims and Jews, because at least it supports other religions' continued existence. By contrast, secularism contains an anti-Islamic sentiment. These people cite the example of France, where strict secularism makes it more difficult for some people to accept the public religious self-identification by Muslims.

The Crucifix in Bavaria

German attitudes toward public religion are still further away from French secularism than are British ones. Recent controversy in Germany has concerned both the wearing of religious dress in schools and whether the state of Bavaria may make compulsory the display of the crucifix in schools (Caldwell 1996).

In France, the normal state of affairs had been, at least in theory, the absence of any religious markers in the classroom, and the signs of religious difference, the Muslim headscarves, introduced into the classroom clashed with secular state officials' expectations. In Germany, and especially in Bavaria, the normal state of affairs was quite different. The state required that all primary school classrooms prominently display a large crucifix.

In 1995, however, the Federal Constitutional Court responded to a suit from a non-Christian ("anthroposophist") family and overturned the Bavarian regulation. The decision set off a storm of protest. The court ruling did not require the crucifixes to be removed, only that schools would not be obliged to hang them. But the furor was intense. Even Chancellor Helmut Kohl objected that the state had an obligation to pass Christian values on to children, and numerous commentators compared the federal court's decision to the Nazis' acts of exchanging crucifixes for swastikas. Some politicians called for disobedience of the court order.

To explain the reaction, it helps to consider how these key religious symbols give public solidity to boundaries between "Us" and the "Other." In France, the Other is either Islamic fundamentalism or religion taking over the state. In Germany, it is the denial of Christian values under Nazi and communist rule. In the United States, it is persecution of religious dissenters by a state-backed church.

The place of religion in Germany traces back to the aftermath of religious wars in the seventeenth century. The German lands adopted the principle that a ruler could determine the religion of his subjects, a principle that tolerated princes, not subjects. It provided for shared practices and beliefs throughout the realm.

This principle continues to claim legitimacy. In 1918, Catholic Bavaria demanded protection against the potential persecution of Catholics in a Germany now two-thirds Protestant. In response, the framers of the Weimar Constitution granted to the German states the right to administer public education. They also gave all registered churches the status of public corporations, to be supported by taxes. These articles were adopted into the 1949 Basic Law, the West German Constitution. The Basic Law continues to be interpreted as the expression of German values that the state should take active steps to promote. The furor over the Bavarian cross decision was thus aimed at a court seen as violating its obligation to promote Christian values.

German attitudes toward religion continue to be shaped by the idea that states could choose between established forms of religion, which meant in practice the Roman Catholic or Lutheran Churches. This historical background has led some Germans to strongly oppose the presence of new religions, or sects such as Scientology. These Germans see Scientology's claims to religious status as a cover for attempts to extract wealth from converts and have led state governments to limit the development of local Scientology branches. By the late 1990s, the controversy had reached international proportions, with Scientologists taking out full-page ads in newspapers in the United States and elsewhere to protest German state suppression of religious freedom.

WHEN RELIGION UNDERLIES LAW

So far, we have seen that states that we would think of as secular in fact are engaged in active dialogue, support, and often regulation vis-à-vis organized religious bodies. Now let me turn to the opposite end of the spectrum, societies (or subgroups within larger societies) that wish, and claim, to follow religious law. In Israel, Jewish courts enforce Jewish law, but the Knesset retains the capacity to define the legal conditions of enforcement. (And in North America, Jewish tribunals enjoy a sometimes ambiguous status with respect to civil courts.) In Indonesia, the state runs Islamic courts alongside civil ones, but the legislature and executive also set the ground rules for enforcement. Finally, in India judges make rulings in family law matters on the basis of the religion of the parties, but they have acted to move interpretations of religious law, particularly Hindu and Islamic, toward more gender-equal terms.

In these and other cases, we cannot simply say that the state enforces religious law; the state and specific individuals and groups with state functions also interpret, modify, and condition the application of religious norms. Religion remains within the confines of a political system, and thus we may consider these states to be secular and to contain a political sphere with its own autonomous norms and procedures.

Gender and Marriage in Israeli Jewish Law

Although in some respects Moses holds the place in Judaism that Muhammad does in Islam, in fact the lives of the two prophets play very different roles with respect to modern authority and law. Muhammad's life casts a very direct and very specific shadow over daily decisions made by jurists, who base their decisions on his statements and actions. Moses delivered the first five books of the Hebrew Bible to his people as the original Torah, but at that point his life made no additional contributions to Jewish scripture.

The Torah has since had a life of its own, accruing layers upon layers of commentary. Indeed, the term *torah* today can refer to the first five books of the Hebrew Bible, or to the entire Bible, or to both the Bible as written Torah and the "oral Torah," further commandments handed to Moses and embodied today in biblical commentaries.

Each commandment in the Torah requires elaboration to make it specific and exceptions to adapt it to changing conditions of life. For example, the commandment to do no work on the Sabbath has required jurists to specify which activities count as work and which do not. The consensus today has it that certain activities, such as carrying an infant or pushing a wheelchair, constitute work when in public but not when in private. Because most Jews consider these particular activities essential even on the Sabbath (when babies and older people also attend worship services), authorities have created nominally private spaces, called *eruv,* within which the activities may still be carried out without violating religious law.

For some Jews, then, understanding Torah and living a religious life requires the interpretive intervention of religious authorities. For certain matters, such as resolving disputes and performing marriages, Jews living in many parts of the world have long had recourse to religious courts. In the Ottoman Empire, Jews had rabbinical courts, empowered to decide matters of marriage and divorce as well as such ritual issues as "carrying on the Sabbath." The courts continued to hold this authority under the British Mandate (1917–1948) and in the post-1948 state of Israel. Israel has continued the Ottoman practice of providing a certain degree of legal autonomy and distinct religious courts to each religious community, including Jews and Muslims.

The place of Jewish law remains contested, however (Edelman 1994). Officially, Israel is a nonconfessional state, meaning that no religion enjoys exclusive state support. The parliament, or Knesset, has final authority over all matters, including religious ones. The law regulating the rabbinical courts, passed in 1953, stipulates that marriage and divorce of Jews will be handled by the courts "in accordance with Jewish law." But who is to interpret Jewish law? Prior to the creation of the Israeli state, political leaders had already committed themselves to granting this authority to Orthodox rabbis, who controlled the courts. In 1947, the executive body preparing for statehood entered into an agreement with an Orthodox body, the Agudah movement, stipulating that the new state would respect the Sabbath, require observance of dietary laws (*kashrut*) in all state institutions, maintain the authority of the rabbinical courts over matters of personal status (especially marriage and divorce), and establish religious schools.

How the remainder of social life would be regulated was left open, and the issue continues to inflame passions on both sides. Many Orthodox Jews see Israel as too secular and try to change social life through direct intervention, some even blocking off streets to traffic during the Sabbath to ensure that Jews follow the law. These men and women see most secular Jews as threatening Israel's distinctive character as a Jewish society. Most of Israel's Jewish citizens indeed consider themselves nonreligious, and they want the freedom to dress as they wish and to drive and visit restaurants and theaters when they wish, including on the Sabbath. They see the Orthodox rabbis as threatening their freedoms. Most of them think that Israel should retain its Jewish character as long as individuals may choose not to observe certain religious rules. What should the character of public life then be? The issue remains subject to debate and, at times, public confrontations.

The same tension emerges over the law to be applied in courts. The Knesset has ruled that the rabbinical courts must decide certain matters, such as the age of marriage, in accord with the statutes passed by the Knesset. Civil courts recognize all marriages conducted outside of Israel if they are in accord with the laws of the land, even if they are not conducted in accord with Jewish law. The rabbinical courts have responded to these pressures by becoming less flexible in their interpretations of religious law, especially on matters of marriage and divorce. Israel has no institutions of civil marriage, and Jews may only be married by an Orthodox rabbi. Jews may not marry non-Jews, nor may they marry people not properly (according to Orthodox rabbis) divorced.

Two resulting problematical questions in Israel (and among Jews in the United States) are as follows: Who is a Jew? What is divorce? Orthodox authorities accept as

Jews only those persons whose maternal lineage (ties through women, starting with one's mother) contains only Jews, or those persons who converted to Judaism under the guidance of an Orthodox rabbi. Thus, many U.S. converts are not recognized as Jews in Israel, and children of Jewish fathers whose mothers either converted or are non-Jews are similarly denied Jewish status for purposes of marriage. But the Israeli government itself recognizes as a Jew anyone sincerely and plausibly identifying himself or herself as a Jew.

This disparity in definition has led to anomalies, such as the treatment of the 35,000 Ethiopian Jews airlifted to Israel in 1984 and 1990. These men and women were granted Israeli citizenship as Jews under the 1950 Law of Return. But the rabbinical courts refused to marry them unless they underwent conversion (and, for the men, recircumcision) on grounds that in the past their ancestors may have married non-Jews. The Ethiopian issue was further complicated by accusations of racism. At one point it was revealed that the blood banks had thrown out all blood donated by the Ethiopians for fear it was tainted with HIV. Finally, the rabbinical courts created a special court to allow Ethiopian Jews to marry among themselves, but still refused to permit them to marry other Jews (Edelman 1994).

Divorce presents additional problems in the gendered nature of Jewish law. Israel recognizes no civil divorce. Jews can obtain a divorce only from the rabbinical court, and the court recognizes divorce only when the husband presents his wife with a document called a *get*. The document, written in a combination of Hebrew and Aramaic, proclaims the husband's act of "releasing" his wife from the marriage. The court must authorize the divorce but cannot deliver the get in the husband's name. (They can imprison a husband if he refuses to grant the divorce but he may still refuse to do so.) If both parties agree to the divorce, then no problem arises. But when the husband refuses to grant it, the wife is unable to remarry. In other countries, including the United States, the Orthodox wife is placed in an anomalous status: She may obtain a civil divorce and legally remarry—and some women do so—but then she is considered by the rabbis to have committed adultery (Breitowitz 1993; Meislin 1981).

Islamic Law in Indonesia

Now I turn to a Muslim society that grants distinct legal rights to citizens on the basis of their religion. Does the claim that Islamic law is based on the Qur'ân and the hadîth (reports of deeds and actions by the Prophet Muhammad) mean that Islamic law is alongside or outside the state? I will argue that, for Indonesia, it is considerations of equity and equality that drive the state and its judges to maintain control over the interpretation of how Islamic law is to be applied. I suggest that this hierarchy of state law over religious law is not unique to Indonesia, but characterizes the workings, if not the explicit policy, of some other countries with Islamic legal systems.

One might expect that some states granting formal autonomy to religious law for some persons would retain their prerogatives to at least modify religious norms, if not overrule them, if they infringed on certain rights. Several sources of normative pressure make such expectation reasonable. International conventions on human rights and women's rights, internal pressures from civil society organizations, and developments within the interpretation of religious law may converge to urge states to adopt such measures. In legally pluralistic states, those that recognize more than one set of legally binding norms applicable to distinct segments of the citizenry, considerations of cross-segment fairness may exert such pressure.

All these sources are in evidence for Indonesia, as described below, but the reforms in Islamic law regarding women's rights in many Muslim-majority societies have meant a partial, de facto convergence of several countries in the way Islamic laws regarding marriage and divorce are applied. Sometimes these reforms are visible in codes, as in the recent case of the reform of the Moroccan code; in other instances they are only discernable through the study of judicial practice, as in Egypt and Iran. My argument is not that equality is thereby achieved, but that a sense that discrimination against women should be at least reduced, if not eliminated, motivates many of these reforms, and that the reforms take place via the state's reserved right to modify how religious law is applied.

Indonesia has an Islamic court system that runs parallel to its system of civil courts (Bowen 2003). Each system hears civil cases in the first instance and on appeal, and allows requests for cassation to be made to the Supreme Court. The Islamic courts only hear cases brought by Muslims. They give legal sanction to marriages and divorces and can hear disputes over inheritance or the division of property upon divorce. The civil courts hear all other types of civil cases and all criminal ones, and also cases involving marriage, divorce, or inheritance brought by non-Muslims. (Special courts also exist for administrative, military, and commercial matters.) The demand for a separate Islamic judiciary was made in part as the right of Muslims to seek a remedy for the discrimination they had suffered at the hands of the Dutch. Islamic judges or tribunals existed in parts of what was then the Dutch East Indies, and in the nineteenth century, the Dutch created uniform tribunals on Java and Madura. But in 1937, the government withdrew the rights of those tribunals to hear inheritance disputes, on grounds that Islam was not the source of the "living law" in Indonesia. The 1989 law creating the courts was thus hailed by some as putting an end to this history of discrimination against a religious group.

More broadly, Indonesia grants distinct rights to its citizens depending on their declared religious confession. The state not only grants legal recognition to Islam, along with a small number of other official religions but also requires that each citizen declare, and indicate on his or her identity card, a recognized religion. (The list was recently extended to include Confucianism.)

If the Islamic courts are limited in jurisdiction to cases involving Muslims, the civil courts not only hear cases involving any and all Indonesians but also emphasize the multireligious nature of the country and of its justice. I recall the manner in which one chief judge of a local civil court in Aceh asked each witness to state his or her religion (required at the swearing-in). When each responded "Islam," he would say *kebetulan,* "as it happens," in order to make of this simple and routine question a didactic moment, an occasion to remind his audience that in his court one might find Christians or Hindus testifying or litigating as well as Muslims, and that this was the nature of justice in Indonesia.

However, the segmentation of the court system also created problems, in part because it suggested that with respect to family law, people could be easily separated into two distinct and sealed communities. Muslims would have their affairs regulated in one court, and those of all other faiths in the other. This idea has two types of difficulties associated with it. First, it creates practical problems whenever a couple or family contains people of different religions, or, more precisely, one or more Muslims and one or more people of another religion, or when a Muslim wishes to marry a non-Muslim. No solution yet exists that would allow marriages of Muslims to non-Muslims to be registered in Indonesia. Second, it may reduce the degree to which people consider themselves citizens first and Muslims, or Christians, second.

Convergence of Norms

In most respects, jurists and politicians in Indonesia have worked to develop avenues along which Islamic law can converge with general norms of interreligious tolerance and human rights. These norms date back at least to statements made by the Indonesian Supreme Court in the 1950s that the new "living law" in Indonesia was one in which men and women had equal rights. Efforts to reinterpret Islamic law so as to guarantee equal rights for women are far from complete, but were important in bringing about substantive reform in marriage, divorce, and postdivorce property settlements. These reforms were within the context of Islamic jurisprudence rather than against it.

Divorce provides a good example of how the state could promote Islamic law and at the same time work to limit discrimination against women within Islam. Current Indonesian divorce law for Muslims did not change the Islamic understanding of how a person brings about a divorce. In that understanding, as a religious law expert or an ordinary person might describe it, the acts brought by a man and those brought by a woman are not equivalent. A husband unilaterally repudiates his wife by uttering the *talaq,* which is valid upon utterance. A wife must appeal to a judge to grant an annulment (*faskh*). (There are other categories, but they are much less frequently applied in Indonesia.)

However, the substantial conditions for granting a divorce are the same in the two cases. In both cases, the initiating party must appear before a judge and demonstrate that one of a specified number of reasons for divorce has been met. The reasons are the same whether the action was brought by the husband or by the wife. The judge may then either grant the wife a divorce or allow the husband to pronounce the divorce formula. The same Indonesian legal terms for "divorce" are used in the two cases, thus masking the underlying Islam-based formal law's asymmetry. All property acquired during a marriage, regardless of title, is divided equally between the husband and wife.

Islamic law experts state that these conditions simply limit how God's word is carried out without contravening it. Most make the same judgment concerning current laws on polygamy, which stipulate that a judge must approve a polygamous marriage before it is legal, and that the first wife must approve of the second marriage, although during the early 2000s there had been a sharp public debate concerning polygamy.

This process of convergence allows different advocates to continue to adhere to their respective, conflicting universalistic positions. Advocates of international human rights and women's rights can insist that men and women enjoy just and equitable judgments. They can point to the changes in Islamic legal practices brought about by Indonesian law as measures to combat discrimination against women—although many would press for the abolition of polygamy. Advocates of Islamic rights and duties can insist that Muslims obey God's commands as set out through the Qur'ân and through the words and deeds of the Prophet Muhammad. Indonesian law also meets this standard. In this way, two or more meta-normative claims, claims about the supremacy of one set of norms over another, can coexist.

Indian Courts and Religious Interpretation

India contributes in important ways to our understandings of secularism. India's constitution proclaims it to be a secular state, but the Indian version of secularism gives religion a central role. Moreover, India was politically and legally constructed around compromises intended to keep various minorities, regions, and language groups enthusiastic about the project of forging a nation.

In the domain of law, these compromises produced what we could call a multicultural or multireligious approach to family law. As is the case with Israel, Indonesia, and some other countries, India directs judges to adjudicate cases regarding marriage, divorce, and certain other aspects of family life in accord with the normative frameworks of one's religious or ethnic group. In India, these groups include Hindus, Muslims, Christians, and members of certain tribes. India's legal system also includes community courts, mosque assemblies, and other sources of law, all subject to appeal within the court system. Judges draw on jurisprudence, statutes, international law, the religious traditions of each religion, and other sources.

Indian judges, therefore, must decide which body of religious law governs the lives of a particular person or family. When judging a Muslim couple, they must determine which legal school (*madhhab*) the couple follows. Most Muslims follow the Hanafi school of Sunni Islam, but some are Shi'ites and in southern India some are governed by the Shafi'i Sunni school. These differences make a difference in some family law disputes; for example, if a Shia woman initiates divorce proceedings, she may be allowed to keep the wealth given to her at marriage, the dower, whereas if she were Sunni (whether Hanafi or Shafi'i) she could not keep this wealth.

Because judges also draw on broader bodies of religious and international law, they have been able to inflect older religious norms in new directions, and in many instances they have rendered religious laws more mindful of gender equality. For example, they now require that Muslim husbands pay their ex-wives alimony until they remarry, rather than, as the older practice required, only three months of support. India's most famous recent civil case, in 1985, touched on this issue. Judges awarded a woman named Shah Bano "permanent alimony" (until remarriage or death) and, moreover, they castigated Muslims for discrimination against women. The subsequent uproar by some Muslims led the legislature to pass an act that limited the period of postdivorce payment to the traditional three months. However, the wording of the law led some judges to subsequently rule that the ex-husband must pay, within three months, a sum substantial enough to provide for his ex-wife until she might remarry! The Supreme Court subsequently confirmed this interpretation.

What has led India's judges to push religious law, Hindu as well as Muslim, in a direction favoring gender equality? One reason surely lies in the relatively progressive nature of judicial culture, but another is the effect of political competition, as some Muslim leaders found in gender-equal views the most effective retort to Hindu nationalist attacks on Islam.

More broadly, as we saw earlier in this book, India's citizens draw on alternative narratives to think about their nation (as do citizens of most nations), including narratives of Indian secularism and a Hindu India. (Thinking about a Muslim nation was displaced onto Pakistan.) Secularism in India promises to keep the state neutral with respect to religions (and in that respect resembles U.S. secularism). The constitution and the positions of most political parties grant equal citizenship rights to all Indians regardless of religious affiliation. India's national movement, associated with Mahatma Gandhi and Jawaharlal Nehru, proclaimed this vision of India, and Nehru's Congress Party is its main standard-bearer.

Hindu nationalism, by contrast, reaches back to a Hindu past to construct images and stories of India's greatness. It has its counterpart in Islamic nationalism, and portrays the creation of Muslim Pakistan as implying that India ought to embody Hinduism. Because over 80 percent of Indians are Hindu, say the advocates of Hindu unity, they ought to set the agenda for politics and society. Now, India's Hindus do not constitute a single political block. Hindus are sharply divided along local caste lines, and often Muslims and lower-caste Hindus form electoral alliances against upper-caste Hindus. But the call for Hindu unity (Hindutva) is intended precisely to forge an all-Hindu alliance despite these divisions.

For Muslim judges and jurists, finding gender-equal versions of Islam afford the best means to argue that Islamic law can have a place in a secular Indian political system. As with their Indonesian counterparts, the Indian legal experts have found ways to apply Islam while recalibrating to fit global norms of equal justice.

Conclusions

When in the 1660s, John Locke wrote his *Essay on Toleration,* he argued for equal rights of conscience for all Protestants, on grounds that the Sovereign could not know what was in their minds and that in any case dissenting Protestants, those not in the Church of England, did not trouble public order. Catholics, obedient to the Pope, and atheists, whose oaths could not be believed, were not included in this plea. In the United States, our early notions of religious toleration today look similar to Locke's and thus quite narrow. It took special promises by John F. Kennedy that he would not listen to the Pope first and foremost to make possible his election, and we have yet to see a Jewish, much less Muslim, president. If today, then, societies in Europe and North America are relatively accepting of religious diversity, this acceptance is but the result of a recent and often hard-fought battle for religious toleration.

I would argue that it is some form of secularism that best permits and pushes a broadening of religious toleration in all countries, and that we need to see secularism as also permitting religious practice. Secularism need not imply antagonism to religions; understood as the political guarantor of equal treatment and respect, secularism may be and probably is the best way to guarantee freedom of religious beliefs and practices. It is, as I hope I have shown, not inimical to the application of religious law or, to put it more precisely, state law that has been inspired by religious traditions and norms.

This particular set of studies and issues reminds us once again that it is only when we look beneath the surface of slogans and ideologies—French laïcité, Indonesian Islamic law—that we appreciate how, in practice, people interpret and live their ideas of what religion is and should be.

Discussion Questions

Is the United States a secular society? Do we have "separation of church and state"? Take the issues surrounding public schools. Some parents think that because we allow local school boards to control schools, they ought to construct curricula according to parents' wishes, which most controversially involves teaching creationist ideas about human history. Others think that because these ideas are religious in origin, they have no place in a public school curriculum. How important is it that everyone learn the same things? Is it a good thing that people can set up alternative religion-based schools or use religion-based home schooling curricula? Does this promote freedom of religion or divide us?

Media Resources

A number of U.S. television documentaries have explored religion in the schools, among them *School Prayer: A Community at War*. The Israeli film *Sentenced to Marriage* examines rabbinical courts in that country, and could be an interesting complement to the film on sharî`a councils mentioned earlier. You can view a 19-minute report from 2004 on French headscarf ban at: http://www.youtube.com/watch?v=kWta4xB4gQ0&feature=results_video&playnext=1&list= PLF9B6D6026F831C1B. A longer and more recent program on the controversy, the first in a series of human rights programs, took the form of a mock trial (I was a witness) and now is available at: http://www.youtube.com/watch?v=Z_cahKQdSI0.

REFERENCES

Abou El Fadl, Khaled (1994). Islamic law and Muslim minorities: The Juristic discourse on Muslim minorities from the second/eighth to the eleventh/seventeenth centuries. *Islamic Law and Society,* 1(2), 143–187.

Ainsworth, Mary D. Salter (1967). *Infancy in Uganda: Infant care and the growth of love.* Baltimore, MD: Johns Hopkins University Press.

Alexander, Jeffrey C. (1982). *The antimonies of classical thought: Marx and Durkheim.* Los Angeles, CA: University of California Press.

Ammerman, Nancy Tatom (1987). *Bible believers: Fundamentalists in the modern world.* New Brunswick, NJ: Rutgers University Press.

Anderson, Jon (1999). The Internet and Islam's New Interpreters. In Dale F. Eickelman and Jon W. Anderson (Eds.), *New Media in the Muslim World* (pp. 1–19). Bloomington, IN: Indiana University Press.

Anderson, Nels (1942). *Desert saints: The Mormon frontier in Utah.* Chicago, IL: The University of Chicago Press.

Apter, Andrew (1993). Atinga revisited: Yoruba witchcraft and the cocoa economy, 1950–1951. In Jean Comaroff and John Comaroff (Eds.), *Modernity and its malcontents* (pp. 111–128). Chicago, IL: University of Chicago Press.

Ariès, Philippe (1974). *Western attitudes toward death: From the Middle Ages to the present.* Baltimore, MD: Johns Hopkins University Press.

Asad, Talal. 1982. *"Anthropological Conceptions of Religion: Reflections on Geertz".* Man 18: 237–259.

Atkinson, Jane Monnig (1987). The effectiveness of shamans in an Indonesian ritual. *American Anthropologist,* 89, 342–355.

Atkinson, Jane Monnig (1989). *The art and politics of Wana shamanship.* Los Angeles, CA: University of California Press.

Auslander, Mark (1993). "Open the wombs!": The symbolic politics of modern Ngoni witchfinding. In Jean Comaroff and John Comaroff (Eds.), *Modernity and its malcontents* (pp. 167–192). Chicago, IL: University of Chicago Press.

Babb, Lawrence A. (1983). Destiny and responsibility: Karma in popular Hinduism. In Charles F. Keyes and E. Valentine Daniel (Eds.), *Karma: An anthropological inquiry* (pp. 163–181). Los Angeles, CA: University of California Press.

Babb, Lawrence A. (1986). *Redemptive encounters: Three modern styles in the Hindu tradition.* Los Angeles, CA: University of California Press.

Bastian, Misty L. (1993). "Bloodhounds who have no friends": Witchcraft and locality in the Nigerian popular press. In Jean Comaroff and John Comaroff (Eds.), *Modernity and its malcontents* (pp. 129–166). Chicago, IL: University of Chicago Press.

Bauman, Richard (1983). *Let your words be few: Symbolism of speaking and silence among seventeenth-century Quakers.* Cambridge: Cambridge University Press.

Bax, Mart (1991). Marian apparitions in Medjugorje: Rivaling religious regimes and state-formation in Yugoslavia. In Eric R. Wolf (Ed.), *Religious regimes and state-formation* (pp. 29–53). Albany, NY: State University of New York Press.

Bayart, Jeans-François (1989). *L'État en Afrique: la politique du ventre.* Paris: Fayard.

Becker, Penny Edgell (1999). *Congregations in conflict.* New York: Cambridge University Press.

Berman, Harold J. (1990). Religious freedom and the challenge of the modern state. In James Davison Hunter and Os Guiness (Eds.), *Articles of faith, articles of peace* (pp. 40–53). Washington, D.C.: The Brookings Institution.

Bloch, Maurice (1982). Death, women and power. In Maurice Bloch and Jonathan Parry (Eds.), *Death and the regeneration of life* (pp. 211–230). Cambridge: Cambridge University Press.

Bloch, Maurice, and Jonathan Parry (1982). Introduction: Death and the regeneration of life. In Maurice Bloch and Jonathan Parry (Eds.), *Death and the regeneration of life* (pp. 1–44). Cambridge: Cambridge University Press.

Bohlen, Celestine (1995). Crying Madonna, blood and many, many tears. *New York Times*, April 8, 1995, A4.

Bokser, Baruch M. (1984). *The origins of the Seder.* Los Angeles, CA: University of California Press.

Boon, James A. (1990). *Affinities and extremes.* Chicago, IL: University of Chicago Press.

Bossy, John (1983). The mass as a social institution, 1200–1700. *Past and Present, 100*, 29–61.

Bowen, John R. (1996). The myth of global ethnic conflict. *Journal of Democracy, 7*(4), 3–14.

Bowen, John R. (2003). *Islam, law and equality in Indonesia: An anthropology of public reasoning.* Cambridge: Cambridge University Press.

Bowen, John R. (2006). "France's Revolt: Can the Republic live up to its ideals?" *Boston Review*, January/February, 29–32.

Bowen, John R. (2007). *Why the French don't like headscarves.* Princeton, NJ: Princeton University Press.

Bowen, John R. (2009a). "Private Arrangements: `Recognizing sharî`a' in England," *Boston Review*, March/April.

Bowen, John R. (2009b). *Can Islam be French? Pluralism and pragmatism in a secularist state.* Princeton, NJ: Princeton University Press.

Bowen, John. (2012). *Blaming Islam.* Cambridge: MIT Press.

Bowlby, John (1980). *Loss: Sadness and depression.* New York: Basic Books.

Boyer, Pascal (2000). Functional origins of religious concepts: Ontological and strategic selection in evolved minds. *Journal of the Royal Anthropological Institute, 6*(2): 195–214.

Boyer, Pascal (2001). *Religion explained.* New York: Basic Books.

Boyer, Paul, and Stephen Nissenbaum (1974). *Salem possessed: The social origins of witchcraft.* Cambridge, MA: Harvard University Press.

Brasher, Brenda E. (2001). *Give me that online religion.* Piscataway, NJ: Rutgers University Press.

Breitowitz, Irving A. (1993). *Between civil and religious law: The plight of the Agunah in American society.* Westport, CT: Greenwood Press.

Brisebarre, Anne-Marie (1998). *Fête du Mouton : Un sacrifice musulman dans l'espace urbain.* Paris: CNRS Editions.

Brown, Diana DeG. (1986). *Umbanda: Religion and politics in urban Brazil.* Ann Arbor, MI: UMI Research Press.

Brown, Karen McCarthy (1987). Alourdes: A case study of moral leadership in Haitian vodou. In John Stratton Hawley (Ed.), *Saints and virtues* (pp. 144–167). Los Angeles, CA: University of California Press.

Brown, Peter (1987). The saint as exemplar in late antiquity. In John Stratton Hawley (Ed.), *Saints and virtues* (pp. 3–14). Los Angeles, CA: University of California Press.

Brubaker, Rogers, and David D. Laitin (1998). Ethnic and nationalist violence. *Annual Review of Sociology, 24*, 423–452.

Burns, J. Patout (1994). The atmosphere of election: Augustinianism as common sense. *Journal of Early Christian Studies, 2*(3), 325–339.

Burridge, Kenelm (1969). *New Heaven, New Earth.* New York: Schocken.

Bynum, Caroline Walker (1987). *Holy feast and holy fast: The religious significance of food to medieval women.* Los Angeles, CA: University of California Press.

Caldwell, Peter C. (1996). The crucifix and German constitutional culture. *Cultural Anthropology, 11*(2), 259–273.

Campbell, Joseph (1949). *The hero with a thousand faces.* New York: Patheon Books.

Cannell, Fenella (2006). Introduction: The anthropology of Christianity. In Fenella Cannell (Ed.), *The Anthropology of Christianity* (pp. 1–50). Durham: Duke University Press.

Cannon, Walter B. (1942). "Voodoo" death. *American Anthropologist, 54*, 169–181.

Casanova, José (1994). *Public religions in the modern world*. Chicago, IL: University of Chicago Press.

Cesari, Jocelyne (1998). *Musulmans et républicains: Les jeunes, l'islam et la France*. Brussels: Éditions Complexe.

Christian, William A., Jr. (1984). Religious apparitions and the cold war in southern Europe. In Eric R. Wolf (Ed.), *Religion, power and protest in local communities: The northern shore of the Mediterranean* (pp. 239–266). Berlin: Mouton.

Christian, William A., Jr. (1989). *Person and god in a Spanish valley* (rev. ed.). Princeton, NJ: Princeton University Press. (Original work published 1972.)

Clark, Francis (1967). *Eucharistic sacrifice and the reformation*. Oxford: Basil Blackwell.

Cohn, Norman (1970). *The pursuit of the millennium* (rev. ed.). Oxford: Oxford University Press.

Comaroff, Jean (1985). *Body of power, spirit of resistance*. Chicago, IL: University of Chicago Press.

Comaroff, Jean and John Comaroff (1986). Christianity and colonialism in South Africa. *American Ethnologist, 13*(1), 1–22.

Comaroff, Jean and John Comaroff (1991). *Of revelation and revolution: Christianity, colonialism, and consciousness in South Africa*. Volume 1. Chicago, IL: University of Chicago Press.

Comaroff, Jean and John Comaroff (1997). *Of revelation and revolution: The dialectics of modernity on a South African Frontier*. Chicago: University of Chicago Press.

Combs-Schilling, M.E. (1989). *Sacred performances*. New York: Columbia University Press.

Conseil européen des fatwâs et de la recherché (2002). *Receuil de fatwas*. Lyon: Tawhid.

Covington, Dennis (1995). *Salvation on sand mountain: Snake handling and redemption in Southern Appalachia*. Reading, MA: Addison-Wesley.

Cragg, Kenneth (1980). *Islam from within: Anthology of a religion*. Belmont, CA: Wadsworth.

Danforth, Loring M. (1982). *The death rituals of rural Greece*. Princeton, NJ: Princeton University Press.

Davis, Winston (1980). *Dojo: Magic and exorcism in modern Japan*. Stanford, CA: Stanford University Press.

Demos, John Putnam (1982). *Entertaining Satan: Witchcraft and the culture of early New England*. Oxford: Oxford University Press.

de Rosny, Eric (1992). *L'Afrique des guérisons*. Paris: Karthala.

Doi, L. Takeo (1986). *Amae:* A key concept for understanding Japanese personality structure. In Takie Sugiyama Lebra and William P. Lebra (Eds.), *Japanese culture and behavior* (rev. ed., pp. 121–129). Honolulu: University of Hawaii Press. (Original work published 1962.)

Donner, Fred. 2010. *Muhammad and the Believers: At the origins of Islam*. Cambridge: Harvard University Press.

Douglas, Mary (1966). *Purity and danger: An analysis of the concepts of pollution and taboo*. London: Routledge & Kegan Paul..

Durkheim, Émile (1995). *The elementary forms of the religious life* (Karen E. Fields, Trans.). New York: The Free Press. (Original work published 1912.)

Durkheim, Émile, and Marcel Mauss (1963). *Primitive classification* (Rodney Needhamn, Trans.). Chicago, IL: University of Chicago Press. (Original work published 1903.)

Earhart, H. Byron (1982). *Japanese religion: Unity and diversity* (3rd ed.). Belmont, CA: Wadsworth.

Eck, Diana L. (1982). *Banaras: City of light*. Princeton, NJ: Princeton University Press.

Edelman, Martin (1994). *Courts, politics, and culture in Israel*. Charlottesville, VA: University Press of Virginia.

Eickelman, Dale F. (1976). *Moroccan Islam: Tradition and society in a pilgrimage center*. Austin, TX: University of Texas Press.

Eickelman, Dale F. (1985). *Knowledge and power in Morocco*. Princeton, NJ: Princeton University Press.

Eliade, Mircea (1954). *The myth of the eternal return.* Princeton, NJ: Princeton University Press. (Original work published 1949.)

Engels, Friedrich (1956). *The peasant war in Germany.* Moscow: Progress. (Original work published 1850.)

Europol (2007). *EU Terrorism Situation and Trend Report.* The Hague: Europol.

Fader, Ayala (2009). *Mitzvah girls: Bringing up the next generation of Hasidic Jews in Brooklyn.* Princeton: Princeton University Press.

Fearon, James D., and David D. Laitin (2003). Ethnicity, insurgency, and civil war. *The American Political Science Review,* 97(1), 75–90.

Feeley-Harnik, Gillian (1981). *The Lord's table: Eucharist and passover in early Christianity.* Philadelphia, PA: University of Pennsylvania Press.

Firmage, Edwin Brown, and Richard Collin Mangrum (1988). *Zion in the courts: A legal history of the Church of Jesus Christ of Latter-day Saints, 1830–1900.* Urbana, IL: University of Illinois Press.

Flynn, Thomas J., M.D., and Charles B. Fulton, Th.D. (2002). *Letter to the editor. Journal of the American Medical Association,* 288(20), 2541.

Foster, Lawrence (1981). *Religion and sexuality: The Shakers, the Mormons, and the Oneida community.* New York: Oxford University Press.

Foucault, Michel (1997). *Ethics: Subjectivity and truth* (vol. 1). New York: New Press.

Foucault, Michel (2011). The Courage of the Self (The Government of Self and Others II): Lectures at the Collège de France, 1983–1984. Houndsmills, UK: Palgrave Macmillan.

Fox, Richard (1989). *Gandhian utopia: Experiments with culture.* Boston, MA: Beacon Press.

Frankel, Marvin E. (1994). *Faith and freedom: Religious liberty in America.* New York: Hill and Wang.

Fraser, Caroline (1996). Mrs. Eddy builds her empire. *New York Times Book Review,* July 11, 1996, 53–59.

Frazer, James G. (1981). *The golden bough: The roots of religion and folklore.* New York: Avenel Books. (Original work published 1890.)

Freud, Sigmund (1930). *Civilization and its discontents.* London: Hogarth Press.

Fuller, Christopher J. (1992). *The camphor flame: Popular Hinduism and society in India.* Princeton, NJ: Princeton University Press.

Fuller, Christopher J. (2003). *The renewal of the priesthood: Modernity and traditionalism in a South Indian temple.* Princeton, NJ: Princeton University Press.

Gardner, Katy (2002). *Age, narrative and migration: The life course and life histories of Bengali elders.* Oxford: Berg.

Geertz, Clifford (1960). *The religion of Java.* Chicago, IL: University of Chicago Press.

Geertz, Clifford (1966). *Person, time, and conduct in Bali: An essay in cultural analysis.* New Haven, CT: Yale University, Southeast Asia Studies, Cultural Report Series No. 14.

Geertz, Clifford (1968). *Islam observed: Religious developments in Morocco and Indonesia.* New Haven, CT: Yale University Press.

Gerbrands, Adrian A. (1967). Art and artist in Asmat society. In Michael Rockefeller and Adrian A. Gerbrands (Eds.), *The Asmat of New Guinea* (pp. 11–39). New York: Museum of Primitive Art.

Geschiere, Peter (1997). *The modernity of witchcraft: Politics and the occult in postcolonial Africa (Sorcellerie et politique en Afrique).* Charlottesville, VA: University Press of Virginia.

Gill, Sam (1981). *Sacred words: A study of Navajo religion and prayer.* Westport, CT: Greenwood Press.

Goheen, Miriam (1996). *Men own the fields, women own the crops.* Madison, WI: University of Wisconsin.

Gold, Ann Grodzins (1988). *Fruitful journeys: The ways of Rajasthani pilgrims.* Los Angeles, CA: University of California Press.

Goodman, Felicitas D. (1988). *How about demons? Possession and exorcism in the modern world.* Bloomington, IN: Indiana University Press.

Graham, William A. (1987). *Beyond the written word: Oral aspects of scripture in the history of religion.* Cambridge: Cambridge University Press.

Guillermoprieto, Alma (1990). *Samba.* New York: Knopf.

Haberman, Clyde (1988). Shinto is thrust back onto the nationalist stage. *New York Times,* June 7, 1988, A4.

Hall, John R., Philip D. Schuyler, and Sylvaine Trinh (2000). *Apocalypse observed: Religious movements and violence in North America, Europe, and Japan.* London and New York: Routledge.

Hammoudi, Abdellah (1993). *The victim and its masks: An essay on sacrifice and masquerade in the Maghreb.* Chicago: University of Chicago Press. (Orig. French 1988.)

Hardacre, Helen (1989). *Shinto and the state, 1868–1988.* Princeton, NJ: Princeton University Press.

Harding, Susan Friend (2000). *The Book of Jerry Falwell: Fundamentalist language and politics.* Princeton, NJ: Princeton University Press.

Harris, Lis (1985). *Holy days.* New York: Collier Books.

Harris, William S., et al. (1999). A randomized, controlled trial of the effects of remote, intercessory prayer on outcomes in patients admitted to the coronary care unit. *Archives of Internal Medicine, 159,* 2273–2278.

Helm, J., et al. (2000). Effects of private religious activity on mortality of elderly disabled and nondisabled adults. *Journal of Gerontology (Medical Sciences), 55A,* M400–M405.

Hertz, Robert (1960). *Death and the right hand* (Rodney and Claudia Needham, Trans.). New York: The Free Press. (Original work published 1907.)

Hiltebeitel, Alf (1985). On the handling of the meat, and related matters, in two south Indian buffalo sacrifices. *L'Uomo: Societa Tradizione Sviluppo, 9*(1/2), 171–199.

Hood, Jr., Ralph W. and W. Paul Williamson (2008). *Them that believe: The power and the meaning of the Christian serpent-handling tradition.* Berkeley: University of California Press.

Hume, David (1993). *Dialogues concerning natural religion and the natural history of religion.* Oxford: Oxford University Press. (Original works published 1779 and 1757.)

Hunter, James Davison (1990). Religious freedom and the challenge of modern pluralism. In James Davison Hunter and Os Guiness (Eds.), *Articles of faith, articles of peace* (pp. 54–73). Washington, D.C.: The Brookings Institution.

Introvigne, Massimo, and Jean-Francois Mayer (2002). Occult masters and the Temple of Doom: The fiery end of the Solar Temple. In David G. Bromley and J. Gordon Melton (Eds.), *Cults, religion, and violence* (pp. 170–188). Cambridge: Cambridge University Press.

Jaeger, Werner (1961). *Early Christianity and Greek paideia.* Cambridge, MA: Harvard University Press.

James, William (1972). *Varieties of religious experience.* London: Fontana. (Original work published 1901–1902.)

Jenkins, Simon (2008). Rituals and pixels: Experiments in online church. *Online—Heidelberg Journal of Religions on the Internet,* 3(1), 95–115.

Johnson, Douglas H. (1994). *Nuer Prophets: A history of prophecy from the upper Nile in the nineteenth and twentieth centuries.* Oxford: Oxford University Press.

Johnson, Paul Christopher (2007). *Diaspora conversions: Black Carib religions and the recovery of Africa.* Berkeley, CA: University of California Press.

Kalb, Claudia (2003). Faith and healing. *Newsweek,* November 10, 2003, 44–56.

Kapferer, Bruce (1997). *The feast of the sorcerer: Practices of consciousness and power.* Chicago, IL: University of Chicago Press.

Kapferer, Bruce (2003). *Beyond rationalism: Rethinking magic, witchcraft and sorcery.* New York: Bergahn Books.

Keane, Webb (2007). *Christian moderns: Freedom and fetish in the mission encounter.* Berkeley: University of California Press.

Kinzer, Stephen (2003). Interest surges in voodoo, and its Queen. *New York Times,* November 20, 2003, A18.

Kipp, Rita Smith, and Susan Rodgers (1987). Introduction: Indonesian religions in society. In Rita Smith Kipp and Susan Rodgers (Eds.), *Indonesian religions in transition* (pp. 1–31). Tucson, AZ: University of Arizona Press.

Kluver, Randolph, and Yanli Chen (2008). The Church of Fools: Virtual ritual and material faith. *Online-Heidelberg Journal of Religions on the Internet,* 3(1), 116–143.

Knauft, Bruce M. (1985). *Good company and violence: Sorcery and social action in a lowland New Guinea society.* Berkeley, CA: University of California Press.

Koenig, Harold G. (2002). An 83-year-old woman with chronic illness and strong religious beliefs. *Journal of the American Medical Association, 288*(4), 487–493.

Koenig, H. G., et al. (1992). Religious coping and depression in elderly hospitalized medically ill men. *American Journal of Psychiatry, 149,* 1693–1700.

Koenig, H. G., et al. (1997). Attendance at religious services, interleukin-6, and other biological indicators of immune function in older adults. *International Journal of Psychiatry in Medicine, 27,* 233–250.

Kuruwaip, Abraham (1974). The Asmat bis pole: Its background and meaning. *Irian, 3*(2), 32–78.

La Barre, Weston (1964). The snake-handling cult of the American Southeast. In Ward H. Goodenough (Ed.), *Explorations in cultural anthropology* (pp. 309–333). New York: McGraw-Hill.

Laderman, Carol (1983). *Wives and midwives: Childbirth and nutrition in rural Malaysia.* Los Angeles, CA: University of California Press.

Lafaye, Jacques (1976). *Quetzalcoatl and Guadalupe: The formation of Mexican national consciousness 1531–1813* (Benjamin Keen, Trans.). Chicago, IL: University of Chicago Press.

Landman, Nico (2002). Islam in the Benelux Countries. In Shireen T. Hunter (Ed.), *Islam, Europe's second religion* (pp. 97–120). Westport, CT: Praeger.

Latour, Bruno (1993). *We have never been modern.* Cambridge: Harvard University Press.

Leibovich, Lori (2000). The online religion with shopping, too. *New York Times,* April 6, 2000, D1, D10.

Leishman, Thomas Linton (1958). *Why I am a Christian Scientist.* New York: Thomas Nelson & Sons.

Leone, Mark P. (1979). *The roots of modern Mormonism.* Cambridge: Harvard University Press.

Lévi-Strauss, Claude (1963a). *Totemism* (Rodney Needham, Trans.). Boston, MA: Beacon Press. (Original work published 1962.)

Lévi-Strauss, Claude (1963b). The effectiveness of symbols. In C. Lévi-Strauss (Ed.), *Structural anthropology* (Claire Jacobson and Brooke Grundfest Schoepf, Trans.) (pp. 180–201). Garden City, NY: Anchor Books. (Original work published 1949.)

Lévi-Strauss, Claude (1976). The story of Asdiwal. In C. Lévi-Strauss (Ed.), *Structural anthropology* (Monique Layton, Trans.) (vol. 2, pp. 146–197). Chicago, IL: University of Chicago Press. (Original work published 1958.)

Lewis, Philip (2002). *Islamic Britain: Religion, politics, and identity among British Muslims* (3rd ed.). London: I. B. Tauris & Co. Ltd.

Lofland, John, and Rodney Stark (1965). Becoming a world-saver: A theory of conversion to a devout perspective. *American Sociological Review, 30*(6), 862–875.

Lukes, Steven (1973). *Émile Durkheim: His life and work.* Harmondsworth, UK: Penguin.

Mahmood, Saba (2005). *Politics of piety.* Princeton, NJ: Princeton University Press.

Malcolm X (1973). *The autobiography of Malcolm X.* Alex Haley (Ed.), New York: Ballantine Books. (Original work published 1964.)

Malinowski, Bronislaw (1954). Magic, science, and religion. In B. Malinowski (Ed.), *Magic, science, and religion and other essays* (pp. 17–92). Garden City, NY: Anchor Books. (Original work published 1926.)

Marx, Karl, and Friedrich Engels (1965). *The German ideology.* London: Lawrence & Wishart. (Original work published 1846.)

Matory, Lorand J. (2005). *Black Atlantic religion: Tradition, transnationalism, and matriarchy in the Afro-Brazilian Candomblé.* Princeton, NJ: Princeton University Press.

Meislin, Bernard J. (1981). Pursuit of the wife's right to a *"Get"* in United States and Canadian courts. *The Jewish Law Annual* (vol. 4). Kinderhook, NY: E. J. Brill.

Metcalf, Barbara Daly (2001). "Traditionalist" Islamic Activism: Deoband, Tablighis, and Talibs. In Craig Calhoun, Paul Price, and Ashley Timmer (Eds.), *Understanding September 11.* New York: The New Press.

Metcalf, Peter (1982). *A Borneo journey into death.* Philadelphia, PA: University of Pennsylvania Press.

Miller, Daniel, and Don Slater (2000). *The Internet: An ethnographic approach.* Oxford: Berg.

Miller, Perry (1956). *Errand into the wilderness.* Cambridge, MA: Belknap Press.

Modood, Tariq (1994). Establishment, multiculturalism, and British citizenship. *Political Quarterly, 65*(1), 53–73.

Momen, Moojan (1985). *An introduction to Shî'î Islam.* New Haven, CT: Yale University Press.

Murphy, Joseph S. (1994). *Working the spirit: Ceremonies of the African diaspora.* Boston, MA: Beacon Press.

Nations, Marilyn, and Linda-Anne Rebhun (1988). Angels with wet wings can't fly: Maternal sentiments in Brazil and the image of neglect. *Culture, Medicine, and Psychiatry, 12,* 141–200.

Newberg, Andrew B., Eugene G. D'Aquili, and Vince Rause (2001). *Why God won't go away: Brain science and the biology of belief.* New York: Ballantine Books.

Nolan, Mary Lee, and Sidney Nolan (1989). *Christian pilgrimage in modern Western Europe.* Chapel Hill, NC: The University of North Carolina Press.

Norton, Mary Beth (2003). *In the Devil's share: The Salem Witchcraft Crisis of 1692.* New York: Alfred A. Knopf.

Obeyesekere, Gananath (1981). *Medusa's hair: An essay on personal symbols and religious experience.* Chicago, IL: University of Chicago Press.

Oe, Kenzaburo (1995). The day the Emperor spoke in human voice. *New York Times Magazine,* May 7, 1995, 103–105.

Palgi, Phyllis, and Henry Abramovitch (1984). Death: A cross-cultural perspective. *Annual Review of Anthropology, 13,* 385–417.

Pargament, K. I., et al. (2001). Religious struggle as a predictor of mortality among medically ill elderly patients: A two-year longitudinal study. *Archives of Internal Medicine, 161,* 1881–1885.

Peacock, James L., and Ruel W. Tyson, Jr. (1989). *Pilgrims of paradox: Calvinism and experience among the primitive Baptists of the Blue Ridge.* Washington, D.C.: Smithsonian Institution Press.

Peters, F. E. (1994). *Muhammad and the origins of Islam.* Albany, NY: State University of New York Press.

Pew Global Attitudes Project (2006). *The Great Divide: How Westerners and Muslims View Each Other,* http://pewglobal.org/reports/display.php?ReportID=253.

Plath, David W. (1964). Where the family of God is the family: The role of the dead in Japanese households. *American Anthropologist, 66,* 300–317.

Pocock, David F. (1973). *Mind, body, and wealth: A study of belief and practice in an Indian village.* Oxford: Blackwell.

Pollock, Sheldon (1993). Ramayana and political imagination in India. *Journal of Asian Studies, 52*(2), 261–297.

Prell, Riv-Ellen (1989). *Prayer and community: The havurah in American Judaism*. Detroit: Wayne State University Press.

Putnam, Robert (2000). *Bowling alone: The collapse and revival of American community*. New York: Simon & Schuster.

Ramadan, Tariq (2002). *Dâr ash-shahâda: L'Occident, espace du témoignage*. Lyon: Tawhid.

Reader, Ian (1991). *Religion in contemporary Japan*. Honolulu, HI: University of Hawaii Press.

Reader, Ian (2000). *Religious violence in contemporary Japan: The case of Aum Shinrikyo*. Honolulu, HI: University of Hawaii Press.

Redfield, Robert (1956). *Peasant society and culture*. Chicago, IL: University of Chicago Press.

Remnick, David (1992). Waiting for the apocalypse in Crown Heights. *The New Yorker*, December 21, 52–57.

Richeport, Madeleine (1985). *Macumba, trance and spirit healing*. Film. New York: Filmmaker's Library.

Robbins, Joel. (2004). *Becoming sinners: Christianity and moral torment in a Papua New Guinea Society*. Berkeley: University of California Press.

Rosaldo, Renato I. (1984). Grief and a headhunter's rage: On the cultural force of emotions. In Edward Bruner (Ed.), *Play, text, and story* (pp. 178–195). Washington, D.C.: American Ethnological Society.

Rothkrug, Lionel (1980). Religious practice and collective perceptions: Hidden homologies in the Renaissance and Reformation. *Historical Reflections*, 7(1).

Roy, Olivier (2002). *L'islam mondialisé*. Paris: Editions du Seuil.

Ruthven, Malisa (1984). *Islam in the world*. New York: Oxford University Press.

Sageman, Marc (2004). *Understanding terror networks*. Philadelphia, PA: University of Pennsylvania Press.

Sageman, Marc (2008). *Leaderless jihad: Terror networks in the twenty-first century*. Philadelphia, PA: University of Pennsylvania Press.

Sanger, David E. (1990). For a job well done, Japanese enshrine the chip. *New York Times*, December 11, 1990, A4.

Saunders, E. Dale (1964). *Buddhism in Japan*. Philadelphia, PA: University of Pennsylvania Press.

Sayle, Murray (1996). Nerve gas and the four noble truths. *The New Yorker*, April 1, 1996.

Schauss, Hayyim (1938). *The Jewish festivals: History and observance*. New York: Schocken Books.

Scheper-Hughes, Nancy (1992). *Death without weeping: The violence of everyday life in Brazil*. Los Angeles, CA: University of California Press.

Schiffauer, Werner (1996). Islamic vision and social reality: The political culture of Sunni Muslims in Germany. In Steven Vertovec and Ceri Peach (Eds.), *Islam in Europe: The politics of religion and community* (pp. 156–176). Houndmills, UK: Palgrave Macmillan.

Schimmel, Annemarie (1973). *Mystical dimensions of Islam*. Chapel Hill, NC: University of North Carolina Press.

Shariati, Dr. Ali (1977). *Hajj*. (Somayyah and Yaser, Trans.). Bedford, OH: Free Islamic Literatures.

Shipps, Jan (1985). *Mormonism: The story of a new religious tradition*. Urbana, IL: University of Illinois Press.

Singer, Milton (1964). The social organization of Indian civilization. *Diogène*, 45, 84–119.

Smith, Robert J. (1974). *Ancestor worship in contemporary Japan*. Stanford, CA: Stanford University Press.

Smith, Robert J. (1983). *Japanese society: Tradition, self, and the social order*. Cambridge: Cambridge University Press.

Smith, Rogers M. (1998). "Equal" Treatment? A liberal separationist view. In Stephen V. Monsma and J. Christopher Soper (Eds.), *Equal treatment of religion in a pluralistic society* (pp. 179–199). Grand Rapids, MI: William B. Eerdmans Publishing Co.

Smith, Rogers M. (2007). Secularism, constitution-alism, and the rise of Christian conservatism in the United States. Unpublished manuscript.

Smith, Wilfred Cantwell (1978). *The meaning and end of religion.* San Francisco, CA: Harper & Row. (Original work published 1962.)

Soares, Benjamin F. (2003). An African Muslim saint and his followers in France. Unpublished manuscript.

Stark, Rodney, and Roger Finke (2000). *Acts of faith: Explaining the human side of religion.* Berkeley, CA: University of California Press.

Statler, Oliver (1984). *Japanese Pilgrimage.* London: Pan Books.

Steinfels, Peter (1992). The vision that wasn't. Or was it? *New York Times,* September 2, 1992, A14.

Sudarman, Dea (1984). *Asmat.* Jakarta: Penerbit Sinar Harapan.

Svensson, Frances (1979). Liberal democracy and group rights: The legacy of individualism and its impact on American Indian tribes. *Political Studies, 27,* 421–439.

Swallow, D. A. (1982). Ashes and powers: Myth, rite and miracle in an Indian god-man's cult. *Modern Asian Studies, 16*(1), 123–158.

Tambiah, Stanley Jeyaraja (1970). *Buddhism and spirit cults in north-east Thailand.* Cambridge: Cambridge University Press.

Tambiah, Stanley Jeyaraja (1976). *World conqueror and world re-nouncer.* Cambridge, MA: Harvard University Press.

Taylor, Charles (1990). Religion in a free society. In James Davison Hunter and Os Guiness (Eds.), *Articles of faith, articles of peace* (pp. 93–113). Washington, D.C.: The Brookings Institution.

Taylor, Charles (2007). *A secular age.* Cambridge, MA: Belknap Press of Harvard University Press.

Taylor, Michael (1982). *Community, anarchy and liberty.* Cambridge: Cambridge University Press.

Trillin, Calvin (1994). Drawing the line. *The New Yorker,* December 12, 50–62.

Trompf, Garry (1995). Pacific Islands. In Tony Swain and Garry Trompf (Eds.), *The religions of Oceania* (pp. 121–222). New York: Routledge.

Turner, Victor (1967). *The forest of symbols: Aspects of Ndembu ritual.* Ithaca, NY: Cornell University Press.

Turner, Victor (1974). Pilgrimages as social processes. In *Dramas, fields, and metaphors* (pp. 166–230). Ithaca, NY: Cornell University Press.

Tylor, Edward Burnett (1970). *Primitive culture* (2 vols.). Gloucester, MA: Peter Smith. (Original work published 1871.)

van Gennep, Arnold (1960). *The rites of passage* (Monika B. Vizedom and Gabrielle L. Caffee, Trans.). Chicago, IL: University of Chicago Press. (Original work published 1908.)

van der Veer, Peter (1994). *Religious nationalisms: Hindus and Muslims in India.* Los Angeles, CA: University of California Press.

Varshney, Ashutosh (2002). *Ethnic conflict and civic life: Hindus and Muslims in India.* New Haven, CT: Yale University Press.

Venel, Nancy (1999). *Musulmanes françaises: Des pratiquantes voiles à l'université.* Paris: L'Harmattan.

Walker, Sheila S. (1990). Everyday and esoteric reality in the Afro-Brazilian Candomblé. *History of Religions, 30,* 103–128.

Wallace, Anthony (1956). Revitalization movements. *American Anthropologist, 58,* 264–281.

Warner, Marina (1996). Blood and tears. *The New Yorker,* April 8, 63–69.

Waugh, Earle H. (1977). Muharram rites: Community death and rebirth. In Frank E. Reynolds and Earle H. Waugh (Eds.), *Religious encounters with death* (pp. 200–213). University Park, PA: Penn State University Press.

Weber, Max (1958). *The protestant ethic and the spirit of capitalism* (Talcott Parsons, Trans.). New York: Charles Scribner's Sons. (Original work published 1904–1905.)

Weber, Max (1978). *Economy and society* (2 vols.). Los Angeles, CA: University of California Press. (Original work published 1956.)

Weisman, Steven R. (1990). Akihito performs his solitary rite. *New York Times,* November 23, 1990, A7.

Werbner, Pnina S. (2003). *Pilgrims of love: Anthropology of a global Sufi Cult.* London: Indiana University Press.

Westermarck, Edward Alexander (1968). *Ritual and belief in Morocco* (2 vols.). New Hyde Park, NY: University Books. (Original work published 1926.)

Wikan, Unni (1990). *Managing turbulent hearts: A Balinese formulation for living.* Chicago, IL: University of Chicago Press.

Wilson, Bryan R. (1961). *Sects and society: A sociological study of three religious groups in Britain.* London: William Heinemann.

Witherspoon, Gary (1977). *Language and art in the Navajo universe.* Ann Arbor, MI: University of Michigan Press.

Wolf, Arthur (1974). Gods, ghosts, and ancestors. In Arthur Wolf (Ed.), *Religion and ritual in Chinese society* (pp. 131–182). Stanford, CA: Stanford University Press.

Wolf, Eric (1958). The virgin of Guadalupe: A Mexican national symbol. *Journal of American Folklore, 71,* 34–39.

Woodburn, James (1982). Social dimensions of death in four African hunting and gathering societies. In Maurice Bloch and Jonathan Parry (Eds.), *Death and the regeneration of life* (pp. 187–210). Cambridge: Cambridge University Press.

Worsley, Peter (1968). *The trumpet shall sound* (rev. ed.). New York: Schocken Books.

WuDunn, Sheryl (1996). In Japan, a ritual of mourning for abortions. *New York Times,* January 25, 1996, A1, A8.

Wuthnow, Robert (1988). *The restructuring of American religion: Society and faith since World War II.* Princeton, NJ: Princeton University Press.

Wyman, Leland C. (1970). *Blessingway, with three versions of the myth recorded and translated from the Navajo by Father Berard Haile, O.F.M.* Tucson, AZ: University of Arizona Press.

Zegwaard, Rev. Gerrad A. (1959). Headhunting practices of the Asmat of Netherlands New Guinea. *American Anthropologist, 61,* 1020–1041.

Zimdars-Schwartz, Sandra L. (1991). *Encountering Mary: From La Salette to Medjugorje.* Princeton, NJ: Princeton University Press.

INDEX